The Ottoman and

Russian Empire

Caucasus

Caspian Sea

Aral Sea

Azerbaijan ⊙ Baku

Bukhara ⊙
Uzbeks   ⊙ Samarkand

⊙ Tabriz

Turkmen

✕ Chaldiran 1510

⊙ Mashhad

Afghans

⊙ Mosul

⊙ Herat   ⊙ Kabul

⊙ Baghdad

⊙ Isfahan   **Safavid Empire**

ire

Dabiq

Euphrates

Tigris

cus

⊙ Basra

⊙ Shiraz

⊙ Hormuz

Baluchi

Indus River

Delhi ⊙

Mughal Empire

Persian Gulf

⊙ Medina

Arabian Peninsula

⊙ Mecca

Arabian Sea

Hadramaut

a

Yemen

⊙ Aden

Gulf of Aden

Indian Ocean

hiopia

Somalia

0   1000

Kilometres

THE HOUSE DIVIDED

THE HOUSE DIVIDED

Sunni, Shia and the Making of the Middle East

BARNABY ROGERSON

PEGASUS BOOKS
NEW YORK LONDON

THE HOUSE DIVIDED

Pegasus Books, Ltd.
148 West 37th Street, 13th Floor
New York, NY 10018

Copyright © 2024 by Barnaby Rogerson

First Pegasus Books cloth edition July 2024

ISBN: 978-1-63936-696-5

10 9 8 7 6 5 4 3 2 1

Printed in the United States of America
Distributed by Simon & Schuster
www.pegasusbooks.com

This book is dedicated to Bruce Wannell (1952–2020), the most enthusiastic traveller of my generation, with an infectious delight in music, mountains, calligraphy, gossip, poetry, controversy, historic monuments and picnics throughout the Middle East. He is missed for all these qualities but also for his scrupulous Islamic scholarship, generously invested into critical readings of the works of his friends.

Sunni, Shia and transliteration of names

Sunni form the majority of Muslims across the world. The Shia account for perhaps 15 per cent, worldwide, and 37 per cent in the central Middle East.

Sunni derives from an ancient Arabic word that translates as 'tradition' or 'trusted path'. Strictly, *Sunni* is the singular or adjective form, but in modern practice it is often used for plurals.

Shia refers back to *Shi'atu Ali* – 'the partisans, or followers, of Ali'. Again, *Shia* (and *Shiite*) is an anglicised form. The word is more correctly rendered as *Shi'i* (as a singular noun or adjective) or *Shi'iyun* (in the plural).

I have followed modern, simplified forms generally in the transliteration of both personal and place names. There is no consensus between the French and English traditions in the translation of Arabic, Turkish and Iranian, so there is a rich variety of spellings. For ease of reading, accents are absent.

Contents

Introduction The House Divided   11

PART ONE The Origins of the Sunni–Shia Schism   23

1 The House Undivided *Medina (622–632)*   25
2 The Protection of Medina *Allegiances, the Constitution of Medina and the Flight from Mecca*   32
3 The Women of the House *The rivalry of Aisha and Fatima*   43
4 Imam Ali: Islam's Perfect Man *The cornerstone of Shia belief and one of the four great heroes that uphold Sunni traditions*   51
5 The Last Revelation and Ghadir Khum *All Shia believe that Ali was publicly blessed by the Prophet as his heir*   59
6 The Death of the Prophet *The fateful chance events of the succession, 632*   63
7 The Rashidun and the Companions of Ali *The four rightly guided Sunni caliphs contrast with the Shia Companions*   72
8 Husayn at Kerbala *The martyrdom of the grandson of the Prophet, 680*   82

PART TWO Medieval Caliphates   95

Map of Umayyad Caliphate (750)   96

9 Umayyads and Abbasids *The Arab Empires: Umayyads (661–750) and Abbasids (750–1258)*   97
10 Shiites Triumphant *Fatimids (909–1107), Qarmatians (899–1077) and Buyids (934–1062)*   105
11 Three Turkic Empires *Seljuk (1037–1194), Mongol (1206–1368) and Timurid (1370–1507)*   111

PART THREE The Emergence of the Three:
Turkey, Persia and Saudi Arabia   123

12 Ottomans and Safavids: The Clash of Neighbours
*Shah Ismail (1501–24), Sultan Selim (1512–20) and
the Battle of Chaldiran (1514)*   125
13 The Consolidation of Iran *Shah Abbas (1588–1629)
and Nadir Shah (1736–47)*   133
14 Enter the Third Force: Wahhabi Arabia
Muhammad ibn Abd al-Wahhab (1703–92)   136

PART FOUR Colonial Night, 1830–1979   147

15 The Misrule of Persia *The Qajar shahs (1794–1925) and
Pahlavi shahs (1925–79)*   149
16 The Kingdom *Ibn Saud and his heirs (1932–75)* 161
17 The Turkish Republic *Ataturk and post-Ottoman Turkey* 173

PART FIVE 1979 Revolutions: The Middle East
Transformed   187

18 Revolution in Iran *The emergence of a Shiite Islamic Republic,
the Iran–Iraq War and modern-day Iran*   189
19 Meccan Insurrection *The 1979 revolt, a return to Wahhabism
and the twenty-first-century reforms of MBS*   208
20 Afghan jihadis *The Russian invasion of 1979, the American
war post-9/11 and the rise, fall and rise again of the Taliban* 220
21 The New Ottomans *Military coups, Islamic popularism and a
yearning to lead the Islamic world once again*   227

PART SIX 21st-century Battlefields:
Syria, Iraq and Yemen   243

22 Syria: Fractured Crossroad *From Greater Syria to
today's war-torn Syrian Arab Republic*   245
23 Iraq in the Balance *The Middle East's key conflict
between Shia and Sunni*   273
24 The Two Yemens *The ancient home of Arabia – and
its battlefield*   308

PART SEVEN The Enemy of My Enemy:
  Egypt, Israel, USA and Qatar   329

25 Once the Leader: Egypt *The view from the Nile*   331
26 Israel and Anti-Shia Alliances *The occupation of Palestine
  and alliance with Sunni Saudi Arabia against Shiite Iran*   341
27 America in the Middle East *From oil industry partners,
  through Cold War allies, to superpower warmongers*   349
28 The Isolated Emirate: Qatar *From pearl fishing to
  a media network*   355

PART EIGHT Far Frontiers: Pakistan, Azerbaijan,
  Chechnya and China's New Silk Road   363

29 Pakistan: The Sunni bedrock *From Islamic statehood
  to the Taliban*   365
30 The Muslim Caucasus: Azerbaijan and Chechnya *Islamism
  in the Caucasus – and Russian foreign policy in the Middle East* 373
31 The New Silk Route: China and the Middle East
  New global alliances as China looks West   379

An Afterword The Middle East After the Gaza War   384

Further reading   391
Acknowledgments   402
Index   404
Timeline of Islamic dynasties   432

THE HOUSE DIVIDED
Introduction

*'And if thy Lord had willed, He would have made
mankind one nation, but they cease not in differing'*
KORAN, 11: 118

The Middle East is home to both unimaginable oil wealth
and a passionate engagement in upholding traditional
religion. This should have produced a region overflowing with
the gifts of peace and prosperity, but the modern Middle East
has been repeatedly rocked by wars, invasions, internal coups,
bloody border conflicts, civil strife and covert operations. The
target one day might be an ayatollah leaving a mosque in Iraq,
the next a scientist on a street in Tehran, then a doctor and
his young son in Karachi, or a refugee camp outside Quetta.
Now and then, the noise comes closer to Europe, as bombs go
off in Istanbul or Moscow and sirens cry out in the streets of
Brussels, Paris or London.

Four of the region's twentieth-century conflicts – 1948–49,
1956, 1967, 1973 – directly involved Israel, but since then
there has been no war fought for that state's survival. Over the
last fifty years, however, military action in the Middle East has
continued unabated, often apparently based on the ancient
internal schism between Sunni and Shia Islam.

To an outsider, the vicious trench fighting of the eight-year-long Iran–Iraq border war (1980–88), the civil wars in Iraq (2013–17) and in Syria (2011–19) seem to have been fuelled by the differences between the two major Muslim sects. Hundreds of thousands of lives have been lost in sectarian civil wars fought out between armed bands of Sunni and Shia in the central heartlands of the region, in the cities of Syria and Iraq. As I wrote this book, five other conflicts were being fought within the Islamic world: in Gaza, Afghanistan, on the coast of Libya, in the Yemen and in Kurdish mountains, while the embers of strife still glow in Algeria, Lebanon and Baluchistan, not to mention truncated Sudan and imploded Somalia.

The causes of these were legion – Yemen is the only one that has clear sectarian roots. But, despite talk of a clash of civilisations, none of these current conflicts is being fought between Islamic regimes and Western nations; instead, it's Muslim soldier fighting Muslim soldier. The Middle East contains 5 per cent of humanity, but over the current generation has produced 58 per cent of its refugees and 68 per cent of battle mortalities. (These figures come from before the invasion of Ukraine.) That is not to say that some of these conflicts haven't been ignited by the intervention of the West. Following the US invasion of Iraq, millions of refugees were driven from their homes, some to escape the cycles of violence, others purposefully terrorised by the massacre of neighbouring villages or the public execution of members of a specific sect, identified in a bus from their identity cards at a roadblock. The massacre of 2 March 2004 was a tragic example of such targeted sectarian hate, when a fusillade of nine car bombs and mortar attacks were launched at Shiite congregations gathering to commemorate Ashura in Kerbala and Baghdad; 178 were killed and another 500 maimed.

The casualty figures in these murderous neighbourhood gang wars will probably never be known, for the internal displacement has been on a vast scale. In Iraq, two million fled their nation during the civil war and another two and a half million were internally displaced. It was communities where Sunni and Shia had for centuries lived side by side that proved most vulnerable, and many of these no longer exist, with the weaker minority expelled. In Iraq, Samarra has been effectively cleansed of Shia, who have been driven south, just as those with a Sunni identity have been driven out of Basra to take refuge in the north. Baghdad lies astride the sectarian fault line and has been divided up neighbourhood by neighbourhood. These turf wars, with their protection rackets, internal gang rivalries and links with political parties, raged most fiercely between 2006 and 2008 in Iraq, then re-emerged with the rise of ISIS in 2014–17, which engulfed both Iraq and Syria. Further destruction was wrought in communities in Afghanistan, Saudi Arabia, the Yemen and Pakistan.

What is it that fuels these destructive bloodbaths? Is the faith division between Sunni and Shia Islam really the central issue, or is it a veil beneath which other power plays are fought – such as the rivalry of nation states and political ideologies? And what role does geography, and an increasingly hostile climate, play in these conflicts? We are just beginning to understand how closely human history follows the graphs of climate change – and this is acutely true for the Middle East. The Arab Spring – the series of anti-government protests that led to armed rebellions in the early 2010s – was reinforced by economic factors, alongside a desire for political change. ISIS paymasters certainly found fertile ground in farming villages, where livings had become impossible amid climate-induced drought. Kings of Jordan and presidents of Egypt have both predicted that the next round of wars will be fought not over faith but water.

❧ ❧ ❧

At first glance the modern Middle East seems to divide easily into two antagonistic factions based on rival interpretations of the Muslim faith and their distinct traditions: Sunni Saudi Arabia (ruled by keffiyeh-wearing Arab kings) opposed by Shiite Iran (ruled by black-turbanned ayatollahs). Standing shoulder-to-shoulder with Saudi Arabia are the Gulf States, backed up to a lesser extent by such Sunni Arab nation states as Egypt and Jordan. The USA and Israel are supporters of this alliance, though obviously neither Muslim nor Arab in their loyalties and so working to their own agendas. The Shiite faction in the Middle East is led by the Islamic Republic of Iran, supported by its allies in Iraq, Syria, southern Lebanon, and North Yemen. Russia and China support this alliance.

But this is not the whole picture, for there is, too, a third faction, a less coherent group, made of such independent-minded Muslim states as Oman and Qatar and the Turkish Republic. In addition, there are international organisations such as the Muslim Brotherhood – and before them, the pan-Arab, secular Ba'ath Party – whose influence needs to be considered.

It's a fiendishly complicated situation to understand, but not an impossible task. For those of us in the West, without affiliation, our first task is to extend our empathy to all sides, to learn to listen both to people and to history. We need to hear the stories that fuel the imagination of the Muslim world, perhaps even to share some of their emotional impact. We should, at the very least, know enough to call our own politicians to account, for their interventions (even when well intentioned) have often backfired.

Although the Sunni and Shia divisions within the Middle East are important, they are matched, and maybe exceeded, by equally strong and enduring divisions based on ethnicity and language – on the three rival identities of Arab, Turk and Iranian. For Turkey, Arabia and Iran have for centuries been the Middle East's three dominant powers. Each has an adamantine sense of its own identity, which coincides with the pride of being a Turk, an Arab and an Iranian. Each comes with its own ancient language, race and thousands of years of history and tradition. In terms of population, the three are also roughly equal: Turkey has around 72 million; Iran 80 million; the Arabian peninsula 78 million (if one includes its migrant workers – many of whom are Muslims from Egypt, Pakistan, Syria and Yemen). The three ethnicities are often considered to mirror Sunni–Shia divides and to fit neatly with the frontiers of modern nation states. Thus, Iran is Persian-speaking and Shiite, Turkey is Turkic-speaking and Sunni, and Saudi Arabia is Arab-speaking and ultra-Sunni. But as we dig deeper, we come upon many fascinating contradictions, present in virtually every chapter of this book. These are the high stress points of the modern Middle East where either faith or race is in conflict with the national majority, in regions that all too often coincide with the position of oil fields.

Turkey is a strong nation state, proud to be the latest in a long succession of Turkic Empires which for centuries have defended Islam. The Turkish Republic is the orphaned heir of the old Ottoman Empire, which ruled the Middle East and Balkans for five hundred years. The frontiers of modern Turkey are but a shadow of this old empire, but it is determined to hold onto every inch of what it has retained, and its rulers are passionately opposed to the south-eastern third of the state breaking away to become an independent Kurdistan. This is the principal reason why Turkey has become so embedded in the recent Syrian civil war, as the Syrian Kurds, who fought so resiliently against ISIS, are seen as closely allied to its own Kurdish independence movement. Turkey also has long-term ambitions to recover its old position as the leading voice in the Middle East.

Saudi Arabia, which invented its militant, fundamentalist form of Sunni Islam – Wahhabism – back in the eighteenth century, has long wished to create a united Arabia. The Saudi Emirate came close to achieving this on two occasions, even before the first drop of oil had been discovered, but was halted by the military strength of external powers. The Saudis, too, fear the influence of an internal minority, for their eastern governate of Al-Hasa, home to all the oil fields, has a large population of Shia. These Shiite Arabs are an oppressed minority within the Sunni kingdom, which helps explain why the Saudi monarchy is so hostile to the expanding influence of the Shiite Islamic Republic of Iran. Before the Iranian Revolution of 1979, there was no Muslim state led by Shiite traditions. But, since 1979 the Saudis have watched the emergence of a Shiite crescent across the Middle East, composed of Iran and its allies. This began with southern Lebanon and Syria, then vastly expanded when a Shiite government was installed in Iraq. Their latest allies are the Zaydi in North Yemen, which has led to the Saudi-sponsored war on the Shiite Houthi Movement.

Iran has not always considered itself a part of the Middle East, for it is proud of its ancient, indigenous culture, with its distinctively Central Asian links, and has a strong sense of its role as a leading intellectual centre of world culture. It has been the seat of many a great empire, and the modern Iranian state is but a shadow of past glories, but even so it too has a particular area of vulnerability. Its wealth would be crippled if Khuzestan, its Arabic-speaking south-west province, were ever separated from the nation. Ethnically, culturally and linguistically, Khuzestan is Arabic not Iranian, though it shares the same Shiite faith as the rest of Iran. And – once again – it is the region that has most of the oil. It was the cause, the prize and the battlefield of the vastly destructive Iran–Iraq War of 1980–88.

So one of the central understandings of this book is that the situation in the Middle East will continue to remain tense because Turkey, Saudi Arabia and Iran do not exercise diplomacy just to win, but to preserve themselves from internal fragmentation. Such struggles are existential. Even if one night the whole of the Middle East decided to renounce all their religious faith and close down the oil fields, there would still be tension the following morning, because of the ancient rivalry between Turk, Arab and Iranian. As we will discover, the only period when this ancient rivalry was calmed was when the entire political structure of the Middle East was threatened with extinction by Western imperialism in the late nineteenth and early twentieth centuries. In this period, ancient animosities were briefly subordinated to a life-and-death struggle for independence against the aggressive colonial powers of Russia, Britain and France.

There can be no simple explanation of the sources of tension within the Middle East. Each nation, sometimes each province, each city, needs to be understood in the light of its own history, its dreams, fears and aspirations. And, while oil fields seem so important in the calculations of the modern world, within the Middle East they have not altered things but merely expanded the arsenals. The essential nature of Sunni Saudi Arabia and Shiite Iran – and their endemic rivalry – was formed centuries before the first barrel of oil was sold.

❊ ❊ ❊

So another of the missions of this book is not just to predict the geopolitical shape of the future but to explore the power of this past. In order to understand the tremendous emotional hold of the loyalties to Shia and Sunni, we first need to hear the stories that every Muslim knows. We cannot skim over the founding era of Islamic history as if it is some Dark Age legend. As anyone who has spent time in the Middle East will be aware, the historical founders of Islam remain vividly alive in the imagination of Muslims. The members of the household of the Prophet Muhammad resonate in the collective memory of Sunni and Shia alike and provide the heroes and villains around which all Muslims navigate their lives. Mecca and Medina of the seventh century CE (first century AH*) glow with compulsive fascination for all believers. It is very hard for those of us who have been brought up in the West to conceive of the passionate engagement of the past with the present in the Islamic world. It is one of the greatest and most surprising differences between the West and the East. In my travels across the Muslim world, I have everywhere stumbled upon history as a living story, whilst in the West we have the luxury of living in the present with no compelling need to uphold the memory of martyrs, heroes and buried civilisations.

It is also important to remember that what keeps Sunni and Shia apart is much less fundamental than what they share. All Muslims recite the same Koran, revere the same Prophet Muhammad, pray, fast and go on pilgrimage to Mecca in the same way. In all major details of the practical demonstration of their faith, they are near identical. Their spiritual visions are also very similar, for most Islamic history has been dominated by rulers who do not fulfil either the Shia or Sunni vision of

---

* I have used the Western CE (COMMON ERA) dating system throughout this book. The Muslim or Hijri calendar was formulated by the caliph Umar in 639 CE (17 AH) and begins with the Hijrah – Muhammad and his followers' migration from Mecca to Medina in 622 CE (1 AH – AFTER HIJRAH). The Prophet's dates are 53 BH – BEFORE HIJRAH (570 CE) to 10 AH (632CE). This book's year of publication, 2025 CE, is 1447 AH.

'rightful leadership'. Shia believe that, before the Prophet was even buried, the Muslim community had lost its divinely anointed and rightful spiritual leadership which would have directed a radically compassionate community. The Sunni are less dismissive but nevertheless believe the rule of good Muslims lasted for less than thirty years after the Prophet's death; they revere only the governance of the first four caliphs – Abu Bakr, Omar, Uthman and Ali. Most modern Sunni scholars believe that the generation who had been taught by the Prophet, 'the Companions', exercised the only period of true Islam. After three generations, this holy period of the pious predecessors – the Salafi – was extinguished.

This discovery – that no real Muslim scholar, be they Shia or Sunni, thinks that the actual rulers of the Islamic world were rightful after the death of Ali in 661 – is important. To an outsider, all those dynasties of Muslim caliphs appear as both political and spiritual leaders, but that was not how they were seen within their own faith communities. Political leadership within Islamic history has often tried to wrap itself up in the cloak of Sunni or Shia spiritual authority but seldom succeeds for long. The 'sultans' are simply the men who hold the power and since 661 have dominated the Islamic world. A handful of these sultans have won respect as military leaders of their community. But the true and enduring heroes of Islamic society (be they Shia or Sunni) over the last 1,400 years are the 'sheikhs', the gentle scholars and venerable elders who have suffered for their faith. They have not sought after office but have slowly earned for themselves the respect of their community, by the practice of their faith, combined with the modesty of their lives and the principled reality of their teaching.

Shia and Sunni intellectuals have now been in ceaseless dialogue with each other for 1,400 years. Over the course of this book, I have indicated a number of occasions when the

Shia intellectual inheritance was about to be placed alongside the four schools of Sunni law. Such a vision of unity, of five schools, has been suggested by many Muslim teachers, especially those who have dedicated their life to pan-Islamic unity. The most obvious human bridge is Jafar al-Sadiq – 'the truthful one' – who was both the sixth imam of the Shiites and a descendant of Abu Bakr, the first Sunni caliph. In his own lifetime (702–765), Jafar refused to accept an official political position from the Abbasid caliph, let alone challenge his right to the caliphate, but rather was content to serve the Muslim community as a simple scholar, albeit one who was treated with enormous respect.

As we will see over the course of this book, the rule of the sultans (literally 'those who possess authority') continues to this day. These men are often labelled 'moderate Muslims' by Western politicians keen to find someone they can talk to and make deals with. In every generation they have been challenged by principled scholar sheikhs to rule with the clear justice of the Muslim faith. This dialogue between sultan and sheikh is at the heart of every dynamic Islamic community, be they Sunni or Shia, Sufi or Salafi. It is what makes the study of Muslim civilisations so continuously fascinating, this quest for the perfect past, when the House was *undivided*, when the Prophet Muhammad led, directed and inspired the first community. If this interests you at all, read on.

PART ONE

The Origins of the
Sunni–Shia Schism

PART ONE

The Origins of the Sunni–Shia Schism

For all Muslims, whether Sunni or Shia, followers of every tradition from Wahhabism to Sufi mysticism, everything stems from the seventh-century Medina household of the Prophet Muhammad. It was in the Medina oasis that the Prophet spent the last ten years of his life, between 622 and 632, a period that every Muslim reveres as the path of rightful spiritual governance. To understand the later divisions, it is crucial to know the historical reality of the Prophet's life, to feel the power of stories Muslims hear from birth, and to learn of the fateful incidents that stopped the Prophet's cousin and son-in-law, Ali, from being acclaimed the rightful leader of the community. These stories set the boundaries and framework of an intellectual mood that has endured for 1,400 years.

All Muslims believe that the Prophet Muhammad was a mortal being, who, orphaned in his childhood, had to earn his keep in his uncle's household, as a shepherdboy and then on the camel caravans. Muhammad's uncle was one of the clan sheikhs of an important tribal confederation of merchants – the Quraysh – which in this period of Arab history dominated the desert trade route that connected the Yemen with the trading cities of Syria. So Muhammad, though poor and illiterate, was an acknowledged member of an important tribe centred on the trading city of Mecca, a significant holy place in pagan Arabia.

Muhammad was naturally drawn to a life of piety and spiritual enquiry, but the gift of prophecy – making him a mouthpiece for the word of God – first visited him as a terrifying revelation at the age of forty. For the next twelve years, Muhammad continued to live in Mecca, but, as he and his followers were persecuted, they migrated to the safety of Medina, a community that had already agreed to protect the Muslims and accept Muhammad as their judge. From this base, Muhammad completed the cycle of revelations that would later be collected as the Koran, which during his life primarily existed in an entirely oral form. All Muslims acknowledge the same Koran, and all study and revere the decisions, judgements and sayings that the Prophet made and which later generations collected as the *hadith*.

It was only at the end of the Prophet's life that we can detect the first fractional differences between Shia and Sunni – the most obvious was a disagreement about who would inherit the leadership of the community after his death. The Shia believe that Ali would have continued the spiritual evolution of the Muslim community which, under the dynamic leadership of a dynasty of holy imams, would have become ever more engaged in the care of the poor and afflicted and the practice of holy poverty. The Sunni concentrate their energy in trying to reconstruct the belief system and practices of the early Muslim community, as it had been led by the Prophet, but also by his 'rightly guided successors', the first four caliphs.

CHAPTER 1

The House Undivided

Medina (622–632)

Between 622 and 632 the Prophet Muhammad lived in the
oasis of Medina. This was the only period in which he exercised
political authority – a time seen as the ideal community – and
it lasted from when he was fifty-two to his death aged sixty-
three. His house was a walled yard, with a prayer hall at one
end – a propped-up affair of timbers and palm trunks leaning
against a solid stone wall – and a scattering of huts at the other,
each lived in by a different wife and partly screened from each
other by curtains. The Prophet had no room of his own, but
every night went to one of his wives. The house was a highly
animated space, which served as mosque, family home, public
kitchen, occasional hospital, store house and meeting room.
Cooking seems to have been done both communally and
privately, so there was a constant bustle around the fetching of
water, firewood and food. At formal times of prayer it could be
as packed as a marketplace, though there were surprisingly few
rules to these times of assembly. Worshippers would stay on
to consult the Prophet about some personal crisis, or spiritual
concern, or to make a petition or tell out a disturbing dream.
The only social rule imposed on his guests was to go home once
fed and not to interrupt the mid-afternoon siesta.

These habits still govern Muslim etiquette: where guests are
always fed, whether it be at a lavish wedding at a sultan's

palace or tea in a simple Bedouin tent. For the house-mosque is the role model for all Muslims. It is the House Undivided, where politics, religion, friends and family all came together under the leadership of the Prophet Muhammad.

I have often thought about this house. I have imagined it not as some pure, white architectural prototype of the first mosque, but bustling with the domestic disorder of a busy household. It would have contained piles of baggage (including at least two campaign tents), bales of reed mats, the coming and going of stepchildren, grandchildren and favourite animals – notably cats, of whom Muhammad was fond.* In one story about the Prophet, he became so exhausted by the animation of his household that he only found privacy by sleeping on a roof.

Camels also shared the compound. Muhammad must have known hundreds, if not thousands, of camels, during the early years of his life, when he worked first as a boy-herder and then on the caravan trails of central Arabia. Kuswa ('split ears') was Muhammad's favourite camel at Medina. He had insisted on buying her from his friend Abu Bakr during their migration from Mecca to Medina, when the two of them travelled with just three camels. It was said to have been Kuswa who chose the location of the house in Medina, for the Prophet had been besieged by so many offers of hospitality in the oasis that he decided not to offend any of his hosts, instead letting his reins slip and so giving Kuswa her head. She rambled through the sandy lanes, eventually selecting a neglected courtyard used for storing dates. Once Muhammad had unloaded his baggage

---

* There are many stories that testify to Muhammad's affection for cats. In one famous incident we hear how, rising before dawn to prepare himself for the first prayers, Muhammad cut off the sleeve of his cloak rather than disturb the slumbers of Muezza. This particular cat had earned this place of honour, by alerting Muhammad to the presence of a viper and so saving his life.

and saddle, he declared that he had found his camp for that night and would move no further. He stayed the next night, and the next, and in due course he purchased it from its owners – a pair of orphans – and over the next months this yard gradually evolved into both his house and Islam's first mosque. Some of the external walls of the yard were reinforced, and various huts and lean-to structures gradually grew up. Fodder must have been stored, for, beside Kuswa and Muezza, there were a pair of racing camels, named Al-Adbaa and Al-Jadaa, and two horses, a beautiful roan mare called Murtajaz ('spontaneous') and a dark stallion called Sakhb ('swift'). In the last years of his life, the Prophet was also associated with a black donkey called Yafur ('deer'), due to his graceful gait. Yafur came to the household, along with Meriem, a Coptic concubine, sent by the ruler of Egypt, known to the Muslims as Muqawqis.*

All sorts of pious and intriguing legends have attached to Yafur: that he could see angels otherwise invisible to human-kind and could talk when he wished to. Other stories explain that he was the last survivor of an ancient dynasty of donkeys who for the last sixty generations had carried a long line of prophets, from Moses in Sinai to Jesus on the road to Jerusa-lem. It was said that, after the Prophet's death, Yafur tried to jump down a well in despair – for he knew that Muhammad was the last of the prophets.

Muhammad also owned an off-white mule called Duldul, whose name (rather surprisingly for such a beloved animal) means 'the vexatious or vacillating one'. Duldul is known to have carried the Prophet through the stormy events of the

* The Prophet had sent the ruler of Egypt a letter in the spring of 628, calling upon the leaders of the war-torn Middle East to unite beneath a shared monotheism. The governor of Egypt in this period was likely to have been a Persian-appointed official, after the Sassanid conquest of Byzantine Alexandria. He replied with a letter accompanied by gifts.

Battle of Hunayn. Victorious generals tend to ride into battle on magnificent dark chargers, like Alexander the Great on Bucephalus, or parade through a conquered city on a stately white horse. A mule is a homely animal of low social stature – infertile and obstinate – and so to ride it at the head of an army is entirely in keeping with Muhammad's renunciation of wealth and title. Mules and donkeys can be ridden bareback without saddles or stirrups, and with both legs swinging on one side. To a Muslim, the image of a bearded old man, trotting along the road on a pale mule or a dark donkey, without weapons or saddlery, still has an impact. For such a man is following the example of the Prophet, one of whose affectionate nicknames was Sahib al-Himar, 'master of the donkey'. Charismatic Islamic reformers like Abu Yazid in the Tunisian Sahara and Ibn Tumert in the Atlas Mountains of Morocco have consciously played on this imagery of the veiled power of a true leader. It stresses the poverty and humility of true Islam, when compared with the gilt and glitter of the cavalry armies of a ruling sultan.

The Shia like to remember that the care of Duldul and Yafur passed down to their hero, Ali, as part of his tattered inheritance. Possession of these two, sad, old animals is both a symbol of the holy poverty Muhammad bequeathed to his spiritual heir, and in some way the insignia of a true Muslim leader. In addition to all the other signs, a Muslim will always be able to recognise a truly holy leader by the poverty of his mount.

❊ ❊ ❊

The Prophet's formal political role in the oasis of Medina was a modest one. This had been agreed within his inner circle in a public oath, before he made his escape from the persecution of Mecca, and was later repeated to an expanded audience and then turned into a written legal document. He was to be the chief arbitrator among the Muslims in the oasis.

One might expect that Muhammad's role as a mouthpiece for the divine revelations of the Koran would have placed him in a position of absolute unquestioned authority. This does not seem to be the case, for, though his followers never questioned the authority of the Koran, they felt free to question any of his decisions that did not come from a divine source.

The Koran was revealed to Muhammad, verse by verse, over a twenty-two-year period and was only authoritatively written down two decades after his death. The first verse was a terrifying experience for Muhammad. It was dictated by the archangel Gabriel. Later Koranic verses often came upon the Prophet when he was unprepared and in some private space – a hut, a tent or a cave; they were sometimes witnessed by one of his wives but never by the ranks of male followers. The prophetic role was never a public performance, or a sermon before the faithful, but occurred within a domestic space. Respect for the sanctity of domestic space has always been an absolute feature of Islamic society.

Muhammad's authority in Medina borrowed nothing from existing examples of kingship. The Arabs were well used to the habits of kings – the magnificent courts of the Byzantine Caesars at Constantinople, or the Persian Sassanid shahs at Ctesiphon, or such princes of the Arabian desert as the Ghassanid, Lakhmid and Kinda dynasties. These recognised all the expressions of royal power: the sumptuous clothing, the cavalry escorts, the gilded ornaments, the palace guards, the hushed ushers, the immense halls in which to wait and the revered atmosphere of a throne room.

Muhammad despised the wearing of silks and brocades, and ornaments fashioned from precious metals, as the assertion of pride. He spurned the long, tailored trousers then closely associated with heroic Arab cavalrymen, and instead wore his clothes loose, and homemade, from cloth that had been spun and woven by his household.

A body of tried and trusted friends, many of them bound by a decade of persecution and the filaments of marriage alliances, formed an informal inner element at the heart of the Muslim community. They could be called upon by the Prophet to lead an embassy, take command of a military raid, act as a missionary, deliver a letter or formally acknowledge the reception of a charitable tithe. They responded to these commands, fulfilled them, and then quietly returned to their family hut in one of the villages of the oasis. There was no palace quarter, no privileged suburb of walled gardens set aside for their use. Nor was there a hierarchy or a system of formal rank, aside from respect for those who had suffered for their faith and professed Islam. Time and time again the Prophet overlooked even this badge of righteous pride and trusted some recent convert with a responsible task. The Bedouin tribes of Arabia, once they had embraced Islam or agreed a peace treaty, were left under the command of their own indigenous sheikhs.

All of this creates an astonishing political role model for future Muslim leaders, Sunni or Shia. It is an example of leadership which requires very exacting standards of accessibility, compassion, humanity and honesty, a life according to the Prophet's heartfelt prayer: 'O Lord, keep me alive a poor man, and let me die poor, and raise me among the poor.' Muslim leaders will on some level always be judged and assessed by their people against the behaviour of the Prophet. They should have the good manners to be able to listen (not just command) and be prepared to share their meals with any man, not just the rich and powerful. In the conduct of their lives, they should remember the words of the Prophet: 'What is pride? Holding another man in contempt.'

They should also be visibly content in the simple pleasures of family life. The narrative of the Prophet's life establishes an ideal role model for a Muslim leader, approaching the wisdom of old age, surrounded by loving children, one or two grandchildren and old friends who have long shared a life of simplicity and modesty and a passionate spiritual quest. No leader should be ashamed of an orphaned childhood, of poverty or of having to work to feed himself as a young man and then to provide for his family. He need not be ashamed of the sparsity of his formal education, either, for as a boy Muhammad lived amongst the herds and the camel caravans and knew no university.

Throughout Islamic history, the gap between the ideal example established by the Prophet and the reality of political leadership has been a continuous tragedy.

CHAPTER 2

The Protection of Medina

*Allegiances, the Constitution of Medina
and the Flight from Mecca*

When Muhammad arrived at the oasis of Medina in the midsummer of 622, he joined a group of just eighty followers from his hometown of Mecca. The Muslims had been financially crippled by a trade boycott organised by the clan chiefs of Mecca, and a small group of believers (including one of his four daughters) had escaped persecution by taking refuge in the Christian empire of Ethiopia. Muhammad had already buried the two most important people in his life, his uncle Abu Talib and his wife Khadija, two years before, in the cemetery at Mecca. Under the persecution at Mecca, he had looked at various options where his followers might feel safe, such as the nearby oasis of Taif. But Medina was chosen after a delegation of its Muslims had come to him and sworn an oath to protect him.

Muhammad had left Mecca under cover of night, protected by the bravery of his cousin, Ali, who slept in his bed outside as a deception, enabling the Prophet to escape near certain death at the hands of an assassination squad put together by the city's pagan clans. For three days and nights, as search parties tried to pick up his trail, he hid in a small cave, accompanied by his old friend Abu Bakr. The Koran records that the two had the divine gift of an unearthly calm.* The two refugees were helped by Abu Bakr's son Abdullah, who would lead the family herd of goats past the cave so that they could take their fill of milk and, as the goats returned in the evening, make certain that their hoof prints buried any tell-tale footprints. On one occasion, it is said, an armed party found the cave, but as the entrance had been sealed by a spider's web, and had a rock dove nesting, they left off searching. On the third day, Abu Bakr's daughter brought food, after which the two men were led to an isolated valley where a Bedouin waited for them with three camels for their long ride to Medina. Muslim story-tellers love these tales, the humble spider and the cooing dove doing their bit for the Prophet and acting as agents of God. The episode also has special relevance for a Sunni audience for the role played by Abu Bakr, the first Sunni caliph.

This journey from the persecution of Mecca to the safety of Medina is the beginning of the history of Islam as a separate community and would later be chosen as the chronological start date of the Islamic era, the Hijrah. The day Muhammad escaped Mecca was 16 June 622, day one of the Muslim era, and from this date the life of the Prophet comes into much tighter focus. Exact dates are not always possible for the Meccan period of his life, and certainly not his first forty years, but after Muhammad arrives at Medina there is a generally accepted chronicle.

This division, between the period of his life in Mecca and the period at Medina, is recognisable within the 114 *suras* (chapters) of the Koran. Those from Mecca are shorter, more powerful and universal. They are full of the sense of God as

---

* 'When the Unbelievers drove him out, he had no more than one companion; they two were in the cave, and he said to his companion, 'Have no fear, for Allah is with us.' Then Allah sent down His peace upon him, and strengthened him'. (from verse 40 of the 9th *sura*).

the creator of the universe, the upholder of heaven and earth and the imminence of the coming Day of Judgement. *Sura* 93 begins with this memorable line: 'By the dawn's early light and by the darkness of the growing stillness of the night: thy Lord has not abandoned you, nor doth he hate you.'

Sura 100 opens with the image of a cavalry horse striking sparks from the stones before turning to reflections on ethical behaviour:

By the war-horse snorting
By the sparkling fire-strikers
By the dawn chargers
Which raise the dust
To pass through the middle-guard
Verily mankind is ungrateful to his Lord
And to that he is his own witness
By his fierce love of wealth.
Does he not know
That when that which is in the grave shall show forth,
And that what is hidden within the breast will be revealed,
And on that day their Lord will knowingly see through them.

By contrast, the twenty-four verses delivered in Medina are longer and more pragmatic, focused on the issues facing the nascent Muslim community, from law to war, marriage and inheritance. They also reveal a conscious awareness of hypocrites within the growing community, a theme which imbeds an innate sense of division within Islam between the genuinely faithful and others.

❀ ❀ ❀

In the orthodox Sunni world there is always a tendency to play up the significance of Mecca, its role within Arabia and the leadership of its dominant Quraysh tribe. Sunni scholars revel in the detailed differences between the fourteen clans of the Quraysh, which include the Prophet Muhammad's own Beni Hashim clan. This partiality is understandable, for one of the key arguments that led to the Sunni caliphate was that Muslim leadership had to come from within the Quraysh.

Shia historians are more aware of historic individuals from outside of Mecca and of Muhammad's close personal connections with Medina. Muhammad's mother Amina, although from a Meccan clan, had been brought up in Medina, in the household of her stepmother, Rughayabah. Her last action as a parent was to take her young son on a desert journey to meet his male relations in Medina. Through his father's side of the family, Muhammad also had strong links with the oasis. He was the great-grandson of Salma bint Amr, a powerful and independent woman from the influential Beni Nazzar clan of Medina. Salma was a woman confident enough to choose her own husbands, of whom Hashim, Muhammad's Meccan great-grandfather, was just one among many. Hashim stayed with Salma on his frequent journeys as a trader but she never moved to Mecca and remained in charge of her own house and business in Medina. Their son, Abdul Muttalib (Muhammad's revered grandfather), was brought up by his mother in Medina until he was old enough to start travelling with his father. As a young man, working on the caravan trails, Muhammad would have got to know Medina intimately. The oasis was a vital staging post on the route north towards Syria, Egypt and Iraq.

Muhammad made his first converts to his new monotheistic religion from Medina during the time of the annual Meccan fair, when he preached to a tent full of pilgrims, probably in 619. By the time of the following year's pilgrimage-fair, the converts numbered a dozen individuals. At the end of the fair, they took a personal oath of loyalty to Muhammad (known as the Bayat al-Nisa) and promised to uphold a moral life worthy of a Muslim. When this group rode back home to Medina, they took with them one of Muhammad's youngest followers, eighteen-year old Musab ibn Umar, later known as Al-Khayr ('the good'). Although Musab came from a wealthy family, he proved himself an exemplary Muslim by following a life of poverty and charity. Empowered by his example, this early group set an extraordinary example of inter-clan harmony.

Within Medina this was particularly noteworthy. For over a century, the oasis had been consumed by a feud between two rival tribal confederations, the Aws and the Khazraj. Their rivalry, relentlessly destructive, culminated at the Battle of Bu'ath, fought just outside the oasis in 617, a bloodbath which threatened the very survival of the oasis. So the harmony achieved by the first group of Muslim converts impressed everyone.

This was the context in which, in 621, a group of seventy-five individuals came from Medina to pledge their loyalty to Muhammad. This delegation included clan chieftains from both factions. The oath took place by moonlight on the rocky slopes of Aqaba, a sacred hill midway between Mecca and Mina. Muhammad's uncle Abbas, who was not yet a Muslim, waited for Muhammad's sermon to be finished and then challenged the delegation from Medina: 'We have protected him as much as we could ... but if you can defend him against his enemies, then assume the burden that you have taken. But if you are going to surrender him and betray him after having taken him away with you, you had better leave him now because he is respected and well defended in his own place.'

Bara ibn Marir, one of the warrior chieftains from Medina, then advanced and, taking the hand of Muhammad in his own, replied: 'By Him who sent you with the truth, we will protect you as we protect our own. So accept our pledge of allegiance, messenger of God. We are men of war, possessed of arms that have been handed down from father to son.' To which Muhammad replied: 'I am yours and you are mine. Who you war against, him I war against. Who you make peace with, him I make peace with.'

Two by two the delegation from Medina, which included a pair of women, advanced to take the Prophet's hand and affirm their oath, which became known as the second pledge of Aqaba, the *bayat* or 'pledge of war'.

This oral oath grew into the first written document of the Islamic world, the Constitution of Medina, which recognised freedom of religion (for three of the clans were Jewish). It also acknowledged that the dozen clans of the oasis would keep their own self-governing structures. Muslims – then in a tiny minority – would become an honorary thirteenth clan under the leadership of Muhammad. No acts of violence would be permitted within the oasis. Muhammad was to be accepted by all the clans of the oasis as the 'arbitrator' of all their disputes. His appointed role was not as a Prophet but as a peace-making judge, a sheikh.

Even after his military victories, which were to follow in the next decade, even after Muhammad had been saluted throughout Arabia as a prophet of God and recognised as a power by the proconsuls of distant empires, he never sought to replace the simple position given to him in this document. He showed no interest in establishing an administration, in drawing up provincial and district boundaries, or in appointing tax collectors, like all other rulers.

Anyone who wishes to understand what makes an Islamic society needs to relish this. Muhammad was not interested in temporal power but wished to teach how all should behave – as individuals to their family, as well as to their neighbours – and how they should struggle to embrace a wider community which includes the old, the poor and the lost. They were not encouraged to pledge loyalty to a new empire, but to invest their fear and hope in an unknowable God who they would meet on Judgement Day.

From day one it is acknowledged that this ethical high ground of Islam will need to be defended by well-armoured warriors experienced in battle. But, while a Muslim leader is recognised as the moral guiding force of society, he does not have to exercise day-to-day control. This made it very easy for Islam to spread its influence across new frontiers. A teacher of the moral truths of the Koran – the imam who leads the daily prayers, or a sheikh – can be welcomed into any self-governing community. The Imam will explain how a good Muslim should live his life. But the old chieftains and power-brokers can keep their place in their society, providing that they can be seen to be upholding the moral guidance of this Islamic leader or teacher. In return, they will give him their military protection and make certain that he is respected as a judge of the last instance. All those messy and often dirty details of running a state can remain with the old bosses.

Islam has never been very interested in the precise detail of political structures, provided its moral code is accepted to stand in unquestionable authority above this political power. This tradition is especially true of the Sunni, and though the Shia yearn for a more politically powerful imam commanding their society, in practice they never got such a man (as we will find out later), so it is perhaps still more true for them.

✳ ✳ ✳

But let us return to the sun-scorched, rock-strewn mountains around the trading town of Mecca. Muhammad has received the oath of loyalty and protection from the delegation from Medina. In a secluded valley, Muhammad and Abu Bakr have mounted their camels, using the third mount to carry their baggage and a vital complement of goatskins filled with well-water. To confuse their enemies they first ride in the opposite direction to Medina, heading south-west, then working their way north along the Red Sea shore until they feel it is safe enough to head due east. It was an eccentric route, but after eight days of hard riding they reached Quba, one of the outlying hamlets of Medina, where they rested for three days of customary hospitality offered to travellers before making their formal entry into the oasis.

Muhammad had been one of the last of the Muslims to escape from Mecca, so practically all of his eighty followers were on hand to welcome him with prayers and tears of joy. They were balanced in number by Muslims who originated from Medina, so Muhammad asked each of the latter to adopt a refugee from Mecca, who they fed and housed, and helped find work. The Meccans were traders and had little experience of gardening in the small but well-worked plots of an oasis, with their intricate system of irrigation beneath the shade of palm trees. But there were plenty of simple tasks that they could perform: working the wells, grinding corn, making mud bricks and weaving the ubiquitous palm rush mats from which walls, ceilings, ground mats and bags were all made. Muhammad himself did not want to show favouritism to any clan, nor be a burden on any, so he chose his penniless young cousin Ali to pair up with.

For the next seven months, the two communities of Muslims – the Ansar ('helpers') from Medina and the Muhajirun ('emigrants') from Mecca – spent the cool of the nights building the exterior walls of the first mosque, which doubled as the home of Muhammad. As a young man, I remember getting off a night bus in an oasis town, and being drawn towards the bright lights, chants and energy of a midnight building project.

It was the construction of a mosque and was being built, it was explained to me with pride, with love, as no-one was being paid and the materials had been funded by local charitable donations. Everyone present was aware of the direct link back to the example of the Prophet's first mosque, and proudly used the example of two gangs of workers, Ansar and Muhajirun, in affectionate competition with each other.*

Once he had a house ready, Muhammad could send messengers to Mecca, to invite the women he was responsible for to join him; in those chivalric days, their passage among the Arab tribes was safe. Then, once the last of the Muslim refugees were safely established in Medina, Muhammad was free to wage war against his enemies in Mecca.

In the spring of 623, the first raiding parties were sent out into the desert, searching for Meccan caravans to pillage. Muhammad, having been persecuted, was now the aggressor. Hamza, his paternal uncle, led this first raiding party of thirty men; they found a Meccan caravan on the Red Sea shore, but it was far too well defended to be attacked. Muhammad himself joined the third raiding party, known as the Waddan patrol, and he used the opportunity to forge the Muslims' first pact of non-aggression with a Bedouin clan.

A month later, the clansmen of Medina joined the raiding parties, as volunteers. The patrols now numbered two hundred and so could contemplate giving battle. This finally occurred at the wells of Badr on 13 March 624 – the twentieth day of Ramadan. A Muslim force of 350 men and seventy camels, again including Muhammad, pursued a rich Syrian caravan, which managed to escape, leaving the Muslim force facing a Meccan army three times their size. The surprise victory of

---

* These same identities were adopted by jihadi warriors in recent times in Syria and Iraq, building their ISIS 'caliphate', an instant connection for the volunteers back to the lifetime of the Prophet.

the Muslims that day is commemorated in three different references within the Koran, and the name 'Badr' has become synonymous with a victory against the odds, assisted by the angels of God.* Ali proved himself the most daring, brave and brilliant of all the passionate young Muslim warriors.

It often comes as a shock, to outsiders, to find that the Prophet Muhammad was so closely engaged in the prosecution of war. He was the aggressor in all of these raids. He was also stepping a little beyond his formal political authority. But the oaths to Muhammad had healed the civil strife between the Aws and Khazraj confederations in Medina and the clan sheikhs recognised that raids against an external enemy would further heal the wounds of the ancient feud.

Muhammad knew, too, that Medina was a place that had for generations been addicted to fighting. He was not interested in wealth or military victory but in the survival and dissemination of his message. However, he was wise enough in the ways of the world to realise that the pagan leadership of Mecca would only be forced to negotiate – and listen to his message – if he struck at the wealth of their camel caravans and the security of their trade routes. Muhammad also realised that he could best recruit an army if he offered the chance of plunder from a desert raid alongside a role in upholding a new ethical vision for the world. If we unpick the details of these raids, it becomes apparent that Muhammad exercised grand strategy more often than battle tactics, time and again avoiding armed conflict in order to build up a network of treaties with the Bedouin tribes, which would gradually isolate Mecca. Once this had been achieved, he began to use desert patrols to bring his message to the tribes. This taught the Arabs to live in peace

---

* 'Badr' was used as a codeword by the Egyptians in their 1973 attack on Israel, as well as in campaigns fought by the Pakistani and Iranian armies.

with their neighbours and to engage in a lifelong battle to protect the weak and feed the poor. But there was always an honourable role for a fighting man, to protect the new ethical community. Muslims consider themselves the people of peace, defended by warriors.

CHAPTER 3

The Women of the House

The rivalry of Aisha and Fatima

In his youth, Muhammad worked as a herdsman on the camel caravans, too poor to support a wife; from the age of twenty-five to fifty, he was a monogamous husband, with a bustling household of children. Then, in the last ten years of his life, he shared his household with eleven wives. These women were a vital and intimate part of the community of Muslims at Medina, performing innumerable functions, while living together in a space which served at times as a hospital, canteen, embassy – and always as a mosque.

It was within this household that the first shadow of the Sunni–Shia schism appears. At its core was the rivalry between Aisha – Muhammad's youngest and most vivacious wife – and his youngest daughter, Fatima. Renowned for her piety, Fatima was married to Ali, Muhammad's cousin, first follower and lifelong companion. Aisha gave birth to no children, while Fatima quickly gave birth to two healthy sons, Hasan and Husayn, both visibly beloved by the Prophet. To complicate things further, Aisha bore a fierce grudge against Ali. And it was her father, Abu Bakr, who would become the First Caliph of Islam, pushing aside Ali's claims to be the true heir.

This makes Aisha one of the most controversial figures in the Islamic world. She is loathed by the Shia, who see her as manipulative, ambitious and vengeful. They will not accept any *hadith* (a reported tradition or saying of the Prophet) if it is sourced back to her memory. The Sunni accept Aisha as a strong character who was genuinely contrite about her failings and an invaluable witness to the character and nature of the Prophet. Her love for Muhammad and her belief in his message was never in doubt, if now and then her individual voice can still be heard above layers of scholarly piety. She believed, for example, that Muhammad had travelled to Jerusalem in spiritual rather than physical form in the Night Journey; she was dismayed by the mass execution of the men of the Jewish Beni Qurayzah clan; and she reacted with spirit when she heard that Zaynab had been given to Muhammad as an additional wife by Koranic revelation, saying, 'Truly thy Lord makes haste to do thy bidding.' But Aisha had a prodigious memory – she is the source for 2,210 *hadith* – and when she died in 678, aged sixty-seven, she had become a fundamental historical source.

By contrast to the fiery, contentious Aisha, every Muslim of whatever creed adores the pious, obedient, suffering example set by Fatima and her mother, Khadija. Muhammad had buried Khadija, his beloved wife of twenty-five years, in Mecca in 620. He was fifty years old at the time and it was the most difficult year of his life, his 'Year of Sorrow', when the persecution of the pagan chiefs of Mecca seemed to be destroying his fledgling community of Muslims. Khadija was older and richer than Muhammad and his intellectual and social equal. Their mothers were third cousins. She was the first Muslim, the first to recognise Muhammad as a Prophet of God after his terrifying possession by the Archangel Gabriel. Before this first revelation, she had lived a highly moral and ethical life, part of her mission as a Hanif – a (pre-Islamic) searcher after God.

While Khadija was alive, Muhammad had no thought of taking another wife, and after her death, though he would marry many women, none stood a chance of displacing Khadija as the great love of his life. Aisha confessed, 'I did not feel jealous of any of the wives of the Prophet as much as I did of Khadija, even though I never met her, for the Prophet used to mention her so very often, and whenever he slaughtered a sheep, he would send the first cuts to the old friends of Khadija.' Muhammad told his household, 'God never granted me anyone better in this life than her. She accepted me when people rejected me; she believed in me when people doubted me; she shared her wealth with me when I became deprived; and God granted me children only through her.' When Khadija's sister Halah visited the Prophet's household in Medina, it was noted how moved he was to hear the sound of her voice, which reminded him of Khadija's. On one occasion Muhammad speculated about his personal hope for paradise, which consisted of nothing more than being alone with Khadija in a reed hut.

Khadija is a curiously modern figure – a powerful, wealthy, independent woman who had had two husbands before she married Muhammad. She had first tested her future husband with a private commercial transaction to see if he matched his high public reputation. Until the Wahhabis of Saudi Arabia knocked down her mausoleum in Mecca, her tomb was a place to visit on the Haj. She was respectfully addressed by pilgrims as the Princess of the Qurayuh and al-Tahira – 'the pure one'. She was the mother of all Muhammad's surviving children, and thus the grand ancestress of all who claim to be of the Prophet's bloodline, through the marriage of her daughter Fatima to Ali. The descendants of Fatima and Ali are venerated in Sunni societies and known as Sayyid or Shorfa, while for the Shia this is the holy bloodline of the imams.

Khadija died before Muhammad migrated to Medina, beginning the Islamic era, so one might imagine that she was a figure equally venerated by both Sunni and Shia historians. But not even this edifying woman is free from the footnote quibbles of rival scholars. Some Sunni historians record that Khadija had children from both of her earlier marriages and claim that she was a forty-year-old widow when she married twenty-five-year-old Muhammad in 595. But she proceeded to have six children with him: a boy Qasim in 598, a daughter Zainab a year later, another daughter Ruqayyah in 601, her daughter Umm Kulthum in 603, then her daughter Fatima and finally Abdullah in 615. This would have made her sixty years old when she gave birth to Abdullah.

The most ardent Shia historians tell a tale with a different nuance: that Khadija was a twenty-five-year-old virgin when she married Muhammad and only gave birth to one perfect child, Fatima, wife of Imam Ali. This account disowns Khadija's three other daughters, maintaining that they were adopted into Muhammad's household as the children of her sister Halah, who had been widowed. One of the motivations for this story is the passionate hatred that the Shia have for anything to do with Uthman (the Third Caliph), who married in succession two of the Prophet's daughters. So this version of history not only downgrades the honour done to Uthman by the Prophet in choosing him to be his son-in-law not once but twice (earning the poetic epithet Dhul-Nurayn – 'He of the Two Lights') but also frames Fatima, Ali's bride, as a unique figure.

Less polemically charged Shia and Sunni can follow a middle storyline. Khadija was a twenty-eight-year-old widower when she married the twenty-five-year-old Muhammad. Older in experience and much wealthier than him, she was otherwise his near equal in age. This would have given Khadija time to give birth to Muhammad's children.

All the chroniclers, however, agree on one fact: that the boys born to Muhammad and Khadija died young, which put extraordinary emotional pressure on Muhammad. In his day, you only existed as an Arab clansman by being a link in the living chain of your tribe, a father to your son and a son to your father. Your *kunya* – your name – was formed by who you were the son of (*ibn*) and father of (*abu*).

All this family history is crucial to understand the emotional tension beneath the Shia–Sunni split, for if Muhammad had left a son, an instantly recognisable male heir, there surely would not have been such a disputed struggle to become his heir. And this desire for a son perhaps also explains why Muhammad, in later life, took so many wives: eleven in all, as well as two concubines. One of the conditions of Islamic marriage is that you should remain content with one wife, if you cannot be equal in your affections. Most Muslims believe that, when the Prophet Muhammad was at home in Medina, he visited each of his wives daily. Certainly, he disapproved of celibacy and delighted in marriage, as a source of mutual pleasure and a bond that helped bind humankind in social obligations.

❋ ❋ ❋

After the death of Khadija, Muhammad's followers proposed that he fill the gap left in his life with two women: Sawdah, a thirty-year-old widow, would run his house and look after his daughters; while Aisha, the daughter of his old friend Abu Bakr, would come to him as a young bride.* In the disturbing

---

* The age of Aisha at her marriage to Muhammad in 624 is contested. Some historians (such as Tabari) write that she was nine, Ibn Ishaq states she was ten, while others believe that this was the date at which she was engaged (in Mecca), but that the marriage this was not consummated until she was sexually mature, aged twelve or thirteen. Twelve had been the age of consent in the Mediterranean and Middle East since the Roman Empire.

environment of the persecution in Mecca, this marriage was postponed. But after the victorious Battle of the Wells of Badr in 624, Muhammad was at last in a position to provide a dowry for his young wife, and he and Aisha were married in a simple ceremony, sharing a bowl of camel milk with their family seated around them.

A few years later, Muhammad took Hafsa as a third wife. Hafsa was an unusual woman within the traditional society of Arabia, fully literate and with a reputation for being outspoken. She is reputed to have been in possession of a written version of the Koran that pre-dates the canonical edition. She married Muhammad after being widowed at the Battle of Uhud. Her father, Omar, offered her to two leading Muslims, Uthman and then Abu Bakr, who rejected her. Muhammad, perhaps sensing a row in the making, deftly stepped in and asked for Hafsa's hand. Like Aisha, she survived the Prophet by thirty-five years and it seems highly likely that most of the *hadith* attributed to her brother Abdullah originated from her experience. There are a number of stories that throw Hafsa and Aisha together as co-conspirators, and this, as well as her status as the daughter of Omar, the Sunni Second Caliph, means that she is not beloved by Shiite historians.

Muhammad's fifth wife, Umm Salamah, was one of Aisha's great rivals. She came into the household as a confident and intelligent widow and was actively wooed by the Prophet. Her father and first husband came from the first rank of Meccan tribal society. Her husband had been an early Muslim who had fought bravely in all the testing first battles against the pagans, dying from his wounds at Uhud. Critically, Umm Salamah also came into the Prophet's life as mother of three young children and, as a widow, gave birth to her fourth child in Muhammad's household. She became a natural companion to Fatima, the Prophet's daughter, and was chosen by her as a guardian for her own children. All her life she remained a passionate supporter of the rights of Fatima and Ali, and was deeply critical of Aisha's involvement in the politics of the succession. She is beloved by Shia historians, but also respected by the Sunni.

In January 627, Umm Salamah and Aisha were selected to be the two wives to accompany the Prophet Muhammad on a military expedition. Muhammad was leading a raid against the Beni Mustaliq tribe, part of the Khuzaa confederation which controlled the trade route along the Red Sea shore. It was a pre-emptive strike, for Muhammad had learned that the Beni Mustaliq were planning to raid Medina. The raid was successful, but it was always necessary to keep one step ahead of the enemy and return to the safety of the oasis before a counter-strike could be made. Just a day's march from Medina, Aisha became detached from the column. She had slipped out of her *howdah* (the leather canopy-like tent in which an Arab woman could travel in privacy) to answer a call of nature, then found herself further delayed as she searched for her onyx necklace. She was so light that no-one noticed any difference in how the *howdah* was swaying and she was not missed. By the time she returned to the desert trail, the column was no longer in sight, so she made her way back to the last night's campsite, the accepted action if you get lost in the desert. There, by chance she was discovered by a handsome young Bedouin herdsman, Safwan ibn Muattal of the Beni Sulaym. Safwan gallantly escorted Aisha back to the Muslim column, but, as she had not yet been registered as missing, the camp buzzed with gossip. This might have blown away, but for the fact that Muhammad was distracted by another new wife (Juwayriyah of the Beni Mustaliq tribe, who had just made peace with the Prophet) and that Aisha had caught a fever so she was taken out of Muhammad's household and nursed at home by her mother. These chance events fed the rumour mill.

Muhammad was troubled by this gossip and waited in vain for some sort of Koranic revelation to clear the air. He also asked various companions for their opinion. Osama, the son of his stepson Zaid, was vehement in Aisha's defence: 'We all know nothing but good of her.' And then it was Ali's turn to speak: 'God hath not restricted thee, and there are many women beside her, but question her maidservant, and she will tell you the truth.' Burayrah, Aisha's maid, agreed that there was no fault in her; 'but that she is a girl, young in years'. Eventually a Koranic revelation exonerated Aisha and created tough new legal standards required for any charges of adultery, with punishments for those convicted of slander. Aisha returned to her marital home in triumph but could never forgive Ali, for to her ears it had sounded as if he was advising the Prophet to divorce Aisha and choose a less contentious wife.

And thus developed the two factions: Aisha (daughter of Abu Bakr) and her three close supporters, Hafsa (daughter of Omar), Saiyah and Sawdah, ranged against Fatima, Umm Salamah and Umm Habiba. It was a rivalry which was to play itself out with ferocious repercussions in the years after the death of the Prophet.

CHAPTER 4

Imam Ali: Islam's Perfect Man

The cornerstone of Shia belief and one of the four great heroes that uphold Sunni traditions

The central dispute between Sunni and Shia is about the rightful succession to the Prophet. Shia is short for 'Shiatu Ali', literally 'Partisans for Ali'. It can come as a surprise, then, to discover that both Sunni and Shia revere Ali. The Turkish Ottoman Empire, always stridently conscious of its Sunni identity, took the two-pointed sword of Ali as its battle flag. The hundreds of Sufi brotherhoods that have existed over the centuries all proudly trace their holy lineage back to Ali, as do the guilds of master-craftsmen throughout the Islamic world. All Muslims honour, respect and try to emulate Ali, be they Salafi or Shia, Wahhabi or Sufi. Ali is regarded as the First Imam of the Shia and the Fourth Caliph of the Sunni.

Ali – Ali ibn Abi Talib, to give him his full name – was the youngest of the children of Abu Talib and Fatima bint Asad. Abu Talib was the Prophet Muhammad's paternal uncle and, as leader of his Beni Hashim clan, a member of the inner council of sheikhs who ran the affairs of the Quraysh tribe of Mecca. The Beni Hashim, as well as participating in the caravan trade, had the responsibility of looking after food and water supplies for the pilgrims who flocked to attend the annual pagan rites in Mecca and in the surrounding hills. After Muhammad lost his mother and then his old grandfather, he passed under the protection of his uncle. This would have been around 586, when Abu Talib was forty and Muhammad just eight years old. Over the next ten years Muhammad worked for his uncle on the long caravan trails that connected Yemen through Mecca with the markets of Syria and Egypt. Muhammad became part of the large family which included three older boys – Talib, Aqeel and Jafar – and three girls, Fakhita, Jumana and Rayta. As a young man, Muhammad fell in love with his cousin Fakhita,* but he was far too poor to be able to contemplate marriage.

As we know, when Muhammad did marry, he and Khadija produced four healthy daughters, but their two sons did not survive infancy. About three years into Muhammad's marriage, Ali was born to Abu Talib and tradition records that Muhammad was the first man to hold the baby. When Ali was five years old, he came to live with Muhammad and Khadija and their young children. All of Ali's brothers and sisters were at least half a generation older than him, so this household must have been much more congenial to the young child, and Ali's presence was no doubt an enormous boon to Muhammad and Khadija in the absence of their own boys. Muhammad was effectively adopting the five-year-old son of the man who had cared for him as an eight-year-old orphan.

Four years later, as a forty-year-old man, Muhammad had his first revelation. The first two people in the world to acknowledge him as a Prophet were his wife Khadija and his nine-year-old cousin Ali. Ali was 'a twin to the Koran', for he literally grew up as the Koran evolved from that first, short revelation to a collection of 114 *suras*. Ali was present throughout that twenty-

---

* Many years later – after his triumphant conquest of Mecca – Muhammad tried to renew this old love affair, and offered to marry his cousin. But Fakhita's husband was Abu Sufyan ibn al-Harith, who had opposed Muhammad for twenty years, both on the battlefield and in verse, so nothing came of this.

year process, and was imbued with the spirit, the language, the instances of revelation and the accretion of certain verses, in a way that was unlike any other man. He had the most extraordinary childhood, deeply immersed in revelation, prophecy, preaching, prayer and theology. This comparatively settled childhood also permitted him to become fully literate, unlike the vast majority of his fellow Arabs.

Although Ali lacked experience of the caravan trails, he never lacked bravery. In 615, as a thirteen-year-old, he helped Muhammad serve a meal to clan sheikhs of the Quraysh tribe, whom the Prophet had assembled in order to explain the nature of his revelations. According to the traditional account, Muhammad asked the assembled company three times if they believed his revelations came from God and whether they could accept him as an Arab prophet. No one answered apart from Ali, who was ridiculed because of his youth. It was a testing experience that revealed the confidence of Ali's faith.

When the following year Muhammad dismissed the three ancient female deities of pagan Arabia as empty idols, half of his followers left him. The Quraysh began to think of ways to silence Muhammad, for in their minds the reputation of Mecca as a trading entrepôt was inextricably bound to its role as a pilgrimage shrine. However, Muhammad's uncle, Abu Talib, though never a believer in Islam, always respected the sincerity of his nephew and insisted that he should retain the protection of his Beni Hashim clan. Thus Ali's father, Abu Talib, protected the life of his adopted father, Muhammad.

Over his youth, Ali watched the majestic authority of the Koran grow, revelation by dazzling revelation. In order to embrace its meaning and to disseminate and protect it, the community of believers would chant the growing extent of the Koran in all-night prayer sessions. By day the believers were increasingly shunned and, for the crime of protecting

Muhammad, all the other clans declared a formal boycott of the Beni Hashim, ending all trading and social connections. Abu Talib made a last attempt to see if he could get his nephew to compromise, in order to lift the ban, but Muhammad was unwavering: 'O uncle! By Almighty God I swear, even if they should put the sun in my right hand and the moon in my left if I abjure this cause, I shall not do so until God has vindicated it or caused me to perish in the process.' Abu Talib looked Muhammad in the eye and replied: 'Go, nephew, and say what you like. By God, I will never hand you over for any reason.'

Muhammad must have yearned for his beloved uncle to convert to Islam. At Abu Talib's death-bed, in 619, some of Muhammad's followers thought they had seen this happen but Muhammad was too principled a man to let sentiment overwhelm his regard for truth. Abu Talib was buried a pagan beside his father. Most of Abu Talib's family remained pagans, too, though one son and his wife now felt free to publicly convert to Islam. With the death of Muhammad's wife, Khadija, in this very same year, Ali emerged as one of the Muslims' central figures, and his continuing support allowed the Prophet to survive another two years of persecution in Mecca.

❈ ❈ ❈

By the summer of 622, the mood in Mecca was perilous. Most of the Muslims had fled the city and, without the leadership of Abu Talib, the conscientious protection of the Beni Hashim was a thing of the past. On the first night of the month of Rabi al-Awwal, Ali secretly wrapped himself in the easily recognisable cloak of the Prophet – a thick shepherd's cloak made from white goat hair adorned with a stripe of black wool – and pretended to sleep on a bench either on the roof or beside the house. He knew he was being watched by a band of fourteen young assassins (one from each of the principal clans in order to frustrate a blood feud), awaiting the chance to kill the Prophet once he left the sanctuary of his home at dawn; they were unlikely to break into a house at night that sheltered women and children. This event is known as the Layla al-Mabit and is remembered as the first night of a new era, dated from when the prophet Muhammad fled the persecution of Mecca. Ali's act of wrapping himself up in the cloak of Muhammad, at risk of his own death, was also a kind of investiture. The mantle, the cloak of the Prophet, is the closest thing to a crown within the Islamic tradition.*

In the morning Ali arose, revealed himself, and was abused and beaten by the assassins, furious that they had allowed Muhammad to escape. Ali had another task to perform for Muhammad, which was to tie up all legal affairs and make certain that all consignments of goods and property had been settled. It would have been a lonely and increasingly diffi-cult time, for eighty Muslims had now migrated to Medina. Ali's last task was to safely conduct his old mother and three women of the Prophet's household, including his future wife, Fatima, to Medina. They were seated within the *howdah* of a camel, while Ali walked beside them, their lone escort across the desert on a ten-day midsummer march.

Ali would have been about twenty-three years old when he arrived in the oasis. As we have noted, all the other Muslim refugees from Mecca had already been paired off with a local

---

* Cloaks believed to belong to the Prophet Muhammad were customarily treated as a mystical treasure and are preserved in shrines in a number of places, most famously in the Topkapi Palace in Istanbul and in the Kherqa treasury at Kandahar in Afghanistan. In recent years, both the Taliban leader Mullah Omar at Kandahar and the ISIS leader Abu Bakr Baghdadi at Raqqa have invoked the ritual of being wrapped in 'the cloak of the Prophet' as a form of public investiture of their political power.

Muslim host, while Ali was formally paired with his cousin, the Prophet. The two of them accepted no charity and worked for their living. This was a period of heavy labour for Ali, who, in addition to running Muhammad's household, rented himself out as a day labourer, breaking stones, hauling water from wells, weeding fields, making bricks and sawing wood.

This period of selfless work is remembered as another of the virtues of Ali, the son of the sheikh of the Beni Hashim, who knew the hunger of poverty, and knew how cold a desert night could become with nothing but a rag to cover yourself. It is a period to which all the craft guilds of Islam look back in affection – a time of holy poverty when the leaders of Islam were proud to labour with their hands, earning their own sustenance by stitching leather and weaving palm fronds. Even in the heyday of the Ottoman Empire, every prince was taught a craft and every sultan practised a trade in emulation of the first Muslims.

As we have already heard, from the first raids, Ali took a prominent role as a warrior. He fought, notably, in the first set-piece battle, at the Wells of Badr, where two battle lines were formed in the traditional manner of a tribal conflict, and ritual insults preceded a trio of champions advancing from each of the ranks. It was important for the community that some of the refugees from Mecca were seen to be risking their lives in the front line, and on the Muslim side the champions included Muhammad's uncle, Hamza, and Ali, his young cousin. The battle was a triumph for the Muslims and for Ali, whose victorious duel with the Meccan champion, Walid ibn Utba, was witnessed by the entire army. After the battle was over, Ali was saluted by the Prophet as 'Hyder Karrar' ('the warrior who attacks time and again'). At the distribution of booty, Ali found himself in possession of a camel, a fine sword and a suit of armour.

A year after his arrival at Medina, Ali asked Muhammad's daughter, Fatima, to marry him. They had known each other all their lives and had both been deeply immersed in the revelation of the Koran and the evolution of Islam. It was usual to employ an intermediary for such matters but in this case Muhammad took on the role of emissary, formally taking Ali's proposal of marriage to his daughter, who had already refused the proposals of two prominent Muslims. Ali had no money for the dowry, fixed at four hundred pieces of silver, but at the last moment this was settled by Uthman, one of the wealthiest Muslim converts, who bought Ali's armour and weapons off him for five hundred silver coins, which would cover both the dowry and wedding meal. Then Uthman, apologising that he was a merchant with no gift for fighting, begged Ali to take back his armour as his wedding gift.

In the next battle, at Uhud in 625, the Muslim army was outmanoeuvred by their pagan enemies, and at one critical momen, the Prophet was cut off from the rest of his army and in mortal danger. It was only the bravery of Ali that protected Muhammad. That evening, the sixteen (or, in some sources, sixty-three) battle wounds of Ali so alarmed the women of the house that Muhammad bathed and bandaged them himself. Once again, Ali's bravery had been an important ingredient in correcting the imbalance between the two Muslim communities, for, when the casualties were counted, seventy men from Medina had died and only four of the men from Mecca.

In the aftermath, Ali was saluted by the Prophet as 'Asad-Ullah' ('lion of God'). Muhammad then unwound his own turban and set down his sword, the legendary two-pointed Zulfiqar ('master of the spine'), and presented them to Ali, whose own sword had been shattered in the battle. Once again, this action of the Prophet is seen as a ritual form of enthronement, in both the Sunni and Shia traditions. The presentation of the sword of an ancestor to a young warrior by a wise old sheikh is how the Ottomans invested each of their new sultans.

During their first year of marriage, Ali and Fatima had continued to hire themselves out as day labourers. They also helped in the running of the complex household of the Prophet. When they finally asked Muhammad for help, he gave them what he most valued, which was prayer. After the birth of Hasan, their first child, in 625, they found a little more privacy by building a hut, away from the Prophet's house. Their second son, Husayn, would be born in 626, followed by two girls, Zaynab and Umm Kulthum. Muhammad was so fond of his grandchildren that, in the last years of his life, they decided to build another hut so that they could be close to his house.

At the Battle of the Trench in 627, the Muslims were faced by such a vast invading army that they were forced to defend Medina with a specially constructed moat. To survive the siege, they needed to maintain a unified defensive position behind this. At one point, the pagan champion Amr ibn Abdu Wudd led a small party of cavalrymen over the trench and taunted the Muslims to come out and fight. His third insult, 'So where is your Paradise now?', was designed to mock their faith and, at this, Ali rode forth to uphold the honour of Islam. After Ali had killed his adversary, in an epic duel, he was acclaimed the greatest warrior in all Arabia.

Ali's bravery and skills were tested again and again in this early period of the establishment of Islam in central Arabia, a fact attested by all accounts, Sunni or Shia. That he was also literate, personally scribing the first Muslim peace treaty, the Truce of Hudaybyah in 628, adds to his indispensability.

CHAPTER 5

The Last Revelation
and Ghadir Khum

*All Shia believe that Ali was publicly
blessed by the Prophet as his heir*

In 628, a mere eight years after fleeing Mecca, Muhammad
would return to the city of his birth escorted by an army of
10,000. The Muslims' advance on Mecca had been precipi-
tated by the Banu Bakr breaking the truce negotiated by Ali,
but in the event the city submitted without resistance. The
Prophet was remarkably merciful with his old enemies, and,
while thousands of Meccans took the Islamic faith, the clan-
based political leadership of the Quraysh was left untouched.

The Kaaba, then as now, stood at the centre of Mecca,
and was filled with pagan trophies, offerings and statues.
Muhammad and Ali gave themselves the task of cleansing
this ancient temple of its pagan furnishings and prepared it
as the centre for Muslim pilgrimage. For the first year, the
Kaaba was shared with the pagan pilgrimage – Muhammad
was campaigning in northern Arabia and asked Abu Bakr to
lead the pilgrimage on his behalf.

In 632, however, Muhammad led the pilgrimage – the first
entirely Muslim Haj and the last performed by the Prophet.
Every action he made was observed, copied and remembered.
At the end of this pilgrimage, Muhammad gave what would

become known as the Farewell Sermon, a fluent summary of the basic obligations, rewards and principles of the Islamic faith. Then sacrifices were made and a vast meat feast was shared amongst all the Muslims, followed by an obligatory period of rest for the pilgrims in their tents.

Today there is no difference between the practice of a Sunni or a Shia, or any of the sects, when they attend the Haj. These rituals have never been forgotten, because every year for the last fourteen centuries (broken only by war or plague) the pilgrimage has been performed. Generations of Meccan guides have been on hand to direct pilgrims as to each of the ritual actions in the proper style and sequence.* Some details might seem to have been inherited from the old ritual actions of pagan Arabia, but this is not a problem for a pious Muslim, who believes that this pagan era itself inherited the rituals that had first been established here by the Prophet Abraham, his son Ishmael, and Hagar, Ishmael's mother.

It is believed by all Muslims that the Prophet received his last revelation on his journey back to Medina. It was not a whole chapter, just a pair of sentences that complete verse three of chapter five of the Koran, which is otherwise largely concerned with diet. These two sentences are of vital importance:

This day have those who reject faith given up all hope of your religion: yet fear them not but fear Me.

This day have I perfected your religion for you, completed My favour upon you, and have chosen for you Islam as your religion.

Muslims do not believe that Muhammad composed the Koran but that he was the Messenger for the divine. So this last

---

* Some of Muhammad's ritual actions during this Haj, such as kissing the black stone, were not understood, but are nevertheless followed.

Koranic revelation informs both Muhammad and his followers that the cycle of revelations is complete. Sunni believe that this final revelation happened on the ninth day of the month of Dhu al-Hijjah; the Shia, that it occurred on the eighteenth. This difference in dates is vital.

For what neither dispute is that, on the eighteenth day of Dhu al-Hijjah, the pilgrim caravan halted at a traditional stop on the desert trail known as Ghadir Khum (after a natural hollow in the rock which trapped rainwater). Below this rock Muhammad ascended a podium made from saddlebags and gave another version of his Farewell Sermon. But this one concluded with a public declaration in favour of Ali: 'O God, be the friend of him who is his friend, and the foe of him who is his foe.' It is an occasion much loved by Shia artists and poets, who believe that Muhammad held up the hand of Ali as he made this announcement. The declaration was followed by a public oath-taking at which all the Muslims placed their hands between the hands of Ali and pledged obedience.

However, here the interpretation of events differs. The Sunni believe that Muhammad was choosing Ali to be the leader of his kinship group – the next sheikh of the Beni Hashim clan – and as *mawla* (patron) of his group of relatives. The Shia insist that the declaration at Ghadir Khum was a universal act and that Muhammad's speech made a specific declaration that Ali was his successor in every aspect of the Muslims' life – the next imam (leader of religion), amir (military commander) and political successor.

The public oath-taking, an action known as *bayat*, has been a primary ritual in all subsequent Islamic societies. And such oaths had taken place on a number of decisive occasions during the life of Muhammad, like a series of legal punctuation points. First there were two midnight oaths at Aqaba; then one after the truce of Hudabiyah; and again after the conquest of Mecca. To the Shia, the oath at Ghadir Khum was given additional authority, for it also included the last revealed verse of the Koran: 'This day have I perfected your religion for you.' For a Shia, this means not just that Muhammad invested Ali, but that this was part of a divine plan for humankind, which would continue to be helped on the way of God by a universally respected leader, the imam.

CHAPTER 6

The Death of the Prophet

The fateful chance events of the succession, 632

Once back in Medina, a succession of events, which included the emergence of a number of rival prophets in different regions of Arabia, vied for Muhammad's attention. But he focused his energy on reversing the Battle of Mu'tah, where his stepson Zayd had been killed by a Byzantine army guarding the frontiers of Syria. Muhammad assembled a cavalry army, which he determined to place under the command of Zayd's young son, Osama. It was not a popular decision, for Osama was only eighteen. Zayd had been the most experienced of all Muslim commanders, yet he had been defeated. Muhammad had to speak sternly to his followers gathered in his house-mosque about this matter: 'You question his leadership even as you questioned the leadership of his father before him, yet he is worthy of the command as his father was worthy of it.'

That night, praying alone over the graves of fallen warriors, Muhammad was more forthright: 'Peace be upon you, O people of the graves. Rejoice in your state, how much better it is than the state of men now living. Dissensions come like waves of darkest night, the one following hard upon the other, each worse than the last.' He was concerned at the state of the Muslim forces, for only 3,000 warriors had assembled at the camp at Jurf, a three-mile ride out of the oasis.

At dawn Muhammad was possessed by a splitting headache, and, though he managed to lead the morning prayers, he was then overcome by fever. Too weak to walk, his cousin Ali and his uncle Abbas escorted him to rest in Aisha's hut. Though it was not her allotted 'day', all Muhammad's wives recognised that this is where he wished to lie down. Muhammad asked Abu Bakr to lead the prayers in his absence. During this period of fever, the Shia believe that only the direct intervention of Omar – a leading Muslim and father of Muhammad's wife, Hafsa – stopped the Prophet from dictating his last wishes about the succession into a legal document. According to this tradition, Omar declared: 'The Messenger of God is overcome with pain. The Book of God is sufficient to us.'

By a great effort of will, Muhammad managed to attend public prayers the following morning, but thereafter he sank rapidly, dying in the lap of Aisha (according to the Sunni) and leaning against the shoulder of Ali (according to the Shia). Both traditions could be true, if the two had briefly put aside their rivalry to nurse the Prophet together. Then the house was overcome by the lamentations of his wives, picked up, echoed and enhanced by the women of the oasis. No matter that Muhammad had always tried to tone down these traditional displays of public grief.

All was disorder amongst the villages and hamlets of the oasis, later recalled as like a herd of lost sheep in a winter storm. One faction of believers refused to accept Muhammad's death, for they had imagined that he would be leading them into the 'End of Times', others hoped that he would be resurrected like Jesus after three days, or ascend into the heavens like Elijah, or return to his followers like Moses after forty days. It seems a group of close companions had decided to keep vigil over the Prophet's body, which had been covered with a thick Yemeni cloak, where he had died, in Aisha's hut.

To make things more confusing, Omar, in his first transport of grief, was threatening to cut off the hands and feet of any Muslim who spoke of the death of the Prophet.

So it was the right of Ali, as the Prophet's closest male kinsman, to reverently wash and prepare his body for the grave. The decision to bury him beneath the floor of Aisha's hut was later justified with references. Maybe the vigil had been allowed to go on too long and in the heat of May, Muhammad's body now needed burying swiftly, without the fuss of a public procession.

It was in this time of disorder, with Ali preoccupied with the burial, that Abu Bakr and Omar – who were to become the first two Sunni caliphs – seized power. Few can doubt that, if it had been left to a formal gathering of the entire Muslim community to choose a successor, Ali would have been chosen. He was Muhammad's closest male relative, his oldest, most intimate follower, his cousin, his son-in-law, the bravest warrior and the father of Muhammad's two male grandchildren. There was also the matter of the very recent public declaration at Ghadir Khum in favour of Ali.

But events moved too fast. Omar and Abu Bakr got to hear about a meeting of the Muslim clans of Medina – the Ansar – who were gathering at the meeting hall of Saad ibn Ubadayah, the warrior sheikh of the Beni Saidah clan who had recently become leader of the Khazraj confederation. Saad was an irreproachable Muslim hero who had fought beside Muhammad in all the principal battles and campaigns and had been one of the very earliest converts to Islam, one of the seventy-five from Medina who had sworn to protect Muhammad at the secret midnight oath of Aqaba.

When Omar and Abu Bakr arrived at this assembly, they were advised to leave the Ansar to their own devices. Why did they not call a meeting of their own – of the Muhajirun, the Muslim men who had migrated to Mecca? They refused this advice and insisted on attending the meeting. They were pleasantly impressed by the passionate Islamic faith of all those present. This was not a meeting that questioned the Muslim faith; it was about clan politics.

When Abu Bakr was permitted to speak, he tactfully repeated the Prophet's many words of praise for the warriors of Medina. But then he declared that they must choose a leader from one of the fourteen clans of the Quraysh tribe of Mecca. He offered no religious arguments for this assertion, but merely suggested that the Bedouin tribes, and the people of Syria and the Yemen, would look down on anyone that was not of the Quraysh. It was a political opinion based on the pre-Islamic prestige of the Quraysh tribe as wealthy, well-known traders throughout central Arabia. Abu Bakr then modestly suggested two outsider candidates – omitting himself and Omar, let alone Ali, the most obvious of all the Quraysh.

Abu Bakr's suggestion caused an uproar, and a compromise was offered: that the men of Mecca elect one spokesman, and the men of Medina, another. But seizing a decisive moment, Omar roared out, 'Who will willingly take precedence over the man that the Prophet ordered to lead the prayers?'

It was a brilliantly timed intervention, and, while the crowd pondered the question, Omar knelt down before Abu Bakr, grasped his hand and pledged his loyalty. The other Muhajirun in their party followed his example and within a few seconds they had entirely won round the mood of the assembly. The men of Medina, warriors who had fought beside the Prophet for the last ten years, one by one advanced to give their oath.

What was foreclosed by these events was the opportunity for this assembly to debate what they looked for in a leader. It could have been a wonderful, empowering example of direct democracy within the existing structures of Arabian society, but it did not happen that way.*

The coup was confirmed at dawn. By the time the believers filed into the mosque, Abu Bakr was in the front rank, ready to lead the prayers which he had been efficiently performing all week. The moment the prayers were finished, Omar stood up and addressed the assembly with his customary formality and authority. He formally repeated his oath of loyalty of the previous night and listed the many acknowledged qualities of Abu Bakr. He had been chosen by Muhammad to lead the prayers in the last week of his life and had been the one who had sheltered in the cave outside Mecca with Muhammad. This event had been referenced by a verse in the Koran which added some dignity to the occasion: 'One of two, when they were in the cave and he said to his companion, "Do not grieve; for God is indeed with us." And the Lord sent down his tranquillity upon them.' Then their supporters acclaimed Abu Bakr as 'Khalifat Rasul Allah' – the successor to the Messenger of God.

For his part, Abu Bakr addressed the congregation with a beautifully composed oath:

> *I have been given the authority over you, and I am not the best of you. If I do well, help me; and if I do wrong, set me right. Truth consists in loyalty and disregard for truth is treachery. The weak amongst you shall be strong in my eyes until I have secured their rights, if God wills it: and the strong amongst you shall be weak with me until I have wrested from him the rights of others, if*

---

* Saad ibn Ubadayah, the Muslim tribal leader who convened the assembly, is customarily reviled. Two tales of his end are related:, one that he was smothered to death that very night by the Muhajirun; another, that he fled from Medina to Syria and was killed by the arrows of the *jinn* (spirits of the desert), enraged by his act of urinating while standing.

God wills it. Obey me for so long as I obey God and His Messenger. But if I disobey God and His Messenger, you owe me no obedience. Arise from your prayer, God have mercy upon you!

❀ ❀ ❀

What is so extraordinary about this vivid narrative of events is that neither Sunni nor Shia disagree in any of the important details. It is acknowledged by both sides to have been a coup. Abu Bakr was an old man, and in two years he would be dead and succeeded in office by Omar, who was much younger. The speed with which they acted may have been supported by inside information received from their two daughters in the household of the Prophet, Aisha (daugher of Abu Bakr) and Hafsa (daughter of Omar). Ali, even if he had wished to attend meetings over these critical twelve hours, could not have done so; as the closest male relative, he was preparing and then burying the body of the Prophet.

So the difference between the Sunni and Shiite perception of this vital series of events comes down to a matter of degree. A passionate Shia will see it as the conclusion of a deeply laid plot to deprive Ali of his rightful succession. A Sunni will think that Abu Bakr and Omar responded to a series of events as best they could. They would probably all agree that Omar forced the pace of the succession in favour of Abu Bakr. A Sunni might contend that he had to do this to frustrate a civil war that might otherwise have erupted in the leaderless Muslim community. Indeed, it is possible to imagine that, without the quick actions of Omar and Abu Bakr, the Muslims of Mecca and Medina might have parted company, incubating conflict among the tribal factions of Medina, and the tension between the early and later believers within the Meccan Muslims. In such a scenario, the

Arab tribes and cities which had so recently accepted Islam and the leadership of the Prophet might have turned their back on the Muslim community. By their prompt action, Abu Bakr and Omar confirmed its unity, allowing the Muslims to dominate all Arabia, and then the Middle East. In the probity of their public and private lives, they also showed themselves worthy successors of the Prophet Muhammad. But this justification cannot be defended by any theological principle. It only becomes legitimate in retrospect, because Omar and Abu Bakr proved themselves successful political leaders.*

In recent years the Shia have toned down their passionate hatred of Abu Bakr and Omar, who in former centuries were formally cursed. But there are limits. For the Shia, their actions destroyed the unity of Islam. The house becomes divided ever after. Ali, as we have seen, had every right to be considered the true heir of the Prophet, by claims of blood, as the Prophet's first follower, and witness to the historic revelation of the Koran. But even more important to the Shia is that they believed Ali had been publicly designated by the Prophet Muhammad as his successor at the moment that the Koran had been completed. Ali's right to succeed Muhammad was part of the divine plan, sanctioned by the same divine spirit that had revealed the Koran to the Prophet: 'This day have I perfected your religion for you, completed My favour upon you.' In this way of looking at things, there is no action of mankind, however well intentioned, however well versed

---

* I have often wondered how important the example of the coup of Abu Bakr and Omar is to the Sunni political imagination. Can it partly explain the military coups that punctuate the political life of so many modern Sunni nation states? Are they all, to some extent, inspired by the example of the first two caliphs? For, in such a world view, a coup might be right, if it brings a wise ruler to power. The oath of Abu Bakr reflects this tradition. He acknowledges that he is 'not the best among you' but 'if I do well, help me'.

in the tribal politics of central Arabia, which should have been allowed to compete with a divine command.

The rejection of Imam Ali is a crucial moment of history and religion for the Shia. And, as we will soon discover, it was the first of many rejections suffered by generation after generation of their divinely selected imams.

The Sunni do not accept the idea of Imam Ali as an aspect of that last *sura*. But they do include him amongst their very greatest heroes. He is part of that assembly of Muslims known as As-Sahabah ('the Companions') whom the Sunni look upon as an unquestioned source of spiritual authority. They alone knew the practice of Muhammad's life; they alone knew the context of each Koranic revelation; they alone were directed in every detail of their life by the active leadership, example and teachings of the Prophet. To the Sunni, the actions of this first community is like a quarry of excellence. All Sunni scholars have dedicated themselves to working out how this first community of believers functioned, and how they kept to the pure practice of the Prophet. Over the centuries they developed a complex ranking system to catalogue the Companions, who as early as 1071 were already listed in a biographical dictionary of 2,770 men and 381 women.*

Sometimes the Sunni, for all their insistence on the absolute monotheism of their Islamic faith, allow themselves to become just a little too uncritically pious about the Companions. They have not exactly been turned into saints, but they are treated as an assembly of virtuous heroes and there are blasphemy laws in many Sunni nations that effectively prohibit discussion of the character of the principal figures. So it certainly doesn't help intercommunal harmony that the Shia community

---

* To be ranked amongst the Companions, an individual had to have met the Prophet, believed in his message and died a Muslim.

effectively ignore, if not actively denigrate, almost this entire collective of heroes. They are the very bedrock from which the Sunni define themselves, and from out of which they have constructed a thousand years of analytical scholarship.

In the eyes of the Shia, the majority of the Companions of the Prophet were flawed witnesses to the coup that imposed the human caliphate of Abu Bakr, Omar and then Uthman over the divinely appointed imamate. Early Islam should have been brought to its spiritual ripening under the leadership of Imam Ali but was instead directed by the earthly rule of the caliphs. The Shia thus look to the future for their heavenly state, while the Sunni quarry the past to try to recover their vision of a near-perfect spiritual community. The Shia believe that the message of the Koran could have been enhanced by a charismatic teacher-leader; the Sunni trust in the text itself.

It is doubtful that the Prophet Muhammad considered the Muslim community he led to be a perfect spiritual brotherhood. The role of hypocrites is attested in many verses of the Koran. Indeed, Muhammad's very last recorded words ('Dissensions come like waves of darkest night ...') is a criticism of this early community.

And so it has proved. Shia and Sunni have an enormous shared emotional sympathy and respect for Ali, the First Imam of the Shia and the Fourth Sunni Caliph, and in all important details practise the same religion as revealed to them by the Koran and taught to them by the living example of the Prophet. But they have very different ways at looking at the same past and different aspirations for the future.

CHAPTER 7

The Rashidun and the Companions of Ali

*The four rightly guided Sunni caliphs contrast
with the Shia Companions*

The years following the death of the Prophet were a period of extraordinary military success for the Muslims. Within three generations, the caliphate would stretch from Spain to South Asia, encompassing all of the Sassanid and much of the former Byzantine Empire and reaching into Central Asia and South Asia. No empire of this size had ever been seen; it was more diverse even than that of Rome or Alexander the Great. The core of this conquest was achieved during the reigns of the first four caliphs, known as the Rashidun – the Rightly Guided. Sunnis revere this period as a golden age of Islamic purity, of enormous importance to their traditions, their lawmakers and their sense of self, for their armies seemed blessed by God.

Before Islam, Arabia had been a poor, downtrodden region, a border zone subdivided by the influence of the three great powers of the day: the Persian Sassanid Empire, the Christian Empire of Abyssinia and the Byzantine Empire. But, as Arab armies fought under the banner of Islam, they became irresistible conquerors. Abu Bakr only ruled as caliph for two years, but this gentle, pious man (much given to weeping during prayer) proved himself a brilliant tactician and a strategic mastermind. After the death of the Prophet, the Muslim community had been faced by revolt across Arabia. Yet, by a dazzlingly confident activism and skilful manipulation of tribal rivalries, Abu Bakr first mastered the rebellions and then conquered eastern Arabia, crushing the army of a rival prophet in a series of bloody battles.*

As a pragmatist, Abu Bakr insisted on collecting a tithe from the Arab tribes, which he framed as the line in the sand. If a tribe refused, they would be attacked; if it was paid, they were guaranteed protection. To give the martial culture of the Arab tribes a legitimate outlet, he encouraged Bedouin armies, operating under their own chieftains, to raid Persian-held Iraq, while he marshalled the tribes of northern and central Arabia and directed them into Byzantine Syria. This campaign had been the fixed intention of the Prophet Muhammad in the last month of his life, but this time young Osama, son of Zayd, was not given the command.

The generals that Abu Bakr appointed were Quraysh fighters of proven worth and had all served under the Prophet. They are lionised figures to Arab Muslims: Amr ibn al-As, the conqueror of Egypt; Muthana ibn Harith, chief of the Beni Bekr tribe, who attacked the Persian Empire; Khalid ibn al-Walid, who won the decisive Battle of Yarmuk against the Byzantine army; and Mughira ibn Shuba, the wily political adventurer from the Thaqiq tribe. You will not find a more dashing, brave, risk-taking and ebullient group of fighters and adventurers in any historical period. They could and did behave with all the chivalric dash of a true Arab knight, but holy men they were not. Nonetheless, it can be difficult for the Sunni not to conflate the dramatic creation of this worldwide Arab empire

---

* The 'Campaign on the Apostasy' was fought against followers of Musaylimah, a tribal leader who claimed prophetic status. It was completed by the spring of 633, the eleventh year of the Hijrah, ensuring Arabia was united under Islam.

of Islam with God's special approval, to link their success in war with the spiritual rigour and righteousness of the first Muslim community. This mood often underwrites the thinking of modern-day fundamentalists. And it has inspired many Sunni scholars to try to return to the imagined purity of this early community, and to again find favour with God.

✻ ✻ ✻

The Shia have a quite different perspective on this period and dwell on the sufferings inflicted on the household of Ali, such as the incident when Omar broke into the house of Fatima to demand that Ali publicly acknowledge the authority of Abu Bakr. Some Shia claim that Fatima was injured in this incident, which brought on the miscarriage of her unborn child Muhsin and contributed to her death. Fatima was also in dispute with Abu Bakr after he became caliph, for he refused to allow her to inherit the oasis gardens of her father, telling her that prophets have no heirs.

In contrast to the Sunni reverence for men of power, the Shia have selected a different set of heroes, their own set of four from this first generation of Muslims. There is no easier way to understand the egalitarian nature of the Shiite tradition, and the way it champions the poor and the downtrodden, than to understand their continuing regard for this curious group of humble and obscure characters: Abu Dharr al-Ghafari, Miqdad ibn Aswad, Ammar ibn Yasir and Salman al-Farisi. They are known as the Four Companions of Ali.

Salman al-Farisi, as his name suggests, was born in Persia, in 568, and studied the mystical traditions of the Zoroastrian faith under his father (who was a priest) before abandoning this heritage to travel across the Middle East in search of God. Salman became a Nestorian Christian before being captured in a desert raid and sold as a slave to an Arab Jewish merchant, who took him to Medina. This brought Salman into contact with the Prophet Muhammad, after which he embraced Islam as the fulfilment of his lifelong spiritual quest. His most famous historical deed was to advise the Prophet how best to defend the oasis of Medina from the siege of a powerful pagan Arab army; it was his defence moat that sheltered the Muslims from a vast force of enemy cavalry who besieged the oasis. Salman is an intriguing role model for the tolerant Sufi and Dervish tradition within Islam, which respects the wandering scholar who might sample all the great faiths of the world before finding Islam.

Ammar ibn Yasir was born in Mecca in 567, and was an early believer, though as the son of a Yemeni slave he had low status in the city and was frequently chastised for his faith. One of his worst persecutors was Abu Jahl, the Prophet's own uncle, who was responsible for the death of Ammar's mother and tortured Ammar 'until he did not know what he was saying'. When Ammar confessed to Muhammad that he feared he had recanted his faith, the Prophet was not concerned with what he had been forced to shout out during his torture but 'what you feel in your heart'. Ammar fought as a foot soldier in all the early battles of Islam and came to be acknowledged as a man of unwavering faith and principle. He never doubted that Ali was the true heir of the Prophet Muhammad and was beheaded for that belief after joining the ranks (as a ninety-year-old soldier) at the Battle of Siffin. A shrine associated with his tomb was long honoured at the city of Raqqa.*

Miqdad ibn Aswad came from the Hadramaut, the eastern-most desert valley within the Yemeni mountains. He was said to have been tall and spindly, with skin that had been burnt

---

* The tomb was very deliberately destroyed by the ultra-Sunni ISIS forces during the recent Syrian civil war.

by a childhood in the desert wastes, a hooked nose and widely spaced eyes. But a beautiful soul was manifested in his voice and he became one of the most eloquent reciters of the Koran, before it was definitively committed to parchment. He was present at most of the great battles of the Arab conquest, not as a dashing warrior, but as a voice that inspired Muslim soldiers.

Abu Dharr al-Ghaffari (also known as Abu Zar) came from a tribe within the Kinnana confederation which inhabited the desert just to the south-west of Medina. He was said to have been the fourth or fifth man to adopt Islam. Unlike many of the early Muslims, however, he refused to profit from the booty pouring in from the conquests and kept true to the simple life and constant charity that he had been taught by the Prophet. Abu Dharr could be blunt to the point of tactlessness about the corruption of wealth and, although he was revered for his faith, he was dismissed as an eccentric and excluded from the inner circle of governance, with its rewards, councils and pro-motions. One of the many stories told of his self-sufficiency and modesty relates how he tried to refuse a gift from a powerful provincial governor (who was trying to test him), replying that surely there were many people in much greater need of this money than himself. When the gift was forced upon him, he accepted it happily, but before the day was over he had gone out into the streets and distributed the unwanted largesse to those in greater need. A messenger sent by the governor to his house the next day was astonished to find not a coin left in his possession. On another occasion, a visitor asked Abu Dharr, 'Where are all your possessions?' to which Abu Dharr replied, 'Sent ahead to my other house' – meaning to the place beyond the grave. Muhammad is said to have compared his soul to that of Issa ibn Maryam (Jesus) and blessed him thus: 'May God have mercy upon you. You'll live alone, die alone, rise from the dead alone and enter Paradise alone.'

These four characters – the despised foreigner, the ugly man from the south, the son of a slave and the blunt, outspoken upholder of truth – create an endearing group of heroes. For, though poor and unsuccessful in the eyes of the world, they each possess exceptional qualities.

❀ ❀ ❀

Through the reigns of the first three caliphs – Abu Barka, Omar and Uthman – Ali remained in Mecca and Medina, immersed in a quiet, contemplative life of scholarship and prayer. He did not publicly oppose the caliphs but turned himself away from the concerns of the world and concentrated on teaching and preaching, explaining the nature of the Koran to a core group of followers. He is widely acknowledged as one of the most important sources when it was decided that the Koran should be written down, rather than kept as a primarily oral recitation.

The Shia believe that many of Ali's teachings have survived, both in oral heritage passed down to his spiritual heirs and as a written document. Three hundred years after his death, the Iraqi scholar Sharif Razi edited a collection of all the surviving oral sources and old transcripts, sayings, letters and written sermons of Ali. Known as the *Nahjul Balagha* – 'The Way of Eloquence' – this can be seen in the home of any literate Shia, two thick volumes occupying the place of honour, lying flat on a protective cloth on the highest shelf in the best room. It contains 241 sermons, 79 letters and 480 sayings. Some Sunni scholars respect it as a valid source for holy law; others argue that it was created in tenth-century Iraq and, while respecting it as one of the canons of Arab literature, give it no doctrinal status.

Abu Bakr was caliph for just two years (632–634) and made certain that Omar would succeed him as ruler. He assembled a council of half a dozen prominent men, asked them their opinion, then appointed Omar as his successor in the mosque at Medina. Omar ruled for ten years (634–644) and, though he frustrated the rule of Ali and is thus no hero to the Shia, he is universally remembered as a pious and exacting Muslim, a stern, implacable, incorruptible ruler who lived simply and humbly. Indeed, among the Sunni, he is venerated as the most capable and perfect example of a Muslim ruler.

It was Omar's armies that achieved the decisive victories in the spread of Muslim rule, notably over the Byzantines at Yarmuk (in modern-day Syria, 636) and over the Sassanians at al-Qadisiya (in modern-day Iraq, 636), after which he organised the governance of the caliphate. Muslim Arab warriors were to live in *amsar* – garrison cities built apart from the old cities of the conquered peoples. At Kufa (in Iraq) and Fustat (in Egypt), the sites of such garrison cities survive to this day. They were designed on a rigid geometric grid with a vast mosque in the centre. The conquered peoples – Christians, Jews and Zoroastrians – were known as *dhimmis* and were protected by Muslim armies in exchange for annual taxes, in the form of a tithe of their harvest (often confirmed in a legal document of submission to the Muslim conquest) and a poll tax. This revenue was paid to the caliph or his provincial deputy and allowed the regime to pay annual salaries to the Muslim armies, as well as providing support for the poor, the widows, the aged and orphans, in line with the teachings of the Koran.

Caliph Omar remained all-powerful, sacking his governors and generals for the most minor infringements, as well as despatching treasury officials to comb through tax accounts. He allowed no favouritism to influence the law courts, insisting on the just conduct of war, proper articles of negotiated peace terms and a graduated scale of salaries. His achievements are codified as the *Awliat-i-Omar*, the forty-one initiatives of Omar. These are not accepted by the Shia.

Towards the end of his life, Caliph Omar worked closely with Ali (who was his father-in-law). When he left on a tour of provincial inspection, he asked Ali to stand in as his deputy. So, when in 644 Omar was assassinated as he bent down to pray in the mosque at Medina, Ali, once again, would have been the natural successor. But instead, an inner council of the six most prominent Muslims – fearing that Ali might overturn the nascent Arab Empire – chose Uthman as the Third Caliph. Uthman, like Ali, was a Companion of the Prophet, and had been chosen by Muhammad to marry two of his daughters by Khadija, Ruqayya and Umm Kulthum. He was seventy years old at his accession, an uncharismatic man, though said to be modest and kind.

While the more liberal-minded Shia might strive to look favourably on Abu Bakr and Omar, few can be persuaded to admire Uthman. The empire that he inherited – and in the early years of his rule expanded – was now vast. However, it soon became apparent that the key posts were given out to his Umayyad family, part of the privileged Abd Shams clan within the Quraysh. Though generous and merciful, Uthman had grown up as a wealthy, entitled individual and he did not respond to the petitions of complaint, even when his clansmen proved incompetent. Deferential delegations became public demonstrations and finally open mutiny. Ali arbitrated a settlement but, having made peace, Uthman's courtier-cousins were soon revealed to be conspiring. The mutineers resolved to strike first. They forced their way into the house of Uthman and assassinated the caliph, accidentally splashing the first copy of the Koran with his blood.

That written Koran had been Uthman's greatest achievement. He had set up an editorial committee that for six years examined every acclaimed reciter and consulted every written fragment. Finally, 77,000 words were gathered and arranged in 6,211 verses, divided into 114 *suras* of unequal length. No attempt was made to order the revelations by chronology, which were instead arranged by order of length. Extremist Shia claim that Uthman suppressed certain verses favourable to Ali, but Ali himself affirmed that 'Uthman acted with the advice of all the leading men amongst us, had I been ruler at the time, I should have done the same.'

※ ※ ※

The morning after Uthman's assassination, Ali was acclaimed caliph, not only as the most fitting Muslim candidate, but as the one man whose authority was respected by both sides in the recent conflict. It is one of the tragedies of the Shiite tradition that Ali, having been deprived of his just rule for twenty-four years, inherited not the undisputed leadership of the Islamic community but a conquest empire riven by rival, mutinous garrisons.

The first and most immediate rebellion was orchestrated by his most implacable rival, Aisha. Supported by her clansmen, Aisha raised a small army that Ali was forced to fight in the Battle of the Camel, a desert skirmish outside the city of Basra in 656. Ali pardoned Aisha after the battle, and she was safely escorted back to her home in Medina by her half-brother Muhammad (the young son of Caliph Abu Bakr), who was personally devoted to the cause of Ali.

The next year, Ali led an army against the experienced Arab army in Syria, which was under the command of Muawiya, one of the many Umayyad kinsmen of the murdered Uthman. Fearing that he might lose his position as the military governor of Syria, Muawiya fomented a confrontation by claiming the traditional Arab right of vengeance for his dead relative. The two armies met at the Battle of Siffin in 657, fought on the north bank of the Euphrates. After four days of fighting, Muawiya realised that he was about to lose and sought a truce by despatching envoys, holding copies of the Koran on the end of their lances to keep the two sides apart. Muawiya secretly allied with one of the two chosen arbitrators, and in the resultant confusion had himself acclaimed caliph by his army.

Some of Ali's most passionate supporters began to doubt him, furious that he should have thought of negotiating with such an unworthy adversary as Muawiya. These principled but increasingly rebellious supporters would become known as the Kharajites ('seceders').* Ali was forced to confront these passionate rebels that summer and 1,800 died at the Battle of Nahrawan. Ali continued to rule as caliph over central Arabia and Iraq from the city of Kufa, but for the last three years of his life the Muslim community was effectively split into three adversarial factions.

Ali was assassinated by a Kharajite as he left his modest house to lead the Friday prayers in January 661. He remained conscious for two days but eventually succumbed, after which his three sons – Hasan, Husayn and their younger half-brother – washed his body and escorted him to his grave. Over the centuries, Kufa would fall into ruin while the city of Najaf grew up around Imam Ali's grave. It is honoured by both Shia and moderate Sunni leaders and is visited annually by around eight million pilgrims.

---

* Kharajite communities survive to this day in Oman, on the island of Jerba in Tunisia and in the Mzab oasis in Algeria. Their puritanical piety has earned them a reputation as scrupulously honest traders. They continue to deny both the Sunni and Shia claims to the historical leadership of Islam, and choose their own imams.

CHAPTER 8

Husayn at Kerbala

The martyrdom of the grandson of the Prophet, 680

After Ali's murder, Muawiya and the family of Uthman held most of the strategic military bases within the caliphate. The next twenty years would be a battle for the soul of Islam. Would the spiritual tradition upheld by the family of the Prophet prevail, or would the warmongering generals and their security forces triumph? From this dramatic crucible of confrontation emerge the principal stories of the Shia tradition, filled with a tragic sense that the good are doomed to suffer in this world alongside an ardent yearning for a true spiritual leadership from a dynasty of martyrs.

It was Ramadan when Ali was assassinated, so the streets around the central mosque were packed with Muslims listening to all-night recitations of the Koran. Ali's son Hasan had a slight speech defect, but that night conquered it as he described his father as a man whose acts were unrivalled and would for ever remain so. He reminded the congregation of his father's bravery, how in battle he had protected the Prophet with his own life. As his legatee, Hasan also formally reported to the people that Ali held no hoard of treasure, just a purse of 700 dirhams that he had saved from his salary in order to be able to acquire a servant for the family. At the memory of the man they had now lost, the congregation wept and pledged loyalty to Hasan, the grandson of 'the bringer of good tidings, the son of the warner, the son of the summoner to God (powerful and exalted) and with his permission: the shining lamp'.

Imam Hasan was said never to have spoken evil of any man. He had performed the Haj twenty-five times, travelling the 250 miles between Medina and Mecca on foot. He remains one of the great unsung heroes of Islam: a pacifist, a pilgrim-walker and a scholar with a totally independent frame of mind. It had been Hasan who stood guard at Caliph Uthman's door, trying to protect him from the mutineers, even though he knew his father might benefit from the rebellion. The Shia might hate Uthman and curse his memory for centuries, but this was contrary to the example of Hasan, their Second Imam.*

Hasan had an innate understanding that mercy, forgiveness and compassion were at the root of Islam. His Islam was such that 'he neither desired evil nor harm to anyone'. When he preached, he summoned from the Koran not a cause for war but a call for peace. He stressed that the lesser jihad, the armed struggle, was just a preparation for the greater jihad, which was the lifelong struggle to master oneself. He quoted *sura* 2, verse 216: 'Warfare is ordained for you, though it is hateful to you.' Hasan was way ahead of his time.

The soldiers of the Kufa garrison wanted Hasan to lead them to war. Young Muslim warriors saw glorious military triumphs in this world as proof of the rightness of their Islam. They could not understand Hasan's determination that Muhammad's message was about the individual's relationship to God. In vain did Hasan preach that 'shame is better than hellfire', that he sought no worldly dominion but to 'seek the favour of God, and to spare the blood of the people'. These words of peace encouraged the soldiers to riot. They broke into Hasan's

---

* Hasan's descendants are exceptionally well chronicled, for most of the families that claim descent from the Prophet Muhammad trace it through one or other of Hasan's two surviving sons, Zayd and Hasan.

house, ripped his prayer mat from underneath him and pulled his cloak off his shoulders. Only the warriors of the Rabia tribe, devoted partisans of Ali, stopped Hasan from being lynched that day, but the violence only made Hasan more determined to end the civil war within Islam.

Thus Imam Hasan relinquished all political authority in exchange for an agreement with his father's adversary, Muawiya, not to harm any of the supporters of Ali, to govern by the book of God and the example of the Prophet. Muawiya for his part agreed that 'the reign would belong to Hasan after him', though this was soon forgotten. In July 661, Hasan and his younger brother Husayn rode out of Kufa and took the road back to Medina. Hasan had ruled for just six months, 'yet I abandoned it, seeking instead the face of God'.

Considered the Second Imam in Shia Islam, Hasan lived quietly in Medina, after his abdication, and died in 670.

✷ ✷ ✷

Muawiya now ruled over all the lands of Islam as the first Umayyad caliph. Tall, tanned and handsome, he was called 'the Caesar of the Arabs' for his ability to charm and persuade, not just command. He promised the Arab armies a vast new horizon of military conquests: an ever-expanding empire.

Throughout his nineteen-year reign (661–680), the centre of Muawiya's power was the city of Damascus. There was no attempt to coordinate the vast military conquests into an Arabic-speaking empire. Each conquered province continued to use its own language, its own officials, its own units of measurement and traditional coinage, usually based on either the gold dinar of Byzantium or the silver dirham of Persia. This was not a doctrinal decision but simply a reflection of the remorseless speed of the Arab conquests. Analysis of early tribute lists shows that Arab garrisons often simply inherited the tithe of harvests and the poll taxes that had previously been paid over to the legions of the Byzantine Empire or that of their Persian rivals.

The simplicity of the Prophet's life and rule was abandoned. Even a deputy governor serving Caliph Muawiya would be surrounded by (as a foreign ambassador reported) 'a crowd of silver-sticks and lectors, and at his gate 500 soldiers mounted guard'. At the beginning of his rule, Muawiya had made the journey to Medina to accept the oath of allegiance from the revered Companions of the Prophet who still dwelt there, but few came to the mosque to pledge their obedience in person. Towards the end of his reign, the caliph tried again, but when they heard he was on the road, the leading Muslims of Medina saddled their camels and decided to check on the state of their flocks in the desert. The first four 'Rightly Guided' caliphs might have been acclaimed in holy Medina, but the Umayyads now ruled from Damascus.

In 680, Caliph Muawiya died, from an illness. He had appointed his son Yazid his successor as Khalifat Allah ('deputy of God'), the title he himself had adopted in place of that of Khalifat rasul Allah ('deputy of the Messenger of God'), used by the earlier caliphs. Less than fifty years after the death of Muhammad, an Arab monarchy had been imposed over the ethical community he had established.

❀ ❀ ❀

From the city of Kufa a succession of messengers made their way to Medina, calling upon Imam Husayn, the surviving brother of Hasan, to claim his rightful place as the head of the Muslim community. Husayn accepted the summons, and so began the most iconic of all the Shia tragedies, commemorated every year in the extraordinary communal mourning that is Ashura. For, as Husayn made his way across the desert, the citizens of Kufa began to think better of their summons. The city was ruled by Ubaydallah ibn Zayyad, an implacable Umayyad loyalist, and, under his watch, not a single youth left the teeming city to join Husayn's caravan.

Instead, Ubaydallah ordered an army into the desert to intercept Husayn and his small body of devoted followers and family, who numbered around thirty horsemen and forty warriors on foot. They had passed freely through lands of the Bedouin tribes, though none of the chiefs, noting the grip of the regime over silent Kufa, would rally their tribe to the cause. The poet Farazdac rode out to warn Husayn of the treachery of Kufa, 'for though the heart of the city is with thee, its sword is against thee'. Still Husayn rode on.

At Kerbala, a detachment of cavalry barred the road to Kufa and manoeuvred themselves to prevent Husayn's small caravan from turning back to Medina. They were then reinforced by four thousand cavalrymen, who encircled their encampment, just above the bank of the Euphrates, twenty-five miles from Kufa. The commander had been ordered by governor Ubay-dallah to deprive Husayn and his supporters of access to water until they had pledged unconditional submission. Despite the crippling thirst imposed upon his family and followers, Husayn refused to submit, though he tried to negotiate a peaceful way out. The dignity with which he conducted himself so impressed the Umayyad cavalry commander that he began to waver in his mission. Shamir, an agent of Ubaydallah, then threatened to take over command if he did not follow strict orders.

On the evening of the ninth of Moharram 61 AH (9 October 680), Husayn ordered his cousins and family to leave the camp and seek refuge with the enemy. This they would not do, even though there was no longer any water in the tents. In the morning they drew themselves up in a tattered battleline, seventy-two men ranged against four thousand. Husayn once again offered peaceful terms. Then his troop rode forward in an attempt to break out of the siege and were cut down by shower upon shower of arrows. Neither Husayn's ten-year-old nephew, Kasim, nor his infant son was spared. The small band of mortally wounded warriors were trampled into the dust by the Umayyad cavalry, which wheeled round to dismount. The heads of the fallen warriors were hacked off and gathered in leather sacks to be spilled out on the floor of the governor's palace at Kufa. As Governor Ubaydallah turned these grim relics over with his staff, one of the old judges attached to his court could not help but cry out: 'Gently, it is the Prophet's grandson and by God I have seen those very lips kissed by the blessed Apostle himself.'

On the tenth day of Moharram, the first month of the Muslim year, Shia communities across the Muslim world commemorate this fearful day. It is acknowledged by both Shia and Sunni as a day of mourning, but the passionate public commemoration of Ashura (literally 'the tenth') is one of the distinctive signs of a Shiite community.

❀ ❀ ❀

The news from Kerbala sent a ripple of horror around the Islamic world. Medina and Mecca now openly defied the officials of the Umayyad caliph, Yazid. An army was sent out from Damascus, bolstered by regiments of Christian Arabs from Syria, to slaughter the defenders of Medina, and for three days they sacked, looted and raped their way through the alleys of the oasis. Then holy Mecca was besieged. Two months into this offensive, the Kaaba was burned to the ground when it was accidentally hit by naptha-enriched arrows launched by the besiegers. The sacred black stone that had been set into the Kaaba wall during the time of the Prophet Muhammad was fractured into three pieces by the heat of the blaze. This stone, believed to be the altar of Abraham, was henceforth only held together by rivets of silver.

At the same time, the forty-year-old Caliph Yazid expired in his hunting palace in the Syrian desert. When news of his death was brought to his army, they halted the siege and prepared to return to Damascus.

It was just fifty years since the death of the Prophet Muhammad. A vast empire had been conquered and an annual tribute of millions upon millions of gold and silver coins poured into the coffers of the caliph's treasury in Damascus to support a salaried ruling class. A hundred thousand Arab warriors dwelt in half a dozen garrison cities, housed in comfort, equipped with the finest weapons, armour and horses and cared for by the labour of slaves in a manner beyond the wildest dreams of their grandfathers. In Mecca, the Kaaba was a burned-out ruin and in a neglected field at Kerbala the headless corpses of the murdered family of the Prophet of God lay buried. It was as if the things of this earth had been won but in the process the kingdom of heaven had been forgotten.

All Muslims feel the horror of this transformation. It helps explain the political fatalism that is so often encountered among Muslim communities. If just fifty years after they had buried the Prophet, the godly rule of the Companions was so decisively overthrown, what hope have we in this more corrupt and less religious age? Did not the Prophet himself declare, 'No time cometh upon you but it is followed by a worse.'

Neither Sunni nor Shia support Muawiya or the claims of his son, Yazid. All Muslims are horrified by the fate of Husayn at Kerbala. The only real difference is in the intensity with which this is felt. If you travel through Shia lands, you will encounter images inspired by Kerbala, be it on the calligraphy of giant black banners stretched across the streets, on figurative wall posters, or amulets and rings. Foremost amongst them is the image of a bloody and riderless horse, exhausted and wounded, being comforted by a small group of black-veiled women. This is Zuljenah, the only survivor of the battle, witness to the death of so many of the menfolk of the family of the Prophet Muhammad.

Similarly, the silhouettes of a dejected column of veiled women being escorted across the desert by a military column shows the women of the encampment of Husayn being marched to Kufa carrying the gruesome relics of the heads of their family. Husayn's sister Zaynab is the heroine of the group, placing herself in the forefront of danger and protecting the ailing life of the only surviving male relative from a callous soldier and the virtue of a young niece from the lust of an Umayyad courtier. When challenged – 'Who are you to object to the orders of Emir Ubaydallah and Caliph Yazid?' – Zaynab simply looks back at them and states that she is 'the daughter of Fatima, the daughter of Muhammad'. Sheltering under her protection, this broken caravan limps its way to Damascus, and thence (according to some accounts) to Ashkelon and on to Cairo. Sayyida (Lady) Zaynab survived captivity for six months, teaching her household the mourning rituals and sermons for her brother Husayn that survive to this day.

There are tomb-shrines to Sayyida Zaynab in both Cairo and Damascus, devoutly visited by Shiite pilgrims all year. They remember the first night after the battle. The tents had been flattened and the women's jewellery had been stolen by soldiers who even tore rings from their ears. There was no fire, no food, no shelter and even the moon was veiled. Zaynab alone possessed the strength to comfort this miserable huddle of widows and orphans. One of her charges, Sukayna, slipped away into the night, wanting to find her father, to whose dead body she told all her woes before falling asleep on him until the dawn. The bodies were left unburied for forty days, until they were secretly buried by the Banu Asad tribe. The site of Husayn's grave was known as Rawzah, 'the Garden', in reference to the paradise of a martyr.

Over the centuries the details of this pitiless tragedy have been recapitulated. One such is the story of Abbas ibn Ali, who, armed only with a spear, determined to get water for the children of the camp. He made his way to the bank of the Euphrates and filled the goatskin but determined not to touch a drop himself until the children had drunk first. Galloping back to the camp, he was intercepted by soldiers but kept his vow not to shed blood. They cut off his right hand, then his left, and finally felled him by shooting a quiver of arrows into his body. Even as he fell, he kept guard of the water-bag (held by his teeth) with the Alam (battle standard) held upright in the bleeding stumps of his arms, lest it fell to the ground. Abbas has become one of the most powerful contemporary heroes of the modern Shiite world. He was a half-brother of Husayn and is affectionately known as Abu Fadl ('father of virtue') in Iraq and Lebanon, and Abu Fazl in Iran and Azerbaijan.*

※ ※ ※

The Shiite lineage descends from the one surviving male member of the family, Ali ibn Husayn Zayn al-Abbadine. He survived years of captivity as a boy and was eventually permitted to retire to Medina. He is acknowledged as the Fourth Imam of the Shia, a gentle, depoliticised mystic whose heritage is

---

* Abu Fazl's example of self-sacrifice is emotionally linked with the suffering of the hundreds of thousands of Iranian soldier-martyrs who fell in the Iraq–Iran war.

Al Sahifa al-Sajjadiyya, a collection of prayers. One of his sons, Muhammad al-Baqir, continued this quietist tradition of gentle scholarship, while another, Zayd ibn Ali (695–740), repeated the bloody experience of his grandfather, responding to the pleas of the people of Kufa to deliver them from oppression and perishing at the hands of an Umayyad army. His example of responding to the call of duty, conscious of the danger, continues to inspire a part of the Shia community known as Zaydis, who remain strong in the Yemen. His body is buried in Iraq and his severed head is revered in Jordan. His nephew, Jafar al-Sadiq (700–765), is considered to be the Sixth Imam of the mainstream Shia. In his lifetime he was acknowledged as one of the greatest Muslim scholars of his age.

The Shia succession after Jafar becomes more contentious, with two lines of descent. That from his son Ismail takes us to his living lineal descendant, the Agha Khan, hereditary leader of the Ismaili community, while that of his brother Musa al-Kadhim, the Seventh Imam, leads us down another family tree of suffering, as four more generations of imams were publicly cherished – but allegedly murdered by their cousins, the Abbasid caliphs of Baghdad. The shrine of the Eighth Imam, Ali al Rida, lies at the heart of the Iranian city of Mashhad, his tomb thronged throughout the year with pilgrims.

The Shia still await the just rule of the righteous imam. Most Shia believe that the historical dynasty of the descendants of Ali ended in its twelfth generation, but that this last imam is the veiled one – the Mahdi, the awaited one, whose reign will come as a sign of the end of the world.

Before his assassination, Imam Ali told his two sons of a dream that warned him of his death. In this dream his body was escorted to the grave by a veiled man who led a camel that bore his corpse wrapped up in winding sheet made from his turban. He warned his sons that, should they ever come across a similar scene, they should not interrupt it. When they witnessed this event for themselves, which happened just as described in their father's dream, they could not resist talking to the veiled man who led the camel, demanding to know who he was. The man lifted his veil and revealed himself to be Ali.

With such popular tales, you get a hint of the complexity of the Shia belief system. The Twelve Imams are historical characters, with mothers and tombs, but they are also in some mysterious way linked to one another. As we will discover in the next chapters, there have been many historical occasions when the Shia prophecies seem about to unfold. So, although the Shia are still waiting for their imam, for their hour of spiritual triumph, there have been many instances when this seems to be about to happen, into our own day.

What is surprising to many is that this historical narrative of events is unchallenged by either Sunni or Shia historians. As must always be stressed, Sunni and Shia practise the same religion, recite the same prayers and venerate the same Koran. Their differences are sometimes just a matter of degree, the choice of which individual you will tell a tale about, and which you will turn away from. But these two storylines create different horizons, different heroes, different aspirations and different approaches to all manner of issues.

PART TWO

Medieval Caliphates

PART TWO

Medieval Caliphates

I t is the stories of the Prophet's family and his Companions, and the events played out amongst the first generations of their descendants, that are most alive in the collective memory of the Sunni and Shia worlds. But the succeeding centuries of Islamic caliphates and empires left enduring marks on the geopolitics of the region. To understand the Middle East in the twenty-first century, there are things we need to grasp from this distant era. The first dynasty of medieval caliphs, the Umayyads, are remembered for their extraordinary empire, stretching from Spain to Central Asia, and their memory is cherished for such sublime buildings as the Dome of the Rock in Jerusalem and the Great Mosque of Damascus. The eclipse of this Arab dynasty is regretted by few and mourned by even fewer, yet there is a yearning for a return to the vast frontiers of this caliphate amongst many pious Muslims, and for a single revered figure to lead the Ummah (the worldwide community of Islam). It is a potent dream that often inspires even moderate Sunni Muslims to yearn for a return of the frontiers of the Umayyad Caliphate and the intellectual authority of the Abbasid caliphate. The Shia, however, have no such doubts about the evil nature of both the Umayyad and Abbasid caliphs.

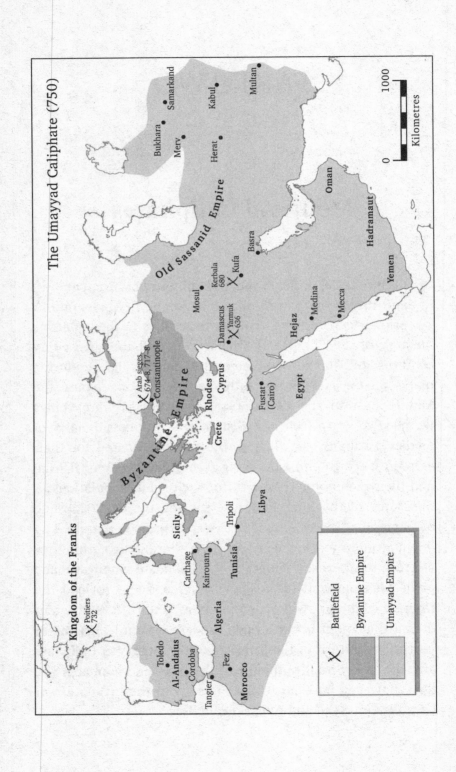

The Umayyad Caliphate (750)

Kingdom of the Franks

✗ Poitiers
732

Toledo
Al-Andalus
Cordoba
Fez
Morocco
Tangier

Carthage
Kairouan
Tunisia
Algeria

Sicily

Tripoli

Libya

Crete
Rhodes
Cyprus

Byzantine Empire

✗ Arab sieges,
674-8, 717-8
Constantinople

Fustat
(Cairo)

Egypt

Damascus
✗ Yarmuk
636

Mosul

Kerbala
680
✗ Kufa
Basra

Old Sassanid Empire

Hejaz

Medina
Mecca

Yemen

Hadramaut

Oman

Merv
Bukhara
Samarkand

Herat
Kabul

Multan

Battlefield
Byzantine Empire
Umayyad Empire
✗

0   1000
Kilometres

CHAPTER 9

Umayyads and Abbasids

The Arab Empires: Umayyads (661–750)
and Abbasids (750–1258)

The Umayyads were Arab tribal lords who knew the reality of power in the Middle East, achieved through their command of army and police and softened by the patronage of salaries distributed by the treasury. They ruled from Damascus and were usually more interested in military conquest – leading a jihad on a far frontier – than in the practice of true religion. The Shia loathe them as godless usurpers and tyrants, the dynasty of Muawiya, who fought against Imam Ali, and Yazid, who was responsible for the death of Husayn at Kerbala. But their empire produced an inspiring succession of military commanders, not least Yazid, who attacked the Byzantine Empire by land and sea and laid siege to Constantinople, a feat that no sultan would equal for the next 750 years.

The dynasty reached its apogee under Abdal Malik, the fifth Umayyad Caliph (685–705), who must be ranked amongst the great leaders of the Arabs. He insisted that the existing languages of administration – Greek, Latin and Persian – be replaced by Arabic, and established the first Islamic coinage, and he built the Dome of the Rock in Jerusalem, now one of the icons of Islamic identity. But he will not get onto any list of virtuous Muslims. It has been argued that the Dome was conceived as an ornate, royal processional hall, where the caliph could receive the formal oath of loyalty, the *bayat*. He built this magnificent domed hall – over an ancient holy place* beside the revered old mosque at Jerusalem – because the pious Muslims of Mecca and Medina had rebelled against his rule and wanted nothing to do with him. In terms of Islamic morality, Umar II (717–720) was the very best of the Umayyad caliphs, for he was genuinely pious, interested in peace and education, and sent out missionaries to his existing provinces rather than plotting another round of military conquests. As his name suggests, he was descended from Caliph Umar (he was a great-grandson through the maternal line), but he had just three years on the throne before he was murdered.

❄ ❄ ❄

The second Islamic dynasty, the Abbasids, ruled as titular caliphs from Baghdad between 750 and 1258. The cultural peak of their dynasty lasted just three generations, but what a golden era that was, when rulers like Haroun al-Rachid (he of *The 1,001 Nights*), patronised poets and philosophers and endowed translation schools. Haroun's princess bride, Zubaida, was loved for her charitable works, which included the construction of shelters and wells so poor pilgrims could walk to Mecca for the Haj.

The Abbasids were relatives of the Prophet, taking their name from Abu Abbas, one of Muhammad's paternal uncles. They were not descendants of Ali and are not considered Shiite imams. However, they came to power by allying themselves with a Shiite rebellion that had emerged out of Afghanistan, led by a mysteriously veiled rebel commander. This rebellion

---

*   It is believed to be the sacred spot where Abraham was preparing an altar to sacrifice his son Isaac, and where the Prophet Muhammad ascended to heaven in the mystical Night Journey (the Miraj).

toppled the Umayyads in 750 but instead of restoring a rightful heir of Ali to the caliphate, the Abbasids seized it for themselves. From time to time, these caliphs might suggest a restoration of authority to the line of true Shia imams, or to make a marriage alliance with Ali's descendants. This idea reached an emotional crescendo when in 816 the caliph Al-Mamun (813–833) chose Ali al-Rida, the Eighth Imam of the Shia, to be both his political heir and his son-in-law. It is a 'what if' moment in Islamic history, when a ruling caliph appeared to be about to heal the historical schism by formally adopting the legitimate Shia heir. But Ali al-Rida died just two years after the declaration. Most Shia believe he was murdered, killed by a poisoned pomegranate, another in the long line of martyred Shia imams.

For most of the Abbasid dynasty, it was power, rather than rightful succession, that mattered. Having risen to prominence on the back of a rebel army from the east, the Abbasids carefully balanced the authority of the old Arab ruling class with other ethnicities, employing Persians and Turks in their army and within their administration. The Baghdad of the Abbasids was a magnificent reflection of this new cosmopolitan society, a city on the banks of the Euphrates that was one of the epicentres of the world. Its rise coincided with a vast expansion in literacy, fuelled by the invention of paper, which was cheaper and easier to produce than leather-based parchment. The fluid lines of Arabic calligraphy worked well on this new medium, and both scholars and merchants liked the fact that ink on paper could not easily be amended. The Abbasids were vital players in the transmission of world culture, be it Greek philosophy or Hindu mathematics, which they translated into Arabic. When the original source documents were destroyed, it was only these Arabic translations which allowed later cultures, including Europe, to regain this lost knowledge.

The Abbasid caliphs also presided over the work of the first great Muslim historians, theologians and Arab grammarians. Abbasid rule provided the necessary patronage and peace for these scholars, as well as a literate, urban audience for their writings. There was a sense of urgency to catch the last oral stories from Arabia and to preserve them in ink. The most important task was to record the *hadith*, the sayings of the Prophet Muhammad, before they got lost. This became a second textual authority which could expand and elucidate the meaning of the Koran. Studying the transmission of *hadith* became a science in itself, as scholars endeavoured to track down who had heard what from whom, following the trail back over 150 years to a reputable Companion or a wife of the Prophet dwelling in Mecca or Medina.

Abbasid scholars were aware that there had been an inflation in *hadith*, as ancient oral wisdom and traditional Bedouin practices became interwoven with memories of the Prophet's conversation. There was a *hadith* recorded for every eight minutes of Muhammad's life as a Prophet and, even when drastically pruned down to the 5,000 most reliable sayings, that still represents five sayings for every week of his public life. There was also a pressing need to record the fluid poetic references embedded in spoken Arabic, where the context is often required to define the exact meaning of a word. The work of a grammarian soon became a vital tool to understanding the Koran. Between 750 and 1500, there were 4,000 published scholars working on Arabic grammar.

It is in this world of urban scholarship, rather than in the magnificent court of the caliphs, that we find the most important Sunni heroes of this period: self-employed scholars, living humbly in courtyard houses off the bustling alleyways of the great Muslim cities. Working together or apart, they collected the legal decisions of the first Muslim judges and the administrative reforms and decisions of the first four caliphs to create guides to the earliest examples of Islamic law and best social practice. The Koran was always the unalterable prime source, but the collections of *hadith* and the example set by the Companions allowed for the creation of a complete code of acceptable practice for devout Muslims. In Medina, Malik ibn Anas (c.711–95) created the Maliki law code which is still followed throughout North and West Africa. Abu Hanifa, the son of an Afghan trader born in Iraq in 767, created the Hanafi lawcode which would became dominant in Central and South Asia and was the official code of the Ottoman sultans. The teachings of Al-Shafi'i, also born in 767, in the Palestinian city of Gaza and later resident in Cairo, now prevail along the shores of the Indian Ocean, along the coast of East Africa and in the Far East. All these schools of Sunni law now exist in amicable tolerance but this has not always been the case. Tribal feuds were once fuelled by marginal differences between the codes, despite the fact that all these founder sheikhs were intellectually and often socially linked to one another.

The fourth and last of these great Sunni scholar-sheikhs was Ahmed ibn Hanbal (780–855), who had personally studied under the tutelage of Al-Shafi'i, who had himself studied under Malik. Ibn Hanbal was obsessed with the task of tracking down the *hadith* of the Prophet and travelled to all the old Arab garrison cities to consult existing collections. What propelled him to popular fame was his opposition to the caliphs – not their political rule but their pretensions to authority on spiritual matters. The Abbasid caliphs had decided to uphold the Mutazalite theological position (on whether the Koran had been created or had existed for all eternity) and sent out a commission to inspect and certify all clerical scholars. Ibn Hanbal would not conform to this inquisition and was periodically exiled, imprisoned and even publicly whipped for his presumption under the reigns of three different Abbasid caliphs – Al-Ma'mun, Al-Mustasim and Al-Wathiq. This principled stance gave him a heroic status in his home city of Baghdad, and when he died in 855 he was escorted to his grave by hundreds of thousands of mourners.

This triumph of the passive, principled poor scholar against the persecution of the man in power stands as the political essence of the Sunni tradition. It was a quiet revolution. The man in power in the palace – calling himself caliph, emir or sultan – would continue to do what he wished, but the one thing that he could no longer touch with impunity was Islamic law. This story of the humble scholar-sheikh refusing to bow before the might of the sultan is a story that has been relived in practically every subsequent generation, in every nation across the Muslim world. So in their different ways the Sunni share the Shia story of the suffering of the truly righteous.

❋ ❋ ❋

Shia scholars were also at work in this period. They put together their own collections of *hadith*, and gathered together the stories, the teachings, the example of modesty and self-sacrifice of Ali and his righteous descendants. The Shias' Sixth Imam, Jafar al-Sadiq (702–65), was a pious scholar whose work was incorporated into both the Maliki and Hanafi traditions. Imam Jafar al-Sadiq's own work is everywhere but nowhere, for, though his scholarship is frequently referenced, no extant book of his has survived the centuries. It is possible to imagine that one day something called the Jafari tradition of Muslim law could be taught. It would contain the Shia vision and be considered as an equally valid intellectual inheritance alongside the four other canonical schools of Sunni law. Such a vision of unity has been suggested by many Islamic teachers, especially those who have dedicated their life to pan-Islamic unity. To add further lustre to his historical appeal, Jafar was descended from both Imam Ali (the first Shiite imam) and Abu Bakr (the first Sunni caliph).

This dynasty of Shia imams, whose spiritual authority passed from father to son (confirmed by a formal act of blessing), continued in the shadows throughout the first 150 years of the Abbasid caliphate. As we have already heard, the imams were observed and sometimes flattered, but hospitality could all too soon morph into a form of house arrest, after which they were imprisoned or murdered. Imam Al-Askari, the last historically chronicled Shia imam, was eleventh in succession from Ali and died in 874. After his death the mainstream of Shiite thought believed in the eventual coming of the Twelfth Imam, who, though in occlusion (spiritual retreat), will return in glory as the Mahdi. Others argued for different lines of descent, which gives us such alternative Shia traditions as the Zaydi or the line represented by the Ismaili Agha Khan.*

❀ ❀ ❀

For all its glamorous lustre, the Abbasid dynasty was actually on the wane within a hundred years of its inauguration. Real power had leached into the hands of Turkic generals, who fought the pitiless civil wars on behalf of rival Abbasid princes. Bajkam was just such a ruthless man, a slave-soldier turned chief of police who restored the tottering throne of the Abbasids by the usual methods (he himself ruled as amir

---

* The Zaydi tradition maintains that the holiest descendant of the Prophet is the most suitable candidate to be their imam, their spiritual leader. Zaydis combine ethical meritocracy with the mystical appeal of a holy bloodline descended from the Prophet Muhammad. The Ismaili tradition is a more rigidly genealogical spiritual monarchy, but also includes an element of selection, as each Ismaili imam selects the heir most fitting to hold office.

from 938 to 941). The military influence of Turkic people within Islamic society is often overlooked, but it was – and is today – arguably just as important, fractious and enduring an influence as the Sunni–Shia rivalry.

Bajkam had taken power in a Baghdad that had been ripped apart by sectarian strife. In the 930s, the city was divided into different quarters, with Hanbali Sunni pitched against those friendly to the Shia. Gang violence spread, linked to different Turkic factions within the army. All over the Abbasid Empire, the outer provinces fell into the hands of opportunistic or capable governors. These provincial governors created new realities on the ground and accepted new titles to legitimise their rule from the otherwise powerless caliph in Baghdad. So native dynasties like the Saffarids ruled over Iran, while from Bokhara the Samanids governed Central Asia.

In Baghdad, the Abbasid dynasty survived until 1258, like an exotic bird in a gilded cage. It continued to exist by rubber stamping the rule of tough, usually Turkic, generals who had risen up through the ranks and found it convenient to their new dignity to be endorsed by the caliph.

CHAPTER 10

Shiites Triumphant

*Fatimids (909–1107), Qarmatians (899–1077)
and Buyids (934–1062)*

As Abbasid power ebbed, something totally unexpected transformed the Islamic world. The Shiite cause had seemed vulnerable and doomed in the time of Ali al-Hadi and Hasan al-Askari, their tenth and eleventh imams – scholar-mystics condemned to a life of house arrest in Iraq. But, in the tenth century, the spirit of the Shiite movement was to re-emerge and dominate three completely separate geographical regions of the Islamic world. The Shiite Qarmatians established their rule over the wastes of the Eastern desert of Arabia in 899. Shiite Fatimid caliphs ruled the central Middle East from their citadel within the walled city of Cairo. And from 934 the whole of Greater Iran fell under the sway of the Buyid emirs. The Buyids did not claim to be descended from the family of Shia imams – they were indigenous Persians – but considered themselves regents, governing on behalf of the lost dynasty of imams.

Although the rule of these states lasted for more than 250 years, these three Shiite empires are not well known. But one of the most fascinating elements about Islamic history is how belief systems and political communities endure. For there are elements from this era of the three medieval Shiite empires which have direct consequences for the political realities of the Middle East today.

❈ ❈ ❈

The Fatimid Empire emerged out of nowhere. Their sudden rise was due to the success of a lone Shiite agent called Abu Abdallah, a charismatic missionary who attached himself to Berber pilgrims from North Africa on their pilgrimage to Mecca. He proved such a wise and learned companion that they asked him to return with them to their home in the Kabyle mountains of Algeria and continue his teaching. From this base, the missionary converted the Berber highland tribes into a Shiite army, determined to put an ancient wrong right, and place a true heir of the Prophet Muhammad, through his daughter Fatima, on the caliph's throne. This army of zealots first conquered all of North Africa, pushing armed columns deep down into the Sahara, before building a fortress city on the coast of Tunisia; it was called Mahdia – a city worthy of the Mahdi. From this base they raided southern Europe and launched a successful conquest of Egypt and the Levant.

Once in power, the Fatimids proved tolerant and internationalist, employing men of talent whatever their religion. One of their most enduring gifts was Cairo's Al Azhar university, which remains the single most respected institution in the Islamic world. The Fatimids' only major doctrinal change was in insisting that Shia textual sources be used in the law courts, rather than those collected by Sunni scholars. The public duties reserved to a Fatimid caliph-imam, however, were similar to those exercised by a Sunni ruler: administer justice, lead the Friday prayers and supervise the religious tithe. The caliph alone could authorise a jihad.

The most public symbol of political authority in the Muslim world was the name of the caliph-imam struck into the coinage and used in the muezzins' call to prayer. Few, though, understood the genealogical claims of the Fatimids to be true heirs of Imam Ali, for there was an awkward two-generation gap in their family tree. And, once in power, they became, as Tim Mackintosh-Smith described them, a 'dynasty of dilettantes, vanishing into books, gemstones, alcohol, racing pigeons, weird alternative medicine, unorthodox sex and sadism. The business of everyday rule they left to viziers.'

After the Fatimids lost power in Cairo, in 1107, a branch of the dynasty managed to survive for another couple of centuries in a handful of fortresses tucked away in remote highland regions. These garrisons stayed true to their Shiite spiritual leaders, notably the Nizari imam, 'the Sheikh of the Assassins'. Fanatical followers succeeded in infiltrating the courts of rival Islamic rulers and effecting public political assassinations. This remnant of the Shia Fatimid Empire was only smoked out of their mountain lairs in a determined war of attrition led by the Mongol Khans in the thirteenth century. The romantic breached walls of their old castellated fortresses can still be found in the mountains of Iran, Pakistan and the valleys of the Lebanon and Syria. But, even after this, the community managed to survive, finding refuge in the remote badlands of Baluchistan for a further few centuries, before finally re-emerging in India as the dynasty of Agha Khans, the hereditary leaders of the worldwide Ismaili community.

❁ ❁ ❁

The authority of the Abbasid caliphs was tested even in Iraq, their dynastic homeland, by a Shiite uprising that sacked the city of Basra. This, the Zanj rebellion of 869, was empowered by African slaves determined to create an ethical Muslim society ruled by a rightful imam. It raged with revolutionary violence and zeal in the flatlands of southern Iraq before it was brutally suppressed in 883. Shia rebels took shelter in the southern reed marshes near the delta.

An offshoot of this revolt prospered amongst the Bedouin Arabs of eastern Arabia, led by Shiite Qarmatians. They established an idyllic-sounding polity in 899, supported by state farms that filled community granaries, exempting the population from taxation and allowing for interest-free loans for those in debt. To discourage hoarding, a token coinage in lead was struck to be used for local transactions. This historical testimony comes from a known Shiite source, the polymath traveller and poet, Nasir Khusraw, the 'Ruby of Badakhshan'. Sunni historians paint a different picture. They concentrate on the horrors of the Qarmatian sack of Mecca in 930, their theft of the sacred black stone from the Kaaba, their massacre of pilgrims and their poisoning of wells. The truth probably lies somewhere in between. The enduring Shiism of this region would be confirmed four hundred years later by the Moroccan travel writer Ibn Battuta, who described the tribes as 'extremist Shia' when he passed through eastern Arabia in 1331. And, indeed, in modern Saudi Arabia, the continued existence of a strong Arab Shiite community in their easternmost province remains one of the most important geopolitical facts on the ground. They are almost certainly the heirs of the Qarmatian Bedouin republic, surviving to disrupt the status quo more than a thousand years later.

❋ ❋ ❋

The Buyid emirs* originated from Dalyan, the fertile, forested region of Iran that runs between the Caspian Sea and the

---

* The multiplicity of Buyid emirates can sew confusion on first encounter, as can the variant spellings – Buwahid, Bowayhid, Buyahid.

Alborz mountains. They saw themselves as regents for the hidden Twelfth Imam and established a loose confederation of brother states, with regional capitals in the Iranian cities of Fars, Shiraz, Iraq and Ray. The rulers of these states did not fight each other, but now and then acknowledged one among their number as paramount leader. They were proud of their Iranian ethnic identity and, though champions of Shiite traditions remained tolerant of all faiths, not even deposing the Abbasid caliph when they controlled Iraq. Some of their pro-Shiite political activity could be childishly sectarian, like the curses against the Sunni caliphs, Abu Bakr and Omar, that in 962 were painted on the city walls. But it was also the Buyids who made a public festival to mark the day of Ghadir Khum and encouraged the mourning processions for Ashura. And they built shrine tombs throughout the land of Iraq and Iran to honour the burial places of the twelve imams. They sponsored the study of Shiite traditions in the Iranian cities of Qumm and Rayy (one Buyid scholar even questioned the genealogical claims of the Fatimid Shiite caliphs whose frontiers brushed against the Buyids in Syria).

The hard result of all these three adventures is that for two hundred years the entire Muslim world was ruled over by three Shiite states, with an impressive array of political forms. The Fatimid caliphate was an absolutist monarchy in theory but in practice was remarkably tolerant, multilingual and internationalist. In their heyday the Fatimids ruled over Egypt, North Africa, Sicily and half of Arabia, while their fleets controlled the southern Mediterranean for two centuries (909–1070). Eastern Arabia and the Persian Gulf were governed by the Qarmatian Bedouin Arab state from 899 to 1077. It was a remarkable, egalitarian political experiment, whose legacy is kept alive by the Shiite regions of al-Hasa within Saudi Arabia and Bahrain. The easternmost Middle East was dominated by the Buyid emirates which ruled over all of Iran, Iraq and Afghanistan for a hundred years, from 945 to 1048, acting as regents for the murdered dynasty of Imam Ali. In terms of art, architecture and intellectual culture, this was an astonishingly creative period for Islamic culture. The ceramics, in particular, with their fine cream-glazed wares bordered with lines of bold Kufic script, are breathtaking.

CHAPTER 11

Three Turkic Empires

*Seljuk (1037–1194), Mongol (1206–1368)
and Timurid (1370–1507)*

Five centuries stand between the astonishing high cul-ture achieved by early medieval Islam – as conjured by Abbasid Baghdad and Fatimid Cairo – and the emergence of Shiite Iran and Sunni Turkey in the sixteenth century, the two powers that still dominate the Middle East. Between-times, the Muslim civilisation was repeatedly attacked by forces from the steppes of Central Asia: highly mobile, Turkic tribesmen, who established three great Empires. The Seljuk, Mongol–Ilkhanid and Timurid states were created by char-ismatic commanders, the latter two by Genghis Khan and Timur (also known as Tamburlaine or Tamerlane), who to modern-day Turks – and the Turkic 'stans' of Central Asia – are heroes, if not genetic ancestors. To the Arabs and Ira-nians and other peoples of the Middle East, these conquerors were seen as a curse from God, repeatedly shattering an effervescent culture and plunging it into darkness.

It is tempting to move swiftly over this period, but to understand the modern Middle East we need at the very least to understand the Turkish perspective. For, in their minds, the first Turkic empire, the Seljuks, was a force for good, riding forth as liberators to destroy the heretical Shiite states and re-establish the Sunni traditions and caliphate. Others might see the Seljuk attachment to Sunni Islam as no more than a convenient battle flag to justify their conquest of the central Middle East. Whatever their motivations, the Seljuks were certainly a force for the good compared to the devastation unleashed by Genghis Khan and his son Hulagu in the thirteenth century, and repeated a hundred years later by Timur.

❀ ❀ ❀

The Seljuks were a confederation of nine clans of Oghuz Turks from the shores of Lake Baikal in the heart of the Asiatic steppe. They served in the Muslim Ghaznavid army which plundered Hindu India, year after year, from military bases tucked into the Afghan mountains. In 1037, the Seljuks struck south into Persia, on their own account, led by Tughril Bey. Tughril freed the Sunni caliph in Baghdad from the rule of the Buyids. His conquests would be expanded by his brother and then by his nephew, Alp Arslan ('the valiant lion'), and reach their apogee under Malik Shah. In 1071, the Seljuks destroyed the army of the Byzantine emperor at the Battle of Manzikert, marking the end of Christian Anatolia and the beginning of a Muslim warrior nation that would become known as Turkey (at roughly the same time that the Normans were conquering Anglo-Saxon England). The Seljuks also proved themselves elsewhere as hero-warriors of a renascent Islam, conquering such Christian strongholds as Georgia and Armenia.

The Seljuks were magnificent builders as well as fighters, and left their historical mark all over the landscape of Turkey and the Middle East: elegant bridges, bold new mosques, tower tombs, castles, city walls and defensible caravanserais in which merchant caravans could shelter. They had a nose for talent, and became patrons to the mathematician-poet

Omar Khayyam and Rumi, both of whom sought shelter under their rule. The most politically convincing of all the Seljuk building projects was the construction of the first madrasas – Islamic teaching colleges.* The greatest of these were the Al-Nazamiyyah and Al-Mustan siriyyah, the latter still the heart of the university in Baghdad. These were deliberately conceived as opulent institutions where the Sunni law codes could be taught to a fresh generation of students – *talib* – destined to become judges and legal advisors to Seljuk princes ruling as provincial governors.

A madrasa stood in the metaphysical shadow of the Prophet Muhammad's house-mosque. But, under the Seljuks, madrasas became an art form, their courtyard cloisters decorated with so many strands of calligraphy, painted and carved in ceramic, plaster and cedar wood. They were endowed with lands to become free-standing charitable foundations, the income supporting professional lecturers and a library. Free accommodation and teaching were offered to students for seven years. In this way, the scholar class was slowly bound into an acceptable form of dependency on the State, happily associated with charity, education and salaries.

The Seljuk Empire lost its unity after the death of Malik Shah in 1092, following which his sons fought each other for supremacy. Smaller Seljuk sultanates, emerging out of this civil war, would survive across the breadth of the Middle East for another two hundred years, coinciding with the period of the Crusader states imposed on the Levant coast from 1098 to 1291. However, the Crusader period of domination lasted for just ninety years before it was broken by Saladin at the Battle of the Horns of Hattin in 1187.

---

* Madrasa is spelled in various forms around the Arab world – commonly, madrasah, madraza, medressa, medersa (in North Africa).

Saladin was neither Arab, Turk nor Persian, but the son of a Kurdish fortress commander. He would betray two sets of masters: first the Sunni Zangid Emirate of Mosul (who were Seljuk allies) and then the Shia Fatimid caliphs of Cairo. He has, however, become a great Sunni military hero, most especially in the light of what was to come.

❊ ❊ ❊

The next Turkic invasion, far more destructive, began in 1206, when five principal Mongol tribes put aside their blood rivalries and swore loyalty to Genghis Khan. The Mongol Khanate was monotheistic, literate and invincible. The tribes had been strengthened by a run of good weather, which had increased the pastures and expanded the herds. By the time of his death in 1227, Genghis Khan ruled an empire that stretched from Korea to the frontiers of Persia.

If you want to hold on to one date, 1258 witnesses the destruction of Baghdad and the execution of the last powerless Abbasid caliph, who was rolled up in a carpet and trampled to death by Mongol cavalry. After the streets had run red, the rivers turned black with the ink of five hundred years of scholarship thrown out as rubbish. However, these merciless conquerors – irritated by such Islamic habits as halal killing, circumcision and the refusal to drink alcohol – did not complete their mission to destroy an entire culture.

Instead, and within three generations, they became Muslims themselves and created one of the most sublime periods of Islamic art, the Ilkhanid. The Mongol Ilkhanid dynasty saw exquisite cultural fusion: Turkic-Persian merging with Chinese influences of Central Asia to enrich the Islamic cultures of the Middle East. It is the cultural label for some of the most beautiful books, buildings and ceramics of any era of mankind.

But it is also the name for the dynasty whose armies destroyed city after city of Iranian culture, flattening both Nishapur and Balkh. It is all very complicated, this mixture of utter savagery and sublime creativity.

The greatest witness to this time was Rumi (1207–78), who has become the world's favourite poet. He was born in Balkh, whose ruins are now located within northern Afghanistan. His extraordinary free spirit and innate internationalism can partly be explained by the obliteration of his homeland by the Mongols. Balkh was destroyed when he was thirteen years old, after which he found refuge in distant Anatolia, in the Seljuk-governed city of Konya. It is possible to hear a reflection of this in the opening lines of his *Mathnawi*:

> Listen to this pierced flute as it sounds its
> sad lament of separation
>
> Bringing men and women to tears since it
> was torn from a bed of reeds
>
> Seeking a heart rent from pain in which
> to share its longing
>
> Like all those who live in exile yearning
> for the day of their return.

If the destruction of his home helped incubate the mystical poetry of Rumi, the obliteration of the great Syrian city of Harran by the Mongols most certainly motivated the scholar Ibn Taymiyyah (1263–1328). A minor scholarly figure in his own lifetime, Ibn Taymiyyah's fame has grown over the last three centuries, for he is the intellectual ancestor of both the Wahhabi and Salafi fundamentalist movements. It is useful to understand his work within its biographical context.

Ibn Taymiyyah left the city of his ancestors as a child in 1269, just before it was obliterated by the Mongols. Harran had been a city of Aramaic- and Arabic-speaking intellectuals for thousands of years. It was important enough to have briefly replaced Damascus as the capital city of the Umayyad caliphate but remains in ruins to this day, with just one vast minaret left standing. Ibn Taymiyyah spent the rest of his life sheltering in Damascus and Cairo, then on the frontiers of the Mongol Empire. They were protected by tough Mameluke sultans who had all started life as Turkic slave boys. Throughout Ibn Taymiyyah's life, no one knew if, when or where a Mongol horde would come back to finish them off. There were frequent and serious alarms when Mongol forces appeared in northern Syria in 1299, 1300 and 1303. To add to the prevailing sense of fear, Christian Georgians, Christian Armenians and such Shia communities as the Alawi and Ismaili only survived the Mongol invasion by becoming submissive allies.

It is against the horrors of this apocalyptic personal experience that one must place Ibn Taymiyyah's scholarship: his lack of trust and fury against both Shia and Christians, his desire to motivate the last remaining Muslims in a jihad to defend their threatened civilisation, and his insistence that fake Muslim leaders should be denounced as Takfir – unbelievers. Though these doctrines have now grown notorious, they would have been understandable in his day, for the Mongol leadership (with the blood of hundreds of thousands of Muslims on their hands) was just then affecting to pose as the leading Muslim sultanate. The conversion of the Mongol Khans to Islam happened around 1295 and seems to have been primarily undertaken for financial reasons, for they had worked out that an efficient collection of the Muslim tithe was now more reliable than plunder as a way to pay the vast armies.

Ibn Taymiyyah denounced the scholarly class of his day as too obedient to such absolute rulers. He argued that a consensus of Muslim scholars had become less important and secure as a source of authority than the historical example set by the Prophet Muhammad and the community of early Islam. This also had the advantage of returning Islam to its Arabic source documents, and downgrading the alien traditions of the royal courts of Turkestan, Mongolia and Iran. Ibn Taymiyyah taught *hadith* studies of the Hanbali legal tradition at the prestigious Sukariya madrasa in Damascus. In terms of the sacred texts, he knew exactly what he was taking about.

Although he is now often depicted as a vengeful cleric, the reality seems more nuanced. He argued for ultimate forgiveness – that hellfire may not be eternal – and proposed legal rules that would have made divorce marginally fairer. Despite his opposition to the worship of Sufi saints, he was an active member of the Sufi Qadiri brotherhood. However, he detested the way that the new ruling class of Turkic and Mongol warriors had debased the simplicity of Islam with their pagan habits and odd traditions, such as appealing to buried saints for intercession as if they were shaman-like demigods rather than addressing their prayers to God. He never married (which was extremely rare for a man of his position), and took a surname that referenced his mother's family not his father's. He was a strange, cantankerous man and would be imprisoned by the authorities half a dozen times for speaking out of turn. He died in Damascus prison in 1328. Tens of thousands of his fellow citizens escorted him on his last journey, to the graveyard of the Sufis.

❀❀❀

In 1347, the Black Death arrived at the docks of Alexandria. Between a third and a half of the population of the Middle East perished of the plague. There were so many deaths in Cairo that the Sultan's treasury became the unexpected beneficiary of thousands of heirless estates. These were auctioned off and the proceeds directed towards building the mosque-madrasa of Sultan Hasan, a stupendous structure that gives not the slightest hint of the suffering which funded it, or that this was a civilisation under any sense of extinction.

For then came the worst of times. In 1380, the armies of Timur surged out of Central Asia, massacring the population of Muslim cities from Isfahan, Herat and Delhi in the east, to Baghdad and Aleppo in the west. Isfahan's population was said to have been reduced to twenty-eight 'towers of silence', each formed of 1,500 skulls. Only skilled craftsmen were spared, and despatched to work on vast building projects in the new imperial capital of Samarkand.

Timur sometimes affected a sympathy for the Shiite cause, as when he condemned the entire city of Damascus to death, but on another occasion affected a Sunni disposition when he determined to punish a Shiite community. He awarded himself the title 'sword of Islam', having expelled the Christian Knights of St John from Turkey and would obliterate the Nestorian Church, then the largest Christian community in the world, spread across Central Asia. Timur desired to recreate the vast domains of the Mongol Empire and married a descendant of Genghis so that his own heirs could share the bloodline of the great Khan.

The destruction and brutality was unparalleled. But, if you wander through museum collections of Islamic civilisation, it is impossible not to salute the Timurid period as a golden age of artistic creativity, certainly in terms of ceramics, architecture and the arts of the book. It is also possible that Timur, a truly monstrous autocrat, a paranoid and pitiless conqueror, may have been the last patron of the poet Hafiz, whose verses are the very pinnacle of Persian literate culture. Timur also befriended Ibn Khaldoun, the great North African historian and political thinker.

After the death of Timur in 1405, his vast, smouldering empire remained under the control of his heirs for a hundred years, before slowly shrinking to become the emirates of Herat and Samarkand. But the overwhelming military superiority of Turkic-Mongolian cavalry armies remained. Babur (1483– 1530), a great grandson of Timur, went on to create the Mughal Empire by conquering half a dozen independent Muslim sultanates across northern India.

The entire population of the Middle East, with Central Asia, Iran and Anatolia, probably numbered around 35 million in the fifteenth century. Western Europe was about equal to this, but both communities were dwarfed by India and China, each with populations of more than 100 million. This makes the triumph of the Turkic warlords in the late medieval world even more remarkable. The population of the grassland steppes was five million, thinly spread over half of their continent, yet they had established their rule over 300 million neighbours. If you were a military analyst at this point in history, guessing at the future shape of world history from its past, everything would point to the continuing importance of the quick-moving, highly mobile cavalry armies of Central Asia. No one would be paying attention to a couple of poor kingdoms on the edge of the world, with their unedifying diet of salted cod and herring. But this was to be the vortex of the next revolution in world history, when the era of horse-power was supplanted by the might of gunpowder, mobile artillery and ocean-going merchant ships.

Fortunately for the survival of Islam, the Portuguese and Spanish kingdoms – who used the instincts of the medieval Crusades to create the first colonial empires – were not alone in their acquisition of these technologies. The conquest of Byzantine Constantinople in 1453 by the Ottoman Sultan was assisted by their own very efficient mastery of the new technology: pounding city walls to dust with artillery bombardments, and constructing coastal artillery fortresses along the straits of Gallipoli and the channel of the Bosphorus that could sink any fleet coming to reinforce the city.

PART THREE

The Emergence of the
Three: Turkey, Persia
and Saudi Arabia

PART THREE

The Emergence of the Three: Turkey, Persia and Saudi Arabia

As Europe slowly entered the world stage in the sixteenth and seventeenth centuries, the Islamic world was coalescing around two empires: Shiite Iran and Sunni Turkey, whose belligerence towards one another only strengthened their contrasting faith allegiances. This was the fiercest period of conflict between Sunni and Shia empires. The war between the competing dynasties of Ottoman sultans and Safavid shahs was intensified by their rival faiths and, as in their modern nation states of Turkey and Iran, partly defined by their ethnic differences.

As this titanic war between neighbours finally burnt itself out, a new force emerged in the south. The Arabs re-emerged through charismatic new dynastic leadership, once again empowered by a radical Islamic creed that also championed a specific ethnic identity. This, after many startling adventures, would become the Wahhabi Kingdom of Saudi Arabia. So, by the end of this period, the three powers that still dominate the Middle East are recognisably present: Sunni Turkey, Shia Persia/Iran and an ultra-Sunni (Wahhabi) Saudi Arabia.

CHAPTER 12

Ottomans and Safavids:
The Clash of Neighbours

*Shah Ismail (1501–24), Sultan Selim (1512–20)
and the Battle of Chaldiran (1514)*

The Ottoman Sultanate emerged from the borderlands of the old Byzantine Empire, which had long been peppered with rival Turkic emirates. The Ottoman sultans had not a drop of Arab blood in their veins, let alone any connection with the family of the Prophet Muhammad. They traced their descent to a thirteenth-century border lord called Osman Gazi, whose father had fought in the Seljuk army. 'Osman', the founder of the dynasty, is a variant spelling of 'Uthman', a name instantly associated with the Third Caliph of the Sunni, and the man most loathed by the Shia. So, from its onset, the Sunni identity of the Turkish Ottoman Empire was deeply embedded.

The Ottomans proved exceptionally efficient in absorbing new technologies, most especially the gunpowder revolution that was creating a new king of the battlefield – artillery. After seizing Constantinople in 1453, they went on to overwhelm all of the last Byzantine outposts, from Trebizond to Mistra.* By this period the Ottoman sultanate had already evolved into an

---

* Trebizond is now in northern Turkey; Mistra was the last Byzantine outpost, at the foot of the Greek Peloponnese.

incredibly efficient military machine, and to finance their wars the sultans nurtured the towns they captured and their tax-paying merchants and craftsmen. They built covered bazaars and *hans* (caravanserais) beside the stout mosques which celebrated their victories, for they realised that by protecting the other peoples of the book (Jews and Christians) they could raise a much greater tax revenue. The Ottomans were proud to be the commanders of a jihad state, and to be both Turkic and Sunni Muslim, but they presided over a polyglot community. The core of their professional standing army, as well as the administrative officials, was formed from slave boys taken as a levy from their Greek and Bosnian Christian subjects. The Sunni–Shia distinction was not rigid, either: Sufi brotherhoods helped knit together this heterodox community and their mystical vocabulary was powerfully loaded with respect for Imam Ali and his spiritual heirs.

❋ ❋ ❋

Meanwhile, in the east, a young prince of the holy blood line of the imams had appeared. Shah Ismail, born in 1487 in the Persian city of Ardabil, was a brilliant military leader and a dazzling poet, whose rhetoric inflamed crowds of thousands. His mystical appeal was enhanced by his being the seventh sheikh of a Sufi brotherhood, the Safavids, that had been respected for generations by both Turkic tribesmen and Kurdish highlanders. He also claimed descent from the household of the Prophet Muhammad through his father's line and from Genghis Khan and Timur through his mother.

His followers saw Ismail as a true Shia imam – the legitimate spiritual leader of the worldwide community of Islam – touched not only with the power of interpreting the scriptures, but the holder of generations of accumulated wisdom. To his ardent disciples, it seemed that he might be the reincarnated spirit of the Mahdi, who would usher in the divine kingdom at the end of the world. His followers became known as the *kizilbas* – the wearers of red hats, both a badge of identity and a crimson mark of potential martyrdom. Ismail offered these followers not just rewards on this earth but inclusion into the Shiite cult of martyrdom, celebrated annually by the month-long commemoration of Imam Husayn's death. When he told his followers that 'No one can be a *kizilbas* unless his heart is pure and his bloody entrails are like rubies', he was demanding total obedience in return for a martyr's death. Their red hats were formed with twelve gussets, to symbolise the twelve imams.

In 1501, fourteen-year-old Ismail declared himself Imam in Tabriz. Within just nine years his *kizilbas* had conquered in his name all the mountains, oases and plains of Persia, and Ismail was Shah of Persia as well as *Murshidi-i Kamil*, 'the perfect master' and 'the Shadow of God on earth.' Architects, artists, poets and engineers were drawn to serve this imaginative ruler who knew how to employ talented men.

His brilliance was born of a passion that could flow equally towards knowledge and terrifying cruelty. Writing under the pen-name of Hatayi ('the sinner'), he is numbered amongst the masters of mystical verse. Yet it was this same passionate searcher after enlightenment who drank from the skull of one of his rivals – which he had mounted like rare porcelain with gilt tracery. Once, having charmed Ottoman ambassadors with his attentions and manners, he made them witness the execution of a learned scholar loyal to the Sunni traditions.

❄ ❄ ❄

In the western heartlands of the Ottoman sultanate, a Shiite revolt erupted in 1511. During the commemoration of Ashura, four thousand *kizilbas* attacked the retinue of the governor outside the Mediterranean port of Antalya. These *kizilbas* acclaimed distant Ismail as their leader. They were joined by thousands of tribal cavalry embittered by the leading role that the Christian-origin Janissary corps, with their ugly fire-arms reeking of sulphur, had acquired within the Ottoman state. Instead of resisting these rebels, the Ottoman garrison stationed in Kutahya (west-central Turkey) joined the mutiny. They impaled their governor, who was then roasted like a pig on a spit.

Stirred on by the report of a Sunni judge, who placed no faith on the loyalty of the city of Bursa, the old capital city of the Ottomans which was just a few days' march from Istanbul, the grand vizier knew he had to act quickly. He placed himself at the head of the Janissaries and advanced to do battle against the tens of thousands of rebel warriors. The disciplined use of firearms by a small professional army triumphed over mere numbers and zeal. The *kizilba* army was driven back from Bursa and routed at Sivas. The survivors sought refuge by escaping further east towards Persia.

The Ottoman ruler, Sultan Selim (1512–20), recognised that if he failed to defeat Shah Ismail it was near certain that his people would, in another province, on another occasion, offer their loyalty to the charismatic young shah-imam in the east. He prodded the Sunni scholars into action. They formally condemned the *kizilbas* as 'unbelievers and heretics. Any who sympathise with them and accept their false religion or assist them are also to be judged as unbelievers and heretics. It is necessary and a divine obligation that they be massacred and their communities be dispersed.'

In 1514, Sultan Selim personally led the Ottoman army across the length of the Anatolian plain. It was an exhausting progress. The public proscription of the *kizilbas* was backed up by brutal force, by massacre after massacre in village after village. It made the sultan deeply unpopular with the rank and file of his own army. At one marching camp, mutinous shots were even fired into Selim's own tent.

On 23 August, the two armies finally confronted each other at Chaldiran, just within the western frontier of modern Iran. Ismail had a vast force of Turkic cavalry under his command, but the battle was decided by Sultan Selim's field artillery. Some five hundred Ottoman light cannon had been chained together in a line, defended by 12,000 Janissary infantrymen. This corps blasted the Shah's army into oblivion, despite a series of desperately brave cavalry charges. Chaldiran deserves to be listed among the most decisive battles in world history, for that day the ancient superiority of the Turkic-Mongol cavalry of Central Asia was broken. It was not recognised at the time, but the message was repeated at Marj Dabak in 1516, when the Ottomans defeated the Mamelukes of Syria and Egypt. Nine years later, it was the presence of mobile field artillery at Panipat (1525) which established the Mughal Empire over India.

The slaughter at Chaldiran shattered the myth of Ismail's God-given invulnerability. Selim advanced into Persia and sacked the city of Tabriz on 6 September, which allowed him to recover some popularity among his soldiers. Even so, his army absolutely refused to advance any further east.

❋ ❋ ❋

The Battle of Chaldiran started the process of creating the hard frontiers – both political and theological – that would define modern Iran and modern Turkey. Persia was to become Shiite and Iranian; the Ottoman Empire was to define itself as Sunni and, later, Turkic. Before 1514, the loyalties, languages, beliefs and identities across the Muslim Middle East had been fluid.

This divorce took a long time and was never total. It still isn't. There is a very large Turkic Azeri minority in north-west Iran and there are many Alevi Shia in south-east Turkey. The influence, habits and traditions of both Iran and Turkey cross the political frontiers in hundreds of different ways. Then there are the Kurds, whose lands still straddle the borderlands of Syria, Turkey, Iran and Iraq. The Kurds see themselves as a people apart, but if they recognise a linguistic and ethnic kinship they know it is with the Iranians, not the Arabs or Turks.

In the great royal palace of the Safavid shah in Isfahan, in the innermost dining room, there is a vast fresco of the Battle of Chaldiran adorning one of the walls. At first sight, it seems bizarre to celebrate a crushing military defeat in so public a place, like depicting the field of Waterloo in the Elysée Palace. But there is a wide understanding that Chaldiran helped create Shiite Iran. If Shah Ismail had won the battle that day, he would almost certainly have advanced west and created a vast Islamic empire. Persia would have been just one of many provinces, and the heady Shiite mystical synthesis with which be began his reign would have been diminished as he became more and more like his ancestors, Genghis Khan and Timur. But this did not happen. The defeat at Chaldiran marked the end of an era. Shah Ismail settled down to rule Persia. The mystical language of his youth was trimmed back. After all, god-kings cannot suffer whole regiments of tribal cavalry to be felled by fusillades of grapeshot fired from a line of five hundred cannons.

In his retirement from schemes of world conquest, Shah Ismail made a pragmatic deal with the Shiite scholars in the university cities. Instead of aspiring to become the living heir of Imam Ali, he would accept their teachings and be Ali's political regent in Persia.

The Persian Shiite scholars had long argued that the holy line of imams ended with the disappearance of the Twelth Imam in 941. This last Imam, Muhammad ibn al-Hasan al-Mahdi, was a mysterious figure, and had as a five-year-old boy gone into hiding after the death of his father, Hasan al-Askari. After almost a lifetime of communicating to a hostile world through trusted deputies, the last of the imams went into a form of spiritual hibernation. This 'great occlusion' is a difficult theological proposition to accept or understand, fFor the Shia believe that their last imam is neither buried, nor alive, but remains an immortal presence. The chain of predestined spiritual authority of the holy dynasty is therefore not broken but reaches back to the moment when the Prophet Muhammad blessed Imam Ali at Ghadir Khum as his successor.

Shah Ismail secured the leadership of this tradition by sending ambassadors to the three intellectual corners of the Shiite world – Jebel Amil in Lebanon, Bahrain in eastern Arabia and to the pilgrimage cities of southern Iraq – and petitioned them to lend him their scholars. Several leading Shiite authorities, including Sheikh Ali al-Muaqqiq al-Karaki (c.1460–1534) and Al Shahid al-Thani (1505–59), both from what is now Lebanon, responded to the invitation to teach in the east. There is not a Shia scholar in Iran who does not acknowledge the debt they owe to these men, who unite them in a 'golden chain' of scholarship that leads back to Al Allama al-Hilli (1250–1325). Al-Hilli had worked in the cities of southern Iraq, collecting scholarly editions of Shiite beliefs and the sayings of the twelve imams, and penned an influential summary of Shia doctrine, *The Eleventh Chapter*, directed to the man in the street, not just the turbaned scholar.

Shah Ismail's son and heir, Shah Tahmasp, who reigned for more than half a century (1524–76), had to quell a rebellion by his own *kizilbas* – supporters who wanted to acclaim him as the Mahdi and kickstart a new round of jihadi campaigns. He also had to frustrate determined invasions by the Ottomans in 1534, 1548 and 1553 and was compelled to use the tactics of a guerrilla commando rather than a shah: to retreat while his enemy advanced and only attack when they retreated. These destructive military campaigns encouraged him to abandon vulnerable Tabriz and move his capital further east, ruling from the city of Qazvin. In the Treaty of Amasya (1555), he agreed to a division of Iraq, Georgia and Armenia with the Ottoman Empire.

CHAPTER 13

The Consolidation of Iran

Shah Abbas (1588–1629) and Nadir Shah(1736–47)

The Safavid Empire was in a weak state when Shah Abbas came to the throne in 1588. In the west, it had lost vast swathes of territory to the Ottomans, and to the north the Uzbeks had taken half of Khorasan. Shah Tamasp had died without an heir and the empire had descended into civil war, leading to a period of misrule by the paranoid Ismail II and further revolt.

Shah Abbas, who reigned for forty-one years, was a brilliant and charming man and a merciless autocrat. He developed a professional standing army, with a core of 12,000 musketeers and 12,000 artillerymen able to deploy an arsenal of 500 cannons. Like the Ottoman Janissaries, this army was recruited from Christian slaves, which he acquired from Georgia and Armenia. He developed an early trade agreement with the Dutch and the English – distant foreign powers that were the enemy of his enemies (Catholic Portugal and Spain) and supplied him with cannons, lent him warships and provided technical expertise. By the end of his reign Abbas had expelled the Uzbeks from Mashhad, reconquered Iraq from the Ottomans, expelled the Portuguese from the fortress-port of Hormuz and advanced his eastern frontier into Mughal India.

Shah Abbas proved himself a passionate supporter of the Shia faith. He not only persecuted Sunni scholars within Persia but destroyed the shrines to their revered scholars, such as Al-Jilani and Abu Hanifa, when he conquered Iraq. He liberated the Shia pilgrim cities of southern Iraq, built a madrasa complex in Qumm and encouraged the leading Shia scholars to continue to engage with philosophy and the poetic, mystical heritage of the Sufis. He turned Isfahan into the world's most beautiful capital city. One of his most celebrated actions was to undertake a twenty-eight-day pilgrimage on foot to the shrine of Imam Ali al-Rida in Mashhad, where he served as a humble sweeper at the sanctuary. It was an act of contrition for his many sins.

His heritage is an extraordinary mixture of beauty, cruelty, sensuality, tolerance and savagery. He murdered or mutilated most of his own family and ordered brutal massacres in Kurdistan and Georgia after he had suppressed national rebellions. For better or for worse, his long and successful reign further cemented the tactical alliance between a military court and an intellectual class of clerics.

※ ※ ※

None of Shah Abbas's heirs could match his political achievements, and after his death the Persian state once again fell prey to its neighbours, including an aggressive attack by Russia, under Peter the Great in 1722–23, and wave after wave of raiding warlords from Afghanistan.

The territorial integrity of Persia was saved by Nadir Shah, who offered an intriguing middle way out of the relentless Sunni–Shia rivalries. Nadir was the son of a poor Turkic herdsman and rose to become ruler of Persia in 1736. He has been likened to Napoleon in his brilliant tactical use of mobile field artillery, and compared to Alexander the Great and Timur for his restless, destructive energy and for the vast range of his conquests.

Still more important, he was religiously tolerant. His rule saw the acceptance of the four Sunni law schools, with the endowment of shrine-complexes, and he seemed on the point of establishing the Shia tradition as the fifth legal school within Islam. He halted the sectarian hate habit of *Sabb*, the ritual cursing of the Sunni caliphs by the Shia.

Politically, in the 1746 peace treaty of Kurdan, Nadir Shah established the frontiers with the Ottoman Empire that have endured to this day. As part of this peace, Shia pilgrims were permitted to travel into Ottoman-governed Iraq, and the old Sunni definition of them as heretics, who could be killed in battle, enslaved or raided at any time with legal impunity, was lifted. Collectively these actions helped to defuse sectarian hatreds and to end the 225-year-long civil war between Sunni and Shia Islam.

Nadir Shah was scarred by his own childhood – he and his mother were enslaved by Sunni Turkoman raiders who felt free to kidnap any Shia they could find – but he may also have been inspired by the more open society he had observed in Mughal India, where in the previous century the Taj Mahal had been built for the beloved Persian Shiite wife of the Sunni Mughal emperor.

This sort of easy-going, multicultural Shiite society did not appeal to everyone. It clearly appalled a young Arab scholar, Muhammad ibn Abdul Wahhab, who visited the city of Basra in southern Iraq during the reign of Nadir Shah.

CHAPTER 14

Enter the Third Force: Wahhabi Arabia

Muhammad ibn Abd al-Wahhab (1703–92)

While the Ottoman and Safavids fought for the soul of Islam and dominion over the Middle East, Arabia, the homeland of the Prophet, was largely in the hands of the indigenous Bedouin tribes. Mecca, Medina and the western half of Arabia had been dominated by the Mameluke sultanate of Egypt. In eastern Arabia, the most important force was the Beni Khalid confederation, which included both Sunni and Shia tribes. However, this tribal patchwork of sheikhs was soon to be subsumed by a new force.

Muhammad ibn Abd al-Wahhab was born in 1703 into an intellectual household in the settlement of Al-Uyaynah in the Najd, a district of eastern Arabia dominated by the Saud clan. The Saud were part of the Beni Hanifa tribe, and were not yet the powerful figures that they later came to be. But they were proud of their domain – the three fortified villages of Ghussaibah, Al-Mulaybeed and Turaif – strung along a dry river bed, the Wadhi Hanifa.

For three generations Muhammad ibn Abd al-Wahhab's family had survived through their knowledge of the Koran and the Islamic law codes. As a youth, Muhammad ibn Abd al-Wahhab joined the Haj to Mecca, and then moved to

Medina as a scholar. The holy city attracted pious intellectuals from all over the Islamic world, who often stayed for years at a time. As was common practice at the time, Muhammad ibn Abd al-Wahhab listened to teacher after teacher in the great mosque, which acted as an open university. There was much to learn – grammar, textual criticism, biography and history – though the chief purpose of all these intellectual endeavours was to be able to recite fluently and better understand the meaning of the Koran and the *hadith*, and the law codes derived from these two primary sources. There were charitable hospices in Medina which provided free lodging for young scholars for seven years. There were also a number of well-equipped libraries and charitable kitchens.

A teacher from Egypt, Muhammad Hayya Al-Sindi, introduced Muhammad ibn Abd al-Wahhab to the Naqshabandi Sufi brotherhood, which taught a system of spiritual self-awareness through eleven personal stepping stones. Another scholar introduced him to the controversial works of the fourteenth-century writer, Ibn Taymiyyah. It was an intense intellectual environment, distracted but enriched by the annual arrival of pilgrims, bringing first-hand news from every corner of the Islamic world. Muhammad ibn Abd al-Wahhab would have heard how the Ottomans stood as a bulwark against the assaults of Christian enemies to the north, such as Russia and Austria, and how in the east there was a troubling meltdown of the old order as the Safavids were replaced by the upstart Nadir Shah, who went on to break the power of the Mughal Empire in India and sack Delhi in 1739.

After studying at Medina, Muhammad ibn Abd al-Wahhab set off into the world to seek work as an expert on the intricacies of Islamic law. This early period of his life is not well recorded, but there are stories of an early marriage, the death of his young wife, local resistance to his teachings and a period at Basra in southern Iraq – a city with both Shiite and Sunni communities – before he returned home to the protection of his family.

Back in Al-Uyaynah, Muhammad ibn Abd al-Wahhab wrote his *Kitab al-Tawhid,* 'The Book of Monotheism', which was to become the core document of Wahhabism. In this text, he set out how Muslims should concentrate the energy of faith on God as the creator and continuous sustainer of the universe. He expressed his abhorrence of any spiritual hierarchy that stood between the humble worshipper and the sole deity. To honour the tomb of a revered saint or a hero-martyr with prayers and supplications, or to accept the spiritual intervention of a holy-man, was *shirk*, a sin which he argued should lead to exclusion from the Islamic community. He explained how these 'hypocrites' should be attacked in this life and were doomed to hellfire and eternal damnation in the next. By 1740, when his father died, Muhammad ibn Abd al-Wahhab had a system of theology which effectively attacked the existing practices of both the Shia and Sunni. Although he preached jihad, this was an internal affair, primarily directed against other Muslims.

It is hard to imagine what the vast and hugely wealthy Mughal Empire of India would have looked like to someone from the pious but desperately poor communities of Bedouin Arabs. Or what they thought of such Muslim rulers as Shah Akbar, the Mughal emperor of India, who toyed with creating a worldwide religion that would syncretise Islam with other faith traditions. There may have been some satisfaction in thinking that the extravagant new edifices of architectural glory were not only spiritually worthless but should be cleansed by destruction, just as the rich stream of pilgrims from India, Persia and Central Asia, who once a year proudly poured themselves across the deserts of Central Asia, were not truly Muslims.

Muhammad ibn Abd al-Wahhab's first attempts to preach his revolutionary creed, to urge on a civil war within Islam, led to attempts to assassinate him. He returned to Al-Uyaynah, where he made a political pact with his local sheikh. Physical protection would be paid for by a creed that could empower a holy war.

Muhammad ibn Abd al-Wahhab then directed three actions which still resonate down the years, and in which can be traced practically every subsequent fundamentalist movement seeking to seize control of an Islamic society. He cut down a holy tree to which women had for centuries tied threads of old cloth while they whispered a prayer of supplication. He next mobilised hundreds of men to demolish the tomb of Zayd ibn al-Khattab, the brother of Umar, the revered Second Caliph of Islam, who was especially dear to the Sunni tradition. And then he ordered the stoning of a local woman to death (she had admitted adultery without shame).

There is little doubt that Muhammad ibn Abd al-Wahhab acted out of a real, personal conviction that he was helping his fellow believers towards salvation. But the chieftain of the Beni Khalid tribe which still dominated eastern Arabia was appalled by his actions. He presided over the mixed culture of the Al-Hasa coast, washed by both Ottoman and Persian influences with a mixed and cosmopolitan population of Shia and Sunni Arabs and Muslim and Hindu merchants from the Indian coast of Gujarat. He overruled the authority of the local sheikh and sent two armed guards – not to kill or punish Muhammad ibn Abd al-Wahhab, but to expel him from Al-Uyaynah.

Muhammad ibn Abd al-Wahhab took refuge in the oasis of Diriyah, ruled by Muhammad al-Saud. This time he took the precaution of preaching privately to the young sheikh, his brother and wife, before launching into any contentious public actions. He found an immediate and enthusiastic ally. Muhammad al-Saud agreed to protect and support the preacher, while Muhammad ibn Abd al-Wahhab formally accepted the military and political leadership of Al-Saud.

Thus was Saudi Arabia born in 1744, in a tactical alliance between a tribal chieftain and a zealous religious reformer, that ancient duality of sultan and sheikh.

In time-honoured Arab fashion, the alliance was confirmed by the marriage of Muhammad ibn Abd al-Wahhab's daughter to Muhammad al-Saud's son, Abdul Aziz. Four of Muhammad ibn Abd al-Wahhab's sons also married into the Al-Saud clan and emerged as dynamic Wahhabi preachers, effectively establishing themselves as a clerical dynasty, the Al-Shaikh, which survives as a power to this day. In 1773, Muhammad ibn Abd al-Wahhab resigned his public position in favour of his sons, but continued to act as a spiritual advisor until his death in 1792.

❀ ❀ ❀

Muhammad ibn Abd al-Wahhab's son-in-law, Abdul Aziz bin Muhammad Al-Saud, proved himself a highly competent warlord, establishing Riyadh as the new capital in 1773.

Then, in 1802, a Saudi prince led a Wahhabi army to storm the Shia city of Kerbala in southern Iraq during its holy annual festival. Thousands of citizens were massacred, while the tomb-shrines and mosques, loaded with centuries of votive offerings, were looted and destroyed. Though this destruction doesn't make it into many Western history books, every Shiite in Iran and Iraq knows about it. It is chronicled in the *Unwan al-Majd*, a nineteenth-century Wahhabi history: 'Ibn Sa'ud made for Karbala with his victorious army, famous pedigree horses, all the settled people and Bedouin of Najd, the people of Janub, Hijaz, Tihama and others ... The Muslims [by which he means the Wahhabis] surrounded Kerbala and took it by storm. They killed most of the people in the houses and the markets. They destroyed the dome above al-Husayn's grave.

They took away everything they saw in the shrine and near it, including the coverlet decorated with emeralds, sapphires and pearls which covered the grave. They took away everything they found in the town – possessions, arms, clothes, fabric, gold, silver, and precious books. One cannot even enumerate the spoils! They stayed there for just one morning and left after midday, taking away all the possessions. Nearly 2,000 people were killed.'

By 1805, both Mecca and Medina had been seized from the Ottomans by Wahhabi armies, and the architectural adornments of centuries of devotion were flattened. This included all the domed shrines raised above the honoured dead in the ancient cemetery of Al-Baqi, which had allowed Haj pilgrims to walk through a living history book of Muslim culture, a gallery of all the great figures of early Islam. It was also the place where the Prophet Muhammad had prayed before his last illness. These were all destroyed, as was the prayer hall established in the cave on Mount Hira where the Prophet had received his first revelation.

In just three years, the Saudi–Wahhabi state had acquired worldwide notoriety, and the undying enmity of both Persian Shiites and the Sunni Ottomans. But a third force had undoubtedly been born, to add complexity to the traditional rivalry within the Middle East. The Saudi–Wahhabi alliance had reformed the Arabs from within their own culture and language and seemed on the point of creating a single, united Arabian state. In the event, it was in fact decades before it was permitted to cohere into the Kingdom of Saudi Arabia.

❋ ❋ ❋

The Ottoman sultan in Istanbul was overstretched on other battlefronts, but subcontracted a war of revenge and reconquest against Wahhabi Arabia to Muhammad Ali, his powerful viceroy of Egypt. Muhammad Ali was an Ottoman officer from Albania who had been posted to Egypt, which he reformed, turning it into an expansionist state. He was another self-made political genius, with a capacity for violence and efficient administration.

Muhammad Ali was delighted to expand his dominions. A modern, well-equipped Egyptian army under the consecutive leadership of his two sons was landed on the Red Sea coast. Mecca and Medina were reconquered in 1811. By April 1818, this Egyptian army had occupied all of the Najd and reduced the Saudi Emirate back to the oasis of Diriyah, which finally capitulated after a nine-month siege. The fourth Saudi emir, Abdullah ibn Saud, was sent back to Istanbul as a captive.

For the next twenty years an Egyptian army remained in control of west Arabia, while also encroaching on the Ottoman Empire in Syria and southern Anatolia. But, in 1840, Ottoman authority was revived and, though Ottoman governors were returned to all the major Arab cities, imperial policy often favoured indirect rule through tribal chieftains.

The chosen Ottoman ally was the Rashidi Emirate of Jabal Shammar, which ruled over eastern and central Arabia from their citadel palace at Hail. They kept a watchful eye on the Al-Saud dynasty but, while remaining faithful allies of the Otto-man sultans, were loyal to the new Arab revolution in Islamic thought. Wahhabism had not withered with the fall of the Al-Saud and remained potent in its central Arabian homeland. It was a form of highly active Islam, involving a commitment to learn and to think, not just to recite and to pray. Its aim was to avoid any superstition, to examine and then tear away inherited piety, and to return to the true sources of religion, the Koran and the *hadith*. In the process, it brushed aside centuries of literary achievement, from such world-renowned poets and theologians as Rumi, Ibn Arabi, Abdul-Qader al-Jilani and al-Ghazali. No monuments were permitted above a grave, and the most pious of the Wahhabi gave instructions that they were to be buried in some isolated spot in the desert – known only to God.

The most dangerous doctrine of Wahhabism was the damning of all those Muslims with whom they did not agree as *takfir* – faithless apostates – who they were entitled to wage war on and to kill, and whose wives and daughters they could enslave as concubines. In other lands, Muslim scholars were appalled. Who were the Wahhabi clerics to judge if a Muslim was an apostate or not? What was their authority, or was it simply providing an excuse for their Bedouin armies to plunder? They noted that Muhammad ibn Abd al-Wahhab, though sincere, was highly selective as a scholar. In his *Kitab al-Tawhid*, he makes very little use of the humane traditions recorded by true family intimates of the Prophet, such as Ali or any of Muhammad's wives. Instead, he preferred to quote second-generation male scholars, who get sixty-one citations, as opposed to just two from Ali and five from Aisha. Despite his outward desire to deliver an Islam based purely on the Koran, he often made use of the more malleable *hadith*. In the *Kitab al-Tawhid*, fifty-seven per cent of quotations are from the *hadith*, against only twenty-four per cent from the Koran.

And, despite his opposition to a spiritual hierachy, Muhammad ibn Abd al-Wahhab's family went on to become the hereditary high priests of Saudi Arabia, and his books their theological testaments. When the Iranian regime wish to denigrate their Saudi opponents, they describe them as *takfiri*. Muhammad ibn Abd al-Wahhab's concept of the *takfiri* was always a double-edged weapon. It empowered him with the right to excommunicate any Muslim that he disagreed with, and to label them as a *kafir* ('unbeliever') who could be killed, robbed or enslaved. It proved a useful weapon in the expansion of the Saudi state, but it has over the centuries served to silence public debate.

The Wahhabi preachers taught that all male adults had to respond to a call of jihad if it was delivered by their recognised emir and confirmed by their sheikh. They were so focused on the Koran that they consciously strove to revere Muhammad as just a man. They cut away what they saw as cult devotions – the celebration of the Prophet's birthday (Moulid), as well as the litanies of prayers and pious listing of his attributes, which they feared were turning Muhammad into a demigod. They concentrated on his perfection as God's Messenger, his total obedience to God and his dedication to putting the Koran into practice. They also liked to stress his illiteracy, which made him just a mouthpiece, not the poetic mind that might have helped form the word order of the Koran.

Muhammad ibn Abd al-Wahhab succeeded in reversing centuries of political and social decline in Arabia and achieved an extraordinary transformation amongst the Bedouin. But the Wahhabis had no interest in the Arab world before Islam, nor in the beliefs and creativity of the rest of the world. They refused to return the greetings of any other spiritual community. They existed within a totally Islamic mindset, with a reputation as vandals, against all created culture, even their own medieval heritage. They had only two periods of interest: the lifetime of the Companions of the Prophet Muhammad, and the present.

PART FOUR

Colonial Night
1830–1979

PART FOUR

Colonial Night, 1830–1979

All the ferocious internecine fighting within the Islamic world – between Ottomans and Safavids, in the Levant, Persia and Arabia – would prove no more than a distraction beside a new external threat from the West. This new set of invaders would not only match the violence of Genghis Khan or Timur, but seek to undermine an entire civilisation. By the early twentieth century, Europe's colonial powers dominated the Islamic world. The first wave – essentially piratical forces – had come from Portugal and Spain, and later Holland, but by the eighteenth century they would be replaced by more serious armies of occupation. France, Britain and Russia each succeeded in carving out sizeable colonial empires from the Muslim world. France conquered most of North and West Africa, and the Sahara, while Russia finally subdued the Khanates of Muslim Central Asia and stormed the mountains of the Caucasus. The British seized control of Mughal India and then extended its control over the Muslim coasts of East and Southern Africa, Malaysia, Egypt and the Sudan, the shores of the Persian Gulf, Oman and half of the Yemen. By the dawn of the twentieth century, only the Turkish Ottoman Empire, Persia under the shahs, and the then backwaters of central Arabia had retained any genuine independence.

Then, over the course of the First World War, things got even worse. France took control of Syria, Britain occupied Iraq and Palestine, and the two powers conspired to dismember the Anatolian core of the Ottoman Empire.

Much speculation has been given to what might have happened had the Islamic world not been riven by the long Sunni–Shia conflict between Ottomans and Persians. What if the lands of Islam had been united under one caliph and able to direct resistance against the pack of European predators? But it had never been that simple. Beneath the glare of faith divisions were powerful ethnic, national, tribal, dynastic and personal rivalries. So it was that Egyptian armies fought wars against both Turks and Arabs, Ottoman soldiers died in the highlands of the Yemen and a Persian shah devastated Mughal India. And the collapse of the Islamic world was due to a stark fact: the military technology of the colonial powers, with their tanks and aerial warfare backed by the resources of the industrial revolution. These advances coincided with the pseudo-science of racism, the dark twin to Darwin's evolutionary theories, such that in retrospect we might call 1850–1950, the descent of colonial night, with no end of brutality and savagery masquerading under the 'advance of Western civilisation'.

The liberation struggles of the 1950s and 1960s toppled most of these colonial empires, but they were immediately replaced by the neo-colonial 'alliance system' established by the USSR and the US over the Cold War. So the intellectual struggle for self-determination was confused by the cultural dictats of these two new world powers, championing either corporate capitalism or command socialism.

CHAPTER 15

The Misrule of Persia

The Qajar shahs (1794–1925) and
Pahlavi shahs (1925–79)

We have seen how Shah Ismail, the energetic founder of
the Safavid dynasty, had turned Persia into a Shiite nation
state, and how it became an expansive Shiite empire under the
leadership of his great-grandson, Shah Abbas, and again under
Nadir Shah. However, each of these zeniths was punctuated by
periods of anarchic confusion, and in the eighteenth century
Persia* became squeezed between the colonial aggressors of
Russia and Britain, and narrowly survived as an independent
nation, protected by its strong indigenous culture.

The decline began in 1747, when Nadir Shah was murdered
by his own bodyguard. His treasury, which included most
of the world's great gems (including the famed Koh-i-Nur),
was dissipated, and part of it funded the establishment of an
independent kingdom in Afghanistan. Iran was fought over by
rival warlords, until eventually Karim Khan Zand established
control, around 1751. He built beautiful mosques and ruled
modestly and humanely as 'regent' on behalf of the rightful
Shiite imams. One can but dream of how Persia might have
evolved under the direction of such an enlightened, indigenous

---

* 'Persia' and 'Iran' are virtually interchangeable, though technically Persia is
merely the influential southern province of a greater geographical entity. Most
historians use 'Persia' until 1979, then switch to Iran. I have followed their lead.

dynasty. However, Karim died in 1779 and his successors were unable to maintain his control. In 1794, the last Zand ruler, Lotf Ali Khan, was toppled from his throne by the Qajar chiefs, led by Mohammed Khan, a eunuch warlord of hardly credible malevolence. It was he who blinded 20,000 citizens of Kerman and who kept the last Zand ruler alive so that he could be tortured for a further three years before his body (already amputated of its limbs) was choked to death.

From their first act to their last, the Qajar shahs were a malign presence. They were also unique in the long chronicles of Persia for presiding over a lifeless period of art, signalled by blowsy floral decorations, mirrored bordello palaces and self-aggrandising royal portraits. The Qajar were obsessed with court rank, jewels, uniforms and thrones, and it is said that any person of talent could be sure of being employed by their court before being murdered as a threat to their grasping mediocrity.* The dynasty remained devoutly Shia but could not claim to be of the bloodline of the imams. The Qajar were Turkic, from one of the seven tribes of the *kizilbas* confederation, and had entered Iran in the thirteenth century, one of the tribes serving within the cavalry army of the Mongol Khans, rewarded with lands on the frontier of Armenia.

❋ ❋ ❋

The nineteenth century was a merciless period for Persia. Two wars against Russia, in 1804–13 and 1826–28, led to the loss

---

* The Qajar were prodigiously fecund. The second Qajar shah, Fatih Ali Shah (1797–1834), who is conspicuous in portraits for the dazzling length of his black beard, kept a thousand concubines, as well as four official wives, and by the time of his death there were 296 princeling grandsons and 292 princess granddaughters. They in turn loyally copied the habit of their grandsire, so that Qajar court genealogies would soon be recording 5,000 descendants.

of a third of the old Safavid Empire, as the dependencies of Georgia, Armenia, Dagestan and Azerbaijan were annexed by the Russian tsar. The Persian state was also bankrupted in its attempt to create an army capable of resisting the Russians, and so became ever more dependent on the British. The British at first appeared to be the good guys, on the side of a strong and independent Persia. But the reality was that their friendship was based on their fear of Russian cavalry armies swooping down on the British Empire in India. In helping Persia maintain its independence, Britain created an invisible protectorate by stealth, and with some financial opportunities attached. British consuls were established in all the provincial cities of Persia and reported to a legation in Tehran, while the British-owned Imperial Bank of Persia (1889–1929) managed the national currency and finances. The British also attempted to establish monopolies, including an attempt to corner the tobacco market.

These capitalist schemes were invariably backed by the Qajar rulers such as Nasir ad-Din Shah (1848–96), always hungry for commission deals to feed their opulent court in Tehran and support an army most often used to guard their palaces and suppress their own people. In many ways, the Qajar had more in common with a medieval monarchy than with the powerful states erected by Shah Abbas or Nadir Shah. The shah of the day was usually content to select his regional governors from a shortlist of powerful tribal chieftains and keep them in obedience by manipulating local rivalries. The occasional emergence of ministers such as Amir Kabir in the 1840s suggest what might have happened under an enlightened leadership, for he imported new technologies, trained up a new generation of scholar officials to master the new sciences and medical improvements whilst balancing the national budget. But he was exiled and killed. By 1890, it was said that in Persia you could rely on the efficiency of just two institutions: the British-run Imperial Bank of Persia, and the six hundred cavalrymen of the Persian Cossack Regiment under the command of Russian officers.

It is the scale of corruption and the weakness of the state which helps make sense of the career of such campaigners for Islamic reform as Jamal al-Din Afghani (1838–97). He was aware that, unless the Muslim world renewed itself, with better rulers and teachers, through argument and internal debate, it was doomed either to be conquered or patronised by the Western powers. Jamal was a Persian Shia from the city of Hamadan but deliberately aspired to escape sectarian labels and so identified as an Afghan Sunni. He held no government office but he was a convincing activist with a powerful intellectual voice who called for an end to the sectarian rivalry between Shia and Sunni and some form of worldwide union of the Islamic world. He taught, argued, debated, provoked and wrote in most of the great cities of the Islamic world, before the authorities were persuaded to move him on. Wisely, he saw his great task as opposing the British, whom he saw as the principal threat to his nation.

❊ ❊ ❊

In the late nineteenth century, the southern shore of Iran was patrolled by the gunboats of the British Royal Navy. Ever since the infamous Wahhabi sack of the holy Shia shrine-city of Kerbala in 1802, the Royal Navy was usually perceived as a welcome presence in the Persian Gulf. These gunboats protected the well-established Arab and Persian trading communities from the predatory raids of Wahhabi Bedouin, as well as suppressing piracy, surveying the coast, drawing up boundaries and making treaties.

By 1905 the winds of change were blowing against the corrupt, inefficient, autocratic Qajar regime. A bad harvest had driven the price of wheat up by 90 per cent and the Russian Empire had just been humiliated in its war against Japan, which inspired the whole world to challenge colonial hegemony. A series of strikes in 1906, led by the educated merchant community, called for a constitution and a Majlis (popular assembly). They were supported by the Shiite clergy. The shah had run out of money to pay the Cossack brigades to suppress this internal call for reform, and Britain at first seemed to support this organic, local, democratic movement, to the extent of sheltering 12,000 reformers within the diplomatic safety of the legation garden in Tehran. But the British gradually shifted their position.

There were two reasons. First, in 1907, the hundred-year rivalry between Britain and Russia – the so-called 'Great Game' of influence fought across Central Asia – had ended as the two enemies joined forces against the threat of German expansionism. The second and decisive factor was the Royal Navy's shift from coal-fired battleships to a faster line of warships fuelled by oil. Britain was riddled with coal mines but controlled no oil fields. But on 26 May 1908 oil was found in south-western Iran in Khuzestan province, not far from the British-controlled waters of the Persian Gulf. British enthusiasm for the Persian reform movement began to wane.

Civil war in Persia briefly led to a triumph of the Constitutionalist Party, but they were betrayed by the outside powers. Russian intrigues (now unopposed by Britain) restored the rule of an autocratic shah in December 1911. Then the First World War effectively divided Persia into two protectorates, the Russians in the north and the British in the south. German agents working out of the Ottoman Empire attempted to raise the Qashqai tribe and lead a revolt that would first throw the

British out of Iran, then raise the Muslims of India in jihad against the Raj. This plot failed. Then the Russian revolutions of 1917 left the British the only military power in the region, as the Russian officers of the Cossack brigade went home to fight on the losing side of the civil war.

General Ironside, the region's commanding British officer, decided that the Cossack brigade could become self-sufficient if its Iranian sergeants were promoted to become officers. He identified Reza Khan as the most forceful of these and, worried by the inefficiency of the old regime and the worldwide advance of Communism, advised him to march on Tehran. Reza Shah seized power in February 1921. He directed a blistering campaign of modernisation which included the adoption of Western dress and the creation of a national language by cleansing Iranian of foreign loan words. Reza Khan poured his energy into creating an army of 100,000 men which could both defend the nation and enforce modernisation. Illiterate villagers, the majority of the nation, were left to their own devices, as were the nomad tribes, which still constituted a quarter of the population. Reza Khan instead concentrated his attention on the cities and big towns. School attendance, which had been just 55,000 in 1922, leapt to 450,000 by 1936. Iran was transformed from within. Having ruled since 1921, he formally occupied the throne in 1925, the first shah of the Pahlavi dynasty (named after the language spoken by the pre-Islamic Sassanid shahs).

❁ ❁ ❁

This modernisation marched side by side with that achieved by the rule of Ataturk in Turkey (1919–38) and that of Ibn Saud (1932–53) in the newly created Kingdom of Saudi Arabia. Ataturk, Ibn Saud and Reza Khan were acknowledged to be the great men of their time, creating new realities through their energy and determination. They were very different in character, in their faith, in their origins, but each aspired to create nation states that could become effectively independent of any external power. None were interested in the leadership of worldwide Islam, and all worked to quarry specific identities – Iranian, Turkish or Arab – from old, multi-ethnic Islamic regimes. Once the new national frontiers had been secured and dissident border tribes disciplined, the chosen battlefield, for Turkey and Iran, was the classroom and dictionary. History was taught as a grand narrative leading to the challenge of building a self-determining, independent nation state. New national languages were created in both countries by purging words of foreign origin. Culture, craft, music, architecture and archaeology were also marshalled to express the enduring struggle for a true, patriotic identity.

Consumed by this inner battle to transform and discipline their own people, the three great nations allowed a period of uninterrupted peace in the Middle East. No wars were fought between them. The age-old Shia–Sunni dichotomy seemed buried, an aspect of the medieval past irrelevant to a modern nation state. Saudi Arabia was emphatically wedded to its rigorous Wahhabi reading of the Sunni traditions, but in both Iran and Turkey the role of religion was deliberately diminished and portrayed as a reactionary interference to the campaign of national regeneration, empowered by education and technical learning. Progress was to be measured in the construction of new dams, roads, railways, schools and hospitals; and by the campaigns for electrification and ever-expanding rates of literacy and productivity, and state-funded industries. Short surnames on identity cards replaced the oral recitation of a proud patronymic, just as armed border posts stood in the way of the seasonal migration of nomadic tribes and of annual pilgrimages.

Although the technical know-how of Western nations was still required at the oil fields, universities, hospitals and industrial complexes, the underlying purpose of this accelerated race towards industrialisation was to get to a position where they could shed, and then match, the West.

In the meantime, the nationalist leaderships learned to balance the influence of the foreigners by playing them off against each other. Ataturk's post-war struggle would have been impossible without arms from Soviet Russia. Ibn Saud made an early tactical alliance with American oil and stuck with it. Reza Shah's regime was financed by royalties fed to him from the British-controlled Persian oil fields. The shah later identified the rising power of Germany as a useful tool with which to try and balance British influence, so in 1937 Iran joined Iraq, Turkey and Afghanistan in the Saadabad pact, which attempted to assert regional independence and side-step the colonial powers. But this assertion of neutrality was brushed aside by Britain in the dark days of the Second World War. In September 1941, Britain and Soviet Russia invaded Iran and sacked the old shah after he refused to dismiss the German staff who ran his railways. It was an especially bleak period in the war for the Allies (Leningrad was under siege) and Iran was the safest route for importing material aid into Russia. The US ultimately pumped a third of all its wartime aid to the Soviet Union through Iran.

For the population of Iran it was a grim expression of political reality. Their Westernising leader had been summarily removed and the vast army that he had so patiently assembled had collapsed. Reza Shah was packed off into exile in South Africa and his young son, Pahlavi, was given the throne, but no-one could have any doubts who stood behind and beside it. (The British had in fact given some thought to restoring the Qajar dynasty, but the legitimate heir, Hamid Mirza, was not suitable, for he spoke not a word of Persian. Under the name 'David Drummond', he served in the Royal Navy throughout the war and then worked for Mobil Oil, as if he knew where the real masters of the world could now be found.)

❊ ❊ ❊

The young Pahlavi Shah had been partly educated in France and Switzerland (whose mountains he always adored). He had a distant relationship with his father, 'the Cossack bully', but a passionately close understanding with his aristocratic mother and twin sister. He had little room for political manoeuvring to begin with, for he desperately needed the support of both Britain and the US to keep the sovereignty of Iran intact. The Soviet occupation of the northern half of Iran during the Second World War had allowed them to create a client Communist Party, Tudeh ('the masses'), as well as to back the creation of two separate republics out of the Azeri and Kurdish provinces of north-western Iran. The final evacuation of Soviet troops from these territories did not occur until May 1946, as agreed between the three powers at the Yalta conference and part-exchanged for Russian dominance over all of Eastern Europe. But, even after the last Soviet soldiers had been withdrawn, the Iranian army had to fight to subdue the two separatist republics in the north. In 1949, the Tudeh party were found to be behind an assassination attempt against the young shah.

These incidents might appear mere Cold War footnotes, but they are vital to understanding the next tragic round of events whose echoes still define our world.

In April 1951, an elderly, well-educated Iranian aristocrat of mildly socialist leanings called Mohammed Mossadeq was elected prime minister and launched a campaign to nationalise the British-owned Iranian oil industry and to attempt some much-needed land reform. These were admirable aspirations, which the young shah should have supported. The British dug their heels in, their technicians left Iran and the lack of oil revenue caused a financial crisis, which greatly increased the political heat. It was feared that the Tudeh party (already in tactical alliance with Mossadeq) was the real force behind a new demand made in 1952 to take command of the vital Ministry of War from the shah. This was a time when the Korean War and the Malayan Emergency were being fought by the West against Communist forces, and it was a real possibility that the Cold War would heat up into a Third World War. In Egypt, the events of Black Saturday in Cairo in January 1952, when all the buildings associated with the British were torched, had been rapidly succeeded in July by the Egyptian officers' coup against the King of Egypt.

So, in the summer of 1953, the fateful decision was made for an American- and British-backed coup to remove Mossadeq, under cover of political street demonstrations, and enable the shah to rule as an autocrat. In the aftermath, a new master now stood in the shadows behind the throne: the USA.

The Americans proceeded to broker a much fairer deal on oil revenue, with a 50/50 split instead of the previous British deal which had paid just 17.5 per cent to the Iranian exchequer. Meantime, the CIA were commissioned to set up a national intelligence and security organisation (SAVAK) to protect the shah from any more assassination attempts. The American oil industry was also invited into Iran to counterbalance the unpopularity of the British-run AIOC (Anglo-Iranian Oil Company). The latter tried to turn over a new leaf and rebranded itself as BP (British Petroleum) in 1954.

In 1955, Iran signed up to an anti-Communist military alliance of Middle Eastern nations, the so-called Baghdad Pact or CENTO. A pseudo-democracy was also set up, with the electorate given a choice between two parties, nicknamed Melliyun and Mardom, the 'Yes Party' and the 'Yes-Sir Party'. But, with oil production increasing and revenue flowing, the ten-year period between 1953 and 1963 proved to be (if only in hindsight) a period of internal peace, prosperity and productivity.

❀ ❀ ❀

The Iranian clergy watched in alarm at this floodtide of Westernisation, but only began to articulate this in 1963, in response to the shah's White Revolution. This was an attempt to break the power of the old urban middle-class intellectuals and ally the shah with the peasantry. Instead, it paved the way for an Islamic revolution. The peasants acquired the right to own the land that they had farmed for generations and were no longer oppressed by their urban, absentee landlords. They also acquired an education. But they were attracted to the Islamic intellectuals with their pride in Iran, not to the corrupt royal court of the shah and his twin sister and their well-oiled parliament of yes-men.

The Shiite clergy proved themselves the chief section of society brave enough to question the regime. They argued that the land reforms and the nationalisation of the forests and mountains went against Islamic law and its fundamental respect for property. One of the leading clerical figures was Ayatollah Khomeini, who was to play the pivotal role in the Islamic revolution of 1979. His 1964 speech hit exactly the right emotional note, as he protested against the legal immunity to prosecution that was being awarded to US citizens based in Iran in this period: 'They have reduced the Iranian people to a level lower than that of an American dog. If someone runs over a dog belonging to an American, he will be prosecuted. Even if the Shah himself were to run over a dog belonging to an American, he would be prosecuted. But if an American cook runs over the shah ... no-one will have the right to object.'

Within a couple of weeks, Khomeini had gone into exile, where he lived for the next fourteen years, in Turkey, Iraq and then France – an alternative force in waiting.

CHAPTER 16

The Kingdom

Ibn Saud and his heirs (1932–75)

The Kingdom of Saudi Arabia, that vast, adamantine space on the map, was the creation, in large part, of a single extraordinary individual. Ibn Saud was one of the great figures of the twentieth century, a tribal chief who first enlarged his Saud clan territories, then annexed three other geographical regions, forging what became one of the world's richest states.

His full name was Abd al-Aziz ibn Abd al-Rahman ibn Faisal Al Saud, but he became known as Ibn Saud once he assumed the leadership of the Saud clan. He was tough, energetic and brave, with a gift for lifelong friendships. He had the ability to listen to advice, to wait on events (a decade if needs be), but then to move decisively and quickly on his own judgement. He kept a court of twenty concubines but also married and amicably divorced a series of young wives, through which he developed the ties of shared offspring with many of the tribes of central Arabia.[*]

He was born on 15 January 1875, the son of a clan ruler consumed by fratricidal conflicts. The most traumatic of these was the Battle of Mulayda in 1891, when the 20,000-strong army of the Saudi Emirate of Nejd was destroyed by that of

---

[*] One of Ibn Saud's closest advisors was his aunt Jawhara, whom he would visit every afternoon, for she had a phenomenal memory for the history of the clans who wove in and out of the triumphs and catastrophes of the family.

the Rashidi emir, their great rivals. The Saudi capital of Riyadh fell and the young Ibn Saud fled with his father to the great desert wastes of the Empty Quarter, where they sought shelter with the Al Murrah tribe – camel nomads who patrolled vast distances to find grazing. Later they spent time as guests with many of the old rulers of the Persian Gulf, including the Bahraini Emir Al-Khalifa and the Kuwaiti Emir Al-Sabah.

Aged eighteen, Ibn Saud left this suffocating life of political exile to become a desert raider. His band grew with each daring success, and withered to a trusted core of forty young warriors with every defeat. It was at the head of this group that Ibn Saud watched over the walls of the old family citadel of Riyadh during Ramadan, when the garrison was distracted by the day-long fast and night-long entertainments. On the night of 15 January 1902, Ibn Saud placed a palm trunk against the Shamsiya Gate to use as a ladder. He then summoned his men to shelter in the house of a friend. He had learned that the governor spent the night with his troops but returned to his household in early morning. So, at dawn, as the citadel gates were opened, the band of warriors made their attack. For many years, the spear thrown by Ibn Saud (coloured with the blood of the governor) was proudly pointed out embedded in the gate of the fortress. The Rashidi garrison were massacred, and the people of Riyadh enthusiastically welcomed back this young prince of the old dynasty. Ibn Saud sent a messenger to recall his father from exile, but when he returned to Riyadh the old man refused to take power, and formally acknowledged his twenty-two-year-old warrior son as the new emir, accepting only the role of imam for himself.

By 1913, Ibn Saud had not only regained control of the Nejd but had conquered most of the eastern governate of Al-Hasa. He was now in alliance with two of the strongest Bedouin tribes of central Arabia, the Mutair and al-Otaibi, and continued the traditional theological alliance with the descendants of Muhammad ibn Abdul Wahhab, who had long been known as 'the Al-Shaikh'. Two members of this dynasty, serving as judges for the towns of Riyadh and Hasa, assisted by a zealot from North Africa and a member of the Shammar tribe, sought to revive the militant spirit of the original Wahhabi movement. Deeming the coast of the Persian Gulf too cosmopolitan, multicultural and tolerant, they determined to establish *hujar* in the deserts of central Arabia – strict Wahhabi villages complete with mosque, school and resident preacher to proselytise and educate the Bedouin tribes. It was originally hoped that these new villages would be self-sufficient, which was not always possible, but the new settlements were nonetheless a great success. The tribal chieftains liked marshalling their clan in one centre, and Ibn Saud could see that this movement, provided with arms and a small subsidy, would provide him with the nucleus of a tough, professional army.

Al-Artawiyah was the first of the *hujar* to be established. It was the geographical centre of the Mutair tribe of whom it was said that plunder and murder run in their blood. The male population of the *hujar* were known as Ikhwan ('brothers'). They wore white turbans (which could be turned into their funeral shrouds on the battlefield) rather than the traditional headdress of the Bedu (the *kufiya* scarf, held in place with a bridle woven of dark hair) and they were encouraged to clip their beards, trim their moustaches and wear their *thobe* (the long cotton robe of Arabia) above the ankle. They avoided music and the use of any silk or gilt embroidery. As good Muslims they abhorred alcohol, but they also never touched tobacco or coffee (substances not mentioned in the Koran or used by the Companions). Like all Wahhabi, they hated tombs and anything that remotely smacked of imagery or decoration. They would not exchange greetings with non-Wahhabi

Muslims, let alone a Christian, Jew or Shia. Wahhabi women were highly restricted, forbidden even to make use of a public well or to shop at a marketplace, which meant that a lot of the initial energy in constructing a *hujar* settlement went into digging private wells for each household.

By 1920, some 52 *hujar* had been established across central Arabia, growing to 120 by 1929, so that one in five Bedouin tribesmen had been recruited into their ranks. Money for the emir of each settlement and arms for his soldiers were provided by Ibn Saud. A good proportion of this came from the British, who in 1915 agreed to supply Ibn Saud with £5,000 in coins each month, topped up by arms and ammunition to wage war against their mutual adversary, the Ottoman Empire. There was tension in financing these fundamentalist warriors with Christian money, but Ibn Saud's competitors, the Hashemite rulers of the Hejaz, were similarly supplied with British gold to lead the Arab Revolt against the Ottoman Empire.

❀ ❀ ❀

Apart from a few desert raids to keep these British funds flowing and to seize control of various exposed Ottoman posts, the Ikhwan remained largely in a state of training throughout the First World War. In their actions, however, they acquired the reputation of slaughtering a defeated army rather than taking any prisoners.

In the aftermath of the First World War, there was a glut of military equipment, and Ibn Saud was ready to take out his opponents. In 1919, an Ikhwan force obliterated the Hashemite army at the Battle of Turabah (on the Nejd–Hejaz frontier), though Ibn Saud was halted from following up this success by the British. In the summer of 1920, Ikhwan armies struck north and conquered the Rashidi Emirate (demolishing their citadel-palace at Hail) and very nearly occupied all of Kuwait in 1920, before launching a succession of raids into Trans-Jordan (1921–22). Again it was only the presence of British bases in both of these small states that halted their conquest by the Ikhwan. British influence had prevented the first Saudi invasion of Hashemite Hejaz, but the region fell in 1925, followed by Saudi occupation of the Yemeni frontier in 1926 and raids on southern Iraq in 1927 and Kuwait (again) in 1928. Without the intervention of British troops on the ground and the RAF in the air, and the Royal Navy on the coast, all of the Arabian peninsula would have fallen to Ibn Saud's Ikhwan armies in these years.

But it is possible that this state would have been too large to have survived. Even the 1925 conquest of the Hejaz had the effect of stirring up an internal schism within the Saudi Kingdom. The actions of the Ikhwan in the holy cities of Mecca and Medina appalled the rest of the Muslim world. Pilgrims had been beaten for playing music and were whipped if they wept at the tomb of the Prophet or prayed at any of the tombs of Muslim heroes. The monuments that marked the birthplace of the Prophet, the house of Caliph Abu Bakr, the house of Muhammad's first wife Khadija and hundreds of revered tombs were demolished. A similar wave of iconoclasm had ripped out the historic monuments of the Hejaz during the Wahhabi invasion of 1805. But, this time, the Ikhwan went on to smash mirrors and to destroy automobiles, telephone lines and telegram posts – for none of these machines were named in the Koran. The annual Egyptian Haj caravan, which escorted gifts to the holy shrine from Cairo, was attacked for sounding a bugle as a morning wake-up call. The Egyptian guards retaliated and killed twenty-five of the more aggressive Ikhwan who had been beating them with sticks.

These actions were witnessed by the entire Muslim world, not only through the presence of Haj pilgrims but because a worldwide Islamic conference had been convened in the holy city that year. Ibn Saud initially proposed that he would rule the Hejaz as a separate kingdom – 'the dual monarchy of Nejd and Hejaz' – and became understandably reluctant to promote his more militant Ikhwan commanders to become provincial governors.

The following winter, 1926, three of the leading tribal chieftains within the Ikhwan movement met at Al-Artwiyah to assemble a list of seven grievances to present to Ibn Saud. One of their seven demands was that the Ikhwan should be permitted either to convert or massacre the Shia population of Al-Hasa; another demanded the destruction of all telephones. Ibn Saud was wise enough not to disagree publicly with these extreme proposals, but instead forwarded them to the *ulema*, a council of fifteen of the most respected Islamic Wahhabi scholars. The *ulema* did their best to fudge things, often agreeing in principle with the Ikhwan but qualifying these decisions with particular instances and practices. These theological prevarications delayed an armed confrontation for a few years, but the three tribal leaders of the Ikhwan began to organise their own raids, without consulting Ibn Saud. These raids, against a British outpost in southern Iraq on 5 November 1927 and into Kuwaiti territory in 1928 and 1929, had undeniable appeal to the rank and file.

The final confrontation between these three extremist tribal leaders and Ibn Saud occurred at As-Sabalah on 31 March 1929. Ibn Saud was well prepared for this battle, for the Royal Saudi Army was now equipped with armoured cars and machine guns, while the Ikhwan rode their camels into battle. Five hundred Ikhwan were killed at As-Sabalah, and another thousand died after a second confrontation in August. After this decisive defeat, the Ikhwan were kept out of the army but recruited into a parallel force, the National Guard – known as the White Guard because for years they kept to their habitual Ikhwan white turban. Since the summer of 1926, Ibn Saud had also been attempting to deflect Ikhwan energies into a moral militia, local committees for 'Encouraging Virtue and Forbidding Wrong' – as viewed through the strict lens of Wahhabi preachers. Ibn Saud also codified the Zakat, the Islamic tithe, to exclude poor Bedouin tribesmen while levying a more aggressive poll tax on the non-Wahhabi population in the two coastal regions. Until oil was discovered, apart from the British subsidies of chests of gold and silver coins, the big cash earner for the Saudi treasury was the Haj pilgrimage.

※ ※ ※

As the world drifted towards the Second World War, the vastly expanded Kingdom of Saudi Arabia was preparing for a period of peace, while the wounds of a civil war were allowed to heal. But the discovery of oil was to change everything, moving Saudi Arabia into a US rather than British orbit, and, of course, radically changing its wealth.

As early as 1933, the US company Standard Oil stumped up £35,000 worth of gold sovereigns as a non-returnable advance on future oil royalties. And it was American geologists who made the breakthrough discovery in 1938, hastening it for sale. It was also American military engineers who built the first Saudi airfields, making Dhahran an operational base by 1944. When Ibn Saud met President Roosevelt aboard an American cruiser on the Bitter Lakes on 14 February 1945, they were confirming an established relationship.

The Roosevelt meeting was not a sinister secret deal, but part of an international fact-finding tour, with the President meeting a number of local leaders, from Egypt and Ethiopia as well as Saudi Arabia, face to face. Ibn Saud was completely clear and outspoken in his opposition to US support for Israel, but did not allow this to impact on allowing a strong role for the US in Saudi Arabia, which continued to run the ever-more-profitable oil industry and equip and train its armed forces.

Ibn Saud died in 1953, having fathered a hundred children, of which forty-five were sons. There was no system of primogeniture, just an understanding that the most senior competent male relative would be chosen by the leaders of the clan and accept their oath of loyalty. Over the following sixty years, six of the sons of Ibn Saud would reign as kings and many others have taken up the reigns of important ministries, which they dominated like medieval fiefdoms. Prince Sultan controlled the Ministry of Defence from 1963 to 2011 and Prince Nayef ruled the Ministry of Interior from 1975 to 2012. Despite Saudi Arabia's reputation for bloody acts of public justice, there was also a simultaneous tradition of inclusion, of curbing the passion of a young rebel by settling them down with a job, a dowry, a wife, a house, and waiting for them to have children.

Ibn Saud's heir, King Saud, did not have the advantage of a poor, adventurous childhood. He was a typical royal prince: intelligent, uxorious, interested in everything and a good communicator, but a bad judge of character and so distracted that he was virtually incapable of finishing any particular task. His mother was of the Bani Khalid, the dynasty who had ruled eastern Arabia since the fifteenth century. He was not a desert puritan, but maintained twenty-five palaces and tended to hide his pale, watery eyes behind dark glasses.

Overshadowing his reign was the deposition of King Farouk from the throne of Egypt in 1952, and the massive popularity of Farouk's successor, Colonel Nasser, and the widespread influence of pan-Arab socialism. With no constitution, no parliament, no trade unions and a reputation for corruption and royal extravagance, Saudi Arabia had much to fear. In February 1958, the Kingdom was accused of trying to bribe Sarraj, a Syrian intelligence officer, with a cheque made out for $2 million to depose Nasser, this cash to be doubled for a kill. He was also toying with political reform (in a haphazard and confusing way) and had anti-American impulses.

Rather than watch the disintegration of the Kingdom's authority, Saud's princely brothers reluctantly conspired to reduce his political mismanagement, and in 1964 replaced him with his half-brother, Prince Faisal. This was not so much a palace coup as the culmination of a six-year-long struggle for control of the important ministries of state achieved through delegations, letters, disagreements and face-saving public agreements. Faisal's mother was an al-Shaikh, and so he was a living example of the two-hundred-year-old Wahhabi–Saudi alliance. Faisal was also backed by the 'Sudairi Seven', a tight-knit group of brother-princes who had benefited from the wisdom, authority and work ethic of their mother, Hussa Sudairi.

Faisal and the 'Sudairi Seven' provided the Kingdom with political direction over the next fifty years. All three subsequent monarchs – King Khalid (1975–82), King Fahd (1982–2005) and King Abdullah (2005–15) – and such influential ministers as Prince Sultan and Prince Nayef – were members.

❁ ❁ ❁

The rivalry between Saudi Arabia and republican Egypt ramped up through the 1960s. The two regimes waged a propaganda war against each other: Radio Cairo promised 'we will make the princes slaves, and the slaves princes', while Radio Mecca focused on puritanical piety. The two rivals backed different political factions in Syria and in the North Yemen civil war. This war, and Communist insurrections in Aden and Darfur, helped bring Saudi Arabia back into the embrace of the West, so much so that the long-running rows with Hashemite Jordan and the British were forgiven – if never quite forgotten.

The military victory of Israel in the 1967 Six-Day War was a shock for the Arab world. It resulted in a truce between Egypt and Saudi Arabia and the oil-rich Arab nations. Saudi Arabia and Kuwait now pledged to support the front-line Arab states, with an annual aid budget of $135 million. The proxy war between Egypt and Saudi Arabia had been halted but the rivalry had not fully ended. It has never been exactly determined if Egypt (perhaps helped by the exiled King Saud) might not have been 'aware' of the June 1969 military coup attempt in Saudi Arabia. This failed coup implicated a hundred young Saudi officers and led to the execution of at least forty of them. The ease with which King Idris was dethroned in the September 1969 coup in Libya certainly gave warning of what could happen in Saudi Arabia if the royal family let go of their political grip. The Saudi monarchy decided it was prudent to keep the National Guard up to strength. It served as an internal balance to their professional army, which had shown themselves to be leaning towards the example set by Colonel Nasser's Egyptian Arab Republic.

The oil embargo of October 1973 was a key moment, the first time that non-Western powers acted as a collective, setting their own oil prices and their own political agenda. Overnight, the Kingdom of Saudi Arabia emerged as a potential new world power. The immediate aim of the embargo had been to halt Western support for Israel, which was rapidly going on the offensive against both Egypt and Syria after the initial Arab victories at the beginning of the 1973 Yom Kippur War. But what began as a diplomatic tactic snowballed into a long-term strategic victory with a 500 per cent growth in oil revenues. The oil minister of Saudi Arabia was now a figure of international importance. There was money in hand for every possible ministerial budget within Saudi Arabia and enough spare cash to buy the leadership of the Middle East. There were funds, too, for the construction of new mosques through the Muslim world (often paired with Saudi-trained imams), and to push forward Wahhabi theology, on a global scale, in colleges and universities.

A giving club was set up by the Kingdom of Saudi Arabia and the Gulf emirates which kept the governments of both Egypt and Syria afloat to the tune of $570 million a year, with $300 million for Jordan and $30 million for the Palestinians. These figures would grow over the decades. There would also be discreetly managed investments in the US and UK. A few trusted banking houses, such as Morgan Guarantee and Chase Manhattan, were commissioned to buy into the US economy. At least $200 billion had been prudently invested by 1981, while leverage could be painlessly acquired by buying up treasury bonds. And, if there was ever a need to, Saudi Arabia had watched with interest what an effective tool this could be. Eisenhower had only to dump British treasury bonds to whip Britain into line during the Suez crisis of 1956.

Then, on 23 March 1975, King Faisal, who had masterminded the delicate balance between Wahhabi theocrats, the massive royal family and a successful oil-exporting economy, was shot. His assassin was a cousin, whose background revealed many of the cracks beneath the surface of the Kingdom. Like many of his generation, he had been expensively educated abroad and found it difficult to reintegrate into traditional Saudi society. His mother was a Rashidi (the Nejd dynasty destroyed by Ibn Saud), while his brother was a religious zealot.

After the accession of King Khalid in 1975, there was a slow but insistent modernising agenda, mostly played out in generous educational allowances and a further vast expansion in ministerial budgets and two brand-new industrial cities. In such comparatively liberal cities as Jeddah, there were plays, fashion shows, four cinemas and women reading news and singing on both radio and television. The Kingdom, it seemed, was evolving in a liberal direction, slowly bracing itself to adopt some sort of formal constitution rather than remain a hereditary monarchy, perhaps introducing a Majlis al-Shura – a consultative council – that had been proposed as long ago as 1964. The Saudi internal security services remained chiefly concerned with monitoring military officers and the professional middle-class elite, 'the PhD set', who would be the obvious beneficiaries of any political transformation. A huge shock was in store.

CHAPTER 17

The Turkish Republic

Ataturk and post-Ottoman Turkey

For five hundred years the Ottoman Empire played the leading role in the Sunni Islamic world. We have seen how often it pitted its strength against its Shia neighbour, Persia, but its capital, Istanbul, stood at the western frontier with Europe, defending the Muslim Mediterranean world against Catholic Spain and Portugal, and its northern frontiers against Orthodox Russia and the Habsburg Empire. The Ottoman sultans also sent fleets and armies to aid embattled Muslim powers in Ethiopia, North Africa and India, whilst protecting the holy cities of Mecca and Medina. For a Turk, this imperial heritage offers up a golden landscape with which to view the past. Many cities throughout the Middle East are still dominated by magnificent Ottoman mosques, palaces, fortresses, holy tombs, madrasas, bridges and caravanserais. The empire remains a potent vision of Islamic unity, with its regard for all four traditional forms of Sunni law and heritage of poetic and artistic culture. As if this is not enough, a Turk will recognise the shadow of the Seljuks – Sunni warriors and creators of empires – as precursors of the Ottoman achievements.

But throughout the Arab world the Turks are not perceived as the heroes. They are coupled with such villains as Genghis Khan and Timur as a curse of God. The defeat of the Mameluke sultanate of Egypt and Syria by the Ottoman Turks in 1516 is still remembered by the Arabs as a catastrophe. In the narrative of the Arabs, the Ottomans were a disdainful caste of uncultured soldiers whose rule destroyed the commerce and intellectual life of the old Middle East. They are remembered for fighting more wars against rival Muslim states than against the Christians, and supported by substantial Christian communities. Throughout the long centuries of Ottoman rule, trade, banking, shipping and industry were left in the hands of Jewish, Greek and Armenian minorities, while their ruthless and obedient Janissary soldiers were recruited from Christian slave boys.

Some Arab historians also deny that the Ottoman Empire was ever the leading Sunni state. The Ottoman claim to act as the caliph of Islam came very late, as a gift of Russian diplomats in an eighteenth-century peace treaty, rather than from the worldwide community of Islam. Arabs deny that the Ottoman Empire was ever the lineal heir of the caliphate. The very last caliph, of the line of the Abbasid dynasty descended from one of the uncles of the Prophet Muhammad, had lived in Cairo in 1516. He was last heard of as a prisoner of the Ottoman sultan in Istanbul.

❋ ❋ ❋

Although a number of Ottoman frontier fortresses fell in the late eighteenth century, the borders of the Ottoman Empire essentially remained firm until the nineteenth century, after which the relentless aggression of Russia and Austria began to make major advances. The emergence of an independent Greece, followed by Serbia, Romania and Bulgaria (all eager to annex Ottoman provinces), resulted in a succession of three Balkan Wars (1912–13). These bloody conflicts were a mere preface to the even greater devastation of the First World War, during which the Ottoman Empire had to protect six separate frontiers: Iraq, the Caucasus, Libya, the Balkans, the Aegean and Arabia.

Western audiences swept up by the story of T. E. Lawrence and the Arab Revolt are often surprised to learn that the Turks had the upper hand for most of the conflict. The Turkish garrison at Gaza succeeded in resisting two British frontal assaults from nearby Egypt, while their garrison in Medina defiantly held out beyond the end of the war. On the Iraq frontier the Turks forced the surrender of an entire British army of 9,000 men at Kut. On the Gallipoli peninsula in 1916, the army of the Ottoman Empire defied the two strongest colonial empires of the time, Britain and France, to march on Istanbul and dictate the terms of their victory. No other Muslim nation had proved itself strong enough to oppose either the French or the British over the previous hundred years, yet, 'on the beaches, on the landing grounds, in the fields and in the streets and in the hills' the Turkish army triumphed.

But, with American support, France and Britain ultimately proved victorious and broke the might of Germany and its allies: the Ottoman and Austro-Hungarian empires.* The 1920 Treaty of Sèvres was dictated by the French and British. They planned to divide the Ottoman Empire into eight pieces and parcel it out amongst Turkish enemies: the Greeks taking the west coast, the Armenians the north-east, the Italians the south-west, while Syria was given to France, and Iraq and Palestine to Britain. It was also imagined that an independent Kurdistan might dominate the south-east quarter of Anatolia.

It was against this fate, after the immense sacrifices of the Balkan Wars and the First World War, that Mustafa Kemal,

---

* America did not declare war on the Ottoman Empire and took no part in any of the campaigns in the Middle East.

later known as Ataturk, summoned the Turks to take up arms once more. He waged war on four fronts, defeating the Armenians in the north-east and the Greeks in the west, after which the French and Italian garrisons evacuated the south. In this, the War of Independence, he had no allies – though the Soviets provided vital shipments of Russian arms through the port of Samsun.

To confirm and stabilise the frontiers achieved by these military victories, Ataturk then pushed through a ruthless series of reforms, designed to enable Turkey to become as strong as any of its Western enemies. The Greek Orthodox Christian minority (1.35 million strong) were expelled, for they were felt to be a potential fifth column who could never be trusted to become loyal Turkish citizens. The Arabic script was stripped out and replaced by a new Latin-based European script. A new educational system was devised, with Western uniforms replacing the ubiquitous felt fez and waistcoat. An orderly ladder of elementary and middle schools was created, which culminated in pragmatic skills to be taught at agricultural and professional colleges. Centuries of social and legal conduct based on the Koran were thrown out and replaced by a law code based on Swiss civil and Italian criminal law.

Muslim law courts and the old Islamic universities, as well as the lodges of the Dervish mystical poets, were closed, and the study of Arabic and Persian literature curtailed. Even the call to prayer was now to be made in Turkish, not the holy language of Koranic Arabic. To put a few dates on the extraordinary pace of political reinvention, November 1922 saw the abolition of the sultanate, March 1924 witnessed the dismissal of the last caliph, sharia law was ended in 1926 and the turban and the fez were banned in 1927. In 1926, Turkish women acquired equal legal rights and then the franchise.

Women first voted in 1930 in local elections, and in 1934 in national elections, which also elected the first eighteen female parliamentary representatives.

The pace of Ataturk's reforms was enabled by an important historical factor. Over the late nineteenth and early twentieth centuries, 800,000 refugees had been driven out of the old European provinces of the Ottoman Empire and taken refuge in Anatolia and Thrace. They understood Western culture. They were descendants of the Muslim administrators and craftsmen who had for centuries dominated life in Crete, northern Greece, Romania, Albania, Bosnia and Macedonia. In the coastal cities and Istanbul, the educated middle-class families had been familiar with French and Italian culture for centuries. These educated Turks formed the bedrock of the new Turkish Republic.

For the mass of the population in the villages and market towns of the rural interior of Anatolia, it was a bewildering period. Despite their pride in the many achievements of the Turkish Republic – the ever-expanding grid of roads, mains water and new electricity power lines, the new schools and universities and jobs – they also fervently wished to remain connected to Islam, and to feel an heir to the old dignity and achievements of the Empire. Ottoman dictionaries were purged of Arabic, Persian and Greek loan words, and the new Latin script further purified the language. Within a generation, no-one could read the inscription on their grandfather's tomb or read the recipes of their grandmothers, let alone swim in the ocean of centuries of Islamic learning.

There was also a madness in the way that the history of the country was taught. Inheritable surnames were forcibly imposed in 1934 in place of the old patronymics, echoing the way in which refugees coming to America were given a random new spelling of an ancient family name by an immigration official. Everyone had to pretend to be a Turk, whatever the complex reality of their ancestry. Ataturk himself knew this was a construct, for he was not born in an Anatolian village but in the bustling Levantine port of Thessaloniki, a Thracian-Macedonian city which included a large Jewish population descended from fifteenth-century refugees from Spain. Enver Pasha, another famous Turkish nationalist hero, had an Albanian mother, while his father's family came from Monastir in Macedonia. General Inonu, Ataturk's chosen successor as president, was half-Kurdish.

❀ ❀ ❀

So modern Turkey is something of an intellectual construct, even for those who were descended from Turkic-speaking families in Anatolia. The Turks only entered Anatolian history in significant numbers in the eleventh century. Yet, however much nationalists might want to think of themselves as descendants of a conquering cavalry army, most Turks will have a strong percentage of Anatolian DNA in their bloodline. Anatolia is one of the undisputed ancient motherlands of the world, the place where the cultivation of barley and wheat, and the herding of sheep and goats, was first invented. Anatolia has always embraced many cultural identities, which includes Georgians, Kurds, Arabs, Armenians as well as Turks. This might seem ancient history, but it has real importance for understanding the modern Turkish Republic and its fissures.

The Armenians are one of the oldest Christian peoples in the world, with their own theology (independent of either Greek Orthodox or Roman Catholic). One of the indigenous people of Anatolia, they tended to live on cultivatable land and became craftsmen, traders and miners, paying their taxes obediently first to the Byzantine, then the Seljuk, empires.

They were superb craftsmen in stone. The Ottoman Empire was founded on a working partnership between the warrior Turks and mercantile Armenians. During the middle of the nineteenth century this partnership slowly dissolved, as the Ottoman leadership, fearing that the Armenians now desired their own state, forged an alliance with Orthodox Russia. In the testing days of the First World War it was decided to destroy the power of the Armenians. Orders were given that Armenian communities were to be assembled, evacuated from any potential conflict zone and marched south to new areas of settlement. But, during these marches, the men were slaughtered and hundreds of thousands of young Armenian girls were abducted, to serve as concubines and housemaids. The murky, blood-drenched history of these local massacres involved Kurdish militia groups, the Hamidiye Alaylari, created by Sultan Abdul Hamid II to perpetrate an earlier round of state-sponsored Armenian massacres in 1894–96.

Despite the silence that surrounds this matter, the facts are a matter of court record. The Turkish ministers directly responsible for ordering the massacres were tried by Ottoman law courts in the immediate post-war period. They were convicted for the murder of hundreds of thousands of innocent non-combatants. In 1914, there were two million Armenians throughout the empire; today, there are probably just 70,000 within the Turkish Republic. Massacre and migration – to the US, France, Lebanon and the Armenian republic in the Caucasus – accounts for the rest, alongside an unknown number of silent Armenians, whose identity is hidden (sometimes even from themselves) behind many a Turkish passport.

The Laz are another Anatolian people and an identifiable ethnic minority, originally Georgians who lived on the Black Sea coast and who converted to Islam over the centuries. They have always found it easy to assimilate into mainstream

Turkish culture, so much so that they are often depicted as the jolly, laughing sea captains and fishermen of Turkish folk tales. And, just as Ataturk came from a Levantine milieu, Erdogan, the current president of Turkey, for all his passionate nationalism, comes from this background.

❋ ❋ ❋

Turkey's most significant – and potent – minority are the Kurds, an ancient people of Anatolia whose territory in the mountainous south-east straddles the modern borders of Iran and Iraq. The Kurds for centuries had served in the cavalry of the Ottoman Empire, which honoured their distinct culture. This partnership was not offered by the Turkish Republic, with its desire to create a one-nation state where all identities would be buried under the pride of being a Turk. Unlike the village-dwelling Armenian farmers and craftsmen, the Kurds traditionally preferred the freedom of tents and huts in the hills with their herds. They trace their descent from the Medes (the empire before the Persians), which is why one Kurdish calendar starts with the fall of the Assyrian capital of Nineveh. Kurds speak a language that is Iranian, not Turkic or Arabic.*

Partly because of this, the Kurds resisted Ataturk's reforms in the 1920s. They were proud of their own identity and did not want to see their ancient Iranian language replaced. Kurdish was associated with all their beloved songs and treasured poetry, which would have to be discarded in favour of the new identity of secular republican Turkey with its Latin script.

In retrospect, it seems possible that a Turkish government with greater sympathy to that identity could have focused on

---

* Kurds are predominantly Muslim, and include both Sunni and Shia. But there are also small communities of Kurdish Yazidis and Jews (the latter – Mizrahis – now mainly in Israel).

their many shared values and won the Kurds over. This was not what happened. Ataturk was in a hurry to modernise in case the nation needed to fight another defensive war for survival. So, instead of being talked to as allies, the Kurds were treated as potential traitors. In 1921, a notoriously brutal army commander, Nureddin Pasha, crushed the Kocgiri tribal region in a three-month reign of terror. It was recognised as a political disaster at the time but the leaders of the Republic did not learn from this mistake.

In 1925, Sheikh Said, a Kurdish Islamic scholar, prepared a list of eleven grievances against Ataturk's reforms. They combined concerns about the proscription of Kurdish identity and the dismantling of Islamic institutions with old-fashioned loyalty to the idea of the Ottoman caliphate. On 6 March, the sheikh raised the standard of rebellion and led 10,000 warriors against a government garrison established within the vast basalt walls of the city of Diyarbakir. Within a few months, the army of the Turkish Republic had destroyed the rebellion and captured the sheikh, who was sentenced to death and hung alongside thirty-six of his followers. It was another tactical mistake, making a martyr of such a man. His brother, Sheikh Abdurrahman, continued the rebellion in the mountains, while in the north-eastern provinces of Van and Bitlis, a battle-experienced old Kurdish Ottoman officer, Ihsan Nuri, led the Ararat rebellion from 1927 to 1930. These rebellions might have become neglected footnotes, for in every instance the government forces, as well as suppressing armed revolt, also made local alliances with rival Kurdish clans.

Except for one more final tragic incident. For, in hardening the antagonistic battle line between Turk and Kurd, the most toxic label of all is 'Dersim, 1937'. The exact narrative is still in dispute, but it seems that a group of men who had delivered a petition of protest to the governor of Dersim province were arrested by the police and killed. A police convoy was then ambushed in revenge, which led to the military occupation of the province. On the evening of 21 March, when the Kurds came together to celebrate the spring festival of Nowruz, a rebellion was launched. It was suppressed, but at least 13,000 Kurds were killed that summer and a further 12,000 sent into administrative exile (one historian thinks these figures should be trebled). That autumn, during a truce, the leader of the rebellion, Seyid Riza, came to talk over the options for peace but was arrested and hung. In consequence, the entire eastern half of Anatolia remained under military rule until 1950 and was forbidden to foreign travellers until 1965.

The leaders of the Turkish Republic have long believed that the Kurds' rebellions were supported by the agents of a malicious foreign power. In 1926, the oil-producing region around Mosul, populated by Kurds and Turkmen, was added to the Arab Kingdom of Iraq, which was under British rule in everything but name. If Britain had not determined to acquire these oil fields, most of Kurdistan might have remained within the country. It might then have remained of sufficient size and territorial integrity to have achieved a proper partnership, or a degree of autonomy, within the Turkish Republic. Turkey would also have benefited from the oil revenue. The Kurds have never had access to the sea, so would always have had to work with at least one of their neighbours to prosper from these oil fields. It is possible to imagine that the Kurds (like the Laz) could have existed as an honoured partner to the Turks.

One of the reasons Britain was able to get away with this annexation (rubber stamped by the League of Nations) was because of Kurdish rebellions in Anatolia. Many Turks believe that British agents helped foment these rebellions for their own nefarious purposes. In the same period, the French added a slice of border territory to the colonial frontiers of Syria and welcomed Kurdish refugees fleeing the new Turkish Republic. Once Britain was sure of its valuable new possession, the shareholding of the Iraq Petroleum Company was divided into attractive slices: 21.5 per cent for France and the US, 52.5 per cent to Britain; the Armenian Calouste Gulbenkian, whose family had been important players in Ottoman and Azerbaijan trade for two generations, was given 5 per cent.

The wounds of Dersim still fester. On 23 November 2011, President Erdogan called it 'one of the most tragic events of our recent history'. It was a brave statement. His leadership of a new Islamist identity within the Turkish Republic seemed at one time to be offering a shared umbrella of values that could unite Kurds and Turks. But, again, this did not come about.

The Kurds are both Shia (in its Alevi form) and Sunni. They have always divided into rival tribes and dialects, a mix made more complex by their region straddling the frontiers between the Ottoman and the Safavid empires, and in modern times (since the 1920s) the borders of Turkey, Iran, Iraq and Syria.*

The Kurdish south-east is the Achilles heel of the Turkish state, which dictates a very clear line with their allies on this issue: if you wish to be our friend, do not interfere with this internal 'south-eastern' issue, and do not support Kurdish independence anywhere else. The nightmare at the back of the minds of all Turkish leaders is that map showing what the Allies intended with their homeland in the 1920 Treaty of Sèvres. The Greeks would be given the western third of Anatolia, the Armenians the north-east, and an independent

---

* In Turkey, the Kurds number around 13 million, or one fifth of the population. There are 2 million Kurds in northern Syria, some 7 million Kurds in northern Iraq and another 7 million in north-west Iran.

Kurdistan occupied the south-east. The first task of every Turkish leader, of whatever political creed, is to guard the nation.

❄ ❄ ❄

The three Muslim states – Persia, Saudi Arabia and Turkey – that we have chronicled in this part of the book are the success stories. It was not easy to survive as a Muslim nation in this troubled period, which the Chinese call the century of humiliations. Independence was never certain and required periods of compromise as well as heroic struggle. Ataturk, Reza Shah and Ibn Saud chose different paths, but not once did any of them think of leading their nations in war against each other. They were content to be the stern father of their people and uninterested in becoming caliph of all Islam.

All the other Muslim states across the globe fell under colonial rule or an imperial protectorate. With one or two exceptions – North Yemen and Afghanistan – these three great powers were the only Muslim nations that managed to resist the worldwide dominance of the west, the colonial night.

PART FIVE

1979 Revolutions: The Middle East Transformed

PART FIVE

1979 Revolutions: The Middle East Transformed

s Lenin observed: 'There are decades where nothing happens; and there are weeks where decades happen.' In the Middle East, 1979 was that time, when three events transformed the region's power-politics. On 16 January, the Shah of Iran was ousted by a year-long uprising on the streets, his secular, modernising autocracy replaced by an Islamic Republic led by the Ayatollah Khomeini, a charismatic Shiite intellectual. On 20 November, the monarchy in Saudi Arabia was shaken to its core by an Islamist uprising in Mecca. Then, on 26 December, a Russian army crossed the frontier into Afghanistan. Turkey, too, was on the brink of civil war, and the following year was reshaped by a military coup.

Nearly half a century on, Iran is still ruled by an ayatollah who was personally appointed by the Ayatollah Khomeini. Authority within the Islamic Republic is shared with an elected leadership, but is ultimately upheld by the Revolutionary Guard, which is deeply committed to upholding a regime with a Shiite identity. The militance of Iran's Revolutionary Guard is the key to understanding the nature of this regime and was formed by the horrific experiences of the 1980–88 Iran–Iraq War, when Iran stood alone against the world.

The events in Mecca in 1979 arose from the Ikhwan tradition that had helped forge Saudi Arabia into a nation, as the rebels, led by veteran soldiers trained within the National Guard, made a fortress out of Islam's holiest of holies, the mosque that surrounds the Kaaba. Though their rebellion failed (and its leaders were killed or executed), politically it triumphed, for the Saudi monarchy executed a 180-degree turn on modernisation, returning to its core identity created by the xenophobic Ikhwan desert warriors and Wahhabi preachers. It was a pause button that remained on hold for thirty-five years, while the oil money kept rolling in, allowing internal opposition to be softened with scholarships and salaries, and secured with US military support. Only in the last decade has any social change reappeared, albeit under an autocratic young crown prince with ambitions to dominate all of Arabia.

The Soviet army entered Afghanistan at the request of the embattled Communist regime in Kabul, which was struggling against uprisings in the provinces. The presence of a foreign army of occupation helped inflame this into a nationwide freedom struggle – one that could also be seen as a civil war, pitching the Islamist zeal of the countryside against secular modernists in the cities. The US, Pakistan and Saudi Arabia formed an alliance that poured aid into fourteen rival Mujahadin resistance groups. It was to be the onset of a civil war that has raged ever since, most recently with the Taliban (the party formed of rural clerics) back in power in Kabul.

To understand the effect of these events on international relations, and their relevance to Sunni–Shia conflict, we need to understand how the story looks from each perspective.

CHAPTER 18

Revolution in Iran

The emergence of a Shiite Islamic Republic,
the Iran–Iraq War and modern-day Iran

In 1977, the Shah of Iran was persuaded by US President Jimmy Carter to tone down the repressive machinery of his authoritarian regime. The Americans hoped a parliamentary democracy might emerge. But the new freedoms instead gave the Iranian people the opportunity to demonstrate how much they had loathed the thirty-seven years of Mohammad Reza Shah's rule and that of his Cossack father, Reza Shah, before him.

At first, a broad-based freedom movement emerged, as democratic parties allied with the Shiite clergy in calling for a new constitution. The first serious demonstration, in January 1978, was led by religious students at Qom, infuriated by a government article dismissing their spiritual leader, Ayatollah Khomeini, as a British spy and mad Indian poet. On the third day of protests, five students were killed by police. The funerals of these martyrs and traditional forty-day mourning cycle provided the opportunity for a new round of anti-regime demonstrations to take place in twelve cites on 18 February. These, too, were crushed by heavy-handed police repression and a new round of memorial marches took place on 29 March, this time in forty-five provincial cities. They were largely peaceful, except in Yazd, where a hundred marchers were killed.

The next round of marches passed off without murderous incidents and, on the day before the fast of Ramadan, held over August that year, the Shah made a speech promising an end to corruption and sacking the head of SAVAK, the loathed security police. It was far too little and far too late, and fatally coincided with a downturn in the economy as the inflation of a previous boom period was curbed by fiscal deflation. During Ramadan, thousands of Iranians claimed to have seen the face of the Ayatollah etched into the moon, and on 4 September, the Eid el-Fitr, the festival that marks the end of Ramadan, turned into a vast protest march. Crowds of half a million possessed the streets of Tehran. On 7 September a smaller but more militant demonstration began to call openly for an Islamic Republic. When this was repeated the next day, soldiers opened fire in Tehran's Jaleh Square, killing eighty-nine people and wounding hundreds more.

Street demonstrations were renewed on 10–11 December, during the heightened emotions of the month of Ashura, when Shiites commemorate the death of the martyred Imam Husayn, killed, of course, by the army of an evil governor working on behalf of a wicked ruler. Millions now marched across the breadth of the nation. The Shah observed the vast crowds in Tehran from a helicopter, and his desire to remain on the throne at any cost began to weaken. He ordered his soldiers to exercise restraint, which might have happened in any event, for no soldier knew how to handle vast crowds of black-veiled women, who could have been their mothers, aunts or sisters. A trickle of soldiers began to leave their uniforms at the barracks and head home to their villages; within weeks this had turned into a stream of 1,200 desertions a day.

The Shah decided to leave the country on a vacation-exile. He had done this once before in his life and had returned in triumph. So, on 31 December, he appointed Shapour Bakhtiar, a liberal aristocrat with some experience of both government office and persecution, as prime minister. Bakhtiar lost his liberal allies in accepting this post but moved quickly to end martial law, dissolve censorship, and disband SAVAK. He announced elections for a constitutional assembly that would be held in three months. On 4 January, a US general, Robert E. Huyser, flew into Tehran to encourage his Iranian counterparts to stand behind Bakhtiar. On 16 January, the Shah flew out.

On the morning of 1 February, an Air France jet delivered Khomeini to Tehran airport. The Ayatollah was greeted by millions of well-wishers chanting 'Emam Amad' ('Imam has come'). Two days later, General Huyser left the country, a signal, to those who could read it, that the US was not going to back the emergence of a military strongman. US Secretary of State Cyrus Vance had been resolutely opposed to direct involvement in a coup, while the US ambassador on the ground had even been discreetly talking to Khomeini.

The crunch came at Tehran's Doshan Tappeh airbase on 8 February, when a body of uniformed cadets travelled to meet Khomeini and publicly pledge allegiance. The next day, two hundred men of the Shah's Imperial Guard tried to reimpose military authority within the now openly mutinous airbase. A column of Chieftain tanks was sent to reinforce them, but their passage was blocked by crowds who poured out into the streets, chanting 'Allah Akbar'. If the tanks had driven forward, it could have become a massacre like Tiananmen Square. But they halted, and by midnight the rebel cadets were in control of the airbase, had broken into the armouries and were distributing arms to the people. Tehran began to organise itself against a feared counter-attack from the Iranian military.

Twenty-two Iranian generals met to discuss what they should do on the morning of 11 February. They decided neither to launch a coup nor support the authority of Prime Minister

Bakhtiar, but ordered the troops back to their barracks. By the end of the day, revolutionary crowds were no longer on the defensive but had surged out to sack police stations and SAVAK offices across the country. SAVAK, over the past decade, had employed 6,000 officers, backed by 60,000 freelance informers. Now they feared for their lives, though their deputy director, Hossein Fardoust, cut an early deal. He would serve both the Shah and the Islamic revolution.

On 14 February, the revolution showed its teeth. General Mehdi Rahimi, Chief of Police in Tehran and deputy commander of the Imperial Guard, was arrested along with three other generals implicated in the repression. They were tried by a revolutionary tribunal and shot on the roof of Tehran's Refah school, Khomeini's headquarters. The US administration woke up to what was happening, but by now it was too late.

❀ ❀ ❀

Ayatollah Khomeini had established a Council of Islamic Revolution the previous November, and it had been actively directing events since his return. The leaders of the Friday prayers in the mosques provided a core of supporters, around which were assembled revolutionary committees – 1,500 of them in Tehran alone. This body of activists created their own political party, the Islamic Revolution Party (IRP), but their strength would be most effectively served in the creation of the Sepah militia, the 'Guardians of the Islamic Revolution'. It was feared that, without their own muscle on the streets, either the old Communist Party, Tudeh, or right-wing groups in the military, would achieve a coup. To further thwart this possibility, Khomeini appointed 'imam agents' to weed out opposition in government administration and the military establishment. Old-regime loyalists who had failed to flee the country were hauled before revolutionary courts that were said to be 'born out of the anger of the Iranian People'. Enemies of the revolution were summarily convicted of either *moharebeh* ('waging war against God') or *mofsed fel-arz* ('spreading corruption on earth') before being executed. Other paramilitary militia groups, such as the left-leaning Islamist People's Mujahedin (MEK), or Fedayeen, were initially allies of the revolution before becoming militant opponents. The revolutionary courts would condemn these old allies as *monafeqin* ('hypocrites'), which had Koranic overtones. By the end of that summer Sepah had grown into the mainstay of the new state. A professional force of 11,000 men, it was funded by the confiscation of the Shah's Pahlavi Foundation, which was renamed Bonyad, the Foundation for the Oppressed. Sepah was immediately put to work quelling a Kurdish revolt and unrest amongst the other non-Iranian minorities – the Arabs in Khuzestan, Turkmen in the north-east, and Baluchi in the south-east.

In the outer, public sphere, a provisional government led by a respected and democratic-oriented academic, Mehdi Bazargan, screened the hard politics of this Islamic revolution from the world. A referendum held on 31 March upheld the Revolution by a vote of 98 per cent. Women kept their right to vote in the referendum, and any subsequent elections, but the Shah's family law reform of 1967, which had outlawed some traditional Islamic practices, was abolished. In the summer, an 'Assembly of Experts' was tasked with writing a new constitution. Fifty-five of the seventy-three experts were Shiite clerics, and they proceeded to create the dazzlingly complex legal edifice of the Islamic Republic of Iran with its intricate checks and balances all watched over by the *velayat-e faqih* ('guardianship of the jurist'). The key role of Ayatollah Khomeini as the first guardian jurist has variously been interpreted: a temporary measure to safeguard the revolution, a new form of constitutional monarchy, a morally selected Islamic president for life, or a tyrant whose oppression would be ten times worse than that of the Shah. Some of the most relevant criticism came from other senior Shiite clerics. Ezzatollah Sahabi was concerned that clerics would inevitably become as corrupt and venal as any politician and lose the respect they had earned over the centuries. Ayatollah Shariatmadari obseved that 'we seem to be moving from one monarchy to another'.

It was this danger – of moderate Shiite clerics joining forces with liberal reformers – which explains the footwork of the next round of Khomeini's revolution. On 22 October, when the exiled Shah sought sanctuary in the US, Khomeini demanded that the 'criminal, deposed Shah' be returned to Iran to face justice, along with his wealth, and an apology from the US. It was not so much that he wanted vengeance, but to establish a confrontational mood. He then despatched Mehdi Bazargan to meet Zbigniew Brzezinski in Algiers, to discuss buying military spare parts from the US; while at home, on 4 November, the US Embassy in Tehran was occupied by radical students.

Khomeini saluted this action as 'a second revolution' against 'a lair of espionage'. Bazargan was humiliated and resigned.* The staff of the American Embassy, blindfolded and handcuffed, became pawns in the Ayatollah's highly political and visual 'US hostage crisis'. On 14 November, the US government froze $11 billion of Iranian assets and stopped importing Iranian oil. Meantime, in Tehran, the release of documents from the US Embassy (even those put through the shredder were slowly pieced together) implicated Iranian liberals as much as it exposed the machinations of America. Khomeini succeeded in

---

* Bazargan, who had earlier argued for the new state to be called an Islamic *Democratic* Republic, opposed the occupation of the US Embassy and 'hostage taking'. He served as a Member of Parliament until 1984, a fierce critic of the 'terror, fear, revenge and national disintegration' of the new regime.

creating just the right mood of nationalist frenzy to win the constitutional referendum vote on 3 December.

Khomeini knew better than anyone that the US Embassy was no bed of hawks. Before his return, he had talked with its ambassador, William Sullivan, who recognised the overwhelming level of support for the Ayatollah within Iran. Sullivan went on to prove himself one of the saviours of the Islamic revolution, forcibly rejecting the idea of a US-backed military coup. The Iranians who interrogated the fifty-two hostages seized were themselves surprised to find that this 'infamous lair of espionage' contained only four identifiable employees of the CIA, none of whom could speak Persian with any fluency.

Then the US administration scored a spectacular own goal. Operation Eagle Claw, on 24 April 1980, saw eight helicopters take off from the flight deck of USS *Nimitz*, cruising off the coast of Oman. It was to be a two-stage operation. An advance base was first to be secured in the empty central desert of Iran. From there, rested and refuelled, they were to make a surprise attack on the US Embassy building in Tehran to recover the hostages. To avoid detection, the helicopters flew in low across a sparsely inhabited coastal region, but three of them developed technical problems and it was reluctantly decided to abort the operation. But, instead of an orderly departure from this secret base, one helicopter crashed on top of another, leaving two burnt-out machines, a cache of classified documents, and nine bodies on the ground. It was just the sort of operation that gave weight to radical Islamist propaganda about US plots, embedded spies, secret bases and covert invasions.

❀ ❀ ❀

A week later, another covert mission was launched against Iran. In London, the Iranian Embassy was seized by members of the Revolutionary Front for the Liberation of Arabistan (Khuzestan). All but one of the terrorists were killed during a night assault by the British SAS, and it was subsequently proven that they had entered the country using Iraqi passports. Three months later, this incident was followed by the Nojeh camp plot, again supported by Iraq. This intended military coup would take place after the bombing of Khomeini's household, and would restore the Shah's designated prime minister, Shapour Bakhtiar. The plot was foiled, 300 were arrested, 144 executed and 4,500 purged from the military.

Both of these plots must have received the approval of Saddam Hussein. He had only formally become the president of Iraq in July 1979 but had been the acknowledged power since the 1968 coup placed his elderly cousin, General Ahmed Hassan al-Bakr, as notional ruler. Saddam Hussein may have been an opportunist, a bully and a thug, but he was also defined by his loyalty to the secular Ba'ath (Arab Renaissance) Party. He may have desired to lead the Arab world but it would be wrong to think of him as a leader of Sunni against Shiite Muslims. Nor did he really aspire to destroy the Islamic revolution in Iran, but rather to use a period of confusion and military weakness to annex the Arab-populated oil region of Khuzestan. This would have immeasurably increased the wealth of Iraq, as well as assuring it access to the Persian Gulf.*

Skirmishes took place along the southern frontier of Iraq and Iran that autumn. On 20 September 1980, Iraq called up its reservists to create an army of 200,000 soldiers marshalled into twelve divisions. On 22 September, air strikes

---

* All Iraqi leaders, whatever their political or religious convictions, have been interested in enlarging their access to the Persian Gulf, which is currently restricted to the narrow Shatt al-Arab channel. The Shatt al-Arab is the jugular vein of Iraq, which can be protected only by capturing territory from either Kuwait or Iran.

were launched against ten Iranian airbases, whilst four military columns struck into south-west Iran. It was an unprovoked attack on a neighbouring nation, designed to annex an oil-rich region – or, in the eyes of the Ba'ath, to unite a lost province to the Arab motherland. Khomeini derisively announced that 'a thief has come in the night, thrown a pebble and fled back home'.

This invasion was not totally unexpected. Indeed, a detailed staff plan to cope with just such a contingency had been drawn up during the reign of the Shah. At dawn on 23 September, 140 Iranian jets struck back at Iraqi airforce bases, and succeeded in destroying twenty jets on the ground. They had been supplied in the air by lumbering Boeing 707 and 747 air-tankers. The Iranian airforce struck again and again over the next few days, and in October succeeded in launching a surprise attack on the al-Hurriyah airbase, near Mosul, with devastating success. Two-thirds of the Iraqi airforce were subsequently withdrawn to the safety of neutral Arab nations.

In October and November 1980, the first land battle, over Khorramshahr, was fought. This was to be the Stalingrad of the Iran–Iraq War. A hundred Iraqi tanks were destroyed in the first battle and each side took at least 7,000 casualties. But it was just the first of a succession of engagements that tore the region apart over the next eight years. The Iranians eventually pushed the Iraqi army east towards the old frontier line, at a vast cost. The Sepah fought alongside the regular Iranian army, as well as martyr-battalions of Basiji volunteers, who on some occasions marched together through minefields to clear a path for the regular soldiers.

As the Iranians attempted to punish their aggressors by taking the offensive into Iraq, the war ground down into a bloody stalemate, and it was the Iraqis' turn to prove themselves steadfast in their defence of national territory.

It is impossible to appreciate the nature of the Islamic Republic of Iran and its leadership without understanding the sacrifices made during this eight-year war. It was worse than the trench warfare of Europe's 1914–18 war and fused a battle-hardened comradeship among its survivors, as well as a sense that they owed it to the fallen to continue the struggle. The Iranians were also aware that the entire Arab world was backing Iraq with loans to buy weapons from the West, who also stood with Iraq. This isolation distilled in both Iran's leadership and people the belief that they would survive only through their own resources and determination.

This sense would be reinforced by incidents such as the Hafte Tir bombing on 28 June 1981. This exploded during a conference of the Islamic Republican Party, killing seventy of their leaders. The Mujahadin, a left-leaning Islamist revolutionary group also known as the MKO, was considered responsible, and over the next two years some 7,000 of their members were hunted down and executed. This was followed by the judicial massacre of 1988, when 5,000 MKO prisoners held in Iranian jails were executed after the Mujahadin had raised a militia to fight alongside Iraq. Soviet loyalists within the Iranian Communist Party were also decimated in 1983.[*]

※ ※ ※

Other odd tactical alliances would be forced upon the leadership of Iran, for the Iranian army had been entirely equipped by the US and the UK over the 1960s and 1970s, and now needed to trade with this 'Great Satan' in order to acquire

---

[*] A Soviet spy called Vladimir Kuzichkin defected to British intelligence in Tehran in 1982, and the British decided to share his information with the Iranians, leading to the arrest and execution of hundreds of Communist Party members.

spare parts to fight Iraq. So they used a variety of international go-betweens, including Chile and Argentina, and Israel ('Little Satan'). This trade was at its busiest between 1980 and 1983 and would become ever more complex once the American Iran–Contra story broke in November 1986.

To make this secret arms trade all the more baffling to the world, the Republic of Iran had been the only Islamic nation, aside from Syria, to respond actively to the Israeli invasion of Lebanon. On 6 June 1982, 800 Israeli tanks and 60,000 soldiers had pushed into southern Lebanon, assisted by marine landings and airstrikes. Within a week, although Iran was itself very hard pressed by the war with Iraq, a thousand Sepah fighters had been flown into the Bekaa valley to train the Lebanese. The speed and confidence with which Iran reacted owed much to the strong personal links between the Shiite scholars of south-east Lebanon and Iran, for the Bekaa valley in the east of Lebanon and the Jebel Amir in the south are among the most ancient strongholds of the Shia faith. It was from here that Arab scholars brought the Shiite faith to Safavid Iran in the sixteenth century. Ali Akbar Mohtashami, who had shared in Khomeini's exile, was the trusted Iranian Ambassador to Syria from 1982 to 1986, directing this operation.

The year 1982 can also be considered the beginning of the close alliance between Syria and Iran, which thirty years later paid back dividends to the Assad regime during the Syrian civil war. Mohtashami may also have been involved with the 1983 suicide bombings against French and US forces in Beirut, which proved efficient in removing foreign garrisons. These operations were executed by the Iranian-influenced Islamic jihad, but, once Shiite clerics had formally decreed that suicide bombs were un-Islamic, no further use was made of the tactic by any Iranian group. In a similar manner, Iranian clerics also declared the use of poison gas un-Islamic and so the Iranian army never retaliated in kind against the Iraqi use of gas on battlefields in 1983–84. Mohtashami subsequently rose to become Iran's Interior Minister.

The 1982 Israeli invasion destroyed the PLO as an armed force in Lebanon, but it also paved the way for a new power. The Hezbollah – the Shia militia of southern Lebanon, trained by Iran – would emerge as a credible force over the 1990s. They proved themselves a challenge to the Israeli army, and after the evacuation of the Syrian army would dominate southern and eastern Lebanon, and do so to this day.

❀ ❀ ❀

By June 1982, Saddam Hussein had withdrawn all his troops behind the old Iraqi frontier. This was clearly an opportunity for a truce, but by now the leadership of Iran wished to destroy Hussein's regime. The Iranian assault on Iraq in July 1982, Operation Ramadan, was followed by the Fajr offensives the next year. The Iranian regime had begun calling for an Islamic revolution in Iraq and recruited several thousand Shiite Iraqis to fight alongside their forces. These men had been recruited from refugee and prisoner-of-war camps and would later become known as the Badr brigade.

These years are as close as the Islamic Middle East has yet got to a widescale Sunni versus Shia confrontation. In 1982, units of the Egyptian and Jordanian army were sent to Iraq to assist their Arab brothers, while Shia-friendly Syria remained Iran's only public ally. Over 1984–85, the war was extended to city centres, as Iran started firing Chinese rockets in retaliation for Iraq's barrage of Soviet missiles. In 1986, the Iranians made a determined attempt to capture the Shatt al-Arab with a series of assaults codenamed 'Kerbala'.

In 1986–87, this vicious struggle began to spread out into the waters of the Persian Gulf and became dangerously international. Iraqi oil tankers started camouflaging themselves as Kuwaiti to avoid attack from Iranian jets, while Kuwaiti ships began sailing under Soviet flags. In May 1987, an Iraqi jet attacked the US frigate *Stark* – by mistake. Then, on 3 July 1987, a US cruiser, USS *Vincennes*, shot down an Iranian passenger plane, flight 655 from Bandar Abbas to Dubai, which they claimed to have mistaken for an F-14 jet. It was flying within Iranian territorial waters on a well-established route when it was destroyed, killing all 290 passengers.

By this period, Iran was financially exhausted. The economy had shrunk by more than half since the revolution and had become ever more dependent on oil. Even that capacity had shrunk, as Iran was only managing to sell three-fifths as much oil as Iraq. An estimated $120 billion in capital assets had fled the country and $200 billion spent on the war. Akbar Hashemi Rafsanjani, an Iranian cleric who was trusted by Khomeini (he had been imprisoned on three occasions by SAVAK), was made deputy minister of war and negotiated a truce. Khomeini described it as 'more bitter than poison to me, but I drink this chalice of poison for the Almighty and for his satisfaction'.

Had the war with Iraq distorted the revolution? Had it left it more violent and repressive, and more in the hands of the Revolutionary Guard commanders who had worked their way up the ranks during eight bloody years of conflict? Or had the Iraq War actually saved the revolution, masking the fiscal, economic and administrative failures of an Islamic government behind a wall of patriotic fervour? Any threat from the Iranian military certainly disappeared as they proved themselves heroic defenders of Iran, while the leftist opposition was brutally purged after their opposition exposed them to the charge of treachery.

It is curious to reflect that Khomeini, a man of religion, ruled for just ten years, almost all of which were clouded by war and violent revolution. The Shah and his father, seemingly obsessed by creating a powerful military, had governed Iran through decades and decades of peace. If you travel anywhere in Iran, you become aware that every hamlet, every village, every town, every city maintains cemeteries for the martyrs who fell in the 1980–88 war with Iraq. It was a war of volunteers, conscripts and reservists that touched everyone.

❋ ❋ ❋

The Rushdie affair again shows that Khomeini was little interested in peace but, instead, determined to assume the worldwide leadership of radical Islam. As he laconically commented: 'Our people made the Revolution for Islam, not to eat more melon.'

Salman Rushdie was an unlikely target for a *fatwa*. A left-wing critic of the establishment in both Europe and the US, his writing opposed the claims of Western cultural superiority in ways that would be familiar to Iran's intellectuals; indeed, the Persian translation of his 1983 novel, *Shame*, had been awarded a prize by a jury appointed by the Iranian Islamic government. No one in Iran took that much notice of the English publication of his next book, *The Satanic Verses* – a complex novel, swirling with multiple inventions and hundreds of allusions and illusions, aside from the Islamic references of its title. But it became an unlikely cause for Asian Muslims in Britain and Pakistan, who denounced the novel's 'blasphemy'. The book was subsequently banned across thirteen countries with significant Muslim populations, including India, Pakistan and Iran.

Khomeini knew that the 'verses' wasn't an issue that the Wahhabi clerics of Saudi Arabia would take up, being concerned that too great an adulation of the person of Prophet Muhammad can distract from absolute monotheism. So, in announcing a *fatwa* – ordering Rushdie's execution – he was able to place Iran at the head of a worldwide Islamic campaign. The *fatwa* was thus an act of foreign policy and a brutal piece of realpolitik. It was read out on the radio on 14 February 1989:

> *We are from God and to God we shall return. I am informing all brave Muslims of the world that the author of The Satanic Verses, a text written, edited, and published against Islam, the Prophet of Islam, and the Qur'an, along with all the editors and publishers aware of its contents, are condemned to death. I call on all valiant Muslims wherever they may be in the world to kill them without delay, so that no one will dare insult the sacred beliefs of Muslims henceforth. And whoever is killed in this cause will be a martyr, Allah willing. Meanwhile if someone has access to the author of the book but is incapable of carrying out the execution, he should inform the people so that he is punished for his actions.*

The declaration was a sensation, as Khomeini had intended. The US and Britain, used to telling the world how to behave, what to think and how to progress, were shocked to the core by this violent challenge to freedom of speech. Britain even broke off diplomatic relations. Ten years after the Islamic revolution, Khomeini was showing the world that he was still its leading radical, and the bold protector of worldwide Islam. He was the only one who could tell the West what they could not do. He had also picked an issue that played to a Sunni Muslim audience, who were often concerned that the Shia showed more devotion to the tragic fates of Imam Ali and Imam Husayn than to the life of the Prophet Muhammad.

Tactically it worked brilliantly to stoke division between the West and the Islamic world. Its noise drowned out the achievement of the Saudi–Pakistan–US alliance, which had helped the resistance in Afghanistan drive out the Soviet army, ten years after their invasion. The Soviet withdrawal was to be announced the next day, but no one was listening to that story with the *fatwa* to talk about.

※ ※ ※

After the war, and after the death of Khomeini in June 1989, Rafsanjani constructed an Islamic economic policy. The state would invest and try to guarantee fair prices in agriculture, for both farmer and consumer. It would own and control the vital oil and defence industries and support the manufacture of cars and farm machinery. The rest of the economy would be open to free trade. Iran boomed throughout the peaceful 1990s and its economy grew by 8 per cent year on year. A strict policy of segregation in primary schools looked like a reactionary decision imposed by the clerics, but actually encouraged families in the countryside to allow their daughters to attend school. Iran had always been a highly literate nation in the cities; now literacy spread in the provinces to reach 80 per cent of the nation. In line with trends observable in other parts of the Islamic world, there was a vast expansion in universities, achieved mainly by independent colleges. And, despite the occasional outburst of rhetoric, Iran's foreign policy calmed down. It was through Iran's influence that a trio of British hostages in Lebanon were finally released in 1990–91.

Iran did not seek to benefit militarily from the Iraqi invasion of Kuwait in 1990, nor intervene when US forces and their allies liberated Kuwait, nor intervene on behalf of the Shiite rebellion against Saddam Hussein in 1991, even though two million refugees fled into Iran. Nor did Iran interfere when Iraq was invaded by the US – apart from one bizarre incident when the entire Iraqi airforce avoided destruction on the ground by taking sanctuary in Iran.

In the Afghan civil war which followed the Russian withdrawal, the influence of Iran was constructive, for it supported Massoud's Tajik resistance and the Uzbek Northern Alliance against the Taliban backed by Pakistan. The Iranians were disgusted by the Taliban's treatment of the indigenous Hazara of central Afghanistan, who were persecuted for their Shia faith. Eleven Iranians from their Mazar al Sharif consulate were massacred alongside their brother Shia by the Taliban in August 1998 – an incident which almost led to war.

So it was natural for Ayatollah Khamenei (Khomeini's successor as Supreme Ruler) and his president, Muhammad Khatemi, to condemn the horrific events of 9/11 (11 September 2001) in the strongest possible terms. Iran subsequently permitted the US to use Iranian airspace for their invasion of Taliban-controlled Afghanistan, and to some extent assisted this operation, lending their influence in the north and centre of Afghanistan. Thus, when President George W. Bush included Iran in his 29 January 2002 'Axis of Evil' speech, it was an unexpected and very public slap in the face. What drove that rhetorical decision – perhaps a desire to please the Saudis – has never been clear.

But the US would not have a monopoly on stupid presidents, especially after Iran elected Mahmud Ahmadinejad, the former mayor of Tehran, in 2005. Ahmadinejad did a good job in representing the thuggish elements of the Sepah and their neighbourhood patrols that enforced public piety to the world. His staging of a conference of Holocaust deniers brought him a rebuke by the Iranian parliament in closed session. His first election, as a poor boy in an ill-fitting suit (set against the wealthy, well-connected Rafsanjani), was probably real; his second, in 2009, was fixed by the regime. It brought the Islamic Republic to the brink of civil strife, as hundreds of thousands of frustrated citizens took to the streets in a series of huge demonstrations dubbed the Green Movement and Persian Spring. It came to the absolute brink of confrontation over 11–14 February, when the regime bused in thousands of Basij from provincial towns to confront the demonstrators in Tehran. In Syria, in 2011, a similar escalation of events would transform the Arab Spring into the Syrian civil war. Iran escaped this fate by a whisker, but in the process Ayatollah Khamenei could no longer pose as a disinterested guardian; he was seen to be part and parcel of the *nezam* – the system. In June 2013, Hassan Rouhani, an establishment lawyer, elected by just over 50 per cent of the vote, was able to open the door to mild reform of the system from within.

Rouhani served three terms as president, but his powers were limited, and his time dogged by the issue of sanctions imposed by the US and its allies over Iran's nuclear programme. It is strange to reflect on why this became such a bogey issue. Throughout the 1970s, the Shah had the full support of the US and Europe in creating a web of twenty-three nuclear power stations, which would have enabled Iran to export electricity. But the nuclear power station programme was disrupted by the Islamic revolution, and then made dangerous by the aerial warfare of the Iran–Iraq War. Only after peace was signed was it possible to continue, with the open assistance of foreign technical companies, sourced from France, Argentina, Germany and Russia. A generating station had been built at Bushehr in 1995 and was finally up and running in 2011.

But meantime the world became aware that Iran, instead of importing all its nuclear fuel, was planning to create its own enriched uranium at a nuclear installation constructed at

Natanz. As a result of this nuclear capability, trade sanctions have been imposed on Iran at the bidding of the US since 2006. Yet Ayatollah Khomeini, and then Ayatollah Khamenei, Iran's current Supreme Leader, have repeatedly declared that nuclear bombs, with their disregard for civilian targets, are against the fundamental teaching and practice of Islam. They made and upheld a similar policy decision against the use of poison gas, and against suicide bombers.

The real issue, of course, is that Iran remains an Islamic republic – and a Shiite power in opposition to the West's allies in Saudi Arabia and the Gulf. For the present, all meaningful political power is in the hands of its ayatollahs. Yet Iran has a constitution and elections and maybe one day the people will be able to select their own leadership. It is a genuine great power of the Middle East, with the largest population (86 million) after Egypt, supported by the world's second-largest gas reserves and fourth largest oil reserves.

In terms of their influence, the leadership of Iran have played a slow but brilliantly effective foreign policy. The lone Shiite power in 1979, the country now stands at the head of an alliance system that embraces Iraq, Syria, southern Lebanon, Gaza and northern Yemen, while its friendship with Russia and China offsets the opposition of the USA and Israel. Iran is the only Islamic state that is prepared to give military support to the oppressed Palestinians.

CHAPTER 19

Meccan Insurrection

The 1979 revolt, a return to Wahhabism
and the twenty-first-century reforms of MBS

For much of the twentieth century, Saudi Arabia's rulers considered potential threats to their power most likely to come from disaffected princes. So, when in September 1979 the police reported the distribution of leaflets calling for the overthrow of despotic agents, the expulsion of all foreigners and a return to the purity of Islam, it was not treated as a security priority. Then, on the first day of the Muslim year 1400 (20 November 1979), a group of five hundred fighters quietly infiltrated the Kaaba mosque at the centre of Mecca. Led by a dissident soldier called Juhyaman al-Otaybi, they declared themselves to be 'The movement of the Muslim Revolution of the Arabian Peninsula'.

The revolutionaries wanted to end the regime of 'drunkards who led a dissolute life in luxurious palaces', to end oppression, corruption and bribery, and to return the Islamic community to 'the golden age of the first century of the Companions'. They were well armed and well trained, many of them having served with al-Otaybi in the National Guard. Al-Otaybi himself came from one of the traditional Hijra settlements of the Ikhwan and his father had fought alongside other members of his tribe at the 1929 Battle of Sabillah. Al-Otaybi was a genuinely pious young man who had studied the Koran and the *hadith*, consulted scholars and set up small study groups with students from the Islamic university. He had even consulted Bin Baz, Saudi Arabia's most popular Islamic scholar.

Crown Prince Fahd – 'Mr Modernity' – was in Tunisia at the time of the attack, while Prince Abdullah, commander of the National Guard, was in Morocco. The first attempt to silence the rebels, led by a hundred armed agents from the Ministry of Interior, was beaten off with contemptible ease by marksmen posted in the minarets. Government forces then evacuated the city of Mecca and over the next two weeks launched a number of attempts to capture the mosque. The regime quickly learned how few of the men receiving their salaries were prepared to die in defence of the monarchy. It also became clear that there was a degree of emotional sympathy, including amongst the clergy of the Saudi regime, for the diehard, young rebels.

The rebel fighters were still in armed possession of the Holy Mosque as the month of Muharram arrived. The Shia of Saudi Arabia's eastern provinces, encouraged by the example of their brethren in Iran, decided to take to the streets with their Ashura processions. In this state of heightened tension, the Saudi National Guard attacked an Ashura procession with clubs, so the Shia defended themselves with stones, after which trigger-happy guards opened fire, killing seventeen and wounding a hundred more. In Tehran the radio announced that 'the ruling regime in Saudi Arabia wears Muslim clothing, but inwardly represents the US body, mind and terrorism'.

It wasn't exactly a call to revolution, but, given the troubled situation within Saudi Arabia, it was never forgiven. The leader of the Saudi Shia community, Sheikh Hassan al-Saffar, who had a consistent record of preaching non-violence, felt it necessary to flee the Kingdom. The Kingdom's Shia had legitimate complaints. They had never been given any good jobs in either the army, police or civil administration, nor ever been permitted in the foreign service or to train as pilots. They were, however, well represented in the tougher jobs within the Saudi oil industry. Eastern Saudi Arabia is officially 45 per cent Shia, but in places like Qataf they number 75 per cent of the population.

In Mecca the rebel fighters made a fortress out of the copious basement of the Kaaba mosque. The Saudi government did not want to damage the mosque and most certainly did not want to be filmed doing so. The image of a Saudi army attacking the Kaaba would have linked the royal family with the universally despised Yazid, Second Caliph of the Umayyads. The rebels were only finally subdued when stun gas was pumped into the basement (on the technical advice of French counter-terrorist experts) and by Saudi forces beefed up by several battalions of Pakistan's special services. Al-Otaybi was captured and he and sixty-two other rebels were beheaded in the public squares of eight different cities on 9 January 1980.

Having executed al-Oytabi, the Saudi regime decided that they needed to embrace his Islamist programme if they were to stay in power. All the modernisations of the last decade were put on hold and then reversed. Women newsreaders were removed; singers were veiled and then removed altogether as all public musical performances disappeared from state media. Cinemas were closed down; and in universities the science, geology and world history courses were replaced by the history of Islam and the study of the Koran. In the meantime, the heirs of Ibn Saud's local committees for the Promotion of Virtue and the Prevention of Vice, the puritanical Mutawa, were given more authority. They started to inspect the identity cards of married couples in shopping malls to prove they were not on an immoral outing, which led to a need to carry a copy of your marriage certificate, as most of the women of central Arabia keep their maiden names. Sweet shops were policed during Ramadan and a relentless high-water mark of puritanical disapproval even required that only men over twenty-one be permitted in a coffee shop, lest they be corrupted by the indiscreet conversation of their elders. There was never a formal law against women driving in Saudi Arabia, or women attending sporting events, or the approved length of a Hijab veil. Public decency was left in the hands of the Mutawa, which is often translated as 'religious police', though this term overstates their literacy and training.

❀❀❀

The Soviet invasion of Afghanistan at the end of 1979 was a gift to the embattled royal regime. They encouraged the next generation of ardent young Saudi Islamist men to go to Afghanistan to assist the Mujahadin, or to Pakistan to lecture refugees in the tented camps. Friday sermons in the Kingdom could concentrate on the violence of Communist atrocities and collecting funds for poor Muslim communities, be they Palestinian, Afghan, Bosnian, Kashmiri or Bulgarian.

For the next ten years there was a successful alliance between the US, Saudi Arabia and Pakistan, fuelled by the suffering of the people of Afghanistan. Saudi Arabia and the US were also on the same side during the Iran–Iraq War and were thrown even more tightly together by the Iraqi invasion of Kuwait in 1990. However, the build-up of US troops in eastern Saudi Arabia (preparing the way for the 'liberation' of Kuwait) appalled the young generation of ardent Saudi Islamists, who had begun returning home after the last Russian troops evacuated Afghanistan in 1989.

Osama bin Laden, who masterminded the 9/11 attacks on the US, was typical of this generation. Those tragic events on 11 September 2001 exposed the dichotomy within the heart of Saudi Arabia, which had always struggled to balance the passionate ardour of Muslim Bedouin warriors with obedience to a hereditary monarchy, and striven to become the leading Muslim nation whilst allying with the US. It was inevitable that some of the hijackers who struck against America on 9/11 would be Arabs, but fifteen Saudi Arabian nationals out of nineteen terrorists was a dauntingly high percentage.

And 9/11 was only the most dramatic instance within a longer pattern of conflict, which included bombing campaigns within Saudi Arabia in 1995, 2003 and 2004. Indeed, between 2003 and 2005 a street war was fought out between the security forces and so called 'al-Qaeda' Islamist fighters, with 200 casualties inflicted by the terrorists and 600 arrests by the security services. It was also a Saudi propaganda department which felt the need to make up and disseminate some of those 9/11 conspiracy theories – those pseudo-scientific rumours about a series of internal explosions within the twin towers, or the holiday suddenly given to the CIA or Jewish office workers that day – in order to take some of the heat off the Kingdom.

In March 2002, however, there was an incident that is now considered a turning point in Saudi Arabian domestic politics. As a fire broke out in a girl's school in Mecca, the Mutawa not only stopped male firefighters going into the school, but even drove the girl students back into the building for being inadequately dressed in a public space. Fifty of these students were injured, and fifteen girls were burnt to death. The Mutawa were immeasurably damaged and discredited.

❀❀❀

Prince Abdullah, one of the many sons of Ibn Saud, was the dominant figure in Saudi Arabia from 1995 until 2015. He was the power behind the throne of his half-brother King Fahd and then ruled himself from 2005. As a young man, Abdullah had commanded the National Guard, which was scattered across every province and recruited men from every tribe. This job made him much more at ease with traditional Saudi society than his intellectual and worldly brothers, allowing him the confidence to start on the slow transformation of Saudi Arabia from an Islamist theocracy to an Arab nation state. He started bringing the religious police and the Wahhabi *ulema* under his authority, while very modestly increasing the role of women and non-royal technocrats. Abdullah continued the traditional Saudi foreign policy of a firm alliance with the US and a close understanding with Pakistan, a Sunni power with military muscle that could be lent to the Kingdom at a moment's notice.

This close alliance with Pakistan was a useful geographical counter in King Abdullah's confrontations with Iran. Abdullah viewed Palestine and Lebanon as provinces of Greater Arabia and opposed the influence of Iran in these regions almost as much for its Persian identity as its Shia faith. Abdullah disliked the Iranian connection with Hamas and was infuriated by the strong alliance between Iran and the Hezbollah in Lebanon. He seemed unaware that both Hamas and Hezbollah had risen to their position of influence and popularity because they had confronted Israel with conviction. Viewed from his perspective, there had been a continuous advance in the influence of Iran in the Arab Middle East, a Shiite Crescent of which his namesake, King Abdullah of Jordan, would also speak.

When the Arab Spring of 2011 erupted, the Saudi monarchy had much to fear. First, President Ben Ali of Tunisia, then President Mubarak of Egypt, then the regime of Colonel Gaddafi in Libya, fell, before civil war broke out in Syria. It is astonishing that there was no major threat to the stability of the Kingdom of Saudi Arabia. One factor is that it is seemingly immune to street demonstrations; the country has no urban square, no historic grid of streets for any group of protesters to march into. It's a nation of cars and motorways and malls.

If popular democracy were to emerge in Saudi Arabia, it would expose the potential strength of the Arab Shia population along the entire shore of the Persian Gulf, and any self-assertion would threaten the political monopoly enjoyed by the ruling families of Saudi Arabia and the Gulf emirates. When the Arab Spring demonstrations reached the island of Bahrain – whose population is 60 per cent Shia but ruled by an autocratic Sunni emir – King Abdullah encouraged and assisted his neighbour, Al Khalifa, in crushing them. After three days of street protests, the tented encampment sheltering the protesters was flattened. Fifty armoured cars injured 300 protesters and killed four on a night that became known as Black Thursday. In the ensuing security crackdown, fifty Shia mosques were destroyed and the emirate occupied by the armed forces of Saudi Arabia, Kuwait and the UAE – once again strengthened by Baluch regiments from Pakistan. It was a convincing demonstration of a club of royal Sunni autocrats working together to destroy the call for democracy and freedom. It was denounced with greater conviction by Iran and Turkey than by any of the Western powers.

❀ ❀ ❀

Revolutionary change in Saudi Arabia came instead from an unlikely direction. In 2015, King Abdullah died and his half-brother Prince Salman, the last surviving son of Ibn Saud, inherited the throne. King Salman had many children from his three wives but had fallen under the influence of one of his youngest children, Prince Muhammad bin Salman. At the age of twenty-four, MBS, as he was known, became his father's principal political advisor.* Using a tactical alliance with Bin Nayef, the prince in charge of the Ministry of Interior, the old king and his headstrong son ripped their way through the traditional fabric of the Kingdom. Princely dynasties that had controlled their ministries like so many feudal duchies were sacked, as MBS brought military, economic and security powers under his control. Promoted over his elder brothers and hundreds of more experienced cousins, MBS took little more than two years to deliver a dazzling series of much-needed social reforms. Saudi women were permitted to drive and to attend sports matches, public concerts with female singers were staged, and bookshop and cinema chains appeared. The legal role of males as 'public guardians' over their female relatives was weakened, and the social tyranny of the Mutawa, the local militia/religious police, ended. As MBS asserted: 'We want to go back to what we were: moderate Islam. Saudi Arabia was not like this before 1979.'

MBS did not stop at social liberalisation, either. New immigration laws were passed and new economic zones imagined. Then, on 4 November 2017, MBS led an anti-corruption drive that swept up 500 previously untouchable members of Saudi

---

* MBS was a deliberate reference to the Crown Prince's political role model, Mohamed bin Zayed Al Nahyan, aka MBZ, the modernising, reformer prince of the United Arab Emirates.

society, who were detained in a luxury hotel until hundreds of billions of dollars of corrupt payments were recovered.

These social, economic and fiscal reforms were not, however, matched by any political reforms. MBS may be a free thinker but he is also an autocrat burdened with princely entitlement. The whole world became aware of how mad that can make a man after an outspoken émigré Saudi journalist, Jamal Khashoggi, was lured to the Saudi Consulate in Istanbul, where he was killed and then chopped into pieces. The incident gave MBS pariah status in the West, at least for a time. Seen within the introverted palace traditions of Saudi Arabia, however, the incident is not so shocking, nor even surprising. Jamal Khashoggi's grandfather had been Ibn Saud's trusted doctor and his uncle was a famously wealthy Saudi arms dealer and broker. For most of his life, he was considered a regime insider, who had taken up leading jobs in the media, probably including intelligence work. So it is possible that members of the Saudi security services considered Khashoggi an out-of-control former officer, if not a traitor in the making.

Notwithstanding, MBS remains very popular with his young Saudi subjects, who respect the fast pace of his social reforms after decades of good intentions. They take pride, too, in Saudi Arabia's new role in world sport. The country has essentially bought golf, taking over the US PGA tour, and is now turning its attention to global football using the seemingly unlimited resources of its Public Investment Fund. To balance his future political stability, MBS needs to assert a strong Saudi nationalist platform to offset his destruction of the old Saudi alliance with Islamist Ikhwan warriors and Wahhabi clerics. They may yet try to strike back, if his reforms weaken, and there are many disappointed royal cousins who might assist them.

This reality is more than enough to explain the arrogant and cruel acts of recent Saudi Arabian foreign policy: the military invasion into Huthi-controlled Yemen, and the manufactured 'Qatar crisis' which attempted to bully the last independent-minded emirate on the Persian Gulf to line up obediently as part of the Saudi team, and not to flirt with Turkey, Iran, the Taliban and the Muslim Brotherhood.

There was also the so-called Lebanon crisis, when MBS seems to have forcibly detained the prime minister of Lebanon, Saad Hariri, in order to dictate his pacts within the country. MBS wants a Sunni Muslim leader like Saad Hariri sooner or later to abandon the political truce with Shiite Hezbollah, the ally of Iran. The Saudis have poured money into rebuilding civil-war-damaged Lebanon and this was their asking price.

These imperious acts all make sense from the perspective of Saudi Arabia. They are attacks on regimes that have some sort of cultural sympathy, military alliance, or other perceived connection with Iran. MBS is deliberately fuelling this tension in order to win the role of leader of the Arabs. He aspires to create a grouping of nations that will stand together under the leadership of Saudi Arabia. Enmity with Shiite Iran on one level is no more than a tool to help construct some sort of 'United States of Arabia'. But it also has an internal logic, for there is always a fear that the Shia population along the Persian Gulf shore will some day assert themselves, especially if democratic freedoms allow this hard-working, oppressed minority to express themselves.

❀ ❀ ❀

The future for Saudi Arabia looks troubled but interesting. MBS (or any other Saudi leader) knows that the rivalry between Sunni Arabia and Shiite Iran is a powerful reality and can be manipulated for political ends. Most of his predecessors have done the same. They backed Iraq in the murderous Iran–Iraq War, which may have fuelled a murky incident in 1987, when 300 Iranian Shiite pilgrims were killed in Mecca during the Haj. In the historically framed imagination of the Shia, the suppression of the Arab Spring in Bahrain in February 2011 was just another cycle of the Kerbala tragedy.

The execution of one of the leading Saudi Shiite clerics, Nimr Baqir al-Nimr, on New Year's Day 2016, added the blood of yet another holy martyr to the Shiite cause. Al-Nimr was an outspoken but scholarly leader of the Friday prayers in his hometown of Al-Awamiyah, in eastern Saudi Arabia, where his family farmed. He had completed his theological education in Syria and Iran amongst moderate teachers. He was a critic of autocracy wherever it was found, be it in Shiite-friendly Syria, Bahrain or Saudi Arabia, and endorsed the need for free elections. What seems to have specifically caused his death was his idea that the eastern provinces of Saudi Arabia were as entitled to call on foreign intervention to set them free as Kuwait had been. He was condemned to death by a court for the crime of 'seeking foreign meddling' and 'disobeying the rulers'. Despite an international campaign, pursued in the UN and through Amnesty, he was beheaded (along with forty-six other condemned prisoners) on New Year's Day, 2016. His body was not given to his family. The news of his execution caused riots throughout the Shiite world.

A Greater Arabia might be a force for stability in the region and might yet prove more tolerant of diversity of belief and different ethnicities than a smaller, more vulnerable nation. Even the briefest glance at Saudi history shows how close they were to achieving this on two occasions over the last two hundred years (1803 and 1922–26). But, in the process of creating this state, there is the danger of a second Iran–Arab war being fought over battle-scarred Iraq and the strategic waters of the Persian Gulf.

CHAPTER 20

Afghan jihadis

*The Russian invasion of 1979, the American war post-9/11
and the rise, fall and rise again of the Taliban*

Afghanistan, locked into the mountains of Central Asia,
has never been considered part of the Middle East, but
with the Russian invasion of 1979, and then the arrival of
America and its allies post-9/11, it became a battlefield
that drew in half the world. Over four decades, its highland
tribesmen, in their long-shirted *shalwar qameez* and Chi-
trali caps, have fought against superpowers equipped with
tanks, helicopter gunships, drones and precision bombing,
with more than half a million casualties and five million
refugees driven from their homeland. But the fighting was
never a straightforward case of Russian military aggression
imposing Communism on a conquered people, nor America
imposing an equally unwanted liberal democracy on a traditional Muslim highland society. All of these conflicts began
amid Afghan civil war.

The first round of foreign intervention started in 1979, when
the Russians involved themselves in a schism between two
factions of the Afghan Communist Party – the Khalq versus the
Parcham. With the support of the Russian 40th Army, the milder
of the two factions of the Communist Party of Afghanistan
took over. They governed the big cities and fielded an army of
up to 40,000 Afghan soldiers. In the daylight, the government

controlled all the principal roads and major valleys. At night, these passed over into the hands of the resistance, who felt entitled to attack not just garrison posts but all the outposts of the government, be they police stations, schools, generating stations or industrial complexes.

Within a few years, the more liberal-minded entrepreneurial middle class had fled from Afghanistan's small towns and cities to the safety of Kabul or to neighbouring Iran or Pakistan. Only the semi-literate peasant farmers remained on their land, ever more deeply attached to the certainties of life: to Islam, to their tribe and their traditions. The mountains (which means about 80 per cent of Afghanistan) were effectively in the hands of the resistance – the Mujahadin – holding out despite the total air superiority of the Russians.

The Pakistan frontier was the supply zone for the Mujahadin. Refugee camps established along the border could nurse soldiers back from conflict and protect their families while they fought. The supply routes and the camps also became battle grounds for Afghan factionalism, as fourteen rival groups waged their own war against both the Afghan Communists and their Russian allies, and sometimes on each other. Money poured in from the US, Saudi Arabia, the Gulf and European states. Volunteers from the Arab world also came to run hospitals, refugee camps, orphanages and supply military aid.

From 1980 to 1985, the Russian army was on the offensive. Operations were launched to cut the supply of arms from Pakistan and to clear the Mujahadin from such strategic valleys as the Panjshir, which commanded the principal highway north from Kabul. Russian troop numbers never exceeded 108,000 men, but, due to the length of occupation and troop movements, more than 400,000 young men would experience service in Afghanistan: of these, 14,453 were killed and 53,000 wounded.

In 1986, two things would alter the nature of the war. Mikhail Gorbachev became president of the Soviet Union and determined to withdraw Russian troops, and the Mujahadin became equipped with Stinger missiles (hand-held ground-to-air missiles). This changed the tactical imbalance of Soviet air command, with 35 Soviet aircraft and 63 helicopters destroyed in a few years of guerrilla war. Between 1988 and 1989, the Russian army was withdrawn.

To the surprise of most observers, the Afghan Communist regime succeeded in keeping its control of the cities and major roads. The Afghan secret police (KHAD) had established militias in the provinces and set up a number of deals which recognised the authority of tribal leaders. The final collapse of this regime did not occur until the spring of 1992 after the Soviet Union had itself imploded and Russia's new leader, Boris Yeltsin, ended the last trickle of economic aid to the Afghanistan regime. A decisive turning point came in March 1992, when the warlord in command of the Uzbek northern third of the country, General Dostum, deserted the regime and joined the Mujahadin alliance.

The four years after Russia withdrew saw half a dozen rival Mujahadin armies battle for supremacy in a savage civil war that devastated the city of Kabul, which had hitherto managed to survive. It was a pitiless, dispiriting period, marked by sudden shifts in the alliances between various warlords. This was not jihad – holy war – and proved to be an even more destructive period than the ten-year resistance, as the armaments acquired for resisting Russian aggression, and captured from government arsenals, were turned against fellow Afghans. Local warlords, deprived of a foreign enemy, were revealed as capricious, greedy gangsters propped up by illegal tolls, checkpoints and savagery.

This civil war was finally ended by the Taliban, who had first emerged in the summer of 1994. Their triumph can only be understood as a reaction to this anarchic period, as local councils of rural clerics, often respected veterans of the struggle, came together to provide an alternative to the rule of predatory gunmen. The first city to fall to – or to be liberated by – the Taliban was Kandahar in November 1994. Within two months they had advanced to take control of twelve of the twenty-eight provinces of Afghanistan, and by September 1996 they had fought their way into Kabul. To celebrate their victory, the old Communist leader, Mohammad Najibullah, was abducted from his hiding place in the UN compound and shot.

※ ※ ※

The Taliban militia was initially composed of 15,000 young war orphans, who stood outside tribal loyalties or obedience to any of the Mujahadin factions. They formed a sort of united Pathan identity, shorn of its tribal factionalism and feudal power structures. The war orphans had mostly been brought up in madrasas – Islamic schools established near the refugee camps and often funded by the Deobandi, a Sunni revivalist movement.* The Taliban followed the leadership of Mullah Omar, who was first acclaimed emir by his young warriors at Kandahar, symbolically draped in the cloak of the Prophet Muhammad kept in a shrine near the mosque.

Brought up through war and suffering, the Taliban delighted in their role as holy warriors engaged in jihad and followed a somewhat unlettered and simplistic desire to

---

* The Deobandi emerged in India in the eighteenth century as followers of Waliullah Dehlawi (1703–62), a contemporary of Muhammad ibn Abd al-Wahhab at Medina. They share the Wahhabis' purity and dislike of saints. In the 1980s and 1990s, they were heavily funded in Pakistan by Saudi Arabia.

return to the times of the first community of believers. Tele-vision, music, images and cinema were banned as they were not mentioned in the Koran, yet they delighted in machine guns, mobile phones and motorised jeeps. They enforced the veiling of women and encouraged men to grow beards and avoid non-Muslims. They would become notorious through public executions and the destruction of what they considered to be idols. They had much in common with the Ikhwan holy warriors who had established Saudi Arabia in the 1920s. Few of their habits made any serious interruption to the traditional lifestyle and subsistence poverty of the vil-lagers, who, with the Taliban, shared an essential distrust of the corruption and administrative arrogance associated with the towns and cities.

The Taliban, in their first period of rule in the 1990s, were recognised as the legitimate government by just three states: Saudi Arabia, Pakistan and the United Arab Emirates. They never succeeded in destroying the power of Ahmed Massoud, the leader of the Tajik resistance in the Panjshir valley, and required the help of al-Qaeda terrorists – who had been given bases in the country – for his assassination. Massoud, who was a natural rival to be the leader of Afghanistan, was killed just before the 9/11 terrorist attacks.

❊ ❊ ❊

Al-Qaeda believed that the 9/11 attacks would provoke the US to intervene in Afghanistan, leading to a world war that would eventually be won by the Islamist militants. In the event, the US invaded in October 2001, backed by virtually the whole world, including, as noted, Iran. Within months, the military authority of the Taliban was snapped and a regime based on the traditional tribal leadership was re-created by the US.

This new regime, well-funded and armed by America for twenty years, fatally undermined its credibility with larcenous levels of corruption, and unleashed a third round of civil war, led by a resurgent Taliban resistance, based as ever in the highland regions. In a bizarre rerun of the Soviet period of occupation, American airpower now supplied the same network of garrison outposts from the same airbases, allowing the central government to control the cities, the big roads and the provincial capitals by daylight. Meanwhile, some 80,000 Taliban fighters ruled the mountains, the night and ultimately commanded the respect of the rural population. After twenty years of escalation, Americans of both political parties tired of war and began talks with the Taliban. On 29 February 2020, the Trump government signed a truce with Mullah Abdul Ghari Baradar, agreeing to leave Afghanistan within fourteen months. Once it was clear that the American forces were really intending to withdraw, the regime collapsed like a house of cards during August 2021.

Abdul Ghari had been born in 1968. He had fought against the Russians from 1979 and against the Americans from 2001. He has enduring connections with the Pakistani intelligence services and is considered one of the historic forty co-founders of the Taliban alongside Mullah Omar. He is from the Popalzai Pashtun tribe, which has often provided the leaders of Afghanistan. Yet Ghari and his victorious Taliban, once in occupation of Kabul, were immediately faced with their own provincial rebellion, led by an ISIS-affiliated group.

❀ ❀ ❀

Afghanistan is a nation made up of five different ethnic groups: Pathan, Tajik, Uzbek, Baluch and Hazara. The nation has always been centred on the power of the Pashtun tribes, though by a bizarre trick of history half of their homeland is incorporated into north-west Pakistan. To make things still more complicated, the Pashtun majority have been spread all over the nation as part of a nineteenth-century policy of nation building, so it is virtually impossible to separate the five ethnic regions into a self-governing confederation of equals. The Uzbeks speak a Turkic-derived language and have always thought of themselves as militantly Sunni. The Tajiks are part of the Iranian language group and consider themselves the most civilised. The Hazara have historically sat on the bottom of the ladder of power and are ethnically allied to the Mongols. They are a much-persecuted community of Shia and occupy the central mountain plateau. Iran has always done its best to try and protect the Hazara.

Afghanistan has always been virtually ungovernable. It is a place of astonishing beauty: mountains upon mountains, riven into thousands of regions by highland valleys, vast scree slopes, wind-blasted plateaus and orchard-lined river valleys. But its own resources are not sufficient to fund a centralised state. Any ruler wishing to govern Afghanistan can only do this by allying themselves, to a greater or lesser degree, with some outside power, who can subsidise government salaries and repair bridges after they have been toppled by earthquakes or floods. Foreign diplomacy is a vital aspect for any Afghan leader wishing to balance the books. In the past they often contrived to offset the influence of various neighbours against one another. In a perennial paradox, as well as expelling foreign invaders, the other essential task that any leader of Afghanistan needs to be able to do is to attract them.

CHAPTER 21

The New Ottomans

Military coups, Islamic popularism and a
yearning to once again lead the Islamic world

The 1970s saw Turkey on the brink of civil war, as political parties fought for dominance. Rival marches were attacked and bombed, leaders were abducted and assassinated, so that by the decade's end more than 5,000 Turks had been killed through political violence. This was a familiar Cold War story of Left against Right, with an additional Turkish element as to who was the true heir to Ataturk's secular republic. The left wanted to get rid of the heavy-handed friendship of the US and advance the socialist dream, while the right dreamed of a pan-Turkic commonwealth to replace the Soviet Union in Central Asia. Those who looked to a return to traditional Islamic values were on the outer fringes. Meantime, there was rampant inflation and a diplomatic impasse following the Turkish military invasion of Cyprus in July 1974.[*]

On 12 September 1980, the Turkish military took control. Previous military coups in 1960 and 1971 were not popular on the streets, but it is now reluctantly conceded that the 1980 coup may have averted civil war. It was impeccably organised by the Chief of the Defence Staff, working through the official

---

[*] The invasion of Cyprus came in reaction to an internal Greek coup on that island, after the fall of the Greek military junta of 'The Colonels' in 1973.

command structure of his colleagues in the navy, airforce, gendarmerie and all four army commands: 1st at Istanbul, 2nd at Malatya, 3rd at Erzincan and 4th at Izmir.

The generals locked up 650,000 activists and banned a total of one and a half million citizens from holding public office. Culturally, it was a sledgehammer, but they did have a political programme up their sleeve, which was fulfilled by a junior government minister, Turgut Ozal, whom they appointed prime minister. Ozal was an unusual character, who understood the language of both the Left and Right, having worked as a trade union official, in state planning and also in the World Bank. He was often compared to Margaret Thatcher, a driven individual from a provincial background with sufficient vision to push through fiscal reforms and neoliberal legislation favourable to business enterprise and foreign investment. These, the so-called '24 January Decisions', were quickly enacted, and after three years had proved sufficiently successful for Ozal to stand and win the election of 1983. He and his Anavatan ('Motherland') Party dominated Turkish politics for the next decade.

Ozal tried to weaken the statist element within Turkish culture, to make government ministers accountable, and pursued a noisy but pacific foreign policy, looking to defuse the historic tension with such old adversaries as Greece and Armenia. His liberalisation of Turkish society also allowed the emergence of a number of mildly Islamist democratic parties. This was not popular with the military establishment, who attempted to deny this new political reality with various decrees – the so-called 'paper coups' attempting to nullify electoral victories by any Islamist democratic party.

The slow collapse of the Soviet Union pulled the Turkish Republic in two new directions – one east and one west – both of which looked very promising. To the east, the new Turkic-speaking nations in Central Asia offered up the promise of new friendships, new allies and new trading alliances. The most friendly and open of these are Azerbaijan, Kazakhstan and Kyrgyzstan, with Turkmenistan and Uzbekistan remaining interested but wary. Meanwhile, from the north and west, the citizens of the formerly Soviet Balkans poured into Turkey to shop for its produce. Ozal joked that Turkey would soon be able to reclaim Thrace, with no need for another round of Balkan wars. The Turks would just reach into their back pocket and buy back Bulgaria. This was a period when the European Common Market was expanding its geographical frontiers ever eastwards. To the liberal elite of Turkey, living in such Westernised and successful cities as Istanbul, Ankara and Izmir, it seemed possible that Turkey might be included.

If social, political, economic, financial and cultural indices had been used to assess a nation's fitness to join the EU, Turkey would have been placed above all the Balkan nations. It was also a lynchpin of NATO that had protected Western Europe throughout the Cold War. However, the bitter antagonism of Greece and Cyprus, and the residual fear of Turkey and suspicion of Islam across Central Europe, made this dream impossible. The rejection of Turkey's candidacy by the European Union, contrasting with the enthusiasm with which any backward Eastern European country with a Christian past was welcomed into the fold, undoubtedly put a powerful reality check on how far the process of Westernisation could take Turkey. It now had to be asked: for what ends?

❊ ❊ ❊

The triumph of Western capitalism in Turkey also proved to be short-lived. Throughout the 1990s, Turkish economic growth and a budgetary deficit was underwritten by massive foreign investment. When this was partially withdrawn, it brought the country to its knees, followed by the collapse of the Turkish banks, which went into a self-inflicted tailspin in 2001. The banks had been gambling profitably for many years on currency exchange rates, which then went horribly wrong. For those with fiscal prescience, 2001 was the Turkish prelude to the crash of the entire Western banking system seven years later in September 2008.

Perhaps too much can be made of the double meltdown of the two Cold War empires. The collapse of the Soviet-Socialist system in 1989 was followed two decades later by the 2008 collapse of the capitalist utopia. It did, however, make it the right time for a Third Way to gain some respectful attention. In Turkey this Third Way had been patiently waiting in the wings: a return to traditional Islamic values, an ethical state, a moral duty to pay tax, combined with a healthy delight in free trade, suspicion of usury and respect for family values. This also came with a renewed respect for the achievements of the Ottoman and Seljuk empires. It was a very attractive package, and easy to combine with the mild state socialism then prevalent in Western Europe, with its public-private partnerships.

In Turkey's particular case, much of the electorate had long been wishing to correct the secular excesses of Ataturk's republic way before the collapse of the Turkish banks. In 1950, Adnan Menderes had won the very first free and fair election with a combination of economic liberalism, an independent but pro-Western foreign policy and a partial return to some of the old Islamic values. Under his leadership, thousands of mosques that had been closed down under the republic were allowed to re-open and the much-hated Turkish language call to prayer was replaced with the original Arabic of the Koran. It was too early, perhaps, for such changes. In 1960, the generals removed Adnan Menderes in a coup, after which he was tried and hung.

To understand how the thread of Islamic political ambition was kept alive through the twentieth century, resulting in the creation of Erdogan's Islamist state, it is important to become familiar, above all, with two key figures – Said Nursi and Fethullah Gulen.

※ ※ ※

In 1960, the same year that Menderes was executed, Said Nursi, a revered Islamic scholar, travelled to the sacred city of Urfa to die, close to the holy birthplace of the prophet Abraham. The generals, concerned that his tomb might become a place of veneration, arranged for his body to be reburied secretly in the hills, in a place known only unto God.

Said Nursi is today something of a litmus test for the inner opinions of Turks. Those loyal to the old secular republic established by Ataturk cannot tolerate any mention of the man. But, for Turks from the poor farming villages and small towns of the Anatolian interior, he is the unsung scholar saint. To his followers he is *Ustad* ('Master') and *Bediuzzaman* ('Wonder of the Age'). To make him a little more controversial, he was a Kurd, born in the far eastern province of Bitlis, where he was educated in the traditional schools of Islamic learning. As a young scholar, he learned Ottoman Turkish as his third language, after his native Kurdish, and Koranic Arabic. He combined an appreciation of modern science with traditional Islamic scholarship, though his central concern was to encourage a moral life. His handwritten commentaries on the Koran, created between 1913 and 1950, are at the heart of the Turkish Islamist movement. He was imprisoned, banished and then placed under house arrest, but his vast corpus of writings survived decades of government persecution. For years they were to be copied out by hand by a small inner circle and secretly circulated among an ever-expanding group of followers. His *Risale-i Nur* – which fill a bookshelf – were not legally printed until Adnan Menderes permitted this in the 1950s.

Said Nursi's teachings fostered a slow-burning provincial resistance to the secular decrees of the republic. His followers had to be cautious, so restricted their energy to running their own businesses, endowing schools and educational charities, and avoided political office and the military. As the gradual economic transformation of Turkey saw illiterate peasant communities from the interior become educated and migrate to the cities, they never lost their traditional attachment to Islam, and were the nucleus from which moderate Islamist political parties emerged in the 1980s. In the Middle East, this sort of social pattern, of a new generation of professionals emerging from the hard-working and pious lower middle class, was the backbone for the spread of the Muslim Brotherhood.

Like the Muslim Brotherhood in Egypt and Syria, the young Islamist politicians and technocrats of Turkey grew up in a society where you needed to hide your full political agenda if you wanted to stay out of jail. And it was from this background that men such as Fethullah Gulen and Recep Tayyip Erdogan emerged.

Fethullah Gulen was inspired by Said Nursi, and his life story shows how traditional Islam survived beneath the radar in the Anatolian heartland. Gulen followed the example of his father and mother, who both taught the Koran in a private capacity so as not to irritate state officials. He was born in 1941 in north-eastern Anatolia, and at eighteen was appointed an imam as part of the liberalising reforms of Adnan Menderes. He retained this job until 1981, but a state-appointed imam was not a prestigious figure just then. In popular imagination they were associated with funerals and stood somewhere between a school janitor and a public notary. They had little in common with an Ottoman Mufti, an urban scholar, presiding over courts and public ceremonials and consulted by everyone.

Gulen and others worked within a network of Muslim educational charities, the most successful of which were a series of provincial tutorial colleges called Isik Evler ('light houses'), which crammed students to achieve the grades to get into university. Undergraduates, especially from poor families, could then make use of dormitory hostels and reading rooms in the cities that were linked to these colleges. Such students were encouraged to form reading groups to study the commentaries of Said Nursi and other Islamist thinkers. They kept in touch with each other through study centres, postgraduate fellowships, cultural institutes and volunteer summer jobs. Over the 1980s this network grew into the six-million-strong Gulen movement, which liked to describe itself as Hizmet ('service') to the community.

The Gulenists looked after their own, nominating one another to sit on a school board or promoting themselves within a ministry or corporation. They supported inter-faith conferences and arranged tours of Turkey for foreign journalists and young politicians, visiting community hospitals as well as ancient monuments. At the height of his rhetorical powers, Fethullah Gulen could pack any football stadium in any province of Turkey with his supporters. I remember seeing him hold the Koran aloft, and just whisper 'Orphan, orphan, orphan!' to a vast crowd. Both the speaker and his tens of thousands of followers were reduced to inarticulate tears, for, in their eyes, the word of God as contained in the Koran was a neglected orphan in modern Turkey.

In 1998, Gulen left to take up residence in America, avoiding the anti-Islamic crackdown that had been ordered by the military. The Gulen movement had been very successful in the US, working within the Turkish expatriate community and had developed a chain of 150 charter schools (including such brand names as Harmony and Cosmos), assisted by a string of think-tank charities: the Niagara Foundation, the Rumi Forum and the Emerging Democracies Institute.

It may be that Gulen dreamed of being summoned back home by his people from exile like the Ayatollah Khomeini, to be greeted at the airport by millions of supporters. His movement was never quite a cult, but like the Muslim Brotherhood there was a culture of secrecy. It has been labelled 'a charismatic aristocracy' controlled by a trusted core of male followers (the Jemaa), whose decisions were screened from the world by layers of 'friends' and 'sympathisers'.

❄ ❄ ❄

The first legal Islamist political parties in Turkey were founded in 1983 and survived a few years before being judged unconstitutional or undemocratic by the secular regime. The breakthrough year for political Islam in Turkey was 2001, the year the banking system collapsed, when the AKP (Justice and Development) Party was established by Recep Tayyip Erdogan, drawing on members of earlier Islamist parties.

Erdogan was born in Istanbul in 1954, and as a young man played for the local Kasimpasa football club – he was nicknamed 'Beckenbauer' for his tendency to plot attacking moves from supposedly defensive positions. He entered local politics, and in 1994 became a young, hard-working and corruption-free mayor of Istanbul for four years. Erdogan was a man of the people who had also endured his fair share of the humiliating authority of the secular state, having once been locked up for reciting a poem. He then won an outright majority in the 2002 national elections, taking two-thirds of the seats in parliament. This convincing support was confirmed two years later in the 2004 local elections, when AKP swept to power in all the Anatolian provinces, their one surviving secular rival, the Republican Party, holding on to its core constituency, the cities and towns in the west.

It was an extraordinary moment in the history of the Middle East. An Islamist political party had won a free election but did not tear up the democratic constitution. Instead, it proved itself an efficient government, pushing through dozens of grand projects and achieving an impressive expansion in the national infrastructure: motorways, tunnels, bridges, dams, canals, water and electricity. Yet, though the AKP won election after election, they never felt secure enough, and slowly but ruthlessly crushed independent voices (imprisoning many journalists), whilst building up their own monopolistic control of all channels of the media.

Erdogan also felt isolated internationally, with Qatar the country's only consistent ally. Turkey's diplomatic isolation did not have to be so complete. Erdogan is a strident speaker when it comes to the claims of Turkey to be the natural leader of the Middle East, or indeed beyond ('Turkey will be the leader of the Islamic world ... The mosques are our barracks, the domes our helmets, the minarets our bayonets and the faithful our soldiers.'). Many of his supporters also thought that it was possible that Turkey could reclaim some of its old authority, internally as well as externally. An Islamist regime had certain advantages over a secular republic. The Republic of Ataturk was defined by its Turkic ethnic identity, which meant that it could never hope to appeal to Kurds, Arabs or Iranians. But an Islamic Turkey could aspire to rise above the divisions of language and race, and appeal to the religion that they had in common. There was obvious political potential in the fact that Said Nursi – the defining spirit behind the Islamist revival – was a Kurd. Fethullah Gulen had always been insistent that the various peoples of Anatolia should come together to celebrate their shared culture.

The Arab Spring of 2011, a decade after Erdogan's rise to power, made things suddenly look very promising for Islamist Turkey. General-President Mubarak was toppled from power in Egypt and Erdogan's natural ally, the Muslim Brotherhood, took over; and, after Syria rose up in rebellion, Colonel Gaddafi was overthrown and killed in Libya. It seemed possible that the Turkish model of an efficient, elected Islamist regime might spread over the entire central Middle East. However, the victory of the Assad regime in the Syrian civil war, and the 2013 Egyptian military coup against the democratically elected Muslim Brotherhood, reversed this picture.

In the first ten years of power, Erdogan and Gulen seemed to work together impressively – the thrusting chief executive and the avuncular chairman. They slowly destroyed the prestige and confidence of the military and intelligence bosses who had been the core of the old regime, a campaign that began with a TV soap called *Valley of the Wolves,* which for ninety-seven episodes aired the idea that Turkish military intelligence and ultra-secular nationalists were in bed with all sorts of villains. In 2007, this fiction turned real when the so-called Ergenkon Plot was exposed: 800 generals, ex-admirals, old ministers and intelligence chiefs were humiliated in the law courts, accused of plotting coups with foreign powers against the state. Some of it was true, but much of it was a witch hunt.

With these sorts of enemies, imagined and real, to unite against, the political alliance between Erdogan and Gulen lasted for a whole decade – until the winter of 2011. By then, Gulenists had become embedded in the Ministry of Interior, the police and law courts, and aspired to positions in MIT, the Turkish intelligence agency. At the same time, there was a vital decision to be made about how to respond to the 'Kurdish

Summer', a season of street demonstrations that had been incubated by the Arab Spring of 2011 but which some feared would break out into another armed uprising, setting the Kurdish-nationalist PKK party once again against the Turkish army. Until that summer of 2011, there had been an armed truce throughout the south-eastern Kurdish regions of Turkey, in place since 1999. There had seemed to be every chance of a permanent peace evolving under the new Islamist umbrella, assisted by government money for development of the region. Gulen was naturally disposed in favour of this pan-ethnic policy.

It appears that Erdogan was not so certain. He had been listening to some very detailed analysis of the changing mood of his nation. After ten years in power, the AKP were no longer the squeaky-clean party of the past. Imams and clerics who had appeared as heroes, persecuted for their faith by the military bosses of the old republic, were now being associated with sexual abuse, with fawning on the state, and with acting piously in their public appearance but not in the sincerity of their private actions. In short, the Islamist agenda was not going to win the next election for the AKP. Erdogan and his party loyalists knew that if they wished to stay in power they would need to combine their existing support base with some patriotic flag-waving Turkish nationalism.

So, between the winter of 2011 and the winter of 2013, a difference in the future direction of policy emerged between Erdogan and Gulen. Erdogan was going to win the approval of Turkish nationalists by confronting, not appeasing, the Kurds. On 17 December 2013, the justice department (dominated by the followers of Gulen) detained fifty-two people closely associated with the AKP ruling elite, of which fourteen were accused of fraud, corruption, bribery and gold smuggling. At the same time, images released on the Web showed shoeboxes packed full of dollar bills being received by members of the governing elite, part of a complex deal, breaking the US embargo on Iran by trading their energy for gold. Some of these images may have been faked, but if the legal case had been allowed to continue it could have become a Watergate, gradually destroying the reputation of close associates of the president. Erdogan struck back. The cabinet was purged and Gulen loyalists in the police force and justice department were sacked.

For the next couple of years this battle continued in cyberspace, as each side tried to discover who was the enemy within. An app called *Bylock*, used by 200,000 Gulenists, was hacked, incriminating 130 senior military officers. This hack was itself discovered, without the other side knowing. The military officers with Gulenist leanings now faced some hard facts. In a matter of weeks, maybe days, they knew they would be summarily dismissed. They would lose their houses and their military pensions. Some would face imprisonment and interrogation; all would lose any chance of state employment and their children would find it difficult to get into universities. They set up a new app, called *Eagle*, which is where the July 2016 coup was plotted.

The certainty of punishment gave this group of officers a cohesive sense of unity and purpose, and they knew they had to act quickly. But they did not have enough time to plan a proper coup. When one of their number defected and told his tale to the national intelligence organisation, the coup had to be suddenly moved forward from dawn (3am is the prime time for these things to happen) to 9pm in the evening. Crucially, they were not able to persuade Hulusi Akar, Chief of the General Staff, to join them. And, without his authority, none of the other senior officers would accept orders from their juniors, even with guns in their hands.

So, between 6pm and 7.30pm on the evening of 15 July, Gulenist elements of the 1st Army and the Turkish airforce went into action against the State, bombing buildings, seizing control of airports, the TRT media building, bridges across the Bosphorus and forcing the TV newsreader to announce a successful coup. Erdogan at this time was enjoying a break in a hotel in Marmaris, but was warned by his brother-in-law, who rang him on his mobile. He headed straight back to Istanbul, making an after-midnight broadcast to the nation by smartphone on his journey, which reached a staggering 84 per cent of the population. He then landed safely back in Istanbul at 4.30am in the morning. By 1.30am, the Admiral of the Turkish navy and the commander of the First Army had assured the president of their loyalty, and the Turkish people poured onto the streets to defend the legitimacy of their elected leader. Next morning, the rebels either resisted (350 were killed) or surrendered. The 2,000 users of the *Bylock* app were arrested, along with 168 out of the 500 generals.

※ ※ ※

All this helped confirm to Erdogan that he should follow a limited foreign policy, protecting his national frontiers as a priority, rather than aspiring to become a worldwide leader of Islam or a role model for the Middle East. Once you take this on board, the subsequent actions of the Turkish army during the Syrian civil war– to control its frontiers and frustrate the creation of a unified block of Kurdish-controlled territory in north-eastern Syria – have their own clear logic. Under such policies, the Turkish world becomes a safer if also less dynamic space, without the vision of Turkic–Kurdish Islamist unity proposed by Fethullah Gulen.

It is widely believed that Erdogan could only fall from power due to a collapse in the Turkish economy. But, in the 2023 presidential election, he defied opinion polls and a wretched economy to win a third term. Three years earlier, he had won a referendum to weaken the powers of parliament in favour of an all-powerful executive president. Islamic populism may no longer be so popular, but he has been able to hold out, helped by control of the country's media.

In regional politics, Turkey is unlikely to become involved in the current Iranian Shia versus Saudi Arabian Sunni conflict unless its national frontiers are threatened. Its main preoccupation remains the minority Kurds in the south-east, and it will do anything to frustrate the creation of an independent Kurdish state in either Syria or Iraq. As the tale of the secretive inner fight between Gulen and Erdogan shows, the man with the internationalist vision of Islam fell at the last fence, defeated by an opponent who understood that nationalism will win against any issue grounded simply on faith.

PART SIX

21st-Century Battlefields:
Syria, Iraq and Yemen

PART SIX

21st-Century Battlefields:
Syria, Iraq and Yemen

S yria, Iraq and the Yemen are crucibles of humanity and have been fought over for five thousand years. In the present century, these three Arab nations – which stand at the emotional heart of the Middle East – have again been overwhelmed by conflict: foreign invasions, insurrections and civil wars. Their people have suffered greatly, but it would be a mistake to see them as the pawns of foreign powers. They have power and influence and their own ambitions, which need to be understood within their own specific context.

To do so, we need to look back – to long-standing factors of landscape, geography and demographics – to follow the path of recent events. With Syria, crucially, we need to recognise that the modern state is the rump heir of a far greater region and civilisation that – with Yemen – is the other original homeland of the Arabs. The strategic junction of two continents and five regions, 'Greater Syria' has been a crucial part of the empires that have arisen along the Nile, or from the Aegean shore, or the inner fastness of Arabia, or the mountain ranges of Anatolia or twin river valleys of Mesopotamia. This historic Syria extends far beyond modern borders, encompassing the states of Lebanon, Jordan and Israel.

Greater Syria was fought over for thousands of years but was largely at peace for the last four centuries, as a part of the Ottoman Empire, up until the end of the First World War. Over the same period, Iraq was a perennial battleground, caught between the two rival empires of faith: the militantly Shia Safavid Empire of Persia, and the Turkic-speaking Sunni Ottoman Empire. By the mid-seventeenth century, the Ottomans had finally emerged victorious, but the Shia Arabs of southern Iraq would remain steadfast in their faith, whatever the costs of political marginalisation.

Yemen, the south-western corner of the Arabian peninsula, was another regular battle region, as the Ottoman Empire tried but ultimately failed to impose its authority over its highlands. The chance intervention of the British, in the 1830s, creating the imperial naval base of Aden, unwittingly helped divide this ancient land into two: South Yemen emerging as a bastion of socialism and internationalism; and North Yemen remaining loyal to the self-governing forms of Zaydi Shia.

CHAPTER 22

Syria: Fractured Crossroad

From Greater Syria to today's war-torn
Syrian Arab Republic

Few nations have had such a long, reckless military history
as Syria. In this landscape, the pharaohs of ancient Egypt
fought the Hittites, King David battled against the Philistines,
Alexander the Great invaded the East, and the Assyrians
'came down like a wolf on the fold'. Then a long succession
of Roman and Parthian conflicts was succeeded by Byzantines
pitted against Sassanids, Umayyads and the Abbasid caliphate.
Seljuks and Fatimids would be followed by Crusaders, Mongols,
Tartars and Mameluke sultanates, until the Ottomans swept all
away, governing 'Greater Syria' until the First World War.

Nor is it simpler if you concentrate on the spiritual history
of the region, for Moses, Jesus and St Paul walked and taught
here, as well as the Prophet Muhammad. Syria is the forgotten
heartland of Christianity, and some churches still use Aramaic,
the language of Christ, in their prayers. When the Turks conquered the region in 1516, every third Syrian was a Christian,
and even today it is one in ten.

Syria's ancient cities have often been rivals in trade, power,
and precedence, making alliances with powerful neighbouring states. They have all had moments of utter desolation and
instances of imperial glory. Antioch was the eastern capital
of the Roman Empire, Tyre was the Phoenician plutocracy

of the ancient world, whilst Acre was so valuable that it was protected by three circuits of Crusader walls. Inner Syria is separated from the coast by a chain of mountains: Mount Lebanon, the Anti-Lebanon and Jabal an-Nusayria. Perched on the edge of this desert steppe are a trail of cities no more than two days' ride from each other: Aleppo, Apamea, Hama, Homs, Damascus, Bostra and Jerusalem. Before Syria was a part of the Ottoman Empire, the region had been a war zone, in a tripartite struggle waged between Seljuk Turks (Sunni), Fatimid caliphs based in Egypt (Shia) and Christian Crusaders.

In recent centuries, the two leading cities were Aleppo and Damascus, capitals of two Ottoman provinces. Aleppo was the acknowledged centre of trade, linked to Tripoli and Alexandretta (the modern Turkish city of Iskenderun) on the Mediterranean, but also to the city of Mosul perched on the banks of the River Tigris. Damascus sat on the edge of an oasis of garden-orchards fed by the waters of the River Barada, a major post on the annual Haj to Mecca, guided by Bedouin tribes.

❁ ❁ ❁

The Ottomans, when not faced with foreign invasion or rebellion, believed in a light hand of governance. In the Syrian provinces, power was concentrated on the governors, or pashas, assisted by small garrisons of Janissary soldiers. The pasha was watched, as well as assisted, by an advisory council of local notables and officers who met four times a week. The *qadi* (chief justice), an independent official directly appointed by the Sultan, acted as another check on the pasha. In the heyday of the empire, a Domesday-style book of useful data was updated every thirty years, giving precise details of the provinces, down to the fields cultivated by each village and the population, assessed by households.

The coast of Syria was chopped into *sanjaks*, smaller districts based on a city-port which had maritime communication with the Ottoman capital, Istanbul. Within the cities there was an internal political system of checks and balances. The urban craftsmen merged with the Janissaries, opposed by a class of urban clerics, merchants and landowners. A third and often unruly political element was represented by the rural sheikhs, upholding the interest of a tribe of Bedouin Arabs, or one of the many ethnic and religious clans that occupied the mountain regions. In the north-east of Syria there were many Kurdish clans; in the north-west hills were highland Alawites (a self-determining fragment of Shia); around Maysaf were Ismailis (another fragment of Shia, obedient to the Agha Khan); while the Bekaa valley and Jebel Amal hills was the bastion of the mainstream Twelver Shia. The slopes of Mount Lebanon were populated by rival villages of Maronite Christians and the Druze, another well-armed and self-governing faith branching off from the Shia.

For these diverse peoples, the modern era of conflict was unleashed in the summer of 1860. French oppression of Muslims in Algeria, Russian actions in the Caucasus, and Christian–Muslim conflict on the island of Crete, had inflamed local feeling in Syria. This turned a routine feud between rival Maronite and Druze villages on the slopes of Mount Lebanon into a massacre, with 11,000 Christian villagers slaughtered in the mountains and an equal number in Damascus.* Christian refugees poured into Beirut and for the first time became an assertive majority in the city. On this occasion, the Ottoman Empire acted with admirable speed. The governor of Damascus and some of his officials were tried and hung for their

---

* The true hero of the hour was Abdel Kader, the exiled leader of the Algerian resistance, who had used his personal authority as a Muslim hero to halt the massacre of Christians in Damascus by the urban mob.

failure to prevent the massacre, and a new *sanjak* of Lebanon was created to give the Christians a sense of security through self-governance.

French annexation of Tunisia in 1881, and British conquest of the Khedivate of Egypt the following year, made Ottoman protection look comparatively benign to most Syrians. This period saw an intellectual renaissance and a vast expansion in publishing and newspaper printing. A popular saying of the time – 'Cairo writes, Beirut prints, Baghdad reads' – expresses this slowly emerging pan-Arab identity. In Istanbul, Sultan Abdul Hamid championed a political programme that looked to the unifying forces of Islam and played up his claims to be caliph, not just the Ottoman sultan.

At the turn of the century, there was an unusually positive wind of change at work in the world, as revolutions in Russia in 1905, in Iran in 1906, and in the Ottoman Empire in July 1908, led to constitutional reforms and free elections. In this period, many Syrians still saw a prosperous future within a reformed Ottoman Empire. In 1908, there were sixty Arab MPs amongst the 275 members of the Ottoman parliament. Tragically, the moment was fleeting, as in 1909 the Young Turks seized power and directed the Ottoman Empire towards a narrow Turkic ethnic nationalism. Their imperial dreams were not centred on a partnership with the Arabs, but on the reconquest of the Crimea, Caucasus and Turkic Central Asia.

❀ ❀ ❀

The First World War was a colossal error for the Ottomans and, for Syria, a triple tragedy. First, Christian Armenians and Assyrians were massacred in the towns of northern Syria. Then the Allied naval blockade, droughts, swarms of locusts and conscription of farm workers into the Ottoman army created a famine, lasting from 1915 to 1918, in which it is thought a fifth of the Syrian population perished. A third disaster was the discovery of compromising letters written during the 1913 Arab conference about dreams of self-government and use of the Arabic language. To the Ottomans, these read like treason and, on 6 May 1916, Jamal Pasha had twenty-one leading Syrian Arab writers and politicians hung in the squares of Damascus and Beirut.*

The Arab Revolt was announced on 5 June 1916. It might have been a marginal affair – another armed insurrection of Bedouin tribesmen in the depths of the desert – but the martyrs were a line in the sand for many Arab officers in the Ottoman army. After the executions of a month before, many of them pledged their allegiance to the Hashemite sheikh of Mecca. The sheikh was backed by British gold and guns, and when the British army broke through Ottoman military positions in the autumn of 1917 there was a spontaneous political uprising throughout Syria. Muslim clergy, Christian bishops and local officials conspired to liberate themselves under the Sharifian flag of the Arab Revolt. Damascus, Beirut, Aleppo and Homs were all first liberated by Arabs, declaring themselves free as the last Ottoman garrisons evacuated their positions. The welcome awarded to the advancing British army was ecstatic and genuine.

Emir Faysal, one of the sons of the Hashemite sheikh of Mecca, was the leading Arab general during the Arab Revolt. In the summer of 1919, he called for elections so that every community would be represented in a National Congress of Greater Syria, whose frontiers stretched from the Taurus Mountains to Sinai. Faysal would later be criticised for the understanding which he made with leading Zionists at this

---

* These Arab martyrs of 1916 are still commemorated each year in Syria and Lebanon, and by a famous (and now bullet-ridden) bronze statue in the centre of Beirut.

time, but he was no traitor to the Arab cause. His promise was made in the context of a Greater Syria, where Jews would be welcomed as another of the minorities within this ethnically rich and culturally diverse region. There were four recognised forms of Muslim belief and thirteen different forms of Christianity in Greater Syria and, if the frontiers of the state were to stretch east to the Euphrates, they would embrace cities such as Baghdad, which in 1917 was 40 per cent Jewish.

It is now difficult to imagine an Arab state that could freely include Shia and Sunni Muslims, indigenous Sephardic Jews, and Christians as equal citizens. But, if there is a 'what if' moment in the recent history of the Middle East, this was surely it. What if the civilised bulk of Greater Syria had enthusiastically embraced the future as a democratic, multi-ethnic, multi-faith community under an indigenous Arab dynasty of holy lineage aspiring to create a constitutional monarchy?

Unfortunately, the European powers had other ideas.

During the First World War, partly to entice Italy to join the Allies, a secret protocol, the 1916 Sykes–Picot Agreement, had been hatched between the British and the French. The French would have Syria and the British dominate Iraq and Palestine, which allowed for the south-west coast of Turkey to be promised to the Italians if they joined the war. So, while the Arabs celebrated a new era of freedom, French troops landed in Beirut and advanced up the Bekaa valley towards Damascus. The British army was already in occupation of southern Syria, now better known as Palestine. No democracy was to be permitted for this new province, which was placed under the rule of a British governor tasked with facilitating Jewish immigration.* The British Cabinet believed a Jewish-dominated Palestine

---

* Sir Herbert Samuel, first British governor of the Mandate of Palestine, was a Jewish enthusiast for a Zionist Palestine as part of the British Empire.

would help them defend both the Suez Canal and guard an oil pipeline from Iraq to the harbour of Haifa. This Jewish state was imagined as a long-term asset for the British Empire.

The Americans, at this time, did their level best to encourage the natural evolution of a tolerant, greater Syrian Arab state and to point out the dangers of this Zionist project. The US-sponsored King–Crane Commission brought back a report that a United Arab Syria was the overwhelming collective wish (85 per cent) of those that they had consulted in the region. The British, French and Italians did their best to strangle this commission and managed to bury the findings of the report, which was not published until 1922.

It was a volatile period. Throughout the summer of 1919, Egypt was poised on the edge of nationalist rebellion, which united Sunni Muslims and Christian Copts (under the Wafd party) against the British. Eight hundred Egyptians would be killed before British troops were back in control of the streets. Meanwhile, another populist movement had formed in Ankara over the winter of 1919–20, and the Turkish national assembly separated themselves from the authority of the Sultan in Istanbul in order to organise resistance to foreign armies of occupation. Set against these events, the French conquest of the recently liberated independent Syrian nation could not have come at a worse time. The Syrians did not think of themselves as an uncivilised people in need of a French protectorate to teach them the arts of civilisation. They had been writing letters to each other for two thousand years before the French learned the craft.

Arab self-government in the inland cities of Syria in this heady period of self-assertion lasted for eighteen months. Then, in June 1920, in accordance with the Sykes–Picot Agreement, French troops marched on Damascus. Ironically, this army of colonial conquest was made up largely of Muslim soldiers, recruited from Senegal, Algeria, Madagascar and Morocco to serve under French officers. At dawn on 24 July 1920, they attacked the Khan Maysalun caravanserai. The young Syrian Minister of War was killed by machine-gun fire from a French tank. Emir Faysal tried to rally further resistance at Daraa (south of Damascus) but was forced to seek refuge with the British in Palestine. Faysal and his brother Abdullah had been betrayed by the British over Syria but were not to be totally deserted by their British allies. Emir Abdullah would rule over the Emirate of Trans-Jordan (the south-eastern quarter of Greater Syria) and within a year Faysal was placed on the throne of Iraq. The two brothers never gave up the hope that they might yet create a United Arab Kingdom.

✼ ✼ ✼

There was nothing positive about the French protectorate of Syria. It is reckoned that, of five billion francs spent there by the French, most of it raised through taxation in Syria, four-fifths was spent upholding their rule. The Syrian people never accepted any French right to govern their nation and actively resisted throughout the twenty years of colonial occupation.

The French, however, had done their Oriental research well. They contrived to cut Greater Syria into small pieces, along lines dictated by existing ethnic and religious rivalries, and, in doing so, hoped to co-opt the support of local tribal leaders. They carved out a completely independent Lebanese state, dominated by their major ally in the region, the Maronite Christian community, based in Beirut and in the highland villages on Mount Lebanon. However, the Syrian Lebanese, even in the hand-picked pro-French administrative council, persisted in calling for the union of Greater Syria under Emir Faysal. The French also supported the formation of an independent Alawite region, an independent Druze county, and set aside another region to be dominated by Bedouin Arab sheikhs in the far north-east. This was what the Roman and the Ottoman Empires had done before them, and it was also inspired by a romantic regard for the old political geography of the medieval Crusader states.

In 1924, a French government of radicals and socialists took power in Paris and started questioning the purpose and expense of the military occupation of Syria. Elections were held in Syria in 1925 to test the popular will. The articulate urban elite of Syria formed the People's Party, which called for an immediate end to French occupation and an independent United Arab Syria. These political demands were matched by a national uprising. In the summer of 1925, the Druze in the Jebel Hauran rose in armed rebellion, followed by the city of Hama on 4 October, after which the rebellion spread to Damascus itself, which came partly under Syrian control. But, by bombarding the ancient city with modern artillery, devastating whole quarters, the French were able to maintain their position. They recruited disaffected young men (especially from the Armenian and Circassian communities) into a local militia and sent them into the alleys of the old city to identify and assassinate Syrian Arab nationalists. After two years of state terror, assisted by aerial bombing, the Syrian rebellion was crushed.

The French were not always convinced that their British allies, present just across the border in Jordan, Iraq and Palestine, had not in some way assisted the Syrian rebels. Certainly the Hashemite monarchs, ruling over both the British protectorates of Iraq and Jordan, hoped to re-create a Greater Syria if the French were driven out. Over the 1930s, the struggle for Syrian independence became political – and split into two antagonistic factions tied to external allies. The Hashemites backed Abd al-Rahman Shahbandar, who set up a secret society, the Iron Hand. He called for a Greater Syria through a union with Emir Abdullah of Jordan until he was assassinated in June 1940. Shukri al-Quwwatli, his principal rival, was backed by the Kingdom of Saudi Arabia. Shukri spoke forcefully on behalf of the Arabs of Palestine, who were being betrayed by the Zionist policy of the British Empire.

In 1936, massive street protests in Syria coincided with the emergence of a new left-wing government in Paris, the Popular Front, eager for a negotiated settlement. They agreed to abandon their attempt to create independent Alawite and Druze cantons, in exchange for recognition of an independent Lebanon, and for the maintenance of airbases and military garrisons. But this compromise was never signed, for the Popular Front fell from power in 1937 and the Second World War brought a return to direct military rule.

France lost even more prestige within Syria by surrendering the cities of Antioch and Alexandretta to Turkey in 1939, and then in 1941 Vichy France offered the use of its airbases in Syria to their Nazi allies. The British and their Free French allies invaded, so a French civil war was fought over Syrian soil throughout that summer. Once in power, the Free French officers forgot all their promises to their Arab allies and it was only under intense pressure from the British that they allowed free elections to take place in July 1943. But the newly elected prime ministers and presidents of Lebanon and Syria were arrested like common criminals that November. The outraged Lebanese created the famous National Pact – an oral (and still unwritten) constitution which allots various key positions in the government to the different religious communities. The president was to be a Christian Maronite; the prime minister a Sunni Muslim; and the speaker of parliament, a Shia.

In Syria, May 1945 saw a conclusion of sorts to this bitter colonial drama, the so-called Levantine Crisis, when the French attacked the Syrian parliament. The Syrian president called upon the British army to intervene, and General Paget had the delicate task of confining his wartime allies to their barracks.

Syria and Lebanon were welcomed into the UN as founding members on 24 October 1945. The last units of the French army finally evacuated Syria the following summer, an evacuation celebrated as the Wedding Day of Freedom in Damascus, whose streets were packed with jubilant crowds.

❈ ❈ ❈

The political future of Syria would soon be inspired by the Ba'ath Party, with its agenda of socialist reform true to their Arab identity. The founders of the Ba'ath came from an impressive array of religious traditions. Michel Aflaq (1910–89) was from a family of Christian merchants but revered Islam as the greatest expression of the Arab genius. Zaki al-Arsuzi (1899–1968), who has some claim to be the original founder, was a scholarly man from an Alawite family settled in Latakia. Salah al-Din al Bitar (1912–80) came from a Damascus-based family of Sunni scholars. The most charismatic and radical of the four was Akram al-Hourani (1912–96), whose Arab family traced its descent back to the family of the Prophet. He was a leading campaigner for socialist land reform against the vast landholdings of Arab notables.

The Ba'ath Party became the dominant ideological movement in the Arab Middle East from 1950. At its simplest, Ba'athism was Arab nationalism empowered by modern education and social reform. The central role of an organised, enlightened state to further national progress was an all-important element. It would clash with traditional Islamic practices, especially over issues like secular education, female emancipation and land reform. As we will later discover, its other principal weakness was that it was determinedly Arab and excluded both Kurds and Turks from its vision of the future – despite their dominating presence in parts of northern Syria and northern Iraq.

The first Syrian election without foreign influence was held in July 1947. The Ba'ath Party had not yet risen to power, so in this period the main political fissure lines were not based on faith or ethnicity, but between a literate, urban elite and the traditional countryside, and between the two rival cities of Aleppo and Damascus. The two cities supported different political parties, the National Party (Damascus) set against the People's Party (Aleppo). These rival parties were locked into a system of alliances with external powers. The People's Party was supported by the Hashemite kingdoms of Jordan and Iraq, while the National Party was backed by Saudi Arabia and Egypt. The kings of Egypt and Saudi Arabia had little love for each other but were united in their suspicion of the Hashemite kings, especially whilst they threatened to become the nucleus of a United Arab Middle East. Jordan was poor on resources, but at this moment in history most of the political leaders of the Middle East were fearful of Emir Abdullah. He was bright, energetic and commanded the best trained of all the Arab armies.

This suspicion of Hashemite Jordan was fully shared by the first president of Syria, Shukri al-Quwwatli of the National Party, who was outspokenly anti-Hashemite, anti-British and open to the influence of Saudi Arabia. Al-Quwwatli was fearful of a military coup and was busily trying to run down the strength and reduce the colossal expense of the Syrian army as inherited from the French colonial regime. When the first

Arab–Israeli War exploded in 1948, President Shukri proved an uninspiring commander. He was chiefly interested in frustrating the plans of King Abdullah of Jordan and preventing the emergence of any charismatic Syrian general.

The military defeat of the Arabs in the 1948–49 war with Israel would haunt internal Syrian politics for the next fifty years. In reaction, Syria would turn itself into a new Sparta, a tough, military society capable of resisting Israel, not only in defence of its own borders but also as a big brother to protect the Palestinian Arabs.

❀ ❀ ❀

At the conclusion of the Arab–Israeli War, the Israeli state was hugely enlarged, with the addition of the Negev. Hashemite Jordan took possession of the West Bank and East Jerusalem, including the Old City, whose Jewish population was forced to leave. The Egyptians held only the Gaza Strip.

In the patriotic chronicles of Israel, this war was a glorious fight for survival, for national liberation against armies whose objective was to drive every Zionist Jewish settler into the sea. In the perspective of the Arabs of the Middle East, it was *al-Nakba*, 'the catastrophe'. Not only did 700,000 Palestinian Arab refugees lose their land, their orchards, their gardens, their homes, but all the Arab states of the Middle East (many of which had just become independent) had been defeated on the battlefield. All Arabs felt deeply ashamed of this, and their leaders blamed one another.

In March 1949, the Syrians, humiliated by the turn of events in Palestine, were the first Arab people to overthrow their own government. Colonel Husni Zaim, who took power on 30 March 1949, was something of a buffoon and lasted only five months before he was shot. He was followed by a succession of president-colonels before a return to parliamentary rule in 1954. It was a confusing time for local politicians, as oil money from Iraq and Saudi Arabia financed rival political parties, further complicated by negotiations about the routes and percentages to be earned by new oil pipelines which involved American oil. But behind all these messy deals there was a union of the Arab Socialist and Arab Ba'ath Parties in 1952 which brought most of the clean, visionary young politicians together.

The real action in shaping the Middle East was happening in Egypt. In 1956, a chance succession of events led to Nasser's nationalisation of the Suez Canal and a bungled British–French–Israeli military operation to seize back control of the canal. Overnight, General Nasser, who had successfully challenged these three great villains, became the hero of heroes. On 1 February 1958, Syria offered to become part of a United Arab Republic led by Nasser, aspiring to create a state strong enough to contain Israel. It could have been the nucleus of a vast Arab federation. But Nasser promptly dissolved all political parties in Syria and appointed an Egyptian general to rule 'the northern province'. The kingdoms of Jordan and Saudi Arabia never saw eye to eye on anything, but the union of Syria and Egypt so alarmed them that they buried the hatchet. Together they backed the Syrian military coup of September 1961 which reclaimed Syrian independence.

❀ ❀ ❀

The next Syrian coup of 8 March 1963 was of a very different order. A group of young Syrian army officers, all members of the Ba'ath Party from poor backgrounds, and all loyal to Nasser, seized power. They initiated a series of social and economic reforms which stripped the old Syrian notables – a couple of thousand interrelated Sunni Muslim families – of their great landed estates, which for centuries had funded their elite status. This revolution was resisted. There were gun battles with Nasserists on the streets of Damascus that July, and the following year the city of Hama rebelled against the secular Ba'athist regime. This encouraged the regime to become ever more radical. In the four years after the coup of 1963, the army was purged of a third of its officers. It was a process paralleled in Iraq, which had also been taken over in a Ba'athist-friendly military coup.

As ever, family and clan relationships proved to be one of the most reliable ways for a new leadership to protect their position, and in Syria this group led to power crystallising around the Alawi Shia. This grouping had always been near the bottom of Syrian society, traditionally taking employment as shepherds, soldiers and servants, before returning to the freedom and simplicity of their mountain homelands. It was easy for the Alawi to trust one another. They shared an inherited resentment of the traditional ruling Muslim Sunni elite from the cities and were attracted to the Ba'ath Party.

Two Alawi officers of forbidding seriousness and commitment to work, Salah Jadid and Hafiz al-Assad, emerged in 1966 as the recognised political masters of Syria. Over the next thirty years, their regime would push through an impressive expansion of the basic infrastructure of the nation. Massive dam projects on the Euphrates provided water and electricity for villages, while land reform enabled a new class of prosperous peasant farmers to emerge. Education and healthcare increased exponentially and there was a fivefold expansion in road building. In all, some 700,000 salaried bureaucrats were incorporated into the Ba'ath Party structure.

The succession of purges of the Syrian officer corps after the 1963 coup had done little to prepare the military for an unexpected war. On 5 June 1967, Israel launched a surprise attack on both Egypt and Syria, destroying both their air forces on the ground within an hour. It was a well-planned and aggressive strike, but, in fairness to the leaders of Israel, it might have seemed that Nasser's series of aggressive blusters on the frontier were leading towards conflict. In retrospect, we now know that the blusters were indeed just that – an attempt by Nasser to remain the leading figure in the Arab world, the strongman of the Middle East. He had no intention of attacking Israel. But the Six-Day War completed the military dominance of Israel. Everywhere, it was victorious, seizing control of the West Bank from Jordan and the Golan Heights from Syria (the day after the 8 June ceasefire).

❋ ❋ ❋

This second humiliating defeat of the Arabs by Israel increased both the radicalisation and militarisation of Syrian society, as well as the Palestine Liberation Organization (PLO), which was then enthusiastically supported by all the radical states within the Middle East.

By 1970, Jordan had reached the brink of civil war with the PLO seemingly on the point of taking over. In what came to be known as Black September, the Syrian leader Salah Jadid ordered units of the Syrian army (albeit dressed in PLO uniform) to cross the frontier and assist the PLO against the Jordanian army. At one point it seemed as if the entire Middle East might become engulfed in this conflict, with Israel and the US coming to the aid of Jordan. Rather than unleash a war for which they were unprepared, the Syrian Minister of Defence, Hafiz al-Assad, countermanded the order for units of the Syrian Armoured Brigade to join the fighting, which allowed the Jordanian army to triumph over the PLO.

That October, Salah Jadid denounced Hafiz al-Assad at the Ba'ath Party conference as a defeatist and called for his expulsion from both party and government. But Assad struck back, and, with his younger brother as Minister of Interior, he proved unassailable. This so-called 'Corrective Movement' established Hafiz al-Assad as sole ruler of Syria.

The Yom Kippur War, the unexpected simultaneous assault by Egypt and Syria on Israel in 1973, can be seen as Hafiz al-Assad's justification for seizing power. Instead of embroiling itself in the confused infighting of a Jordanian civil war, Assad was leading the Arab world, hand-in-hand with Egypt, in a bold frontal attack on the real enemy. The Yom Kippur War is often considered to be something of a triumph for the Arab armies, but it was also a sacrifice. The Syrian army lost 870 tanks and 3,000 soldiers, and in the end the most decisive weapon in the Arab arsenal was neither its tanks nor its airforce jets, but the oil embargo organised by the Kingdom of Saudi Arabia. It proved to be a weapon that was powerful enough to attract the wholehearted interest of the US in trying to establish peace in the Middle East.

Syria hardly had time to recover from the wounds of the Yom Kippur War before the Lebanese civil war erupted in March 1975. This civil war is fiendishly complicated, but the heart of the conflict was a struggle waged between the armed militias of the Maronite Christians of Lebanon and the PLO. After their expulsion from Jordan in 1970, the PLO made increasing use of their network of refugee camps and military training camps in Lebanon. They wished to become influential in Lebanon in order to wage border raids and rocket attacks on Israel, but their hosts feared that they aspired to seize control of a new homeland. There were many other elements thrown into the conflict, for it was also a class struggle between the rich elite of old notable families and the urban poor, and had elements of Cold War rivalry. Lebanon was then the financial, educational, social, mercantile, diplomatic and media centre for the Arab world. So each Arab nation had particular interests and local allies in the Lebanon. This allowed for the age-old jostle for dominance between the different elements of the Lebanese ethnic mosaic, as factions of Christians, Sunni, Druze and Shia battled for advantage, the whole thing given an opaque twist through political schisms and gang rivalries within these clans.

The Syrian army was invited into Lebanon in the autumn of 1978 as part of a pan-Arab peacekeeping force, but Israel did not think they were controlling the PLO so decided to enter the fray themselves. In the summer of 1982, an Israeli army cut through the hill country of southern Lebanon with surgical ease in order to lay siege to PLO-controlled West Beirut. Ten thousand were killed in this campaign, which also resulted in Israel's greatest PR disaster, the massacres in the Sabra and Shatilla PLO refugee camps. The actual killings were perpetrated by Maronite Phalangist militia taking revenge on the PLO for the recent assassination of their commander, Bashir Gemayel. The Israeli army merely held the perimeter walls of these two camps, but it was a merciless, bitter aftermath to their invasion, for the PLO had already begun to pull out of Beirut that summer. Everyone seemed to have blood on their hands, so the American army came in as part of a new peace-keeping force. Their presence did not last long, after their barracks was hit by suicide bombers.

It was at this point that Hezbollah started to emerge in southern and eastern Lebanon as a determined and disciplined militia force. Initially formed to protect Shia villages, they were trained by Iranian Revolutionary Guards. As fellow Shias, they were natural allies of Hafiz al-Assad, coming as he did from the clans of Alawi Shia. Hezbollah proved themselves a dogged opponent to the Israeli army, which had occupied a buffer zone in southern Lebanon when they withdrew from Beirut.

❊ ❊ ❊

Armed resistance to the Assad regime within Syria was formed from disgruntled offshoots of the PLO (seeking revenge for Black September and the exodus from Beirut), embittered members of the old Sunni class of notables and the Muslim Brotherhood. The Brotherhood had been founded in Egypt but had spread through the towns of Syria after Independence.

The first reported incident of armed resistance to the Assad regime was the shooting of thirty-two military cadets in June 1979. The next year, in June 1980, an attempt was made to assassinate the president, who was to be caught between the crossfire of two machine guns and a pair of thrown grenades. Hafiz al-Assad kicked one of these out of harm's way himself, while a bodyguard threw himself over the other.

Shortly after, the president's younger brother, the Interior Minister, ordered the killing of all members of the Muslim Brotherhood held in the Tadmor prison near the ruins of Palmyra. This massacre was in due course revenged by the shooting of seventy Ba'athists in their homes in the city of Hama, in February 1982. This action cleared the city of all regime loyalists and allowed a group of Islamist militants, the Fighting Vanguard, to seize control of the old city. Hama, with its dense network of narrow alleys and traditional courtyard houses, whose roofs connect together, was a natural warren for an urban resistance movement. The Assad regime claim to have evacuated the city of all citizens before they launched their counter-attack. Other accounts suggest that regime forces were repelled, after which Hama was cordoned off, bombarded with artillery and then attacked by tanks. Casualty figures vary between 3,000 Islamist gunmen killed in street fighting to 40,000 citizens buried in the wholescale destruction of the city. In many ways the Syrian civil war (which was fought largely from 2011 to 2017) was a continuation of the Hama uprising of 1982.

Although the Syrian regime had been fighting a war on two fronts – in Lebanon and Hama – it started to benefit from the complex international situation. The 1979 peace treaty signed between Egypt and Israel had led to the expulsion of Egypt from the Arab League, leaving Syria as the one Arab frontier state that refused to sign a peace with Israel, unless it promised a simultaneous settlement for the Palestinians. The Iran–Iraq War had also removed any fear of Iraqi interference in Syrian politics. Syria's steadfast alliance with Iran in those critical eight years of complete isolation helped establish an enduring friendship.

The slow collapse of the Soviet Union after 1989 had an initially peaceful effect on the Middle East, for it removed the Cold War element from the complex webs of rivalry. The increasing demonisation of Saddam Hussein by the US also helped take the heat off Syria, which in its heyday had harboured dozens of terrorist groups and sponsored many bombings. The main ripples on the surface of Syrian politics were court gossip: whether Hafiz al-Assad's young brother Rifat, or his eldest son Basil, was his most likely political heir, and which cousin or nephew controlled which part of the economy or which branch of the intelligence services. Like some scene from a tragedy, brother Rifat was seen to move too decisively towards the presidential office when Hafiz al-Assad was ill. Though pardoned for this half-attempt at a palace coup, he never recovered his position. Then the swaggering, cocksure heir Basil died in a car crash. So it was his younger brother Bashar, training to become an eye surgeon in London, who was eventually recalled to the presidential palace in Damascus when his father died in 2000. Bashar al-Assad was just thirty-four years old.

❀ ❀ ❀

Bashar was not the only hereditary heir to a revolutionary republic. At this time there were a whole bunch of similar candidates in their sleek Italian suits. In Libya, in Iraq and in Egypt the university-educated, well-spoken sons of the old brutal boss all looked as if they might take over, while in the meantime benefiting from a bonanza of mobile-phone contracts and car-import licences.

Bashar al-Assad presided over Syria on what seemed a slow arc of reform. The old spartan regime of Ba'athist Syria certainly needed some fiscal and social liberalisation. It was saddled with a socialist command structure, with deep budgets committed to the defence and security ministries, and a political culture completely lacking in mercantile innovation. Bashar also strove to reduce the regime's reliance on Alawite clan loyalties. Sunni merchants and Christian financiers were co-opted into governmental structures, and he neatly avoided a confrontation between secularists and Islamists on the headcovering appropriate to females by leaving the choice up to the individuals. Diversity and tolerance became buzz words to explain to the world Syria's unique position. Bashar's 'Damascus Spring' served to unearth a new generation of Syrian activists, but many of these self-identified reformers found themselves locked up, little over a year later, the news buried by the events of 9/11.

There were some other unexpected hitches to the process of liberalisation. The noisiest of these was the hundred-ton bomb which killed Rifaq Hariri, prime minister of Lebanon, in February 2005. He had annoyed the Syrian regime by refusing to renew the presidency of Emile Lahoud. The Syrians trusted Lahoud (a Maronite Christian with a long military career) as their man in Beirut. But the bomb incubated a street march – the so-called Cedar Revolution – of a million Lebanese citizens, calling for an end to Syrian military occupation. By the end of April 2005, 14,000 Syrian soldiers, police and intelligence officials had evacuated their offices.

A year later, however, in July 2006, the political clock was set back by the Tammuz War, a thirty-four-day battle by Hezbollah against the Israeli invasion of southern Lebanon. The steadfast resistance of Hezbollah turned them into the heroes of the hour, not just in Lebanon, but in the wider Arab world. For Israel it proved another international disaster, as all the reconstruction projects achieved in Lebanon since the civil war were attacked with a fury that the rest of the world could no longer understand. Hezbollah's victory was moral, not tactical. They survived the Israeli onslaught and, despite high casualties, continued to resist. They were also beginning to engage with Lebanese democracy, despite its many constitutional imperfections. The Shia of Lebanon now had two dozen representatives in Lebanon's 128-seat parliament, which has given them two or three ministerial posts in most of the recent coalition governments. Syrian tanks might have left the orchards of Lebanon, but their closest allies were now firmly embedded in the power structure.

This recognition of the Shia minority as part of the governing structure of Lebanon was opposed by Saudi Arabia, which in one form or another had generously bankrolled the rebuilding of Beirut after the destruction of the civil war years. Saudi Arabia wanted to undermine the strong position that

Hezbollah had achieved, but to do so would be to remove one of the essential props that now held Lebanon together.

❀ ❀ ❀

Water, or the lack of it, is one of the many ways to explain the Arab Spring in Syria. A prolonged drought from 2006 to 2010, coupled with decades of over-extraction of underground water, had impoverished and progressively ruined thousands upon thousands of smallholding peasant farmers, who were otherwise the proudest boast of thirty years of Ba'athist governance. Casual rural labour evaporated and swelled the cities with disgruntled, unhappy, poor young men.

There was also something in the air, that ripple of optimism in every generation that encourages people to believe that change is possible. Such a mood had transformed the Middle East in 1979 and had again resurfaced. Mobile phones and the Internet made communication easier and, just at that moment, less controllable by instruments of government. The election of the first African-American president of the US in January 2009 also set new standards of hope.

Arguably it all began in Iran, as the so-called Green Revolution filled the streets of Tehran with protesters against the results of the June 2009 presidential election. Then, in the winter of 2010, the self-immolation of a young Tunisian street trader in front of the office of the provincial governor of Sidi Bouzid lit a chain of street protests that brought down the dictatorship of Ben Ali, President of Tunisia, in January 2011. This Jasmine Revolution of Tunisia spread to Egypt (where it brought down Mubarak), Libya (where it toppled Gaddafi, with Western military assistance), Bahrain and Syria. It alarmed the rulers of Saudi Arabia, Iran and Israel, all of whom were horrified by the emergence of popular democracy in the Islamic Middle East.

The Arab Spring reached Syria in March 2011, emerging at first, not in the prosperous big cities, but in small towns most affected by the drought. The arrest of some teenage children, caught by the police writing political graffiti on a wall in Daraa on the Jordanian frontier, motivated a demonstration calling for their release. There was a real and touching concern to get these children out of the police cells and away from the habitual degradation meted out by the security services. After four protesters were shot dead, 20,000 took to the streets the following day. The three symbols of government authority – the governor's office, the Ba'ath Party headquarters and the security service barracks – were attacked. On 23 March, the security service counter-attacked, raiding a mosque that was being used as an emergency hospital for those who had been wounded in the street demonstrations. Fifteen were killed in this raid, after which the protests spread all over Syria.

On 30 March 2011, Bashar al-Assad delivered a speech to the Syrian parliament. There were no apologies and no promises of reform. Instead, the delegates (and the nation) were given a long, factual lecture about the difficulties of governing Syria over the last decade. Syria was surrounded by dangerous, predatory and aggressive foreign powers, their plots, spies and conspiracies. Assad pointed out how Iraq, Lebanon and Afghanistan had been devastated by recent events. These facts were only too true, but the protest marches escalated, especially on Friday afternoons after people had gathered for the noonday prayers. If one event lit the spark of civil war, it was the arrest of thirteen-year-old Hamza al-Khateeb during a protest march in Deraa in April, and the return of his tortured and mutilated body a month later. By the end of July, there were 2,000 casualties. Elements of the Syrian military had started to defect to form the Free Syrian Army, which was determined to protect its revolution from the regime.

The fighting in the first twelve months of the civil war was bloody and confusing. Neighbourhood militia were often formed to protect their own communities from violence and looting, but then had to choose between revolution or regime. Villages and cities were split in half: central Damascus remained regime; the outer suburbs went for revolution. The balance of power between the regime and the rebels was almost evenly balanced, though the pro-democracy element of the Arab Spring was soon overshadowed by militant Islamist fighters. Saudi Arabia and the US backed different Islamist groups, with others supported by Turkey and Qatar, probably to the tune of $100 million in that first year. The regime was assisted by volunteer fighters from Iran and Hezbollah, probably not very important in terms of actual numbers of boots on the ground, but they helped keep control of the vital roads from Damascus to the ports of Beirut and Latakia.

By 2014, after two years of fighting, 200,000 had been killed, three million Syrians had fled the country (600,000 into neighbouring Jordan, 1.2 million into the Lebanon) and around six million had left their homes and become internally displaced.

❋ ❋ ❋

The emergence of ISIS, initially from the rebel-held city of Raqqa in April 2013, completely changed the equation. ISIS were extreme – in their claims to be founding a new caliphate, in their worldwide appeal (at least 20,000 foreigners joined their army as volunteers), and in the brutality and visibility of their public executions. Captured Yazidi women were treated as slave concubines, Shia prisoners of war were executed, captured foreigners were accused of spying and beheaded. Most foolishly of all, the Kurds were attacked, rather than treated as a potential neutral force. For those with an eye for historical detail, the homemade black and white ISIS war banners looked remarkably similar to those of the Saudi Ikhwan in the 1920s, as were their choice of victims. The Ba'athist Assad regime suddenly looked like the moderate good guys.

The presence of over 2,000 volunteers from the Caucasus in the ranks of ISIS helped the Russians decide to become active players. By September 2015, Russian special forces were on the ground in Syria directing targeted air strikes. This was not going to be another Afghanistan. Russian casualties were comparatively slight, with no more than 200 soldiers killed on active duty. But, with the assistance of Russian airpower, hill by hill, village by village, the rebels were subdued, eventually falling back (in a series of truces) to their stronghold of Idlib, between Aleppo and the Turkish frontier.

The Americans and their Western allies also became involved, in support of the Kurds, who had carved out a state for themselves in north-east Syria and offered effective resistance to ISIS. Here, however, things become more complex. The chosen ally of the Kurds of Syria was not the Kurds in Iraq, but the Kurds in south-eastern Turkey, so supporting them was like waving a red flag at the Turkish Republic, already angry that its own rival Islamist allies* were in retreat.

From a distance, the Syrian civil war seems a classic case of Shia against Sunni: on one side, the military alliance of the Shiite Hezbollah, the Alawi–Shia Assad regime and elements of the Iranian Revolutionary Guard; on the other, various groups of militant Sunni Islamist militia, supported

---

* Al-Nusra became the leading coalition of Syrian Sunni Islamist fighters, backed by Turkey and Qatar, aggressively anti-Shia but subtly distancing itself from both Al-Qaeda and ISIS's worldwide jihad militancy, whilst sharing a similar Wahhabi–Salafi ideology.

by such Sunni nations as Saudi Arabia, Turkey, the UAE and Qatar. Dig a little deeper and you find elements that go against this reading. The Syrian regime is Ba'athist, the last supporter of a secular pan-Arabic union across the Middle East. They are clearly not a natural political partner to the Islamic Republic of Iran, ruled by a constitutionally embedded clergy. Furthermore, the Sunni nations interfering in Syria are divided into two antagonistic factions: Saudi Arabia and the Gulf emirates on one side; Qatar, the Muslim Brotherhood and the Turkish Republic on the other. Viewed through the lens of history, Turkey and Saudi Arabia come with a long back history of ambitions, interference and rivalry in the region.

Everyone agrees that, if there was a free and fair election tomorrow, a Syrian political party allied to traditional Sunni Islam would win hands down. But key players in the region, such as Saudi Arabia with its Gulf allies, and the military regime in Egypt, would be very opposed to this. They wanted to win an armed civil war, not to usher in an Islamist democracy, which is the most likely political force to topple them from their thrones.

Nor should we forget the crucial role of the world powers. The US and its European allies declined to interfere in the Syrian civil war with the same decisive burst of airpower with which they destroyed Gaddafi's state in Libya. This lack of involvement was decisive in allowing the Syrian regime to survive, especially once Russia had decided to enter the war in September 2015. Two years later, it had been won.

❋ ❋ ❋

There are limits to how far Syria's alliance with Hezbollah and Iran can go. Syria has a majority Sunni population. Somehow, this majority must eventually be included in the governance of the nation, if Syria is to find long-term stability. At the same time, it would be foolish to imagine that the Ba'athist–Assad regime, victors in a fierce, long and closely fought civil war, might be in the mood to give away political ground. Russian influence is almost certain to continue, however committed they have become in the war against Ukraine. And, if Basher al-Assad was blown up by a bomb, his younger brother, the battle-tested Maher, one of the regime's most effective military commanders, would be likely to assume power.

Neither Saudi Arabia – nor Israel – would likely welcome Syria becoming a free nation, with its own self-determining Islamist Sunni government. However, if such a thing were to happen, Turkey would be keen to step forward as a protective big brother. Saudi Arabia is already troubled by the role that the Shiite Hezbollah have acquired, but the Shia are only a fifth of the population of the Lebanon and need to work together with the other faith communities to retain their position. It is unlikely that Iran is going to turn the Lebanon into a distant province of a Shiite Persian Empire with a naval base in the Mediterranean.

Whether the nearly independent canton of the Kurds will survive in north-east Syria against the enmity of the Turkish Republic and the slowly regathering authority of the Syrian regime, time will tell. It proved to be a valiant base for operations against ISIS, but the track record of the loyalty of the US towards allies of convenience in the Middle East is not encouraging.

CHAPTER 23

Iraq in the Balance

*The Middle East's key conflict
between Shia and Sunni*

Iraq lies at the centre of the Islamic world and any equation of power in the region. A few hours' drive from its capital city of Baghdad brings you to Jordan, Iran, Turkey, Saudi Arabia, Syria and Kuwait. Iraq has oil, it has water, it has agriculture, it has culture, and too much history. Iraq also has people: some forty million, of whom three-quarters are Arab and one quarter Kurd. The Arab population is divided 60 per cent Shia, 40 per cent Sunni. There are minorities – Yazidi, Assyrians and Turkmen – scattered amongst both Arabs and Kurds.

The nation has always been determined by its elemental geography. The word 'Iraq' is derived from both the Sumerian word for 'the city' and Arabic for 'the bank', as in riverbank; just as to the classical world Iraq was Mesopotamia, 'the land between rivers'. The course of the two great rivers, the Tigris and the Euphrates, has determined the fate of Iraq's cities. This is one of the cradles of humankind, where the wheel and writing were invented, astronomy and arithmetic first taught, and where the first cities arose, and then were dramatically expanded by canals.

The Euphrates flows out of the mountains of Anatolia in modern Turkey, sweeping through eastern Syria on its way south. There is no natural geographical frontier along this river course and the many crumbling walls and castles were all failed attempts to create a political frontier, for the upper Euphrates serves as a fertile umbilical cord that connects Iraq, Syria and southern Turkey, now and in the past. The Tigris also begins in Anatolia but is additionally fed by five tributary rivers that drain the mountains of Iran, intimately interconnecting Iraq to the highland cultures to its east. Iraq has never stood apart in the way that Egypt does, with the Nile cutting its long course through the inhospitable Sahara Desert. Instead, it is a place that has drawn people and cultures, expanding along these river highways to become an empire and battlefield.

Where the Euphrates and Tigris come almost together, in the centre of Iraq, are two natural nodes of power, the modern cities of Baghdad and Basra. These have been key for a thousand years, controlling separate provinces, with a third northern province ruled from the city of Mosul, a tripartite division that corresponds to the dominant modern divisions of Sunni, Shia and Kurds. Even in ancient times, the three were rival kingdoms – Assyrians, Babylonians and Sumerians.

In light of the region's long history, therefore, it is not so surprising to find Saddam Hussein, the late president of Iraq, who came from the Sunni heartlands of the geographical centre, campaigning in the north against the Kurds and in the southern marshes against the Shia, to enforce his authority. When he invaded other nations – Iran in 1980, Kuwait in 1991 – he was doing so for reasons that every single ruler of Iraq for the last five thousand years would immediately recognise. He was seeking to assert the unity of geographic Mesopotamia, which arguably includes Khuzestan (in Iran) and Kuwait. Certainly, he was seeking to strengthen the country's Achilles heel, the Shatt al-Arab, Iraq's very limited access to the sea on the Persian Gulf, through which every Iraqi merchant ship, every oil tanker, has to sail. The Shatt al-Arab is controlled on its west bank by Kuwait, and on its east by Iran.

Any ruler of Iraq sees two hands around the throat of Mesopotamia in these geopolitical frontiers. To the east you have Arab-populated Khuzestan, in south-western Iran, while to the west you have a small Arab state, the Emirate of Kuwait. Many Iraqi historians consider that Kuwait floated away from the motherland due to the machinations of the British East India Company in the eighteenth century, working their will on a town filled with exiles from the Iraqi merchant city of Basra, then under siege. And here is a condundrum in the recent history of Iraq. The 1980 Iraqi invasion of Iran through Khuzestan (in order to seize control of the east bank of the Shatt al-Arab and some useful oil fields) got the support of most of the world, including Saudi Arabia, the Gulf States and the US. Yet the 1990 Iraqi invasion of Kuwait (in order to seize control of the western side of the Shatt al-Arab and some useful oil fields) incited the opposition of those same powers, leading the US and its European allies to launch the First Gulf War.

The motivations for the Second Gulf War of 2003 are perhaps even harder to understand, from any moral or geopolitical standpoint. In this war, the US destroyed Iraqi forces for a second time, then conquered and occupied Iraq. It was a demonstration to the world – perhaps for the last time – of the overwhelming power of the US military machine, with the British as bit players, in reaction to the American trauma of 9/11. Yet it was a war waged against the wrong nation.

❀ ❀ ❀

But first, a reminder of some pertinent episodes from the early modern history of Iraq. As we have already seen, the highly civilised Abbasid capital of Baghdad was sacked by the Mongols in 1258. The river first ran red with the blood of a quarter of a million civilians, then black with ink when the contents of its public libraries were thrown into it. For the next 250 years the grazing land of Iraq was fought over by rival Turkic warlords, including the bloodthirsty conquests of Timur, consciously following in the footsteps of the Mongols. And then came the two-hundred-year war between the Turkish Ottomans and the Persian Safavids.

This was just as merciless a war for the civilians as previous conflicts. The Safavids in ascendancy could put whole Sunni cities to death, while their Sunni Ottoman foe did the same to Shia cities. The Ottoman sultan, Selim the Grim, 'cleansed' the Shia faithful along his military line of march, while Shah Ismail eradicated the whole Sunni population of Baghdad when he seized control of the city. The tomb shrines of the Sunni scholars became an architectural litmus test of dominion. The mosque associated with the tomb of Ibn Hanbal was destroyed by the Shia in 1508, restored to glory by the Ottoman Sultan Suleyman the Magnificent (who led his army in person into Iraq) and then wrecked again in 1624 by Shah Abbas. By and large, the Ottomans were not as savagely destructive as the Safavids. As mainstream Sunnis, they respected the sanctity of the Prophet's family, so the tombs of Imam Ali at Najaf and Imam Husayn at Kerbala were adorned with gifts and not destroyed. The Safavids finally ceded control of Iraq to the Ottomans in the 1639 Treaty of Zuhab, leading to almost three hundred years of rule from Istanbul.

During the Ottoman–Safavid wars, the urban population of Iraq had declined. Indigenous Jews and Christians often survived more easily than their Muslim neighbours, as traders and urban craftsmen. The other great survivors were the Arab tribes in the countryside. If your wealth could be counted in herds, and your home was woven and highly mobile, there was a much greater chance of avoiding invading armies and tribute collectors. The Arab tribes were also courted by many of the invaders, not only as cavalry to serve in their armies, but to guarantee the safety of the desert roads. In the countryside, the authority of the tribal chieftains was paramount.

The Ottomans divided Iraq into its traditional trio of provinces, and appointed governors, known either as pasha or vali, to rule from Mosul, Baghdad and Basra. The governor was a great public figure. He ruled through a resident garrison of Janissaries, young foreign soldiers despatched from the distant capital, paid in silver coins that bore the name of the ruling sultan, whose name was also respectfully referenced in the Friday prayers. But an intriguing cross-current of Iraqi politics was that although it was a recognised province of the Ottoman Empire, in practice many of its links with the world – in terms of trade, migration and a vast annual flow of Shiite pilgrims – was with Iran to its east. Throughout this period Baghdad was a quarter Jewish, and a centre of Jewish scholarship and finance. The merchants of Basra were mostly Sunni. They were engaged with a very large geographical horizon, trading with China, India and the British East India Company.

Iraq benefited from an explosion of administrative efficiency in the mid-nineteenth century when the Ottoman Empire was reforming itself. New schools, libraries and hospitals emerged out of existing Islamic charitable foundations, creating an infrastructure that was desired, paid for and cared for by the urban communities. The first printed newspapers appeared in this period – *Al-Zawra, Al-Mawsil, Al-Basra* – encouraging an expansion in literacy, while continuing to reflect the tripartite nature of Iraq. There were nods, too, towards political representation. By 1908, there were sixty Arab MPs sitting in the 275-seat Ottoman parliament in Istanbul and there were enough Arab officers within the Ottoman army for them to form their own club. By and large the Shiites in southern Iraq tended to be indifferent to these connections with the reform-minded Ottoman Empire, regarding the Ottoman sultan as a usurper in his assumption of the title of caliph. So a career within the Ottoman army or a seat in parliament were dominated by Sunni Arabs, Kurds and Turkmen from central Iraq.

❋ ❋ ❋

When a military coup placed three strident and ambitious Turkish nationalists in charge of the Ottoman Empire in 1913, the British feared that their dominant position in the Persian Gulf might be overthrown. They occupied Basra in the first months of the First World War, in October 1914. The old rivalries within Iraq were forgotten at this act of aggression. The Arab tribes in the countryside supported the Ottoman 6th Army while Shia clerics stood with the Sunni *ulema* and echoed the call for a worldwide jihad against the British.

However, the Arab sheikhs were horrified by the brutality of modern warfare, as their young warriors were mown down by the machine guns and howitzers of the British at the Battle of Shu'aiba in April 1915. After this military victory, the British army determined to seize Baghdad, but instead found themselves cut off at Kut. The surrender of their forces, in April 1916, after the failure of the Gallipoli landings, was a low point in British military prestige. The Arab Revolt led by the Hashemite sheikhs – in alliance with the British operating out of Egypt – was not supported within Iraq. Nevertheless, the British did finally triumph and, in March 1917, had occupied Baghdad. The next year, the Ottoman 6th Army was destroyed within Iraq as an effective fighting force. In May 1918, Kirkuk to the north was also occupied.

In the absence of Ottoman rule, the internal politics of Iraq now revealed themselves. In the far south, a Shiite emirate emerged after the region was evacuated by the Ottoman army. In the northern hills, a tribal notable, Sheikh Mahmud Barzanji, declared an independent Kurdish state. In the centre of Iraq, the British had been welcomed as liberators in 1918, for they had promised self-determination and independence, but after two years of military occupation it became clear that they were planning to add Iraq to their vast Indian Empire.

In 1920, there were two simultaneous revolts. One was led by Sunni Arab tribes along the Middle Euphrates whilst a quite separate revolt erupted in the Shiite south, supported by senior Shia clerics. In the background were potential regional powers, such as the Emir of Kuwait, Mubarrah al-Sabah, who looked interested in taking a slice of Iraq. Sheikh Khaza'il of the Muhammara was meantime plotting to create an independent Emirate of Khuzestan from the Arab-speaking southern province of Iran.

The British concentrated their forces on the Sunni Arab revolt in the Middle Euphrates, bombing villages from the air and killing Iraqi warriors with machine guns mounted on armoured cars. They then put forward the Hashemite Emir Faysal, commander of the northern army of the Arab Revolt, as a candidate for the throne of Iraq. The country had not been independent since the fall of Baghdad in 1258, so it was an exciting prospect. Faysal was from the bloodline of the Prophet, so, although he was not Shia, he was at least a Sayyid. As an Arab prince, he was not popular with the Kurds, who wanted their own independent state, while most of the Sunni Arab notables thought of him as a carpetbagging interloper from the Red Sea. Faysal was, however, intelligent and had some experience of politics, for he had served as an Arab MP in the old Ottoman parliament. He diligently toured the country, talking to all communities about their options. He explained that, although the British military occupation of Iraq might never be loved, they were better than the French, who had just invaded Syria. Iraq at that time also had need of a strong military ally, with the Turks to the north, the Persians to the east and the Saudi Ikhwan raiding in the south. The British organised a referendum, held in 1921, which gave King Faysal 96 per cent of the vote.

❋ ❋ ❋

Faysal had plans. The security core of his Iraqi Kingdom would be 600 Iraqi soldiers, veteran troops of the Ottoman Empire who in some cases served under him during the Arab Revolt. They were not the sons of the tribal sheikhs, but had been recruited from the educated middle class of the cities and were overwhelmingly Sunni. They understood the need for unity and obedience and found it comparatively easy to transfer their loyalty from an Ottoman sultan to a Hashemite king. The force came with a commander, Jafar al-Askari.

Jafar, a great bull of a man, Mosul-born and the son of an Arab colonel in the Ottoman army, had seen action in the victorious Ottoman Gallipoli campaign. But the execution of twenty-one of the leading Arab intellectuals in 1916 by the Turkish governor of Syria encouraged him to switch his loyalty decisively to the Hashemites. Faysal took a great personal risk in trusting this career Ottoman officer with so much responsibility but Jafar proved himself worthy. His brother-in-law, Nuri al-Said, a fellow officer in the Ottoman army, also switched loyalties and became the Chief of Staff.

Faysal, Jafar al-Askari and Nuri al-Said proved themselves to be a formidable team. They were adept at allowing other individuals their time in the limelight, and did not seek to monopolise public office, but were content to manage affairs for the long term. Nuri al-Said remained a mainstay in Iraqi politics, on and off, until 1958.

The Iraqi regime was faced with many problems. The most pressing was that, although Faysal and his ministers accepted the need for a close military alliance with the British, this neo-colonial protectorate (mandated by the League of Nations) was fantastically unpopular with their people. The other great issue, and one which dominates Iraqi politics to this day, was the fate of the Kurdish north and the Shia south. The population of Iraq in 1921 was then about three million: 52 per cent Shia Arab, 20 per cent Kurd, 20 per cent Sunni Arab and 8 per cent comprising Jews, Assyrian and Chaldean Christians, Turkmen and Yazidi. The new regime first won the allegiance of the Sunni Arabs, co-opting the sheikhs of the great Arab tribes with the customary rewards of land and administrative jobs, as well as 40 per cent of the parliamentary seats.

Meanwhile in the north, the British were manoeuvring to invalidate Turkish claims to Kurdistan, in order to get their hands on the Kirkuk oil fields in Mosul province. The British took the Kurdish leader, Shaikh Ahmed Barzani, out of the prison in which they had placed him and installed him as governor of Sulaymaniyah. They then promised self-government to the Kurds and asked the League of Nations to send a fact-finding mission to rubber stamp what they had already established on the ground. The Turkish Republic has never forgiven Britain for the theft of the oil-rich province of Mosul, and to this day the area is one of the tinderboxes of the Middle East.

The Ottoman Petroleum Company of Mosul was renamed the Iraqi Petroleum Company and registered as a British company. The French were given 23.75 per cent, the US another 23.75 per cent (divided between Mobil and Standard Oil), while Royal Dutch Shell and Anglo-Persian (the corporate ancestor of BP) took 23.75 per cent each, with 5 per cent set aside for the deal-broking Armenian, Calouste Gulbenkian. The 20 per cent stake in the company that had been assigned to Iraq at an early stage of the talks had evaporated by the time the negotiations were completed. Oil royalties, however, gave the government of Iraq a useful stream of revenue, which by 1941 had allowed for the expansion of its army to 43,000 men.

This Iraqi army was trained and armed by the British and backed up by the presence of two RAF bases. They were soon put to work. Once the Mosul situation had been sorted, the idea of self-government for the Kurds was quietly shelved, and the RAF and Iraqi army were sent into action against them. In July 1924, Sheikh Mahmud Barzanji sought sanctuary in Iran, from where he directed an armed struggle until 1931. In 1932, the sheikh was forced to seek shelter in Turkey, where he was arrested. This frontier war in the Kurdish hills suited the British just fine. It gave the new army something to do, an enemy to fight, and allowed Britain to look like a useful ally to the Iraqi regime, not just its puppet master.

Shia scholars in southern Iraq denounced the whole Mandate structure as a sham, created entirely for the benefit of the British. And they were right. Even after the British had granted the Kingdom of Iraq its independence in 1932, it still reserved the right to supply (and sell) arms, to operate the RAF airbases as sovereign territory, to occupy Iraq in time of war and to oversee all foreign policy. So the Shiite clerics advised their people not to take part in the elections, which would give tacit acceptance to a puppet regime.

Sullen animosity grew violent over the summer of 1927, when the Iraqi army fired on a Shia procession. Instead of being punished for this massacre, the officer in charge was promoted. To make things worse, a government employee had published a book that rubbished Shia traditions. So the

Shia majority tended to avoid service in the national army. The Yazidi and Assyrian minorities felt the same reluctance to surrender their young men to conscription, which gave ambitious young Sunni Arab army officers the chance to crush these provincial rebellions and work themselves up into a righteous fury about traitors.

Within this new ruling class of Sunni Arab officers, there was debate about the future direction of Iraq. The Watani-yya ('people of the nation') were Iraqi nationalists. They were inclined to be interested in the grand Mesopotamian past, and aware of the influence, both good and bad, of Persia and Turkey in the making of modern Iraq, which meant there was room for Kurds, Shia and Christians to feel part of the vision. The Qawmiyya ('unity of the Arabs') were equally proud of Iraq but saw their nation as the natural centre of a much more powerful independent empire of Arab nations. They looked back for inspiration to the Abbasid caliphate as well as forward to an Arab intellectual renaissance. Unity or some form of close alliance with Arab Syria and Arab Jordan was part of this vision, which would also boost the Sunni Arabs within Iraq from a minority into a majority.

These two intellectual factions mixed with other loyalties – socialists and Communists – but all had hatred of the British protectorate in common. The hand of the British, manipulating Arab politics for their own narrow ends, could be traced on a map, following the pipeline by which the British were stealing the oil from Kirkuk and funnelling it across the Syrian desert to the Palestinian port of Haifa, where it fuelled the British fleet in the Mediterranean.

As ever, all Iraqi patriots were united by the situation on their southern frontier. If Iraq was to be defined by its Arab nature, then surely the Arabs of Kuwait and the Arabs of Khuzestan were part of the nation? If Iraq was to be defined by natural geographical frontiers, then Mesopotamia must include Kuwait and Khuzestan. On this matter, both the Wataniyya and the Qawmiyya thought as one.

❋ ❋ ❋

King Ghazi, who inherited the throne after the death of Faysal in 1933, had none of his father's experience. However, he was much more popular with the people, for he publicly criticised British rule in Palestine and claimed Kuwait as a lost province of Iraq. His death in a car crash in 1939 was popularly considered to have been the work of British secret agents.

The first of many military coups was plotted in 1936 by General Bakr Sidqi, probably with the support of King Ghazi. Bakr Sidqi looked to the example of Turkey and Iran, both at the time being forged into modern nation states under the autocratic command of a military leader. He aspired to modernise Iraq in a similarly forceful manner. In military campaigns waged within Iraq, first against the Christian Assyrians in 1933 and then the Shia in the south in 1935, he had proved himself a brutally efficient general. As a half-Arab, half-Kurd officer with a network of Turkmen soldiers, the general also seemed a living example of a new Iraq, forged from all its communities. He might have proved so, but he was shot in August 1937, on the orders of a cabal of seven senior officers, concerned that he was promoting too many of his Turkmen and Kurdish followers within the army.

In the Second World War, a group of young Iraqi officers known as the Golden Square attempted to rid themselves of the hated British. In April 1941, they backed a coup led by an old general, Rashid Ali, and called for a jihad against the British Empire. But, although Britain looked on the verge of defeat at this point in the war, their Axis allies were too far away, and too committed elsewhere, to be able to aid the conspirators effectively. Thirty plane-loads of arms did arrive in Mosul, but the British reacted decisively and crushed the coup. It was the ancient Jewish community of Baghdad who suffered most from this thirty-day emergency as two days of looting and lynching known as the Farhud left 180 Iraqi Jews dead and hundreds wounded. The misguided fury of these mobs was seeded by anxiety about the fate of Arab Palestine, whose 1936–39 revolt had also just been crushed by the British.

Kurdish diplomacy needs to flow in many directions, as they seek any ally to assist their struggle for independence. This was especially true during the Second World War, when the Russians occupied northern Iran in agreement with the British. The Soviet occupation established a socialist republic in the north-west of Iran, which inspired a Kurdish revolt across northern Iraq in 1945, led by Mustafa Barzani, younger brother of the leader of Kurdish resistance, Sheikh Ahmed Barzani. The Iraqi army defeated this rebellion, and the Kurdish fighters were forced to withdraw back over the mountains into Soviet-occupied Iran, where they supported the short lived Mahabad Kurdish Republic. This was itself defeated in the summer of 1947, but the Soviet Union continued to support these Kurdish rebels until 1958. It was an unlikely alliance: a highland chieftain working with the Stalinist bosses of Soviet-ruled Central Asia.*

As we have seen, the end of the Second World War was followed by the evacuation of French troops from Syria in 1946, which brought a renewal of hope for some sort of Arab union,

---

* This tale might be considered a distracting footnote in the history of the Middle East, except that it did have important ramifications. The Kurdish resistance movement (the KDP) would become politically radical during its period of exile within the Soviet Union. By 1951, it was calling for land reform, and the rights of workers and peasants, which encouraged Arab military elites within the Middle East to keep to their old Western alliances.

further ignited by the publicised 1948 withdrawal of British troops from some of their bases in Iraq. However, when the secret military clauses were revealed, it was clear that British military influence remained. Massive street protests erupted, which led to the imposition of martial law, and feelings were further inflamed by the Arab–Israeli War of 1948–49. Iraq had sent 15,000 men to assist their Arab brothers in Palestine, but they were given no effective leadership.

Nuri al-Said, the Iraqi political strongman over this entire period, had foreseen some of the likely problems of the Arab–Israeli War and made certain he was out of office, neatly sidestepping responsibility for the Arab defeat and the post-war recriminations between the political leadership of Jordan, Syria and Egypt. Instead, despite being seen as a pro-Western, anti-Communist leader, he gained respect as the Iraqi politician who took back control of the oil industry. Iraqi oil production increased by 400 per cent and government revenues by 600 per cent between 1951 and 1958. Nuri al-Said pledged that 70 per cent of this new largesse would be invested in long-term infrastructure and development projects. Side by side with this fiscal windfall, he had been patiently co-opting the southern two-thirds of the nation into employment in the schools, hospitals and ministries. This was reflected, too, in his cabinet, half of whom were Shia. There was by now a sufficiently large, literate middle class for a functioning multi-party democracy to operate. By the summer of 1954, Iraq was a solvent and independent nation with a constitutional monarchy, an articulate press and an almost free electoral system. In retrospect, these were to be the golden years of liberty and freedom of speech in Iraq.

Egypt's July 1952 military coup, which deposed King Farouk and established a republic commanded by Colonel Nasser, was watched with passionate interest by young officers in Iraq, who saw how popular this coup had been on the streets of Baghdad. Four years later, with the Suez crisis, Nasser was the hero of the entire Arab world. This was followed by the spontaneous union of Syria with Egypt (and later Yemen) to form the short-lived United Arab Republic. Nasser and his pan-Arabic vision flew in the face of Nuri al-Said's patient attempts to build a strong national identity for Iraq, which could unite people of different faiths and races, and his decision to take Iraq into the Baghdad pact (an anti-Soviet military alliance of Turkey, Iran, Pakistan and Britain) was loathed by the people of Iraq, who saw that it was in some way opposed to Nasser. When units from the Iraqi army were loaned to protect Lebanon and Jordan, it seemed that Iraq was now openly working as the henchman of the hated British, against the Arabs as led by Nasser.

These political pressures, which had been building up for decades, could no longer be contained. On 14 July 1958, a military coup struck against the Iraqi regime. It was clearly modelled on Nasser's coup in Egypt.

The violence of the revolution in Iraq was a shocking indication of the levels of anger that had built up beneath the veneer of the British-manipulated constitutional monarchy. In Egypt, the khedive had been escorted to his ship and saluted as he was sent off into exile. In Iraq, the old prince regent, the young King Faysal II and old Nuri al-Said were shot and their bodies dragged through the streets, defiled and strung up as formless carcasses. The patriotic fury against the long period of British rule had finally found its expression.

※ ※ ※

Abd al-Karim Qasim, the brigadier behind the 1958 coup, was not a democrat. He wished to rule as a populist strongman like Nasser and described himself as *al-Zaim al-Awhad* ('sole leader'). Qasim's father had been a humble Sunni Arab farmer from south of Baghdad, while his mother was a Shiite Kurd. Like so many dictators, he had endured a fatherless childhood.* In the countryside, a social revolution was ignited, urging peasants to rise up against the three thousand landowners who owned half the agricultural land. Oil revenue was flowing, which allowed Qasim to fund an impressive expansion of housing schemes and new schools for the poor. Qasim made alliances with the radical forces in the Arab world and invited both the Iraqi Communist Party and the Ba'ath Party into the regime.

The Ba'ath Party, influential throughout the Arab world as we have seen, tended to attract young, professional Arabs who had risen by their own merits and opposed the monopolisation of power and wealth by the old landowning families, allied with merchants and tribal chieftains. The Ba'ath were secular, intellectual and socialist, but were also political pluralists and not doctrinaire atheists like the Communist Party. One of the most impressive features of the Ba'ath was how they transcended the faith divisions of the Middle East, not just Sunni and Shia but also Arab Christians.

On 9 February 1963, the Ba'athist faction within the Iraq army mounted a successful coup. Qasim had survived so many attempts to kill him that by this stage in his life he slept on a camp bed in his office in the Ministry of Defence. His bullet-ridden corpse was exhibited on television to prove that the charismatic boss of the last five years was truly dead. His colleague from the 1958 coup, Abdal-Salam Arif, now emerged as the general-president.

---

* Saddam Hussein was also a fatherless child, growing up under the protection of his uncle, a passionate Ba'ath Party loyalist.

The Ba'ath Party, in the ascendant, were permitted to expand their own militia, which grew to a force of 30,000. An Orwellian double-think was emerging to cope with the splits, schisms and rivalries which were emerging across the Arab world. Everyone on the street could agree on 'Arab Freedom, Arab Unity and Arab Socialism', but what exactly was it that separated the political creed of a Nasserist from a Ba'athist? And what was the exact nature of the doctrinal issue that split the Syrian Ba'ath Party from the Iraqi Ba'ath Party in 1966? And, with Nasser still ruling in Egypt and the Ba'ath Party now in power in both Syria and Iraq, why was a United Arab Republic not emerging?

The answers were written over any map of the Middle East. Iraq was on the eastern edge of Arabia, and Egypt its western edge. Neither looked geographically destined to be the centre of any emerging pan-Arabia. So the purges and dawn arrests continued and, without any certain political answers, there was a return to a modern form of tribalism. The President of Iraq found it convenient to appoint a member of his own Al-Jumaila tribe as commander of the elite Republican Guard, who then used his tribe as his principal recruiting base. Similarly, in the summer of 1964, General-Vice President Ahmed Hasan al Bakri made certain that his young cousin, one Saddam Hussein, became the new secretary of the Ba'ath Party, to keep a close watch over the militia commanders.

The Ba'ath Party moved from being a junior partner into the seat of power. The Communist Party were initially courted, but this proved to be just a tactic to help identify the full extent of their membership, before they were purged from government posts and arrested. Rival factions of Ba'ath, Nasserist and other types of Marxists and Communists would also be taken out – complete with show trials and public hangings of spies, terrorists and traitors. In 1966, the Ba'ath Party split into rival

Syrian and Iraqi factions which would pursue their vendettas in the streets of Lebanon, in the Palestinian refugee camps, and amongst the Arab diaspora in Paris and London.

In the north of Iraq, the new regime behaved to a now well-established political formula. Peace with the Kurds was proclaimed and was followed by talks on such safe subjects as federalism and cantonal self-administration, but stuttered to a halt over who was going to hold a gun and bank the oil money. The regime then tried to divide the Kurds, by creating a pro-government faction. Fighting was renewed, and in the spring of 1969 Barzani's Kurdish militia hit the vital Kiruk oil fields. After a summer military campaign put the Iraqi army back in control on the ground, Saddam Hussein, a major power in the land but not yet president, settled down to secret negotiations. He agreed a four-year truce, which would lead to a final-status referendum on an independent Kurdistan. Barzani was to be allowed to keep command of his militia but agreed to withdraw them to the safety of Iran. It seemed a workable solution, but, to make the result certain where it mattered, Saddam Hussein organised the migration of loyal Sunni Arab workers into the Kirkup oil fields, so that these would remain part of Iraq, come what may.

In the south, the regime had continued Iraq's well-established interference with Arabistan, their term for the Iranian province of Khuzestan with its Arabic majority population. This annoyed the Shah, who decided to get tough on the exact line of the Iranian frontier along the Shatt al-Arab, which encouraged the Iraqi regime to lean on their own local Shia leadership to publish an official condemnation of Iranian foreign policy. But the Shia scholars refused to get involved in a squabble over frontier maps. The regime then overreacted to the customary independence of the Shia scholars, and in April 1969 expelled

20,000 Shiites from the university-shrine city of Najaf. They were judged to be Iranian, not Iraqi, in their loyalties.

The battlelines of two conflicting loyalties had now been disastrously drawn across southern Iraq. The Ba'ath Party, working with many secular-minded Shia, now attempted to destroy the influence of the clerics, who for their part had proclaimed a *fatwa* against membership of the party. But mass expulsions and arbitrary arrests created their own mood in the south, which led to the more defiant political stance of the new Shiite Ayatollah of Iraq, Muhammad Baqir al-Sadr. As a Baghdad-born Iraqi, he could not be labelled a meddling foreign scholar from Iran.

In other affairs the regime proved more subtle. It achieved the well-managed nationalisation of the Iraqi oil industry in 1972 so that, by 1975, the government was receiving $8 billion of oil revenue a year. Some 40 per cent was spent on military and security, but that left more than enough with which the state could provide food, housing and medical care for the urban working class and poor farmers. Saddam Hussein also pushed forward with campaigns to provide education and employment for women. In 1972, a pact was signed with the Soviet Union. This not only ended the long internal Ba'athist versus Communist feud within Iraq but guaranteed a reliable source of arms and placed Iraq squarely within the international alliance of progressive socialist nations. An abortive internal coup over the summer of 1973 gave Saddam Hussein (whose elderly cousin was now the president) the opportunity to purge the security services and place his own men in key positions of power, among them his half-brother, Barzan al-Takriti. The 20,000-strong Takriti clan became ever more associated with power. A few years later, a cousin and a brother-in-law of Saddam would also be promoted to high office.

In terms of tanks and jets destroyed, the 1973 Arab–Israeli Yom Kippur War seemed a critically important conflict, but, with the benefit of historical distance, it is not so much the fighting but the truce enforced by the Saudi-led Arab oil embargo that is important. All of a sudden, the Arabs found a weapon that could work, and in the process completed their long struggle to possess their own oil industry. It also marked the emergence of Saudi Arabia as the new lynchpin of Middle East politics. Egypt had disgraced itself as an independent-minded leader of the Arabs by making peace with Israel at Camp David in 1978 and becoming a paid-up ally of the US. The aspirations of both Iraq and Syria to take up the place occupied by Nasser (who had died in 1970) is another clue to understanding the fierce regional rivalry between the two Arab nations.

❋ ❋ ❋

As we have seen, 1979 was a crucial year in the Middle East. It is the birth of our confused era and was also the year that Saddam Hussein formally took over as president of Iraq from his cousin, though he had held power as deputy ruler since the 1968 coup. The pan-Arabic cause continued to be championed by the Ba'ath Party but in all other ways Saddam Hussein followed a consistently Mesopotamian agenda. He was often depicted in military uniform, but in fact he was one of the very few rulers of Iraq not to have had a military career. His rise to power had been entirely within the Ba'ath Party, albeit within its security apparatus.

Saddam Hussein's ascent to power gave some gory hints of what was to come. His elderly cousin, President Hassan al-Bakr, was about to end the rivalry between the Ba'ath regimes of Syria and Iraq by signing a treaty of union. But Saddam was determined to rule and hurriedly forced his old cousin into retirement before arresting and torturing Abdel Hassan, the permanent secretary of the Revolutionary Command Council. In a televised scene that repeated the drama of Stalin's Great Purge of the Communist Party in 1937, Abdel Hassan, broken by torture, denounced sixty Ba'ath Party members for a supposed 'Syrian Plot'. As their names were read out, the television camera caught the stumbling rise, confusion and anxiety written all over their troubled faces, as they hurriedly left the council chamber. Not all were killed, but those who were pardoned were encouraged to denounce other party members and form volunteer execution squads. This bloody purge of the party led to 500 executions.

Encouraged by the success of the Islamic revolution in Iran, in June 1979 the Shiite clergy of southern Iraq reacted against state repression with an unusual level of confidence and organisation. Street protests spread beyond the Shiite core of the holy cities of Najaf and Karbala, to engulf the southern suburbs of Baghdad itself. Their marches were suppressed by 5,000 arrests. By October 1979, leading members of the Shia clergy were starting to think in terms of a determined opposition movement to Saddam Hussein's regime. The headquarters of the Al-Dawa Party, which had been established as a Shiite political party in 1957, and long experienced state persecution, was formally based in Tehran.

On 3 April 1980, a grenade was thrown in Baghdad by an agent from Iran, in an assassination attempt against the deputy prime minister, Tariq Aziz. It failed to take out its target. On 5 April, the leading Shiite scholar, Ayatollah Muhammad Baqir al-Sadr, was arrested, followed by his sister, Bint al-Huda. They were taken from their homes in Najaf for interrogation in the Ministry of Defence buildings in Baghdad to try to prove a direct line of command between the Shiite scholar clergy of Iraq, the Al-Dawa Party in exile in Iran and this terrorist grenade attack. According to some emotive accounts, Saddam Hussein personally involved himself in these investigations, and Bint al-Huda was raped before her brother, who then had an iron nail hammered into his skull, before he was shot. To anyone brought up within the Shiite tradition, this brutal martyrdom at the hands of the 'Power' comes as no surprise. These two are referred to as the martyrs of 9 April, a date which, ironically, marked the fall of Saddam Hussein twenty-three years later. No Western leader condemned Iraq for the killings, which were followed by the expulsion of 40,000 Shia, accused of being Iranian not Iraqi, from the south.

❋ ❋ ❋

Saddam Hussein launched his invasion of Iran in September 1980. He and most Iraqis understood this not as a war of Sunni against Shia, but as an attempt to expand the country's narrow access to the sea on the Shatt al-Arab. Maybe Saddam also dreamed of annexing to Iraq the rich oil fields of Khuzestan with its majority Arab population, but he would have known that this would come at a cost. It would have made the Shia majority in Iraq even larger, for virtually all the four million Arabs in Khuzestan are Shia.

The Iranian armed forces had long been considered the best trained and equipped in the entire Middle East, but since the revolution its officer corps had been decimated by arrests, exile and political purges. Saddam Hussein had good reason to believe that Iran had weakened itself. He had never served in the army and this must have seemed an excellent chance to prove himself a military leader. The plan was for a quick, decisive invasion: occupy a substantial amount of Iranian territory, agree a truce and then settle down to a negotiated peace, giving Iraq control of the Shatt al-Arab.

As described earlier, it didn't work out in this way. The spirit of the Iranian armed forces was instantly revived by a surprise attack from an external enemy. Iran held back the Iraqi attack and then launched its counter-attack.

In 1980, Iraq had been sitting on reserves of $30bn. After three years of war this had all been spent and replaced by a foreign debt of $25 billion. The catastrophic expense of waging war had been further exaggerated by a collapse in the oil price (down from $26 a barrel in 1980 to $9 in 1982). Iraq was only able to continue the war due to the backing of Saudi Arabia and the Gulf emirates, who had always been wary of Iranian power, and had become especially worried since the Iranian Revolution. Suddenly the Iran–Iraq War, which had been about territory, took on a new dimension. An alliance of Sunni Arab nations began to collect behind Saddam Hussein.

The catastrophic destruction of the war went almost entirely unreported in the West. There was lukewarm US support for Iraq, but only because they hated the clerical regime in Iran even more, as summed up by the infamous quip by Kissinger: 'It's a pity both sides can't lose.' One thing is certain, however. The major industrial powers made fortunes selling war material, often to both sides, especially once they started firing long-range missiles at each other. By 1988, Iraq had built up $80 billion of debt. A similar financial meltdown faced Iran, and so the two sides reluctantly agreed a ceasefire.

Two facts emerged during the fighting. Shiite Arabs in Iran had remained loyal to Iran, while the Shiites of Iraq had also remained loyal to their own country. National identity had proved stronger than ethnic or faith divisions. However, the Kurdish KDP under Barzani had sided with the Iranians and were treated as traitors by Saddam Hussein. After the war ground to a halt, the full weight of Saddam's battle-trained army was sent to the northern hills in the bloody Al-Anfal campaign. The figures are disputed, but perhaps as many as 100,000 Kurds died and 80 per cent of the Kurdish villages associated with the resistance were flattened. Kurdish fighters were forced to seek refuge wherever they could – even within the Republic of Turkey.

Although there had been no Shia risings in Iraq during the war, this period did witness the emergence of the Al-Badr Brigade in Iran, recruited from the tens of thousands of Shia expelled in 1969 and 1980. This group of Iraqi refugees, who had already suffered for their faith, were a fertile recruiting ground. Their numbers, and their professionalism, were enhanced by military volunteers from the tens of thousands of Iraqi soldiers who had been captured and made prisoners of war. At the end of this war, these fighters could not return to Iraq, for they would be certainly shot as traitors. They remained in Iran with strong personal relationships to many of the leaders of the Iranian Revolution. However, they were to return to Iraq more quickly than any observer could have possibly predicted.

❀ ❀ ❀

After the Iran–Iraq War had ended, Saddam Hussein faced a challenge: how to keep his authority over the world's fourth largest army in the aftermath of a military defeat, and how to inspire the nation with his leadership. Taking possession of Kuwait was an obvious solution. As already noted, this was a long-term policy goal for all leaders of Iraq, and expansion into Kuwait would tick a number of domestic boxes for Saddam, proving him both the dynamic leader of an ever-greater Mesopotamia and a Ba'athist leader creating a pan-Arab super-state. He also had a war loan to pay off, which would be quickly resolved by the annexation of the

Kuwait oil fields and the cancellation of Iraq's war-loan debt to Kuwait.

Relations between the US and Saddam Hussein were then close and, as Iraqi troops began to mass on the southern border with Kuwait, a delegation of five influential senators came to talk to him. Then, on 25 July, US ambassador April Glaspie told Saddam that 'we have no opinion on Arab–Arab conflicts like your border disagreement with Kuwait'. Back in the US, Senator John Kelly, part of the delegation, confirmed that the US had no joint defence treaty with Kuwait. Saddam Hussein's decision to invade Kuwait may not have been given the green light by the US, but these statements suggested amber rather than red.

So, on 2 August 1990, Iraqi tanks rolled across the frontier. It was a gamble that very nearly paid off. The international media and political leadership were on holiday, and initially it seemed that President George H.W. Bush did not want to fight on the ground. But two key US allies helped change his mind: King Fahd of Saudi Arabia and the British prime minister Margaret Thatcher both talked up the dangers of letting bullying dictators get away with it. They argued that the evacuation of the Russians from Afghanistan in 1989 and of the Argentines from the Falklands in 1982 had established a pattern for world peace, where sabre-rattling dictators were opposed. Bush had fought as a young man in the war, had served as head of the CIA, as an ambassador and as vice-president, so knew the full range of options at first hand. By 12 August, Saddam Hussein began to realise that his gamble had not worked. He tried to camouflage his failure by posing as an Arab hero and offered to withdraw from Kuwait if Israel withdrew from the West Bank.

There was no deal. That summer President Bush patiently put together a diplomatic alliance that would be the zenith of the US working as the global policeman. He received the backing of the UN and could also be clearly seen as responding to a call for assistance from the independent Kingdom of Saudi Arabia. By 31 October, an allied army of 400,000 troops was in position in the Persian Gulf, from an alliance of thirty states, including Arab kingdoms and Western democracies. On 29 November, the UN authorised the use of armed force, set to a diplomatic deadline of 15 January. It was a glorious day of the new world order, orchestrated by the global assembly of the United Nations. But not before Saddam Hussein had fired forty-two Scud missiles at Israel, a move which won him kudos on the streets of the Arab world, posing as a Saladin-like warrior leader to the Palestinian Arabs. Saddam may have hoped that Israel would launch a quick counter-strike against Iraq, which might have fractured the alliance of Arab nations with the US. It did not work, but in the process he made himself powerful enemies, who would never forgive nor forget this attack.

Victory on the ground was achieved in the first 100 hours and a ceasefire was called after just forty-two days of conflict. The Shia in the south, and the Kurds in the north of Iraq, took the opportunity of Saddam Hussein's defeat to rebel. In April 1991, UN Resolution 688 changed the rules on the ground within Kurdistan by creating a no-fly zone north of the 36th parallel. This was actively policed by the air forces of the US and its Western allies. Although two million Kurds had fled over the Iranian and Turkish borders to escape the fighting, the removal of airpower from the military equation changed the situation. By October 1991, the Iraqi army had withdrawn from the Kurdish northernmost provinces. Free local elections were held in May 1992, with the vote evenly split between two rival Kurdish parties, the KDP and PUK. The KDP (Kurdish Democratic Party) and its Peshmerga militia is led by the Barzani family (Masoud, son of Mustafa, and his nephew Nechirvan); it has historic links with the Turkish Republic and an enmity with the PKK Kurdish resistance in Turkey. The PUK (Patriotic Union of Kurdistan) looked to Iran and occasional support from the Al-Badr Brigade. They established control of different border passes and indulged in lucrative oil smuggling, profitably pursued with some of their old enemies within the Iraqi regime. In 1996, the Kurdish regional government came to an agreement with the Iraqi state, accepting 13 per cent of national oil sales.

Both the KDP and PUK were supported by militia armies of 80,000 men but managed to maintain a truce rather than launch a Kurdish civil war. In 2005, these various ad hoc arrangements were codified in a new constitution which created the Kurdish Regional Government, effectively divided into two separate emirates, each with their own international airports. Although an attempt to annex the Kirkuk oil fields and to declare complete independence was defeated, this was the best deal yet achieved by any Kurdish community. It is a possible role model for the Kurds in Syria, Turkey, and Iran. Any grand talk of an independent, united Kurdistan needs to bear in mind that even the Kurds of Iraq are split into two. The two Kurdish states in northern Iraq have strong working relationships with Iran and Turkey. In the past they have been rivals to the Kurds of south-eastern Turkey, who are the allies of the Kurds of northern Syria.

❋ ❋ ❋

A less visible long-term consequence of the First Gulf War was incubating itself in Saudi Arabia. Groups of young Saudi military volunteers, back from their victory over the Russians in Afghanistan, offered to guard the borders of their homeland,

and if need be help liberate Kuwait from the invasion of the secular Ba'athist regime of Iraq. There would be no need to call in assistance from the hated Western powers. They could do the job on their own, like their grandfathers who had served in the Ikhwan.

Saudi Arabia was one of the very few Arab (as well as one of the very few Muslim) countries in the world that had never been colonised, invaded or occupied by any Western army, or suffered a protectorate. As the homeland of the Prophet Muhammad and the two sacred cities of Medina and Mecca, it felt to the young men an especially acute disgrace that Saudi Arabia should now need the support of the West to defend itself from an Arab neighbour. But these ardent offers from volunteer fighters were not so much spurned as never even answered, as hundreds of thousands of American troops poured into the eastern half of Saudi Arabia.

The young warriors, many brought up within urban middle-class families, hardened their hearts and began to disassociate themselves from the affairs of the world, in order to plan a new Islamic state. Their leader, Osama bin Laden, was a quietly spoken Saudi Arabian of good family, who had spent time in Afghanistan helping the Mujahadin fight the Soviets. In 1992, he left his homeland and took up residence in Sudan before moving back to his old comrades in Afghanistan, becoming the emotional fulcrum linking like-minded groups and individuals under the banner of Al-Qaeda. The primary attraction was the opportunity for men to fight for what they considered to be a noble cause, to be part of an old tradition that embraced Arab pride, Wahhabi militarism and Salafi theology, but involved a new strain of internationalism, enabled and inspired through the technology of the Internet and the mobile phone.

The Al-Qaeda plan was to escalate a clash of civilisations by attacking America and her worldwide network of military bases. On 7 August 1998, bombs blew apart two US embassies in East Africa, and in October the USS *Cole* was attacked off the coast of Yemen. This was followed by 9/11, when the cell of nineteen Al-Qaeda terrorists hijacked four internal US passenger planes and flew them into New York's Twin Towers and the Pentagon. Fifteen of these terrorists were Saudi citizens, two came from the Gulf, one from Egypt, and one from Lebanon. There were no individuals or any organisational connection with either Iraq or Iran. As George W. Bush, son of George H.W. Bush, and now the US president, would later admit: 'One of the hardest parts of my job is to connect Iraq to the war on terror.'

✤ ✤ ✤

The Second Gulf War was nonetheless a direct corollary of 9/11, as the terror attacks became universally known. America had been quietly proud of its role as the world's peacemaker during the 1990s, but overnight the small international wars that it had undertaken in faraway countries had migrated to its home soil – so unexpectedly, so violently, and directed at an innocent trading city and its unsuspecting inhabitants.

The reaction of America to this outrage against its domestic sanctity, its military, political, diplomatic and financial sovereignty, was bound to be complex. Its actions in the end were as much emotional as strategic. The invasion of Afghanistan less than a month after 9/11 was rational: to seek out and destroy the men who had masterminded this terrorist attack on American civilians. The desire to attack Iraq is more difficult to understand. There were no Iraqi citizens involved in 9/11. So why did the Second Gulf War happen? It seems that the US wanted to exact more vengeance, and the regime in Iraq was already labelled as an enemy. Pehaps there was also some emotional linkage between the Scud missiles that were launched by Saddam Hussein at Israel in 1991 and the events, ten years later, of 9/11, both of which were brought to the world on live TV. The story used by the Western intelligence services to justify this war, that Saddam Hussein was harbouring weapons of mass destruction, was a lie, but one that cleverly used memories of his Scud missile attacks to stoke up fears.

The Second Gulf War saw the US and its allies defeat the Iraqi forces for a second time, and then conquer and occupy Iraq. It was a demonstration to the world of the overwhelming power of the American military machine. A hundred thousand casualties in Iraq, not to mention the chaos the war unleashed in its wake, was the price that someone had to be pay 'for awakening a sleeping giant filled with a terrible resolve'. It was just a pity that the wrong people were punished.

American foreign policy adopted the mantra of regime change and had a curiously inappropriate example in mind. Back in 1945, they had constructed liberal, free-trading nation states in their own image from the most unpromising of materials, from Nazi Germany and imperialist Japan, so one of their principal aims was to strip the Ba'ath Party surgically from the body politic of Iraq. It was an odd decision, for in many ways the Ba'ath, with its dedication to an Arab intellectual renewal, its enthusiasm for female education, its tolerance of all religions, and its 'United States of Arabia' aspiration, had much in common with 'the American dream'.

In effecting this post-war policy, the US effectively destroyed the existing police, military, civil service, education, and intelligence services. Iraq, in consequence, was threatened with anarchy. So the Americans looked to impose a new regime that hated the Ba'ath but also had internal discipline. The Al-Badr Brigade seemed to fit the bill, so they selected its veteran leader, Jabr Bayan, to be the new interior minister. This meant that, for the first time, Iraq would be ruled by members of its Shia majority. But there were two problems. Firstly, by their very nature, as a force that had been on the opposite side of the Iran–Iraq War, the new masters would be hated by even the mildest-mannered Sunni Arab. And, secondly, the Al-Badr Brigade revered the leadership of Iran. They had served the very men who now directed the militia and intelligence services that are the ultimate power in Iran. At a stroke, the US had handed over the long-term future of Iraq to their even greater enemy, the Islamic Republic of Iran. It was the most decisive shift in the balance of power within the Middle East since 1979.

However, not all Shia Iraqis were as naturally in tune with the Iranian leadership as the members of the Al-Badr Brigade. There has always been a quietist, intellectual Shia tradition centred on the city of Najaf which eschews politics. Many believe that they hold to the true line of Shiite theology, and that Ayatollah Khomeini broke rank with his political engagement. Such Iraqi ayatollahs as Al-Sistani and al-Khoi and their intellectual heirs may one day help reform the Islamic Republic of Iran, and take the clerics out of cabinet and put them back in the mosques.

Another strand of Shia intellectual leadership in Iraq was represented by Muqtada al-Sadr, whose infamous Mahdi army militia opposed the American occupation. Muqtada inherited an extraordinary mantle of respect from his father and his intellectual aunt, both martyred by Saddam Hussein. His Mahdi army evolved out of the vacuum of authority after the American conquest, when mobs looted the streets. It began as a self-help group of 500 young scholars protecting Shiite communities in Baghdad, but grew into a state within the state. Muqtada al-Sadr has clearly proved himself a politically ambitious man, so that some of the respect won by the martyrdom of his pious father is beginning to wash off, especially as he has begun to cooperate with Iran.

As well as transforming the regime, the American military occupation delivered the first free elections for fifty years. The elections produced an outstanding majority for the Shia, very largely divided into the two political factions described: the old boys of the Al-Badr Brigade and the party that represented Muqtada al-Sadr and his allies. The old Sunni Ba'ath elite in government, the military, the police and the intelligence services were out on their ear, having lost their jobs, pensions and positions of respect. They were replaced by Shia politicians, backed up Shia militia and a Shiite minister of interior.

It was almost inevitable that there would be some sort of Sunni Arab backlash, which would need to seek support from the larger Sunni world. An insurrection at Fallujah during 2004, supported by international volunteers, was one of the early flashpoints and helps to explain the later emergence of ISIS, which achieved such an astonishing ascent to power in the summer of 2014, when it came to control such substantial cities as Mosul, Tikrit, Raqqa and Deir el-Zour. ISIS was an alliance of Sunni Islamists working with the professional military and security skills of discharged members of the old Ba'athist regime. It could also easily identify local allies within the Sunni Arab forces fighting in the Syrian Civil War, which had erupted in 2011 in the wake of the Arab Spring.

❊ ❊ ❊

One of the most intriguing features of ISIS was the level of international support that it received. Up to half of its soldiers were unpaid foreign volunteers, numbering around 30,000 individuals, of which perhaps half were likely to be active at any one period. These volunteers were recruited by an innovative international propaganda campaign waged on the Internet. Like all Islamist groups, ISIS concentrated its theoretical attention on the very earliest period of Islam and on the present day. There was to be a return to the daily life of the caliphate (their leader, Abu Bakr al-Baghdadi, shared the name of the very first Sunni caliph), with universal gold dinar coinage, and such traditions as enslaving captured enemy women as concubines.

ISIS were keen on millennial prophecies about the 'End of the Days', and on the mysterious traditions about the coming of the Mahdi, who will usher in the Day of Judgement. The name of their online magazine, *Dabiq*, which published fifteen issues between July 2014 and July 2016, was itself a reference to these events, for Marj Dabiq in northern Syria was historically one of the candidates for the last battle at the end of the world. It references one of the *hadith*, which prophesies that 'The Last Hour would not come until the Rumi [Western soldiers] occupy Dabiq. An army consisting of the best [soldiers] of the people of the earth at that time will come [to counteract them] from Medina.'

ISIS recruits could pledge their obedience in online inter-views. They were rewarded with violent video films: the execution of Shia prisoners of war, the slaughter of Yazidi men and enslavement of Yazidi women, the burning alive of a Jor-danian airforce pilot, and the execution of a dozen foreign journalists and aid workers accused of being spies. Though these films disgusted the leaders of the Western world, they were popular amongst the young online supporters of ISIS and referenced Salafi scholarship to the actions of Abu Bakr, the First Caliph, and his Ridda war.

Thousands of volunteers came from Chechnya and other regions of the former Soviet Union, backed up by recruits from such outwardly moderate Muslim nations as Turkey, Tunisia, Jordan and Morocco, and also from Europe. This internationalisation had been a feature of those who volunteered to support the Mujahadin struggle in Afghanistan. Initially they were an ineffective force in combat, though useful for garrison support, propaganda, urban patrols and fundraising.

The spectacular speed and success of ISIS in creating a new state on the upper Euphrates valley, which straddled the Syria–Iraq border, created a unique response. This working alliance included the US and its NATO allies, Russia, various Shia and Iranian militia groups, Kurdish freedom fighters and a handful of Sunni nations such as Jordan and Pakistan. Turkey largely stood to one side, incapable of assisting the Kurdish militia in northern Syria or of abandoning its Islamist allies in the Syrian civil war. Russian forces concentrated their efforts within Syria, the Pakistani army policed the Saudi border, and the US was responsible for at least 80 per cent of the targeted air strikes on ISIS positions, backed up by its Western allies, France and Britain.* Ground intelligence was provided by small squads of special forces working with Kurdish and Shia militia.

After three years of airstrikes, ISIS as a geographical state was destroyed. The self-proclaimed caliph, Iraqi-born Abu Bakr al-Baghdadi, was killed on 27 October 2019 in north Syria. In the aftermath, it became clear just how many of the effective military leaders of ISIS came from the dismantled Ba'ath Party and the old Iraqi intelligence services. There was also a core of Sunni Turkmen from northern Iraq, just the sort of candidates whose grandfathers would have served in the

---

* France had strongly opposed the Second Gulf War, unlike Britain, which under Prime Minister Tony Blair had given full support and provided troops for the invasion and subsequent occupation.

army of the Ottoman sultan, then taken office under Faysal. Such are the unforeseen consequences of regime change.

The emergence of ISIS was a direct consequence of the establishment of Shiite rule in Iraq. It would clearly be wise to allow the Sunni Arab population in the north-central provinces of Iraq some sort of regional self-government, in something of the manner in which it has been given to the Kurds, in order to deter the emergence of a new version of ISIS. But, looking back over the modern history of Iraq, one can locate very few instances where the old Sunni ruling class behaved with any compassion towards the Shia.

One knock-on effect of Shiite majority rule in Iraq has been to encourage the Shia minority in the emirates of the Persian Gulf and in the eastern provinces of Saudi Arabia. This has increased the pressure on the existing rivalry between Saudi Arabia and the Islamic Republic of Iran and led to the persecution of those Shiite minorities. Optimists look to the long future, to the emergence of a new generation tired with the corrupt regimes of old men. And perhaps, with the friendship of Iraq in the bag, the leaders of Iran will become less isolated, and the quietist Iraqi traditions of Shiite theology might encourage the clerics of Iran back into the colleges. Perhaps.

CHAPTER 24

The Two Yemens

The ancient home of Arabia – and its battlefield

The Yemen is the ultimate home of all that is valued in Arab culture, be it poetry, architecture or the long-trailing genealogy of your favourite dun-coloured mare. And it is an astonishing, beautiful land, with stern, bleak mountains rising in row after row of monumental terraces, and, at the edge of all this monumental drama, a vast sand desert, suddenly and unexpectedly broken by bright-green oasis valleys. Yet, so much beauty, so much cheerful hospitality, so much poverty and pride, is combined with centuries of violent conflict. The current round of fighting began in 2014 as a civil war but has now morphed into a proxy war between a Saudi Arabia-led Sunni military confederacy and Shiite Iran. Over the last decade, it has killed 50,000 soldiers and at least 6,000 civilians. If we are looking for a modern Sunni–Shia faultline, the Yemen is significant.

The simple explanation of this conflict is that Saudi Arabia fears the establishment of a Shiite state in the Yemen, which would create a dependent ally of Iran on its south-west frontier. The Sunni confederacy that the Saudis have armed and support claim to want to re-establish the legitimate government of the Yemen (now in exile in Aden), ousted from the capital of Sanaa by a Shiite insurrection by a Houthi movement that call themselves *Ansar Allah* ('supporters of God'). For their part, the Houthi would claim to be an Islamic, nationalist rebellion, fighting for Zaydi Shiite rights, and in 2012 helped topple the corrupt regime of President Ali Abdullah Saleh, who had plundered Yemen of a reported $30–60 billion in two decades of rule.

The emergence of a Shiite Yemen might appear as yet another enlargement of the crescent of Shiite states, and as part of a mutating war zone of Sunni–Shia war in Lebanon, then Iraq, then Syria and now in the Yemen. First the slow enlargement of the Shiites and then the Sunni counter-attack. There are commentators who see this as a round in a Middle East war that will tear the region apart before engulfing the world. Yet there is also a less alarming reading of events. For this is not the first time the Yemen has split into two, or fought a civil war or toppled a regime by assassination, coup or conspiracy. These things have happened often in the Yemen. It is a land where tribal and clan affiliations remain more important than political or sectarian affiliations. And, to add to all the confusion, we might remember that thirty years ago the Kingdom of Saudi Arabia was supporting the same tribes that they are now attacking.

❁ ❁ ❁

Looking back over the past half-century or so, Yemeni political history begins with a Socialist coup against the monarchy of the imam in 1962, which was followed by the Aden Insurrection (1963–67), which expelled the British. Then, in 1972, came a brief border war between the two Yemens; a coup in 1974; two presidential assassinations; a brief civil war in 1979; union in 1990; a rebellion in 2004; a border skirmish in 2009; the Arab Spring in 2011; and a fixed election in 2012. All were interwoven with Houthi rebellion in the north that survived the assault of six government campaigns before finally taking control of the capital, Sanaa, in September 2014. This was followed by civil war – a new round of odd alliances – followed by the intervention of a Saudi-led military coalition, Operation Decisive Storm, from March 2015. This began as a proxy war, fought by fighter pilots, border patrols and naval interceptor craft, but escalated as the Sunni alliance landed marines to occupy the Red Sea port of Hodeidah.

In this campaign, Saudi Arabia claimed to be supporting the 'official government' of President Hadi, a general who was the only candidate in the 2012 election. The Saudis and their Sunni Arab allies* alleged that Iran was creating a proxy Shiite state in the Yemen, which had begun to launch missile strikes against Saudi cities. If you look at a military map of the Yemen, and the division of the country into power blocks, you will notice that it almost exactly follows the old frontier between North Yemen (with the capital, Sanaa) and South Yemen (based on the port of Aden). The Houthis control the north, Hadi supposedly controls the south (which is actually divided into two factions), while other groups control parts of the Hadramaut in the east.

This civil war has now displaced two million Yemenis and driven a quarter of a million refugees from the country. The nation's GDP has been cut in half and government revenue crippled; even before the war, average income was around $2,500 (compared to $21,000 in neighbouring Saudi Arabia). Yemen is only preserved from famine and starvation by the loyalty of its migrants. There is a widespread diaspora that for hundreds of years has sent Yemeni seamen, scholars and traders to seek their fortune in Britain, California, Malaysia, Indonesia and the Gulf. This diaspora sends home an estimated $3.5

* The Saudi forces were reported to include planes from Egypt, Morocco, Jordan, Sudan, Kuwait, the United Arab Emirates, Qatar and Bahrain

billion a year to keep their cousins, old folks and motherland from total ruin. The aid agencies also help.

✤ ✤ ✤

Yemen's highland tribes freely accepted Islam during the lifetime of the Prophet. In the centuries following, political control changed often, as the coastal regions (easily accessible to any invader) split off from the mountains, or the south separated from the northern highlands, or the Hadramaut in the east asserted independence. There were also moments when a Greater Yemen emerged under a single ruler and expanded its dominion over the Red Sea shore. In the eleventh century, the Sulayhid rulers appointed a governor to rule over Mecca, a memory still cherished in the Yemen and for centuries remembered in the annual Yemeni Haj caravan to Mecca, led by a *mahal* (an unridden camel) bearing an ornate litter as a gift to the sacred but subject city.

What is most enduring in the Yemen are the tribes. The Hashid and Bakil of the northern highlands have an identity that goes back at least a thousand years before they were converted to Islam by the preaching of Ali. It was these tribes who accepted a young refugee prince and scholar as their first Zaydi imam in 893. They established a sense of religious and political identity, characterised by a strong sense of justice against corrupt rulers, that remains valid in Yemen to this day.

The Zaydi tradition within Islam is labelled Shia, though it follows a middle way between Shiite and Sunni positions on a number of issues. They honour (and do not curse) the achievements of Caliph Abu Bakr and Caliph Omar, while feeling free to question the way these first two caliphs assumed power instead of Ali. The Zaydi also do not believe in a strict succession of hereditary leaders of the Islamic world, passing spiritual authority from father to son. Instead, they suggest that the family of Muhammad and Ali provide a natural pool of leadership for the Islamic world, but that it is up to the community to choose those who appear most valiant and 'the most versed human knowing the Holy Book of God'. The Zaydi are sometimes known as The Fivers, for, though they honour all the family of the Prophet (revering Ali, his sons Hasan and Husayn, and Husayn's only surviving son, Ali ibn Husayn Zayn al-Abbadine), they also delight in the example of their choice for the fifth imam, who was Zayd ibn Ali.*

Zayd ibn Ali was born in 695 in Medina, a fourth-generation descendant of the Prophet through Ali and Fatima. He had grown up surrounded by the tales of the martyrdom of his family, most especially of his grandfather, Husayn at Kerbala, which took place only fifteen years before he was born. He could not watch the community being led astray and in 740 rode east to Kufa, in answer to the call for the leadership of a just man. Like his grandfather before him, he found the people who had summoned him melted away, angered, it is said, by his refusal to claim the authority of sacred kingship. Zayd was simply content with the honour of being of the family of the Prophet and a reputation as 'most versed human'. Like his grandfather, Husayn, he carried the purity of his conviction into a battlefield in southern Iraq, where he was struck down by an arrow, and then beheaded and crucified.

Different strands of the descendants of the first Zaydi imam of Yemen have come and gone over the centuries, some establishing themselves as absolute monarchs, others simply serving

---

* Zaydi communities arose in eastern Arabia, Muslim Andalucia and Morocco under their Idrissid, Saadien and Alaouite dynasties. The Zaydis differ in many ways from the Twelver Shiites of Iran and are arguably closer to the Shafi Sunnis (who make up the majority of Yemen's Sunni population).

their communities with religious advice. In times of danger, the Hashid and Bakil tribes were praised as 'the two wings of the imamate', though at other times a ruling Zaydi imam would find the outward, public loyalty of these two tribes combined with an equally determined desire to remain free. In periods of danger, the two tribes have proved themselves, again and again, to be the heroic vanguard of Yemeni identity.

When the Shiite Fatimid dynasty, ruling from Cairo, tried to enforce their rule over the Yemen in the eleventh century, the Zaydi imamate in the northern mountains never submitted, even though both states were Shiite. A century later, another Egypt-centred empire, the Sunni Ayyubids, set out to conquer all Yemen; they achieved mastery, but failed in the northern mountains. In the sixteenth century, the Sunni Ottomans sent an armada of ninety ships, concerned that, if they did not seize hold of the Yemen, a Crusader army from Portugal would do so. They achieved the conquest at a vast price, losing 70,000 soldiers in capturing and garrisoning Sanaa; however, they again found they could not effectively occupy the northern highlands.

Two hundred years later, the Turkish Ottoman Empire once again tried to seize control of the Yemen. An army was landed in 1849 and after twenty-five years finally took control of Sanaa.

❀ ❀ ❀

Yemeni resistance to this well-equipped modern army came from the Hashid and Bakil tribes of the northern mountains, who led a national rising against the Turkish garrison in 1876 and again in 1890. By 1904, they had re-established the rule of a Zaydi imam, Yahya Muhammad Hamid ed-Din al Mutawakil. His state, with its theocratic underpinning, managed to negotiate the troubled waters of the twentieth century by signing a truce with the Ottoman Empire in 1911, with the Italians (who had occupied Eritrea and were invading Ethiopia) in 1926 and with Saudi Arabia in 1934. The one power that the imam refused to acknowledge was the British in Aden, though in practice (if not in principle) an accepted frontier had been established back in 1904.

The Zaydi imam combined firm rule at home in the Yemen with the policy of sending bright young youths to study in such cities of Arab culture as Baghdad and Beirut. It was hoped that they would come home and help to modernise things. That was the theory. In practice, the returning graduates found their suggested reforms ignored and became revolutionaries. Imam Yahya was assassinated in 1948, which encouraged his successor, Imam Ahmed ibn Yahya, to isolate the Yemen from all contact with the outside world. After Imam Ahmed's death (in his own bed), his son, Muhammad al-Badr, inherited the Zaydi imamate but was immediately confronted by the coup of 1962. This had been masterminded by Nasser's chargé d'affaires, Abd al-Wahad, as part of a dream of a United Arab Republic centred on Egypt.

Over the next eight years, a little-reported civil war was waged in the northern mountains of the Yemen. The Imam's cause was backed by Jordan and Saudi Arabia with British military assistance. UK prime minister Harold Macmillan wanted the British presence to be officially deniable, so much of the work was contracted out to a group of ex-SAS officers, whose most important function was to supply the Royalist forces with arms through air-drops and by camel caravans. During this civil war, the Yemeni Royalists had been allowed to recruit volunteers from Asir, the three south-western provinces of the Saudi Arabian Kingdom, which are largely populated by tribes loyal to Zaydi traditions. They served under their tribal elders, who placed themselves under the command of Imam Badr's uncles, Prince Hassan, Prince Abdallah and Prince Mohammed bin Mohsin.

Nasser had backed his republican allies in the Yemen (who had dutifully petitioned him to be allowed to join the United Arab Republic) with a garrison of 70,000 Egyptian soldiers. In the aftermath of Israel's decisive victory against all the Arabs in the Six-Day War of 1967, Nasser began to realise how the Yemen campaign had distracted from the threat from Israel. In a meeting at Khartoum, the King of Saudi Arabia and President of Egypt ended the Yemen civil war with a handshake, after which both leaders agreed to abandon their local allies. The last Imam of Yemen, Muhammad al-Badr, continued to fight on for two more years, before retiring to a small house in Kent, in the UK, to pursue a life of piety.

Abdul Rahman al-Iryani, a principled judge who had the decency to oppose both the autocratic rule of the old Imam as well as the violent coup of the republicans, was anointed as the new president of Yemen in 1967. A good man, he helped broker peace between the Saudis and Communist South Yemen, before being removed from power by a coup in 1974. His two successors were despatched – by a bullet and an exploding briefcase – and would be replaced by President Ali Abdullah Saleh. His long rule over the Yemen (1978–2012) can be partly explained by tribal allegiance. He was supported by Sheikh Abdullah al-Ahmar, the long-serving speaker of the house and the chief of the Hashid tribe.

Leadership of the Zaydi community passed to the party of Al Haqq ('the truth') and especially to an articulate Member of Parliament, Sheikh Hussein Badreddin Houthi, one of the eight sons of Badr al-Din, a Zaydi scholar. Houthi was brave enough to criticise the corruption of President Ali Abdullah Saleh's regime in the 1990s, way before there was any national consensus. And then, in the summer of 2004, after the arrest of 604 Houthi followers outside a mosque, followed by the death of twenty-five supporters, fighting began. Sheikh Hussein was killed in September and his body buried within a state prison, to prevent the growth of a cult.

Armed resistance from the Houthi movement was now led by Sheikh Hussein's two brothers, Abdul-Malik and Yahya. The movement supported the 2011 Arab Spring demonstrations, which seemed on the point of dethroning President Ali Abdullah Saleh and his regime, who had become as unpopular as Mubarak in Egypt, Gaddafi in Libya and Assad in Syria. The Arab Spring also sought an ethical foreign policy, where a freely elected, Islamic leadership could speak the truth about Palestine and other issues. The Houthi movement had now advanced from protest to a national cause. Saleh, who had been deposed, even tried to ally himself with the movement over the summer of 2015, in an attempt to ease himself back into power. He was killed in December 2017 after being accused of plotting with Saudi Arabia to destroy his new allies.

The Saudis had, by this time, seen a significant Iranian Shiite footprint in the Houthi rebellion. In this, they may have been over-concerned. It seems likely that Iran, perhaps through the Hezbollah in Lebanon, assisted in the overseas training of some Houthi militia, and a small number of missiles were fired from the northern Yemen into Saudi Arabia in 2018. But that may have been more symbolic than targeted strike. The initial source of Houthi arms was most likely the impressive arsenal that Saleh had built up by pursuing (or pretending to pursue) the war on terror on behalf of the USA. Saleh had been a skilful operator. He had encouraged dissident tribes in the interior of Yemen to host al-Qaeda-like Islamist terrorist groups, purely to extract arms and technical gadgets for their 'suppression' from the USA. Now and then terrorist incidents happened and government counter-strikes were launched. Saleh also appears to have employed Islamist hitmen to take out political rivals in the old Socialist-Communist regime in southern Yemen.

One of many intriguing elements about the Houthi movement is that it is not passionate about the political union of North and South Yemen. The Houthis acknowledge the need for a federation to bind the two Yemens in peace, but they are also sufficiently aware of the differences to wish to make a slow, cautious progress on his issue.

❋ ❋ ❋

The current civil war, intensified by the military actions of the Sunni–Arab alliance, has divided the country in two. The area that freely offers its loyalty to the Zaydi Islam championed by the Houthis largely follows the old frontiers of the imamate. The region of the Yemen that respects the government of President Hadi is the entity previously known as South Yemen, with its main city the port of Aden. Within South Yemen, there are also separatist movements and elements of al-Qaeda.

Aden – South Yemen – was governed for six generations by the British. Their rule was never liked, though a few individuals – Bertram Thomas, Harold and Doreen Ingrams* – came to be cherished for their knowledge and love of the region. The British came to the Yemen as alien conquerors, but with very modest ambitions: to control a strategic port on the seaway between the British Isles and the British Empire in India. In 1839, the Royal Marines landed and seized control of the port of Aden from the local ruler, the Sultan of Lahej. To hide such a crime behind a public virtue, the British occupation pretended to be suppressing piracy. However, within a few months they revealed their determination to stay by the zeal with which they

---

* Doreen Ingrams has been described as 'the last and greatest of Arabian imperial lady travellers and a pioneer post-imperialist'.

destroyed the military column that the sultan had sent to take back possession of this ancient Yemeni port.

Aden was a useful stopping place for an empire based on the control of the seas, midway between Suez and Bombay. The British turned it into a coal-bunker (in the days when a ship burnt 700 tons of coal per cruise) and an Indian Ocean naval base. Aden was also turned into a tax-free port where alcohol, opium, silver coins and guns were sold openly and coffee acquired. It was a boom town, similar to those other free-trade entrepôts of the British Empire, Hong Kong and Singapore. In the process, the British destroyed the trade for all the other old harbour towns of the Yemen.

In 1960, Aden was the world's second busiest port for refuelling ships. The British had no interest in extending their rule over the interior and maintained their authority in the port of Aden with a garrison of 15,000 troops. A network of individual peace treaties with nine tribal lords (backed up by modest annual payments of gold coin) proved just about adequate to police the hinterland. This was both running an empire on a tight budget and a classic implementation of divide and rule. The southern region of Yemen, sometimes called the Aden Protectorate, compromised the Sultan of Lahej, the Emir of Bihan, the Emir of Dhala, the Fadhili Sultanate and the sultanates of Wahdi Haban, Yafa, Aulaqi and Wahidi Balhaf. The Southern Arabia Federation would later emerge as an umbrella organisation for these principalities. This was very similar to the patchwork of emirates along the shore of the Persian Gulf (which would become the UAE), where the British also exercised paramount influence.

The key difference between the emirs along the Persian Gulf and those in southern Yemen was that there was no oil with which to strengthen the hand of these fledgling states. The other great difference was that the bustling port-city of Aden had created a perfect environment for Arab nationalism. The city was independent of any sultanate yet linked with every centre of Arabic culture. It had a working class of dockers and an educated elite (mostly graduates from the two showcases of Western academic culture in the Middle East: AUC, the American University in Cairo; and AUB, the American University at Beirut). The Arab community in Aden was inspired by Nasser and well-educated in the cut and thrust of politics by watching the bloody progress of the Arab nationalist struggles in Algeria and Palestine. They understood the need for discipline, secrecy and obedience. By co-opting both local Communists and Ba'athists they created a 500-strong unit of Aden-based Arab nationalists.

They were determinedly militant. They desired not just to be independent but publicly to defeat and humiliate the British before the world. They wished to expel the British in a bloody armed struggle which would then place them in a position to overthrow the regime of the imam in North Yemen. There was a local rival, a moderate group connected with the trade union movement called the PSP, the People's Socialist Party.

During 1962, the last pieces fell neatly in place, to help prepare a national and revolutionary struggle against the British regime and their feudal allies in southern Yemen. An umbrella group, the National Liberation Front, had been created to unite over a dozen separate organisations for the coming struggle. The 1962 coup in North Yemen had overthrown the imamate and now offered the nationalists a local ally who could provide arms as well as secure military bases for the forthcoming struggle. The Aden-based Arab nationalists had also begun to use their clan connections to radicalise the tribes of the interior. The Aden Insurrection of 1963 was launched with a grenade attack at Aden airport and a traditional rebellion by the Radfan tribe on the frontier of southern and northern Yemen. By 1965, the nationalists had established six command centres in the interior and directed over 1,372 incidents with which to weaken the British military occupation.

Aden was the potential point of weakness for the nationalists, because it was the only part of the country that the British desired to retain. If the British had used the brutal instruments of state terrorism perfected by the French to pacify the city of Algiers during the Algerian Struggle for Independence, they could have inflicted major damage to that small core group of 500 Arab nationalists. But the nationalists struck first. They targeted the Special Branch, the few Arab police officers loyal to the British, and the most experienced Arabic-speaking British officers. Having assassinated these men, they then proceeded to intimidate and radicalise the local Arab administration, gradually extending their influence over the 15,000-strong South Arabian (Federation) army and the Aden police force.

These tactics proved highly effective within the city-port of Aden. The British were also faced with a tidal wave of passionate Arab nationalism across the length and breadth of rural southern Yemen. British forces were also weakened by a loss of imperial resolve. This process had begun with the independence of India, was vastly accelerated by the debacle of the Suez War and completed by prime minister Harold Macmillan's 'wind of change' speech, which he had delivered in Africa in 1960, after which, all over Africa, dozens of British colonial territories and protectorates moved swiftly towards independence.

By 1966, Nasser had become suspicious of the independent mindset of the Arab nationalists in Aden and created FLOSY (Front for the Liberation of Occupied South Yemen). This was to be more moderate and subservient to Egyptian policy. The Arab nationalists had also begun to divide themselves into two bitterly antagonistic wings – a right wing dominated by the Ba'ath Party, which dreamed of pan-Arabic unity; and the Left, who saw Arab nationalism as just the first blow in a class struggle. By 1967, these antagonisms within the Arab insurrection had become public, as street battles were fought for the control of Aden. Then came the catastrophe of the Six-Day War with the defeat of all three of the Arab front-line states by Israel. After 1967, Nasser began to turn away from his heavy-handed interference in the Yemen. Then, to add a further twist to the confusion, the Aden Police effectively went on strike, and revealed to the British the full extent of their Arab nationalist allegiance.

Faced with incipient civil war, the Arab officers within the supposedly pro-British Southern Arabian (Federation) Army declared their obedience to the invisible leadership of the Arab nationalist struggle in Aden. These officers were then used as ambassadors by both sides, in secret negotiations which concluded with the unilateral declaration of the People's Republic of Southern Yemen on 30 November 1967.

The Aden Insurrection had achieved its objective: the humiliating destruction of British power during a four-year-long nationalist struggle. It is often placed beside Algeria and Vietnam as one of the turning points of post-colonial history. But, compared to these other wars, casualties were light: 227 British soldiers and 2,000 Arab resistance fighters.

❋ ❋ ❋

The peace would prove to be rather harder to win than this war. The closure of the Suez Canal during the Six-Day War effectively halved the handling trade of the Port of Aden, while the closure of the British military base after Independence put 20,000 Yemenis out of work. The £60 million that had been pumped into the national economy by Britain also ceased. Over the next two years, 80,000 skilled workers left Aden as the economy shrank. Only the BP refinery continued to work, a blatant symbol of Western capitalism, yet also a vital remnant of the old prosperity.

The new government of the People's Republic of South Yemen was stridently radical. It gave voracious support to the Palestinian struggle and the small Arab nationalist cells embedded in the Gulf States. It sought alliances with China and Russia, and aspired to close friendships with Cuba, Korea and Vietnam. Army regiments were given new identities, such as 'First of May', 'Che Guevara' or 'Ho Chi Minh', and women were recruited into the military. The historian Abdal Fattah Ismail raked through the long centuries of Yemeni history, identifying leftist heroes and rightist criminal reactionaries, to make a new syllabus for the schools to teach.

The regime remained deeply opposed to Nasser's Egypt, let alone such class enemies as the Arab monarchies in Jordan and Saudi Arabia. They also strove to break the influence of Islamic clerics in their society, liberate women into a position of social and political equality and destroy the power of the tribal sheikhs. Those sheikhs who had worked for the British were driven into exile (if not lynched), and landowning families legally restricted to twenty acres of irrigated land, which allowed the surplus to be distributed to peasants who had previously worked it.

It was an extraordinary period of dynamic change which would eventually create some form of free and secular education, state healthcare and welfare. South Yemen was poor, but in this period it was also zealous and incorruptible. One of its most impressive achievements was the campaign to improve literacy. Students were urged to share their new learning over the long summer holidays and challenged to educate five individuals; there was even a period of street agitation when the people demanded their government reduce salaries in order to concentrate resources on building colleges. But the regime was also dominated by internal debates as to the virtues of Maoism or Marxist-Leninism, and exercised an aggressive foreign policy. Britain had been prepared to continue some sort of minimal aid budget, but not if it was to be spent on exporting revolution to their Gulf allies. South Yemen grew into an ever poorer state, albeit one with an impressive lack of difference between a worker and a government minister.

Under a very different form of leadership, South Yemen might have emerged as the Singapore of Arabia, or at the very least a rival to Beirut and Kuwait. In the end, Aden was only sustained by becoming a Soviet naval base.

South Yemen also helped to polarise the politics of Arabia. The arrival of tens of thousands of middle-class refugees, telling of the ruination of their ancient houses and culture, had a major impact. In North Yemen it probably contributed to the massacre of the Left by the republicans after they emerged victorious in the long guerrilla war with the royalists in 1968. The fate of the old royal families of southern Yemen undoubtedly stiffened the resolve of other Arab monarchies to fight the prevailing Socialist wind.

The regime did try to export revolution, providing support for the Dhofar Liberation Front on their eastern frontier. The first sparks of the Dhofar rebellion had been fired in the summer of 1965, followed the next year with an assassination attempt on the old sultan as he inspected his troops. But between 1967 and 1970 the rebellion, aided by southern Yemen and its allies, advanced on every front. By 1970, they had succeeded in bottling up the authority of the old Sultan of Muscat and Oman,* Said bin

---

* In the nineteenth century, Dhofar had come under the rule of the Sultanate of Muscat and Oman, despite a 500-mile-wide desert between the regions.

Tammur, to little more than a barbed-wire enclosure stretched around the regional capital of Salala.

Dhofar is a place apart. If the winds of history had blown in another direction, it could have evolved as an independent emirate, maybe in league with the Hadramaut, with which it shares much. Culturally, Dhofar, like the three Yemeni provinces within Saudi Arabia, must be considered to be part of historic 'Greater Yemen'. Dhofar is the Ophir of the Bible, and the local Arab dialect carries direct connections with the language of the ancient Himyarite kingdom of the Yemen. Regional politics are dominated by the Qara and Kathir tribes, or rather by the factions and clans within them.

All seemed to be going well for the Dhofar revolution until Prince Qabus deposed his father in a bloodless palace coup in 1970. Qabus had been trained at the British military college of Sandhurst and understood the need to win the war on the ground. Qabus's mother was from Dhofar and he was able to make immediate use of his tribal cousinage to add useful allies to the beleaguered government forces. He also had sufficient oil revenues with which to fight a long war, and the money and charisma with which to win over old enemies. Despite their many tactical failures in the Aden Insurrection, he was also prepared to make use of the British. Over the next ten years, he employed a thousand British officers and a seconded unit of the SAS to train and initially lead a new national army. Alongside them, he also employed officers from Pakistan and recruited men from the Baluch tribes (Baluchistan is the other side of the Persian Gulf from Oman and occupies the poor frontier region between Iran, Pakistan and Afghanistan). On at least one occasion, in the winter of 1973, an Iranian regiment, well supplied with helicopters, also fought on the ground.

The tribal core of the Dhofar insurrection was gradually isolated from the support of South Yemen. The first step had been for the new Omani army to secure their own lines of communication, after which they set up secure zones where the tribes could be policed and won over with health, education and employment. The third stage in this methodical campaign was to patiently observe, then cut off, the supply lines of the insurgents, so that the rebels would be isolated and forced to engage in a fixed battle. It helped that the northern frontier was closed to the rebels by the desert – the Empty Quarter – and the Kingdom of Saudi Arabia.

It was a long war, waged from 1970 to 1978, and, though the victory of Sultan Qabus might look inevitable in retrospect, it was less certain at the time, as monarchies elsewhere (Egypt, Iraq, Libya) had toppled before the high tide of Socialist revolution.

The Dhofar war completed the bankruptcy of the already cash-strapped People's Republic of Southern Yemen. They desperately needed to take over an oil-rich kingdom if they were going to survive financially. Abdul Fattah Ismail (known as Al Faqih) had been the regime leader since an internal coup of 1969. He was deeply committed to the armed struggle and had supported both the insurgency in Dhofar as well as infiltrating Communist bands into North Yemen. By 1980, this expensive game of spies and insurgents was over. His Soviet allies persuaded him to go to Russia (for his health), which allowed Ali Nasir Muhammad to concentrate on the domestic situation.

When Abdul Fattah Ismail flew back to the Yemen in 1986, he was to be greeted at the airport by Ali Nasir Muhammad, but, just before the two leaders could kiss each other's cheeks, their bodyguards opened fire on each other. This was just the first of the many bloody gun battles that year which killed up to 10,000 and sent 60,000 into exile, and would defy political analysis. Southern Yemen was in great danger of imploding from civil war into a failed state, just as Somalia was at this time, on the other side of the Red Sea. By 1990, there was no Cold War rivalry with which to exploit foreign aid, as the USSR had bankrupted itself. There was also the matter of the discovery of a small oil field which straddled the frontier of South and North Yemen.

❖ ❖ ❖

The union of the two Yemens in 1990 may have been the one action that ultimately saved South Yemen, but at the high price of domination by northerners, who the southerners had been used to looking down upon as ill-educated, reactionary hillbillies. This resentment simmered, and periodically blew up in assassinations, a failed coup or another round of civil war.

South Yemen still totters between bankruptcy and its continued sense of a worldwide mission, between regional anarchy (which at times seems to revive the old frontiers of the old sultanates) and a desire for a unified Greater Yemen. It is also proud of its decaying but real social, cultural and educational achievements. It has been waging a long cultural war against tribalism, yet no political analysis of the civil wars and coups makes much sense without knowledge of the clan rivalries within the elite.

As even this brief skim over the surface of events in the Yemen makes clear, it would be misleading to identify South Yemen as a bastion of Sunni orthodoxy, just as North Yemen cannot be considered a Shiite protectorate of Iran. Nor is it easy to identify any government that is the legitimate expression of the people, which continues to make tribe and family the only institutions that anyone can engage with and trust. That the Yemen should have been selected as one of the battlegrounds of a Sunni Arab alliance against Shiite Iran would be absurd, if history had not already shown us how often the Yemen has been the chosen battleground of so many empires.

PART SEVEN

The Enemy of My Enemy: Egypt, Israel, USA and Qatar

PART SEVEN

The Enemy of My Enemy: Egypt, Israel, USA and Qatar

T hree other leading players in the Middle East – without whose backing there is no lasting peace – are Egypt, Israel and Qatar. Some of their actions are threaded through preceding chapters, but here we follow the stories from their own particular frameworks. Each of them are key manipulators of the levers of influence, fearing some of their neighbours, while seeking to influence others, establishing and maintaining a tactical web of alliances across the region. The Shia–Sunni schism is not a major issue in any of their political calculations, but they are all highly attuned to the balance of power between the three regional powers: Iran, Turkey and Saudi Arabia. Egypt has the population; Israel has military muscle and unconditional support from the USA; Qatar has the money and talks to everyone. They do not work together, but they respect each others concerns.

Egypt, though funded by Saudi Arabia, the Gulf States and the US,* succeeds in keeping its own counsel as the cultural epicentre of the Arab world. Qatar is fearful of falling under

---

* Since the Second World War, $960 billion, a quarter of all US foreign aid has gone to five countries: Israel ($312.5 billion), former South Vietnam ($184.5bn), Egypt ($183.7bn), Afghanistan ($158.9 billion), and South Korea ($120.7 billion).

the control of Saudi Arabia, so likes to keep an open door to all possible allies, be they Turkey, Iran or the US. Israel is a very close ally of the US and for the moment is attempting to create a working relationship with Saudi Arabia and the Gulf States, united by their hostility to Shiite Iran, the only power in the Middle East that is independent and militarily competent. Israel's strident anti-Iranian foreign policy – and its presentation of a nuclear-armed Iran as an existential threat – seems intractable, but is not inevitable, nor a strategic necessity. Iran and Israel were under-the-counter allies during the Iran–Iraq War.

CHAPTER 25

Once the Leader: Egypt

The view from the Nile

'The one thing that could take Egypt to war again is water.' So said Anwar Sadat, Egypt's third president and a dominant force in the country since helping Nasser overthrow King Farouk. It is a cliché, but the River Nile is the central fact of Egypt's identity. Viewed from the ground, the vibrant, verdant valley is an indestructible life force, a place where you can grow anything at any time of the year. Viewed from the air, it is a miracle of nature, a sliver of bright green slicing through the yellow sands, black mountains and red rocks of the vastness of the Sahara Desert. The Nile valley allows Egypt to support a population of 100 million, four times that of Saudi and the Gulf States combined. Within the Arab world, Egyptian singers, writers, film-makers and artists have always been the most innovative and most admired. Egypt is also a cultural beacon to Arabic-speaking North Africa – Libya, Tunisia, Algeria and Morocco – to its west. To the south, Egypt has a more complex role, for here its cultural eminence is mingled with thousands of years of imperialism, both enlightened and predatory, over Sudan, Ethiopia and East Africa.

Egypt is a Sunni nation, enriched by a remnant population of the indigenous Coptic Christians (around 10 per cent), who are directly connected to Egypt's gloriously ancient past.

The Copts are a fascinating community – heirs to a faith tradition quite as old as the rival Orthodox and Catholic churches – but are politically powerless.

Egypt has been a great power for four thousand years but has also suffered periods of domination by outside forces – 300 years under the Turks, followed by seventy under the British. This has created a complex historical background, with a recent past dominated by struggle against colonial oppression. But, as you dig deeper, you unearth great strata of pride, confidence and determination. The Kingdom of Egypt (also known as the Khedivate), an independent dynasty embued with Ottoman culture, flourished from 1805 to 1952, and at times seemed poised to become the new principal power in the Middle East.* In the nineteenth century its armies campaigned with remarkable efficiency in Arabia, Syria, Greece, Anatolia and the Sudan, so the imposition of a British military protectorate (1882–1956) was furiously resented.

❋ ❋ ❋

Other chapters in this book have noted the huge influence of Colonel Abdel Nasser, ruler of Egypt from 1956 to 1970 and still the greatest hero of the modern Arab world. Nasser was the man who stood up to Britain and its allies, France and Israel, during the 1956 Suez crisis – and managed to triumph. In these dark days, when it seemed possible that enemy forces might advance from the Suez Canal and assault Cairo, he found his authentic voice as an impassioned Egyptian orator.

---

* Mohammed Ali founded the Kingdom in 1805 but was only ever given the title of Wali by the Ottoman sultan. He liked to use the title of Khediva ('Viceroy'), but that was only officially granted to his successors. In 1914, the Khedivate lost its curious self-governing status as an autonomous province of the Ottoman Empire and became a kingdom, at the dictation of the British.

He had already learned to think on his feet. On 26 October 1954, having survived eight bullets fired by an assassin, he famously continued a speech with the words, 'My countrymen, my blood spills for you and for Egypt. I will live for your sake and die for the sake of your freedom and honor. Let them kill me; it does not concern me so long as I have instilled pride, honor, and freedom in you. If Gamal Abdel Nasser should die, each of you shall be Gamal Abdel Nasser.'

Nasser not only empowered all of Egypt to stand fast and be brave. He also inspired the entire Arab world through his 'Voice of the Arabs' radio broadcasts, which were listened to by the poor and virtually illiterate masses. The technology worked in his favour, for in the 1950s the first cheap transistor radios were being produced and sold. His picture was found in pride of place throughout the Arab world, from the souks of Marrakech to the back alleys of Mosul, from a grand villa in Lebanon to the stone towers of the Yemen. His articulate call for Arab unity would later be nuanced into a complete political programme, which combined a rejection of Communism and its wholescale land reform with the maintenance of a free marketplace supported by an empowering state-directed socialism mapping out industrial projects and new cities. Nasser seemed to be carving a distinctive path for the Middle East, a third way that respected Islamic and Arabic heritage and kept a friendly distance from the crushing embrace of the Soviet Union or the US.

It helped that Nasser's political speeches were often prefaced by the spiritually charged love songs of the adored Egyptian singer Umm Kulthum, who shared his political aspirations. They were an extraordinary double act – one that dipped into the archaic speech of classical Arabic and yet relished the intimacy of street dialect. So powerful was this that the people of Syria spontaneously decided to dissolve their nation state and join Egypt in creating the United Arab Republic (UAR) in 1958. When Nasser made a visit to Damascus that February, hundreds of thousands of Syrians spontaneously poured out onto the streets to welcome him, and carried him, still seated in his official limousine, on their shoulders. Later, the people of North Yemen petitioned to join this UAR, and such newly independent Arab republics as Libya (under Colonel Gaddafi) and Algeria (under Ben Bella) were delighted to recognise Abdel Nasser as their guide and to acknowledge his leadership.

After the defeat of the Arab front-line nations in 1967's Six-Day War – which began with the destruction of the Egyptian airforce on the ground – Nasser was at first unable to communicate this bitter truth to his people. It was not until four days later, on 9 June, that he formally announced the catastrophe over the radio and the next day tendered his resignation to the people. They responded by filling the streets of Cairo and demanding that he remain their leader – even in abject defeat. It was a moment of grandeur and humility. In the last years of his life, with the UAR broken (both Syria and Yemen had reclaimed their independence), he poured his energy into the Arab League; he died after chairing the summit in 1970. Five million of his fellow citizens bore his body to its grave. Three years later, his successor, Anwar Sadat, redeemed the defeat of 1967 by launching a surprise attack on Israel, together with Syria – the so-called Yom Kippur War of October 1973.

Egypt has declined since Nasser and its decades of glory as the unmistakable leader of the Arab world. It now plays the role of the poor cousin, being patiently and continuously bailed out by well-meaning relatives. Annual subsidies from the US (around $1.3 billion a year) and the oil-rich Arab nations balance the national account book, which staggers under a vast mountain of debt.* When the country's radical Muslim Brotherhood president, Mohamed Morsi, was ousted in 2013, both Saudi Arabia and Kuwait rewarded the new military regime with annual grants of $4 billion. But Egypt deserves this support, for in terms of population and its vast cultural reach it remains at the centre of the Arab-speaking world. Al-Azhar University in the historic centre of Cairo remains the acknowledged global centre of Sunni Islamic scholarship. There is also the influence of its Sufi brotherhoods, who have the allegiance of around a third of Egyptian male Muslims. There are between forty to eighty annual Sufi celebrations in Egypt, some drawing more followers than the annual Haj.

❈ ❈ ❈

What happens in Egypt will later happen in the rest of the Middle East. This was most certainly true of the Arab Spring, which, though incubated in Tunisia, reached its most volatile and public manifestation in Egypt, with the people taking possession of Cairo's Tahrir Square. It helped that the comparative poverty and population density of Cairo – unlike the motorway-laced suburbs of the oil-rich Arab world – allowed 400,000 concerned citizens to be within marching distance of the centre. The demonstrations were sustained by a working alliance between urban liberals and influential Islamist organisations such as the Muslim Brotherhood, but were only made possible by the apolitical stance of the army, which had become disenchanted with President Mubarak.

---

* Egypt's public debt is $282 billion which is locked into a spiral of escalation by the fact that the government spends $58 billion a year but only receives $37 billion of revenue. Public debt is now well over 100 per cent of GDP. Fiscal alarm bells are meant to be rung at any peacetime state going over 60 per cent.

Mubarak was an air-force commander who had helped rebuild the Egyptian force after 1967 so that it was able to operate effectively in the Yom Kippur War of 1973. He rose to become deputy to President Anwar Sadat, helping form a new alliance with Saudi Arabia and the US, and breaking with Syria and the Soviet Union. Mubarak's great error was that he did not groom a political heir other than his son, Gamal; an affliction – to love, trust and favour your family without measure – that has so often derailed an otherwise capable Arab politician.

After the fall of Mubarak, an election was held in 2012 and won by the Muslim Brotherhood. The first democratic election since the end of the monarchy, this resulted in a narrow victory for Mohamed Morsi, who became the republic's first non-military president. Morsi had some passionate supporters abroad, especially in Turkey (also led in this period by a freely elected non-military Islamist leader, Recep Erdogan), and the government was enthusiastically bankrolled by Qatar. Morsi's foreign policy gave public support to the long-oppressed Palestinians and made friendly overtures to Hamas in Gaza and Hezbollah in Lebanon, which alarmed nations that considered these as terrorist organisations.

Morsi was also interested in talking to Iran, rather than joining the Sunni–Arab alliance led by Saudi Arabia. He had a vision of a modern, universal Islam that was not locked into two adversarial camps. He was proud of his rise to eminence through education (he had been taken to school by his father, a poor farmer, on the back of a donkey) and knew all about America, where he had lived for three years, completing his training as a space-rocket engineer in California.

Opposed by Saudi Arabia, the Gulf emirates, Israel and the US, Morsi's government became increasingly autocratic. In

July 2013, public demonstrations were used by the Egyptian army to mount a coup, and General El-Sisi, who had previously served as both director of military intelligence and defence minister, took power as president. He had worked in Saudi Arabia, the UK and US: a safe pair of hands for the allies.

The Sisi regime is financed by Saudi Arabia, the Gulf emirates and the US. It has forged a nuanced, Egyptian-centred foreign policy and resisted the projects of his Saudi allies, such as the invasion of Yemen. But the various levels of Saudi leverage on Egypt should not be underestimated. A recent survey has tallied up $27bn of Saudi investments, spread over 2,900 projects, aside from the remittances of the three million Egyptians who work in the Kingdom.*

❊ ❊ ❊

But for the actions of the Egyptian army, it is almost certain that the Muslim Brotherhood (and other Islamist organisations that share its objectives) would have emerged as the dominant political force in Egypt.

The Muslim Brotherhood (Al-Ikhwan al-Muslimun) was founded in March 1928 when six workers from the Suez Canal port of Ismailia asked Hassan al-Banna, a learned, charismatic young scholar-teacher, to help them understand their own culture. They were disgusted by British rule, by the Levantine morals of their port city and the aloof Islamic scholarly class. So Hassan al-Banna created a populist self-help community, with evening reading classes and prayer sessions, practical assistance and intellectual enquiry. It blended the energetic example of the Scout movement with

---

* The Egyptian army itself owns (and controls) huge amounts of the country's infrastructure and business.

a Trotskyist-like cell structure and the traditional practices of a Sufi brotherhood. Members of the Brotherhood saw themselves as following that first egalitarian community of Muslims in the oasis of Medina. Interested supporters could progress to 'affiliate' status and then be promoted to 'organiser' before finally reaching the life-long commitment of 'working brother'. Within a decade of its foundation there were 200,000 Muslim Brothers, and by 1948 they numbered two million. A council of 100 senior brothers made decisions, which were implemented by an inner committee, chaired by a supreme guide. The Muslim Brotherhood also established branches in the other Arab nations of the Middle East without ever losing their innate Egyptian identity. They aided the Palestinian Revolt of 1936–39 against British rule and were involved in Black Saturday in 1952, when the hated British presence within Cairo was physically burnt out with the torching of 700 buildings.

The Muslim Brotherhood came within an inch of attaining power. Both Nasser and Sadat had served as members of the Brotherhood's paramilitary wing (Al-Tanzim al-Khass) during their youth, before slipping out of touch with the organisation sometime between 1947 and 1950. This was a confusing political period, when both the Egyptian monarchy and socialists were attempting to infiltrate the Brotherhood, which led to a spate of assassinations and revenge killings. Hassan al-Banna was shot by two gunmen in 1949, after which Sayyid Qutb emerged as an influential spokesman. He was a fascinating and complex man who had been appalled by the sexuality and greed of Western society which he had observed at first hand on a scholarship to America. He was also among the first to recognise the genius of the Egyptian novelist Naguib Mahfouz. At one time Sayyid Qutb seemed set to become the intellectual muse behind Nasser's revolution, but he would later call for violent jihadism to topple the Egyptian state and in 1966 was executed in prison.

So Islamists in Egypt – be they Muslim Brotherhood or fellow travellers – learned to operate discreetly, often working within the structure of charities, schools, hospitals and institutes. The Brotherhood was most able to flourish amongst middle-class professionals in provincial cities, outwardly apolitical, committed to family life (women wear the veil, or at very least a close-fitting headscarf), and advancing their way in society through education and hard work.

The Brotherhood has always been a rival of the secular Ba'ath Party that led Syria and Iraq, while also suspicious of Wahhabi scholars controlled by the Saudi state. One of their key figures was Sheikh Yusuf al-Qaradawi (1926–2022), who was born to a poor family in the Delta region of the Nile, and had been inspired as a young man by the preaching of Hassan al-Banna, whom he described as 'brilliantly radiating, as if his words were revelations or live coals from the light of prophecy'. Sheikh Yusuf had the distinction of being thrown into prison by both King Farouk and President Nasser, and denounced both Saudi Wahhabism and the autocratic rule of Assad in Syria and Gaddafi in Libya, as well as the oppression of the Palestinians by Israel. Sixty million Muslims would regularly watch him on Al Jazeera TV shows, talking about sharia and life. When, in 2011, Yusuf returned to Egypt, from a long exile in Qatar, he was greeted by a million well-wishers, and then led prayers followed by two million. He was considered a radical extremist by the US and Europe.

This Islamist political tradition within Egypt is opposed by the Egyptian army, which has ruthlessly crushed all opposition, most noticeably in the 2013 massacre at Rabiah Square. Yet it is a mistake to label the army as secular, like Ataturk's Turkey or the Ba'ath Party. It is totally Muslim, Sunni and

Arab in its loyalties, and defines itself as patriotic. This army views itself to be the guardian of an Egypt that has needed to be protected from outside enemies for the last five thousand years.

CHAPTER 26

Israel and Anti-Shia Alliances

*The occupation of Palestine and alliance with
Sunni Saudi Arabia against Shiite Iran*

Once, walking in the hills of southern Syria, trying to find
a way down to the Yarmuk river, where the Byzantine legions
had been decimated by an Arab army during a sandstorm, I
overheard a snippet of conversation between my Syrian guide
and a local farmer, who had come to warn us that we were
close to the disputed frontier on the Golan Heights. Without
pointing with his hands, he tossed his head to indicate that the
other side of the valley was *mamlakat al-yahud* – 'the kingdom
of the Jews'. Those same words could have been used by an
Assyrian, Seleucid or Roman. They acknowledge the Jews as
a part of the historical landscape – no matter that they were
spoken with an edge of hatred.

The ancient Jewish kingdoms in the Levant were destroyed
by the Roman Empire but for 1,400 years Jewish communities
survived as a tolerated minority throughout the Islamic Middle
East. However, the energy to create a new state of their own in
Israel did not come from these disparate Mizrahi communities
but from Ashkenazi Jews in Central Europe and Russia.
Fuelled by centuries of persecution, a Zionist movement was
determined to establish a homeland where Jews felt safe. In
the mid-nineteenth century, 45 per cent of the worldwide
population of Jews lived within Poland and Russia. The

wealthier, long-established Jewish communities in London, Paris, Vienna and Berlin were romantically inclined to support this venture but more likely to give money than to send their children to work as settler-farmers in Palestine. So, right from the start, the Zionist movement was an alliance of well-funded and articulate intellectuals (often highly assimilated Sephardim from Western Europe) allied on the ground to tough Ashkenazi settlers (from Russia and Eastern Europe). The project finally fell into place when a patron emerged in the middle of the First World War. British politicians, their imagination fired by biblical history, shared some of the Zionist vision, but were motivated by realpolitik. They wanted a reliable local ally in the Levant to protect a new oil pipeline to Haifa, which could fuel its fleet and reinforce its control over the Suez Canal. The Zionists were prepared to work with Britain, for they had no other options.

The British envisioned a Jewish state that might become another loyal, self-governing white dominion within their Empire. Their 'dominions' – Canada, Australia, New Zealand – had all been formed by the colonial appropriation of the lands of indigenous people, so dispossessing the Palestinian Arabs from their ancient homeland was imperial business as usual. The British were only strategically interested in the coast and, to try and make themselves less hated by the indigenous Arabs, they ordained in 1921 that the eastern half of Palestine would be part of the new Arab Kingdom of Jordan, created from southern Syria.*

This made the British hated by Zionists as well as Arabs. For the ancient Jewish kingdom of David and Solomon, the nursery of the Hebrew faith, are the hills around Jerusalem and the

---

* This action was a partial apology for the British betrayal of the promises they had made to the Hashemite sheikhs for the creation of an independent Arabia during the First World War.

Jordan valley. Once it became clear that British policy would not give them this ancient fatherland, sections of the Zionist movement, notably the Irgun, then regarded as terrorists, started to split off. They made their ambitions abundantly clear with the map on their badge of identity, which showed both Palestine and Jordan as the Jewish homeland. Lehi (also known as the Stern gang) was an even more militant Zionist group, which would later achieve spectacular assassinations and actions against the British.

At the end of the First World War, there were 66,000 Jews living in Palestine west of the Jordan river and 573,000 Muslim and Christian Arabs. Between 1921 and 1936, the Jewish population grew sixfold by migration to reach a self-sustaining level of 370,000. Most of Israel's leaders – military, political and security – have had roots in this first generation of inter-war Ashkenazi Zionists. The majority of the Jewish settlers recognised the need actively to support the British military administration, and kept their emotional sympathy with Irgun and Lehi to themselves. During the 1936–39 Arab Revolt, a Jewish militia army, the Haganah (10,000 soldiers backed up by 40,000 reservists), was raised to support the British.

The Zionists had never lacked zeal but their determination to succeed was reinforced by the appalling fate that had fallen upon the Jewish communities during the Second World War, when two-thirds of the entire population of European Jews – six million helpless civilians – had been systematically murdered by the Nazi regime. So, as the British, weakened by the war, dismantled their empire, they made the decision to evacuate Palestine in 1948 and leave the two communities to fight it out amongst themselves. This criminal irresponsibility was not specific to the Levant, for millions would also suffer as India and Pakistan violently separated themselves into two nations, and the British would also surrender their responsibility for the Greek civil war that they had partly engendered. As already described in the chapter on Syria, Israel emerged as a nation state from three rounds of fighting over 1948–49. It then was the aggressor in two wars with its Arab neighbours – Suez in 1956 and the Six-Day War of June 1967 – but in the last great testing struggle, the Yom Kippur War of 1973, faced a simultaneous surprise attack by both Egypt and Syria.

In the process of these wars and countless border incidents, Israel has pushed the frontiers of its state further inland. The extent of its territory, even after seventy years of conquest, still does not look very extensive on a map. It is the same size as Wales or Rhode Island, has no mineral resources to speak of and restricted access to fresh water. Yet, in just two generations, it has created a highly effective army and military intelligence, and one of the world's most technologically advanced manufacturing centres, specialising in arms, computers and telecoms. Israel's greatest asset, however, has been the unstinting diplomatic, financial and military support of the US. Israel receives a waterfall of American aid – $260 billion from 1946 to 2022 – and has enjoyed customs-free trade since 1985. This has been achieved by persistent and artful propaganda. Before the Second World War, the political culture in the US was indifferent to Jewish issues, if not actively anti-Semitic.

❊❊❊

Israeli national interests have always been well served by divisions within the Middle East, which might otherwise combine against it. As noted, the rivalry between the three royal dynasties – Hashemite Jordan and Iraq, the Kingdom of Saudi Arabia and the kings of Egypt – was an opportunity skilfully exploited by Israel over the 1948–49 war. This was followed by rivalry between the new Arab socialist republics and surviving hereditary monarchies, and later by the feud between Ba'athist Syria and Iraq, which kept Israel's two most determined enemies apart. In 1970, Jordan was engulfed in the Black September emergency and then Lebanon was consumed by civil war. The Iran–Iraq War of 1980–88, followed by the invasion of Kuwait, the two Iraq wars, civil war in Syria, and now the rivalry between Iran and Saudi Arabia fought out in the Yemen, have kept Israel's potential enemies distracted, disunited and diminished. The Israeli security and intelligence services have a great reputation as masters of espionage and covert operations, but they did not have to do much more than observe the self-destruction of their Arab enemies. Indeed, Israel has frequently prospered from the sale and discreet delivery of arms to different factions within the Middle East.

Israel is not afraid of war. It was born as a nation in arms. National service within the Israel Defense Forces has been one of the major unifying factors in creating a nation from streams of immigrant settlers from every corner of the world. Israel has also succeeded in reviving Hebrew as a living language, but it is a pragmatic nation where English, Arabic and Russian are used to communicate on roadsigns, radio, TV and trade.

Optimistic foreign peacemakers, and even a few old Israeli generals, dream of restricting Israel to its pre-1967 borders with the addition of Jerusalem in exchange for a long-term peace with its Arab neighbours. It is an aspiration that a patriotic, secular, second- or third- generation citizen of Israel, cherishing the jobs and beach life of Tel Aviv, might share. But it is to ignore the gravitational pull of the historical imagination that has driven the whole Zionist project. Every new settler knows that to make 'aliyah', to migrate to the homeland, means reviving the ancient Jewish kingdoms of Judaea and Samaria. An Israeli politician might delay it or deny it, but they can never put a permanent halt to the Zionist desire for Jewish settlement of the West Bank. A decision to abandon this dream in favour of a long-term peace with the Palestinians is one that threatens to divide the Jewish population in two. It has already caused prime ministers and presidents to be assassinated.

Likud, the current ruling party of Israel, is the lineal heir of Jabotinsky's Irgun. Even when they were a powerless group of Jewish settlers who felt threatened by their Arab neighbours, the Irgun decided to fight the British rather than accept that Israel would not rule over the Jordan valley. Since those days, they have waged half a dozen victorious campaigns, so their determination has not diminished. And, as I write, Likud is ruling Israel in coalition with far-right and religious parties.

In terms of pragmatism, rather than political rhetoric, the idea of a genuinely independent Palestinian state is dead in the water. The surviving Palestinian communities of the West Bank seem destined to become like Indian reservations in the US, with Gaza existing as a militant city-state. History might well prove us wrong in the long term, but in the short term this is their accepted fate in the diplomatic chancellries.

Yet the Palestinian diaspora – displaced from their ancestral villages, their ancient olive groves, their stone-built mansions, their orchards of lemons and oranges – is a brilliant, mobile, articulate and creative force. If you scratch beneath the surface of many an Arab magazine, bank, art gallery or publishing house, or meet a creator of dictionaries, a novelist, a visionary designer, or the man who turned Al Jazeera into a worldwide phenomenon, you will find a Palestinian. Having lost their homeland, they are pouring their restless energies into work and education. There must be a future for these people.

❀ ❀ ❀

It is not easy to understand why Israel should be so violently invested in opposing Iran, thousands of miles to the east. Looked at through the long, long lens of history, they were old allies against Assyria, Babylon, Rome and Byzantium. And in recent years they have had a common interest in opposing any expansionist Arab state. Throughout most of the Iran–Iraq War, the sale of Israeli arms, technology and small parts kept the Iranian airforce in existence.

Israel could have a grievance, it is true, about the generous way that Iran has funded Hamas, the elected Islamist government in Palestinian Gaza. Hamas took up the stridently militant Palestinian baton in 1993, when the PLO signed the Oslo Accords with Israel. The other grudge that Israel holds against Iran is its support – logistical, financial and diplomatic – for Shiite Hezbollah. Iran is certainly the patron of the Hezbollah of southern Lebanon. But the leaders of Israel know that the true reason for the rise of Hezbollah was as a direct reaction to Israel's invasion of Lebanon in June 1982. In conversation they will also privately acknowledge that the rise of Hezbollah finally brought stability to the northern frontier of Israel, as well as to Lebanon.

Given that Israel already has a nuclear deterrent, its vociferous denunciation of Iran's nuclear ambitions is largely a diplomatic agenda. It is a valuable tool for dividing the Muslim world, and for making Iran the pariah of the Middle East, not Israel. It also plays well to America. The US retains a sense of shame about its failures in Iran. The fall of the Shah, followed by the hostage crisis in Tehran and the bungled military attempt to rescue them, happened just four years after America's humiliating collapse in Vietnam. So, when the leader of Israel tours the world trying to build up a coalition of allies to impose something drastic on Iran, the love for Israel within America just keeps on growing.

This anti-Iranian rhetoric appeals just as much to the oil-rich monarchies of the Arab world, with whom Israel has recently been forming a new understanding. The combination of Arab largesse and Israeli technical know-how could make a terrific force. Nothing but good would come of a world where Israel feels less threatened and where the Arabs are encouraged to invest their abundant revenues in homegrown industries, building regional self-sufficiency and investing in their own domestic environment, rather than in London and New York apartments or armed training camps in someone else's desert. But it is a deeply unpopular policy on the Arab street, seen as a betrayal of the Palestinians by cynical, oil-rich Arabs, and strengthens the appeal of Islamist sheikhs.

Arab acceptance of Israel would allow the country to become a dynamic and useful part of the Middle East. Israel could even gradually wean itself off its unhealthy dependency on the US. Probably, the relentless inclination to advance the frontiers of Israel eastwards will make this impossible. But it would be foolish to underplay the one issue that brings Israel and Arab together – their mutual antipathy to Shiite Iran. This is a vital element in understanding the tensions between Sunni and Shia in the Middle East.

However, the October 2023 Hamas attack on southern Israel, launched fifty years after the Yom Kippur War, will put back any attempt to make alliances between Israel and the moderate Arab Sunni states (as was the likely intention of Iran, backers of Hamas).*

---

* This book went to press in October 2023, a week after the attacks. See the Afterword on p.384.

CHAPTER 27

America in the Middle East

From oil industry partners, through Cold War allies,
to superpower warmongers

Any discussion of the dynamics of Israeli influence in the Middle East must inevitably merge with that of its sponsor and guarantor, the USA. America is, for Iran (and others in the Middle East), 'The Great Satan' and Israel 'The Little Satan'. And yet it was not always so. US influence in the Middle East in the first half of the twentieth century was largely benign, and especially when compared to France or Britain. The US did not take place in any campaigns in the Middle East during the First World War and played no part in the colonial land grab following the Ottoman collapse. It was the American geologists Max Steineke and Thomas Barger who discovered and began the exploitation of Arab oil in the late 1930s and early 1940s, and American expertise that created the oil industry in Saudi Arabia and the Gulf.

After the Suez crisis of 1956, the US replaced Britain as the dominant foreign power in the Middle East. This could have been positive for the region if not for their obsessive Cold War rivalry with the Soviet Union, which meant that from 1955 to 1990 the principal division between the nations of the Middle East was not about religion (Shia or Sunni) or ethnicity (Arab, Turk or Iranian), but who supplied its weaponry and military advisors. It was not Nasser's domestic policies that estranged

Egypt from the US, but his decision to buy arms from the Soviet bloc. At the height of the Cold War, the socialist Arab republics of Egypt, Syria, Yemen, Somalia, Libya, Algeria and Iraq were all armed by the Soviet Union, while the hereditary monarchs who ruled over Iran, Saudi Arabia, Oman, Jordan, Ethiopia, Morocco and the emirates brought their weapons from the US and its allies. Turkey traded with both sides.

Israel, initially at least, was the odd one out in Cold War alliances. It had been supported by both the USSR and the US in the war of 1948–49 and was initially governed by a socialist party that had much in common with the Soviets, while many original Zionist settlers spoke Russian. Israel's opportunistic military alliance with the French and British colonial empires in the Suez crisis of 1956 would be condemned by both the USSR and US, so the diplomatic field was still wide open in the late 1950s. Then, as Egypt, Syria and Iraq became Soviet allies and backed revolutionary struggles, Israel launched a diplomatic offensive which succeeded in forging an extraordinary close alliance with the US. It is so strong now that it seems inevitable. However, in the 1950s the five million Jewish Americans represented just 1.5 per cent of the US population and were not a major political force. But somehow a strong connection was forged and steadily enhanced by the political lobbying of AIPAC (American Israel Public Affairs Committee). Military success, too, played a part. Americans were impressed by the Israeli forces, be it the Six-Day War of 1967 or the 1976 counter-terrorism raid on Entebbe. The Israelis came to seem like natural American allies.

During the Cold War, the US and USSR fought a series of proxy wars in the Middle East, as attested by the carnage of the Lebanese civil war and the (now almost forgotten) bloody campaigns fought out in the mountains of North Yemen and the hills of Dhofar (Oman). In 1970, before Egypt went into the American camp, there were 20,000 Russian troops on Egyptian territory and a string of Soviet naval bases on the coast of Syria, Somalia and Aden.

By 1979, the superpowers had both begun to lose their grip, but what really changed the geopolitical map was the Islamic revolution in Iran. At a stroke the US lost one of its most important allies and reliable trading partners in the Middle East. And for the first time there emerged a Muslim nation determined not to become a subsidiary ally of either the US or USSR, at whatever cost. In November 1979, American alliances in the Middle East were further shaken by the revolution that nearly toppled the monarchy of Saudi Arabia. Then, right at the end of 1979, the Russian 40th Army occupied Afghanistan. The American leadership feared that Pakistan (so intricately linked with Afghanistan) might topple into the Soviet bloc and that the Russians might establish a naval base on the eastern periphery of the Persian Gulf. Instead, after ten years of war in Afghanistan, the Soviet Union began to implode.

The American-led liberation of Kuwait in 1990 (after its invasion by Iraq), its invasion of Afghanistan (to punish the perpetrators of 9/11) and its invasion of Iraq in 2002 (for no good reason) all showed the awesome reach and capability of this world power with its big stick. Regimes and armies could be liberated or destroyed in a matter of weeks, in a hellfire of guided missiles and intelligent rockets. What has been less obvious has been how each of these three decisive military victories have ended up benefiting their enemies.

Having preserved the independence of the Gulf emirate of Kuwait by expelling the Iraqi army, the Americans, much to their surprise, found themselves hated by many of the Arabs whom they thought they had been protecting. The establishment of US military bases along the shore of the Persian Gulf was seen as a humiliating form of dependence by many within

Saudi Arabia. So, bizarrely, it would be America's closest Arab ally that would provide most of the young terrorists eager to attack emblems of American power, culminating in 9/11.

Having watched how the costs of the ten-year-long war in Afghanistan helped bankrupt the Soviet Union, it was bizarre of the US to decide to place this affliction on themselves with their own military occupation. The American desire for some spectacular blood vengeance in revenge for 9/11 was understandable, but, if there was ever a case for a military campaign that had a quick in and out, this was it. Instead, the Americans became embattled in the country for twenty years.

The US intervention in Iraq was a still greater self-inflicted wound. After it had destroyed the Iraqi state and encouraged democratic elections, the US discovered that they had created a new Shiite nation in natural sympathy with Iran, while the Sunni rump of Iraq transformed itself into ISIS, an experiment in a pathologically violent and reactionary Islam. These two rivals hated each other with a murderous zeal, but one thing they had in common was a desire to roll back the frontiers of America's worldwide imperium.

❊ ❊ ❊

How could these strategic blunders happen? The US government has no fewer than sixteen intelligence agencies, with 850,000 employees funded at the cost of $50 billion a year. But, at a presidential level, foreign policy decisions are all too often framed as the relationship between a specific nation and the US. Bill Clinton's words of advice to a visiting foreign politician were simple: 'Hug us close'; George W. Bush framed it, 'Either you are with us, or you are with the terrorists.' America wants loyalty most, and its presidents rarely have the capacity to understand the regional picture. In the Middle East, the perception is that there is only one ally that can be totally relied upon, and that is Israel. It has a reputation for getting the job done, quickly, efficiently and, if need be, quietly.

Democratic presidents, who get most of the traditionally liberal Jewish-American vote and influence, nurse their public relationship with the state of Israel. They are, in theory at least, a liberal and restraining influence on Israeli policy (though with seemingly little effect on the current Netanyahu government). Republicans have a stranger constituency, with fervent support for Israeli occupation of the West Bank from the millions of American Christian fundamentalists invested in biblical prophecy. They will always have both ears open to the concerns of the oil, defence and aircraft industries, which means the security of the Persian Gulf – as well as the lucrative markets of the emirates and the Kingdom of Saudi Arabia – is slightly higher up on their policy agenda. So there are just two absolutes in America's foreign policy in the Middle East, shared by both parties: the security of Israel and the security of the Persian Gulf.

In the past, these internal policy debates could become heated, as they impacted America's ability to contain the Soviet Union and the threat of world Communism. Some analysts argued that American support of Israel had driven half of the Arab states into the arms of the Soviet Union, while others thought that American support of the oil-rich Arab kingdoms had done this even more effectively. America's reputation for hypocrisy and double-dealing will be found to rest on the essential incompatibility of being both a friend to Israel and a friend to the Arabs. The Arab oil embargo of 1974 really brought this message home, so much so that since then the facts have been changed on the ground.

After 1974, the US decided on a massive internal investment in shale extraction, which made America self-sufficient in oil.

This makes the security of the Persian Gulf less of a life-and-death issue for American foreign policy. It is still important, but it is no longer 'thumb-on-the-jugular-vein' vital.

Which brings us to a crucial fact about understanding the problems of the modern Middle East. The antagonism between the Saudi-led Sunni faction and Shiite Iran is not against key American interests. The Sunni–Shia rivalry could actually offer US foreign policy the opportunity to square the circle – to draw its two hitherto-antagonistic allies (Israel and Saudi Arabia) closer together. It could, however, just as easily blow up in their face, confirming the hatred of Shiite Iran and Iraq for America, and increasing the chance of an Islamist revolution within the Arab Sunni heartlands, and the toppling of America's last remaining Arab monarchical allies.

The other option? Hold out the hand of friendship to Iran and put some mild pressure on Israel to make a lasting peace with the Palestinians.

CHAPTER 28

The Isolated Emirate: Qatar

From pearl fishing to a media network

Qatar is a small but glittering presence on the chessboard of the Middle East. The emirate is staggeringly wealthy, with the largest average income in the world ($106,000 a year), the third-largest gas reserves and a sovereign wealth fund stacking up more than $100 billion. No native Qatari pays tax, and all physical labour is performed by powerless migrant workers (90 per cent of the population of around two and a half million). Yet, with all its cash, Qatar also dares to be different, to march to its own tune, rather than keep loyally in step with the Kingdom of Saudi Arabia like its Emirati neighbours, Kuwait, Bahrain and the UAE. It has a lively foreign policy and is not afraid to purchase anything or anyone who has a price.

In June 2017, Qatar was confronted by a list of thirteen demands from its Sunni Arab neighbours. These allegedly included severing ties with the Muslim Brotherhood, Hezbollah, al-Qaeda and ISIS, cutting relations with Iran, ending a Turkish military base, and closing its media operation, Al Jazeera. Qatar refused to agree, denying that it was funding any terrorist groups. It was then put into isolation, with Saudi Arabia, Egypt and the Gulf States severing diplomatic relations. There was talk of the Saudis symbolically cutting a canal along their land frontier to float this problem neighbour off from the rest of Arabia. As it was, Qatar was expelled from Gulf councils and placed under a cultural and economic blockade. The Saudis also made some offbeat claims, suggesting that Iran's Revolutionary Guards were running the internal security of Qatar's palaces, even though Qatar is the only other Arab country that is officially Wahhabi.

Qatar's chief crime was that it had refused to join the Saudi-led alliance against Shiite Iran and instead ran its own open-door diplomacy with the powerful neighbour to its north. There is pragmatic reason for this, for the two countries share possession of South Pars/North Dome, the world's largest natural gas field with reserves of fifty-one trillion cubic metres. Its second considerable crime in the eyes of its neighbours is that it has consistently backed various Islamist populist parties throughout the Middle East and supported the democratic protest movements that came to the fore during the Arab Spring, as well as the Muslim Brotherhood in Egypt and Erdogan's Islamist leadership in Turkey. All these elected Islamist politicians tend to distance themselves from the sectarian Sunni–Shia split and believe in a worldwide Umma of the faithful. But they are also all outspokenly critical of the regimes supported by the West and strong vocal supporters of the Palestinian struggle against Israel. Qatar had been prepared to bankroll the elected Muslim Brotherhood regime in Egypt to the tune of $5 billion a year.

Qatar also maintains some form of relationship with most of the militant Islamist groups – the Taliban in Afghanistan, Hezbollah of southern Lebanon and Hamas in Gaza (which cover a full range of Muslim beliefs, almost to the point of contradiction) – as well as being a major funder of selected Islamist resistance groups in the Syrian and Libyan civil wars. Qatar is believed to have provided over $3 billion to the various factions within Syria that oppose the government. Their argument is that it is always important to keep the diplomatic door open, while its opponents blame it for recklessly funding terror and fuelling civil war. It is an argument that could also be laid at the door of Saudi Arabia. Indeed, many conflicts in Syria have been fought out between gunmen funded by Qatar against those funded by Saudi Arabia.

Qatar's third offence in the eyes of its neighbours is Al Jazeera. Since 1996, the emirs of Qatar have funded this outspoken, free-thinking TV news channel, which has become the single most important opinion-former in the Middle East. Al Jazeera has captured worldwide audiences from the BBC and CNN, not to mention the turgid, self-censoring state-owned media channels in the rest of the region. It reaches an audience of one billion people and operates film and documentary divisions across eighty global offices. It began as an accidental good deed, when the ruling emir of Qatar, faced with the closure of the much-loved Arab-language service of the BBC World Service, decided to support a group of journalists thrown out of their jobs with a loan of $137 million.*

Yet, when you look a bit closer at Qatar itself, it seems that this open-minded regime only works as its external face. Qatar is not ruled by any electoral body but governed by an autocratic monarchy. The occupant of this sovereign throne is changed by secretive coups within the palace. The last emir, Hamad bin Khalifa al-Thani, who ruled from 1995 to 2013, got to the throne by deposing his own father, who had himself acquired the throne in a 1972 coup against his cousin (who was on a hunting trip in the mountains of Iran). The current ruler, Sheikh Tamim bin Hamad al-Thani, emerged as ruling emir after the sudden resignation of his father in 2013,

---

* Wadah Khanfar, Al Jazeera's brilliant founding director general, is like many talented technocrats at work in the Gulf, a refugee from Palestine. More than half of the Palestinians watch Al Jazeera as their station of choice.

which happened live on TV. No one had identified Tamim, the British-educated fourth son of a second wife, as a likely heir. According to Gulf gossip, he won the throne 'because one brother played, and the other prayed, too much'.

Al Jazeera might be free to report the misbehaviour of any Arab monarch or president, but it never criticises Qatar's ruling al-Thani family. And, while Qatar appears to follow an attractive, non-aligned middle path in its public foreign policy, it is very much in the Western camp when it comes to domestic security. Qatar is the willing host to two US bases.

❋ ❋ ❋

This all seems very confusing, until you look at the history, and realise that Qatar is the Cinderella of the Gulf. Once a humble pearl-fishing dependency of the island emirate of Bahrain, its small peninsula comprised just four townships, squeezed for tribute by their overlords in Bahrain, by a Turkish garrison at Basra and by raiding parties of Wahhabi Bedouin. The al-Thani family rose to prominence through their quick wits in dealing with these multiple threats.

The dynasty's acknowledged founder was Sheikh Jassim al-Thani, who ruled from the 1840s until his death in 1913. He corresponded with all three Muslim powers – the Ottoman Sultan, the Persian Qajar shah and the Egyptian khedive – while simultaneously intriguing with the British in order to become independent of the emirs of Bahrain. He was succeeded by Abdullah bin Jassim (his fifth son, triumphant over eighteen rival siblings), who seized the opportunity presented by the forced evacuation of the Turkish garrison in 1915 to become master in his own land. In the midst of the First World War, he risked signing a formal treaty with the British, and it is this 1916 agreement that is the foundation charter of Qatar as an independent emirate, the ninth of the Trucial States.

The new state was not an obvious prize. The cultivation of pearls had been the mainstay of its economy for the past five thousand years and this trade was largely destroyed by the global Great Depression in the 1930s and the Second World War. However, oil had been discovered in Qatar in 1935–38 and, although the wells were capped for the duration of the war, al-Thani negotiated a respectable royalty deal with the Anglo-Persian oil company. Qatar would be able to pay for itself for the next hundred years.

Politically, the late 1950s and early 1960s were a testing time for the al-Thani sheikhs, faced with the progressive socialism of local oil workers (not yet replaced by migrant workers from South Asia) and the Ba'ath Party antagonistic to a hereditary regime so openly allied with the British. But, by sharing Qatar's oil wealth with other traditional families, who became bound in loyalty to the regime, and tight control of the police and army, the al-Thani survived.

In the 1970s, the US took over from the British, making use of Al Udeid as an airbase and turning Qatar into one of three anchorages for the US 5th Fleet. These overseas military bases helped Qatar to remain independent of the UAE, which was emerging as a proto-nation state from the feudal tapestry of the Trucial Emirates. But the Qataris realised that not even US military power is immortal, and began to hedge their bets, welcoming a small Turkish military presence. This infuriated such neighbours as Saudi Arabia, with its old antagonistic history with the Ottoman Empire. But the 2017 row with Saudi Arabia has propelled the current emir into unexpected popularity at home. A street graffiti portrait of their ruler, currently known as Tamim al Majd ('the Great') has become a national badge.

All rulers of Qatar know that their emirate is desirable and vulnerable, and that they cannot defend themselves without outside allies. Only by the deftest diplomatic footwork will they succeed in maintaining their independence, but this has been what they have been doing for hundreds of years. Diplomacy and negotiation is in the blood. The country's independent foreign policy also helps bind the small indigenous population together in loyalty to the regime and has the advantage of employing potential internal critics in glamorous international affairs, not least in the country hosting the FIFA World Cup in 2022. Is there room to hope that Qatar will eventually allow the principles of its foreign policy to influence its own system of government? It is not impossible. Qatar has always had to negotiate with many neighbours and understand many identities. The mother of the current emir is Moza bint Nasser al-Missned, the daughter of the old leader of opposition to the palace.

It is possible both to admire the energy and individualism of Qatar but also to taste the irritation of its neighbours.

PART EIGHT

Far Frontiers: Pakistan, Azerbaijan, Chechnya and China's New Silk Road

PART EIGHT

Far Frontiers: Pakistan, Azerbaijan, Chechnya and China's New Silk Road

There are a clutch of Muslim nations, on the furthest frontiers of what anyone might term the Middle East, whose fates directly impact the balance of power in the heart of the region. We have already seen that Pakistan has time and again served as a military bolster to reinforce the authority of various Sunni Arab states, as well as the role it has played in the wars of neighbouring Afghanistan. But what of its own needs and aspirations in this complex world?

To the north, Chechnya and Azerbaijan in the Caucasus have been often overlooked in the story of the Muslim world. They were conquered by Tsarist Russia, but before that were distant provinces of Greater Iran. Their histories, little known to the West, are significant in understanding the recent narrative of events in the Middle East. They are certainly key to Russian policy in the region, with its perceived threat from the Islamists of Chechnya. It was this, as well as the opportunity to keep an old ally and a Mediterranean base, that drove Russian military support for Syria in the war against ISIS.

Finally, we look to the nation that has been playing an ever more dominant role in the Middle East. China, for all its vast territories, lacks significant oil and gas reserves of its own and depends on imports from both Iran and the Gulf. And, like Russia, it fears its own domestic Islamists, whom it has been oppressing in Xinjiang province.

CHAPTER 29

Pakistan: The Sunni Bedrock

From Islamic Statehood to the Taliban

Pakistan is one of the bedrocks of Sunni Islamic power, set in firm partnership with the Kingdom of Saudi Arabia. Pakistan has the manpower, military and the bomb; Saudi Arabia has money, and Mecca. Each claims a commitment to establishing 'pure' Islam throughout the world, funding mosques and exporting imams and radical Islamism. Pakistan was founded on its faith, designed as the safe homeland for India's minority Muslim population after Independence. This image of a nation united by faith – *Pakistan* literally means 'the land of the pure' – is one that has been projected during its long periods of autocratic rule by generals who have turned themselves into presidents, notably Zia al-Huq (1977–88) and Pervez Musharraf (1999–2008).

The military in Pakistan is the glue that holds this nation of 230 million people together. It is associated with middle-class decency and an orderly career, in contrast to the political parties dominated by wealthy clans of landowners and corrupt clerics. The defence establishment is vast, directly employing 600,000 men, not including militia and volunteer reserves, and the army has been tested in two border wars and innumerable confrontations with India, and within its own dissident mountain provinces. At critical moments, this military muscle has been hired out to other Sunni Muslim nations, such as the 40,000 soldiers that secured the internal security of Saudi Arabia in 1979–80. The Pakistani military have also served in actions to bolster state authority in Oman, Jordan and Bahrain. This is all part of an old pattern of historic relationships between the southern shore of the Persian Gulf and the northern shore – Baluchistan.

Government finances in Pakistan are propped up by foreign aid (notably from the US and Saudis) and are almost entirely earmarked to pay the military and civil service. The domestic economy is supported by a vast diaspora of Pakistani talent beavering away in the back offices of the world. Four million 'overseas Pakistanis' work in the Middle East, 1.5 million in the UK and some 500,000 have made it to North America. It is reckoned that, every year, $20 billion of remittances are pumped home to support families and put the young through school.

In essence, if not always in practice, Pakistan is the largest Muslim democracy in the world. It created its own purpose-built modern capital of Islamabad to step outside the ancient rivalry between the powerful provinces of Punjab and Sindh. The Punjab has a population of 110 million (60 per cent of the country's population); the southern province of Sindh adds a further 47 million. Sindh has a high percentage of Shia, so there are at least 40 million Shia Muslims in Pakistan. Sindh is also the province that has consistently supported the Islamic-Socialist party of reform (PPP), headed by the Bhutto political dynasty. So what at first sight might appear a rock-solid Sunni nation state is actually sitting on its own internal schism, containing a Shia minority associated not only with a specific region but also with radical political alternatives.

In addition to these two central provinces, the Northwest Frontier Province is home to 35 million Pathans, and the equally wild south-eastern region of Baluchistan houses 12 million Baluch. These two borderland provinces can be seen as heroic role models of ethnic self-governance and anarchic badlands at one and the same time. Both regions are determinedly tribal and mostly Sunni, but nothing is entirely straightforward. The numerically small and mountainous province of Baltistan has a Shia majority.

※ ※ ※

Zulfikar Ali Bhutto – left wing, Shia and from Sindh – won the leadership of Pakistan in 1971, after the traumatic war and secession of Bangladesh. He initiated a nationalisation campaign, in keeping with the prevailing socialist spirit of his age. It was ultimately disastrous, but initially exciting, coupled with land reform, trade-union rights and a massive expansion in state education. But Bhutto's socialist policies were combined with some chilling acts. He sent the army into Baluchistan to quell the tribal rebellion of 1973 and to strengthen his Islamic credentials with the electoral masses; he also declared Pakistan an Islamic Republic that year.

Fatefully, Bhutto backed militant Islamists in the Pathan border region of Afghanistan, in order to outflank Afghan President Daoud Khan's 'Pashtunistan' campaign, which aspired to reclaim Pakistan's north-west frontier province for the Afghan motherland. His security chiefs selected their new Afghan allies – Gulbuddin Hekmatyr and Ahmed Shah Massoud – with fine discrimination, for twenty years later these two charismatic leaders would prove themselves to be the most militarily efficient and politically astute commanders of the Afghan Mujahadin. It is interesting to note that these two leaders were already in command of an armed guerrilla resistance – against their own socialist government – five years before the Russian invasion. The Pakistan intelligence services had also embedded an element of divide and rule with their two Afghan clients, for Hekmatyr was a Pathan while Massoud was a Tajik. Both studied engineering at Kabul University and were rivals even then, if only on the basketball court.

By 1977, Pakistan itself was spiralling out of control. Bhutto's economic policies had shrunk the economy and he had become increasingly despotic, even with politicians whose social policies he shared. That year he was overthrown by a military coup organised by General Zia-al-Huq. Bhutto was put on trial for the assassination of a political rival and was hung in April 1979, against worldwide appeals for clemency.

No-one imagined that Zia, a stolid, unimaginative general, would last long in power. By the standards of the Pakistani ruling class, he was a model of middle-class rectitude. Even as a four-star general he had been content to live with his family in a modest bungalow, proud of the example of Muslim decency set by his own father, a trusted clerk who worked for the British military. As a young officer, Zia had served beside British colleagues in the jungles of Burma and Malaya. He had also shown great courage and resource while working for King Hussein of Jordan during Black September.

But General Zia's grip on power was immeasurably reinforced by the events of 1979: the fall of the Shah, the insurrection in Mecca and the Soviet invasion of Afghanistan. The 1979 insurrection in Mecca was quelled with the assistance of several Pakistani regiments, which secured General Zia the gratitude of the entire royal family of Saudi Arabia. This important friendship was further strengthened by the Soviet invasion of Afghanistan. Suddenly Pakistan became the place where the Western and Islamic world met, and through which the West could support the struggle of the Afghan Mujahadin against Russian Communism.

A trickle of aid for the Mujahadin promised by President Carter became a flood under President Reagan, first matched, then doubled, dollar for dollar, by Saudi Arabia and its Gulf allies. It all passed through Pakistan as funds both to buy arms for the Afghan resistance and to support the millions of Afghan refugees who had fled from the civil war. The intricate tribal politics of Pakistan's north-west frontier province became ever more labryinthine, for there were fourteen different Afghan Mujahadin factions fighting the Russians.

The ten years of the Russian invasion of Afghanistan was the golden period of the US–Saudi–Pakistan alliance. Thousands of well-meaning Western aid workers came to work in the refugee camps and in headquarter offices in Peshawar, outnumbered by some 30,000 foreign Muslims who came to fight alongside the Afghan resistance movements. Osama bin Laden was one of those volunteers. An old friend of mine remembers having a civilised chat over a cup of tea with him, as they tried to find ways to stop their medical aid convoys being pillaged by 'bandits in league with the Pakistan intelligence service'. This period also witnessed the emergence of the Taliban from a string of madrasas – Islamic schools – that were educating Afghan and Pakistani orphans to become warriors of the faith like their heroic fathers, who had been martyred by the atheist Communists. The movement took its name from the *talib* ('students') of this network of madrasas.

❋ ❋ ❋

General Zia also recruited thousands of Islamists into government service and imposed a Sharia board on the judiciary to enforce *hudud* ordinances, with their Koranic punishments for such crimes as *zina* (extramarital sex) and consumption of alcohol. He also brought the Islamic madrasa system under the fold of the State and created a succession of blasphemy laws. His principal domestic failure was the imposition of a compulsory *Zakat* tax – a 2.5 per cent 'donation' to be taken out of every bank account on the first day of Ramadan. This arbitrary act of state bureaucracy was a disaster, for it transformed a self-motivating Islamic virtue – the giving of alms – into an item of the state budget. It also brought out the biggest Shia demonstrations in Pakistan's political history, through the streets of the principal cities in 1983 and again in 1984. Zia eventually backed down from enforcing this 'reform', but it had disastrous long-term effects.

Previous to this, there had been no way that a Shia citizen would need to distinguish themselves legally from a Sunni neighbour, but now the Shia could register themselves in order to avoid paying this extra 2.5 per cent tax and be in charge of their own almsgiving. This produced an extraordinary surge in the perceived number of Shia within Pakistan, which began to alarm the Sunni-centric regime.

The state also began to fear that the Shia, encouraged by the power of neighbouring Iran, would become more assertive. To frustrate this, the Shia community was humiliated in an annual cycle of bombings, targeted assassinations and lynch-mob-like riots. Shia festival processions were attacked with nail grenades and their mosques destroyed by firebombs; or, on some of out-of-town back road, a local bus (packed as ever in Pakistan) would be stopped by hooded men, emptied of passengers and the Shia identified and taken aside to be killed. By the late 1980s, four militant Sunni Islamist groups had emerged which were capable of executing this sort of violence: Sipha-e-Sahaba (SAP), Lashkar-e-Jhangvi, Josh-e-Muhammad and Lashkar-e-Tayyaba. A decade later, they had splinted into over eighty 'Punjabi Talibans – each as psychotic as the other', according to the Islamic scholar of Pakistani origins, Ziauddin Sardar. The security services were perceived as doing little to prevent such attacks and sometimes suspected of involvement.

Perhaps the most chilling of all the massacres was at Gilgit in May 1988, where communal violence had exploded over the different timings of Ramadan. Four days after this had calmed down, the *Pakistani Herald* would report: 'Low-intensity political rivalry and sectarian tension ignited into full-scale carnage as thousands of armed tribesmen invaded Gilgit along the Karakoram Highway. Nobody stopped them. They destroyed crops and houses, lynched and burnt people to death in the villages around Gilgit town. The number of dead and injured was in the hundreds. But numbers alone tell nothing of the savagery of the invading hordes and the chilling impact it has left on these peaceful valleys.' Casualty estimates vary, but between 400 and 700 Shia were killed in Gilgit-Baltistan province. Shiite self-protection militia began to emerge all over Pakistan.

On 8 August 1988, the Shia community leader, Arif Hussain Hussaini, was assassinated. Then on 17 August, the military aeroplane carrying President Zia-ul-Haq, as well as the US ambassador, the head of the US military and a whole court of Pakistani generals and aides, crashed soon after takeoff. No one knows who was responsible for this accident but it was rumoured to have been a last-minute decision by a Shiite pilot determined to take his revenge. So, even in Pakistan, outwardly one of the bedrocks of Sunni orthodoxy, the hidden Sunni–Shia schism had the potential to split the nation and turn murderous.

The death of Zia-ul-Haq allowed the return of Pakistani democracy, though much of Zia's *Nizam-e-Mustaf* ('The Rule of the Prophet') Islamist framework remains in place.

One of Zia's hand-picked young technocrats, Nazim Sharif, survived as the centrist figure of Pakistani politics over the next generation, governing his nation through three terms of office (four, if you include that of his younger brother). Nazim

Sharif's periods of office would alternate with that of Benazir Bhutto, the charismatic daughter of Zuflikar Ali Bhutto. Benazir Bhutto would win the 1988 general election, Sharif the election in 1990, but Benazir was back in office in 1993.

In order to hold power, Benazir knew that it was wise to identify herself in public as a Sunni. By contrast, her two brothers, Murtaza and Shahnawaz, had sought a more militant identity, helping to create the Shia group Zuflikar, which was at least partly funded by Gaddafi's Libya. Shahnawaz died in Paris, possibly poisoned, whilst Murtaza was shot dead in a police incident within Pakistan in 1996, which helped discredit his sister. The rising levels of political violence led to another period of military rule, presided over by general-president Musharraf (1997–2007), pushing through the prevailing policies of economic liberalism that made him popular with the USA but increasingly isolated at home.

In the run-up to the 2008 elections, Benazir Bhutto was assassinated. Her leftist, Sindh-based PPP (Pakistan Peoples Party) won the election and her political heirs attempted to create a more liberal, and devolved, parliamentary democracy. But ultimately the winning cocktail for Pakistani politics is a hard-working technocrat or handsome cricket star to work in close alliance with the leading conservative party representing Sunni political Islam, and not to touch the vast slice of the national budget that upholds the military. So, although old General Zia-ul-Haq is everywhere reviled, his political imprint survives.

CHAPTER 30

The Muslim Caucasus:
Azerbaijan and Chechnya

*Islamism in the Caucasus – and Russian
foreign policy in the Middle East*

Russia's relationship with the handful of Muslim peoples
nestled in the Caucasus Mountains on its southern border
plays a small but important role in the current complexion of
the Middle East.

The Caucasus, a concertina of mountain ranges between
the Black Sea and Caspian Sea, have long been one of the
frontiers of Islam. In the south, you can follow a mountain
stream that will eventually join the Tigris or the Euphrates,
and flow down to the warm waters of the Persian Gulf. In the
north, the grazing lands at the foot of the mountains beckon
ever onwards, into the grass oceans of the Asian steppe. It is
an ancient land, where winemaking and cheesemaking were
first born and where Noah's Ark is remembered to have landed
after the flood. A perennial frontier, it has been fought over for
millennia by Persian, Ottoman and Russian empires, and even
today its isolated valleys are home to a bewildering number of
indigenous languages, dialects and peoples.

Between 1864 and 1867, the Russian Empire expelled
all Muslim peoples from the north-western provinces of the
Caucasus. The Tsarist court had been greatly concerned about

agents of France and Britain establishing local allies here during the Crimean War of 1853–56. A decade after this war was over, Russia decided to end this strategic concern. The operation took over three years. An estimated 400,000 Muslim Circassians died in the process of forcible eviction, and perhaps 1.5 millon people were cleared out of their ancient highland homes and driven towards disease-ridden encampments along the Black Sea shore. Ship-loads of impoverished refugees were then deposited on the shores of the Ottoman Empire, where they eventually found land to farm. The city of Amman, the modern capital of Jordan, was one of the many chosen areas for their settlement. The ultimate fate of a Muslim people under a Christian empire was well advertised throughout the Middle East and the Ottoman Balkans, repeating the experience of the Muslims of Spain.

❋ ❋ ❋

The Chechens have never got a good press in the West. This embattled nation of around a million people has seemingly contributed more than its share of diehard volunteers to every manifestation of Islamic jihadi-terrorism, be it fighting along-side the Afghan resistance with the Taliban, with ISIS, or in infamous terrorist incidents in Russian cities. But you cannot aspire to understand the mentality of a Chechen fighter with-out realising how deeply their identity has been caught up in this tale of the Russian destruction of Islam north of the Caucasus Mountains.

Chechnya and the neighbouring nation of Dagestan are perched on the summits of the northern face of the Caucasus Mountains. They have never been ruled by a monarch, for they are composed of over a hundred *teip* (clans), all 'free and equal like wolves'. The clans only fully converted to Islam in the seventeenth and eighteenth centuries, as Russian armies were pushing them south. This was the period when battles for control of southern Russia were being fought on the far horizons, and in 1818 the Russian fort of Grozny was planted in Chechen lands by General Yermolov.

Resistance to the Russians was led throughout the century by a line of learned warrior chieftains, the most famous of whom was Imam Shamil. They expanded the resistance from their own clans to create a Caucasian-wide national identity, and, in organising the highlanders to fight against Orthodox imperialist Russia, these men did more to convert the pagan mountain communities (to Sunni Islam) than anything that had happened over the previous thousand years. Imam Shamil was finally forced to surrender in 1859, but towards the end of his life he was permitted to go on the Haj. He was greeted like a hero throughout the Ottoman Empire and died in Mecca, where he was buried beside early martyrs of the Islamic faith in the cemetery established by the Prophet Muhammad. In the Caucasus, Islam is a faith that has always been connected with the noble struggle of highland chieftains against a rabble of alcohol-drinking Christian merchants and their freebooting Cossack allies.

The recent series of Russian–Chechen wars continued this theme after a lull of a hundred, mainly Soviet, years. These wars of the 1990s and 2000s caused an exodus of most of the Russian Slavs who had migrated into the region over the last century. But it was the suppression of Chechen terrorist operations in Russia which helped President Putin emerge as the patriotic leader of his nation. It now seems clear that it was evidence of the large numbers of Chechen fighters volunteering to fight in the ranks of ISIS that was one of the key reasons why the Russian leaders decided to involve themselves so decisively in the Syrian civil war. Echoes of Tsarist Russia's expulsion of the Muslims continue to make themselves felt in the Middle East in the twenty-first century.

❋ ❋ ❋

Azerbaijan contradicts all the stereotypes: a nation that is both secular-leaning and entirely Shiite. It is one of the oldest oil-exporting nations in the world, and also the oldest Muslim democracy (it gave women the vote in 1919, before the US and most of Europe), even if it is currently flattened under the hereditary presidency of Ilham Aliyev. Ilham is the third generation of a family which emerged to prominence under Stalin's wartime administration.

Azerbaijan is ethnically a Turkic nation but one that has been deeply embedded in Iranian culture for thousands of years. It is linked with north-western Iran, which has a very substantial Azeri population and many shared cultural heroes and historical monuments. The castle of Babak, for example, the quintessential Azeri nationalist hero, who led a Shiite rebellion against the Abbasid caliphate in the ninth century, stands across the border in Iran. Babak, 'the Young Father', declared that 'It is better to live for a single day as a free ruler than live for forty years as an abject slave', and in the best Shia tradition died horribly for his faith, having been betrayed to an Abbasid general.*

Babak remains a potent image for modern Azerbaijan, which is locked into a long-running border war with Christian Armenia over the control of various mountain valleys. It is an intractable conflict, complex and ferocious, which has seen massacres on both sides of the frontiers. Armenia is backed

---

* Babak's legs and arms were cut off, after which he was sewn into a cow's skin, which gradually dried and contracted, slowly smothering the dismembered hero as he swung on a gibbet.

by Russia in this conflict and it might be supposed that Iran would be on the side of its Shia neighbour. However, hard-nosed Iran, keen to work with Russia in other areas of the world, such as Syria, seems content to observe the current mess. Iran may also be cautious of Azerbaijan becoming too powerful, lest it look south and start befriending Iran's own Azeri internal minority in the north-western provinces.

Cast adrift by both Russia and Iran, the Azeri have naturally turned towards Turkey. There is a hotline between the two presidents and much public talk of two nations and one people. This is supported by a logistical fact on the ground, which is that SOCAR (the Azerbaijan state oil company) sends its crude oil from Baku across eastern Turkey to be shipped. Azerbaijan has also developed a trading relationship with Britain, which sells armaments and pharmaceuticals to the Azeris and, through BP, is enabling a new round of offshore oil and gas exploration.

❋ ❋ ❋

Russia, of course, is not so much a nation as a continent, even in its post-Soviet make-up. Its territories cover six-million-square-miles, sliced up into eleven time zones; this is twice the size of either the US or China, though its population, at 144 million, is half the US and only one tenth that of China. Even before its invasion of Ukraine, its economy was relatively modest: in terms of global GDP it ranks twelve in the world and has become ever more dependent on oil and gas exports, the only two products that the Middle East really does not need. In the high days of the Soviet Union in the 1970s, Russia's allies in the Middle East included Egypt, Syria, Algeria, Libya, Iraq, Somalia and South Yemen. Only the relationship with Syria has survived intact.

So, viewed from a diplomatic perspective, Russia did well to support the Syrian regime with such military conviction in the second phase of Syria's civil war. This was costly (though not in Russian lives) but seems to be paying dividends. Russia kept use of its Syrian naval port in the eastern Mediterranean, and increased its standing with Turkey, Saudi Arabia and the Gulf States – even though they were effectively supporting other Syrian factions. A strong understanding with Iran was also achieved during the war.

CHAPTER 31

The New Silk Route: China and the Middle East

New global alliances as China looks West

The global powers – the US, Russia and China – have, over the past decade, firmed up their relations with the key Middle East powers of Saudi Arabia, Turkey and Iran. Russia is now strongly allied with Syria and Iran and can talk straight with Turkey (though they back different allies in the region). The US remains allied with Israel and Saudi Arabia and the Gulf emirates and is relentlessly (perhaps irrationally) opposed to Iran. China, for its part, is keen to trade with everybody in the Middle East, due to its own strategic needs for oil. It would like to forge a good working relationship with Pakistan, Iran and probably Oman, and perhaps, also, to forge a common policy with Russia and Iran in order to counter American influence.

China will soon become the biggest single importer of oil and thus ever more interested in the security of the Gulf sea-lanes.* So, as the US talks about disengaging from its role as the world's policeman, China seems likely to step up. This is a radical change in the Middle East, for China had been deliberately excluded since the Second World War by the

---

* China currently trails the US as the world's largest economy at $15 trillion to $18 trillion. American dominance, however, may not last another decade.

active opposition of both the Soviet Union and the US. In consequence, it has something of a blank slate, historically, in its Middle East relations. It had never had to choose between supporting Israel or Palestine, nor whether to trade with the wealthy monarchies or back the earnest socialist republics with their five-year plans.

China would like to capitalise on this tradition and uphold its non-aligned third way, as the superpower without enemies. But there are already issues stacking up. China imports 50 per cent of its oil and gas from the Middle East, so its relationship with Iran is likely to grow. Iranian oil can be sent overland to China and is not dependent on the security of the sea-lanes. Iran is also an integral part of Asia and at some point could become a useful ally in helping China police this vast continent. It harbours bitter memories as an ancient civilisation occupied and bullied by both Russia and Britain and dominated by America – a history that chimes with the Chinese experience. Both states are determined that this will never again happen.

To appreciate China's foreign policy in the Middle East, we need to look at the map of the world afresh. We might envisage the vast coastline of China opening directly to the freedom of the Pacific Ocean, but from a Chinese perspective; its sea routes are watched over by a string of US military island bases (Okinawa, Bonin and Guam) linked to long-term American allies in Japan, South Korea, Taiwan and the Philippines. Things look even more unsatisfactory to the south, for all the world's maritime trade (most especially Middle East oil being exported to the Far East) is funnelled through the Malacca Strait, a jugular vein for the Chinese economy, once again controlled by a cocktail of American allies – Singapore, Thailand, Malaysia, Indonesia and Australia. The Malacca Strait is the busiest in the world, used by more than 90,000 ships a year, and is 500 miles long, narrow and shallow.

As a result, China has been engaged in a long-term project that is intended to reopen the old silk route with the benefit of modern engineering and infrastructure. Iran's eastern neighbour, Pakistan, is a key beneficiary and partner in this vastly ambitious scheme. In 2015, China announced a $46 billion project to build roads, railways and a pipeline which would connect China with Gwadar, a vast new port on the south coast of Pakistan, which it will lease for an initial forty years. It will be insulated from the occasional troubles of lawless Baluchistan by a 25,000-strong security force.

China will probably wish to establish another safe port, maybe even a naval base, closer to the Persian Gulf. It will be wary of the political complications of the central Middle East and will be more interested in developing a friendship with a small nation that has an Indian Ocean or Red Sea shore – possibly Yemen or Oman (both threatened by their powerful Saudi Arabian neighbour). For the moment, China has spread its bets, both politically and geographically, and is working on partnership deals with four ports: the tiny port-state of Djibouti, Duqm (in Oman), Jazan in Saudi Arabia and Ain Sokhna in Egypt. The Chinese also have a growing commercial understanding with the UAE, which currently hosts 250,000 Chinese workers and has bilateral trade of around $60 billion.

In 2023, it appeared that the patient nature of Chinese diplomacy in the Middle East was coming of age, when it brokered a deal between Shia Iran and Sunni Saudi Arabia, encouraging them to reopen diplomatic relationships. This is an exciting and entirely positive initiative, reducing the tension in the Middle East. Both Iran and Saudi Arabia are autocracies, and unlikely to wish to embarrass China in its two no-go areas – any interference with the Muslims in China, especially the Uighur in Xinjiang (Chinese Turkestan) – and any linkage of the Arab Spring with the 1989 massacre at

Tiananmen Square. Only Turkey, wrapped up in distant day-dreams of a confederation of Turkish-speaking peoples, is outspokenly in support of the Chinese Uighur claims for self-determination. However, Turkey is a minor trading partner with China, with practically no export trade. They are unlikely to become close friends.

Those who might want to drive a wedge between China and the Middle East have an obvious cause to hand, the fate of the Uighurs, the indigenous Muslim population of Chinese Turkestan. The 12 million Uighurs comprise around 60 per cent of the population of Xinjiang. They are predominantly Sunni. Over the past decade, their religious identity has been ruthlessly suppressed by the Chinese state.

So a key figure from the recent past we are likely to hear more about will be Ma Bufang (1903–58), the charismatic Chinese Muslim general whose family dominated the region for a generation. He kept the Soviet Union at bay when it backed a small East Turkestan Republic on the Russo-China border during the Second World War, opposed the influence of both Tibet and local Buddhist communities, and repelled a Japanese invasion. At the peak of his influence, he commanded a fiercely loyal army of 50,000 soldiers, including the last great body of militarily effective cavalry, which allowed him to hold out against the Communist victory longer than any of Chiang Kai-Shek's allies. From 1950 to 1958, Ma Bufang was in exile, trying to find funds and allies (spending time in Egypt, Saudi Arabia and talking to the USA) to support the simmering Muslim rebellion against the Communists from 1950 to 1958.

❋ ❋ ❋

China is interested in promoting peace throughout the Middle East in order for it to buy the oil and gas it needs at the right price. Wars and political uncertainty have always increased prices. At the moment China has no enemies in the Middle East – curiously, the same position as the USA of a hundred years ago. America gradually destroyed its position as a trusted go-between by becoming too supportive of Israel, the one trusted ally it had identified in the region as sharing a notion of political democracy. China would do well not to follow this example, to fall in love with no cause or creed or nation, but to trade with everyone, and tolerate those nations who want to shop around to diversify their suppliers of armaments. China will also have an enormous advantage over the USA if it does not lecture and assess its regional allies and trading partners on liberty, transparency and justice, let alone the implementation of democracy and other liberal freedoms.

An Afterword

The Middle East after the Gaza War

I completed the final edits of The House Divided in October 2023. Earlier drafts had been three times longer, and the book had taken several years to write, and many decades of research and travel. I then set off to Rome, for a break; the war between Russia and the Ukraine dominated the news and, for once, the Middle East seemed quiet. I spent the day of October 7 exploring the ruins of the ancient port of Ostia, when I heard news of the Hamas massacres outside Gaza. By the time I returned to London, the Israelis had launched a revenge attack on Gaza, and the Middle East was set off into a new whirlwind of violence.

I was instantly aware that my history book would become both peculiarly relevant and out of date. My UK publishers added a brief note to say that the book had gone to print a week after the initial events in Gaza. Now, six months later, I am sending it off to press in America, with the Middle East in turmoil, the Israelis' war on Gaza having carried far beyond Israel and Palestine, with rocket assassinations in Lebanon, Syria and Iraq, and the old scars of the Sunni–Shia schism, which I had chronicled as history, reopening as fresh wounds.

In the Western media, this new Middle East crisis has seen Iran depicted as chair of a threatening Shiite alliance that embraces Syria, Iraq, the Houthi of northern Yemen and the Hezbollah of southern Lebanon. All the members of this so-called 'Axis of Resistance' are indeed influenced by Iran, yet they are also self-determining entities. Each wishes to be seen as the trusted ally of the Palestinians and to prove to the world that they belong to the true Muslim community that protects the poor and the oppressed at whatever cost to their purse. The other side, by implication, are the party of hypocrites, so often referenced in the Koran. Nothing is simple, however. The Palestinian fighters in Gaza – Hamas and Islamic Jihad – are emphatically Sunni in their belief traditions, while it is Shiite forces that have lent them active support.

The Sunni Arab nations, led by Saudi Arabia and its allies in the Gulf, and backed up by an outer circle of supporters such as Egypt and Jordan, might go very public on the rhetoric, but do nothing practical or militant to help the Palestinian resistance lest they anger the USA and Israel. It is, of course, true that these nations have much to lose, and as close neighbours of Israel are highly vulnerable. Israel, supported with weapons and finance from the US, could destroy the air forces of Egypt and Jordan, should they engage militarily, just as they did in the Arab–Israeli Six-Day War of 1967.

Off to one side of these two Middle East alliances stands a third power grouping – the Turkish Republic, working in tandem with Qatar. These powers, open to both the West and the Arab world, may do their best to broker a peace and can use forceful rhetoric in their criticism of Israel and the US. Qatar proved itself a vital player in the November 2023 truce that led to a release of some of the Israeli hostages held in Gaza, exchanged for imprisoned Palestinians. Qatar has also been quietly paying the salaries of teachers and doctors in Gaza for years, so has a long track record of engagement, alongside its more contentious policy of giving the Hamas leadership a safe haven. The Turkish president, Tayyip Erdogan, became increasingly outspoken as the war on Gaza continued, issuing a joint statement with the Palestinian President Mahmoud Abbas that asserted 'Netanyahu and his crazed administration have been openly carrying out genocide against Palestinian people.' Turkey's intelligence chief pointed out, early in the war, that there was clearly no universal standard of morality at work, for the powers that supported Ukraine against Russian military invasion were those that approved the destruction of Gaza by Israel. Turkey is a cornerstone of the NATO alliance so now and then they can say things that will be listened to.

Meantime, distant explosions also rattled the interest of the world, with targeted Israeli airstrikes in Syria, Lebanon and Iraq. Rockets were even briefly exchanged between Iran and Pakistan. But what caught the most interest were the Houthi attacks on shipping in the Red Sea, in support of Palestine, which triggered strikes on northern Yemen by the USA and the UK. The Houthi of North Yemen follow the mildest brand of doctrinal Shia, and had just endured nine years of assaults from a Sunni military alliance led by Saudi Arabia and the UAE. So the Western missiles unleashed upon them proved a boost to the morale of the regime and hugely popular on the Arab street. It made them look to be truly on the side of the party of God. Though, again, one must peer behind the smoke. Before this recent spate of rocket attacks, the Houthi were close to signing a truce with Saudi Arabia; and their forces do not control the Red Sea coast of Yemen.

Iran, the country that Israel and the US pretend to hold responsible for Middle East conflict, has been largely detached from any direct involvement. However, a mysterious exchange of missile fire between Iran and Pakistan once again exposed how connected things are within the Middle East. Iran and Pakistan share a desert frontier that bisects the wild landscape of Baluchistan. In Iranian terms, the province of Baluchistan is a minority Sunni region always a little at odds with the country's majority Shia population, while, in a Pakistani context, Baluchistan is a militantly Sunni province that borders the province of Sind, which is both rich and radical and Shia. Opportunities for misunderstandings and covert operations are considerable in such border regions, where either religion or ethnicity are in conflict with the national majority.

The current conflict between Israel and Gaza is horrifying, day by day. On 7 October, when 1200 Israelis were killed and around 240 taken hostage by gunmen surging out of Gaza, everyone in the Middle East knew that the military response from Israel would be overwhelming. Few, however, can have expected Israel's revenge on Gaza to be so comprehensively drawn out into a total war, levelling homes, public buildings and hospitals, and displacing and then starving the entire population. After five months of war, more than 32,000 Palestinians have been killed by Israeli military action within Gaza. Not so much an eye for an eye and a tooth for a tooth, but thirty-fold.

The Gaza war is deeply shocking, but it is not surprising. Most of the Gaza Strip's 2.1 million population come from families driven from their ancestral villages during the 1948–49 war, the Naqba ('catastrophe'), as it came to be called by Palestinians. The Israelis knew that they were hated by these Palestinians for seizing their land, but imagined this hatred would dwindle, 'for the old die and the young forget.' It is now 75 years since Israel's victory, but their hope that the Palestinians would forget their lost homes and migrate to find better lives elsewhere, have proved false. It is true that the 'notables', the well-educated middle-class Palestinians (from the cities of Haifa, Ramallah and Jerusalem), have become a diaspora of talent scattered across the world. But the reverse happened in places like Gaza where a powerful new nationalism was born from working class Palestinians shorn of their previous clan loyalties and village identities, and led by their own indigenous and ever more radical leaders. To such people the current conflict in Gaza is no more than the continuation of the 1948–49 war, now into the third generation. The Israeli army has invaded Gaza a dozen times since 1949, and has always tried to crush whatever form of Palestinian resistance had emerged, be they labelled Fatah, PLO, PFLP, Islamic Jihad or Hamas. Talk of a two-state solution, beloved by foreign peacemakers, was rarely (some would say never) seriously entertained by Israel, other than as a temporary truce in the long, slow march to create the Zionist homeland.

Some observers believe that a one-state solution for Israel–Palestine is more likely: that once Israel has become sufficiently secure and confident (from the scale of its military victories, its alliances, economy and expanded frontiers), it will be able to integrate indigenous Palestinian Arabs into the life of a single unitary democratic state. We are all free to dream that this efficient, well-governed Israel – including all of historic Palestine – could eventually be the core of a free trade zone, combined with Jordan, Lebanon and Syria. However, the violence in Gaza has put such optimistic visions back another generation or two.

In terms of diplomacy, the most striking fallout of the Gaza war is the death of the so-called Abraham Accords, the US-brokered attempt to ally Saudi Arabia, the Gulf and the Sunni bloc with Israel, in order to confront and demonise Iran. Although much can be made of the differences between the Shia Axis of Resistance and the passive Sunni nations, the invasion of Gaza has actually drawn the entire population of the Middle East together, in emotional sympathy with the fate of the Palestinians, mirrored by hostility to Israel and its American enablers.

This, in itself, is a shift in history. Unlike the colonial villains, France and Britain, the USA was the good guy in the Middle East for the first half of the twentieth century. Its dominance of the free world was absolute, under such men as Eisenhower, and it further strengthened its position over the second half of the twentieth century. But, in the 1960s, through its involvement in Cuba, Vietnam, South and Central America, and its tacit support for Israel's Six-Day War of 1967, the US in its foreign affairs became an empire first, and a democratic republic second.

The USA's three most recent tactical victories imposed on the Middle East – the liberation of Kuwait (1991), the invasion of Afghanistan (2001) and the invasion of Iraq (2003) – now mark the high water of American military reach, and they were undermined on each occasion by its failure to listen to the mood and the opinion of the street. Meantime, new realities are being formed by the resurgence of the two great economies of the ancient world, China and India, reinforced by a working alliance with Russia and Iran. Alongside this is the long term US military strategy (shared by all its political leaders) to prioritise the Pacific, and to encourage the leading military powers in Europe – Germany, France and Britain – to become more proactive.

The violence of the conflict between Israel and Palestine catches at the conscience of the world and seems so elemental that it can monopolise our attention. But, while it is the most reported upon conflict, it is in fact just one of half a dozen points of tension within the wider Middle East. In terms of battle casualties, it is much less destructive than what has been happening over the last decade in the Yemen, let alone the civil wars that have ripped apart Syria, Iraq, Lebanon and Afghanistan, or the one that is currently raging in Sudan.

389

For the slow news that could yet transform the Middle East, we need to look further and deeper: at how the Syrian regime will deal with the Sunni majority of their nation; if Iraq will be able to stay true to its own traditions or remain a client of Iran; if the Gulf Emirates will ennoble their middle class with a political voice; if the Kurdish emirates recently established in northern Syria and northern Iraq will survive; and if in Egypt some political genius will emerge to melt the standoff between the Egyptian army and the Muslim Brotherhood. Nor should we forget that the centre of the picture will always be framed by the political evolutions of Iran, Turkey and Saudi Arabia – each of which is acutely aware that if they do not play the Great Game with their utmost skill, what happens in their own borderlands of Khuzestan, Kurdistan and El Hasa could break their nations.

Barnaby Rogerson, April 2024

Further Reading

This is a highly selective bibliography, with an emphasis on modern and accessible books. It is divided into the eight parts of this book but, obviously, many recommendations cross boundaries and time zones.

PART ONE: The Origins of the Sunni–Shia Schism

For general Islamic history, three good introductions:

Karen Armstrong, *Islam: A Short History,* Orion, 2000.
Reza Aslan, *No God but God*, Heinemann, 2005.
Malise Ruthven, *Islam in the World,* Oxford UP, 2006.

For more on the specifics of the Sunni–Shia divide:

John McHugo, A *Concise History of Sunnis & Shi'is,* Saqi, 2017.
Toby Matthiesen, *The Caliph and the Imam: The Making of Sunnism and Shiism,* Oxford UP, 2023.

For the life and household of the Prophet Muhammad:

Karen Armstrong, *Muhammad, A Biography of the Prophet,* Harper, 1991.
Martin Lings, *Muhammad – His Life Based on the Earliest Sources,* Islamic Texts Society, 1991.

Ziauddin Sardar, *Reading the Quran*, Hurst, 2011;
  Mecca: The Sacred City, Bloomsbury, 2015.
Montgomery Watt, *Muhammad at Medina*, Oxford UP, 1956;
  Muhammad at Mecca, Oxford UP, 1956.

Primary sources:

Muhammad Ibn Ishak, *The Life of Muhammad (Sirat al-Nabi)*.
  This work of Ibn Ishak (699–761) survives with two different
  early commentaries – that of Abd al-Malik ibn Hisham and
  Abd ar-Rahman ibn Abd Allah as-Suhayli.

Al-Tabari, Abu Jafar Muhammad ibn Jarir, Ta'rikh al-Rusul
  Wa'l-muluk, *The History of the Messengers and the Kings*, 39
  vols, State University of New York Press, 1985–99.

PART TWO: Medieval Caliphates

Hugh Kennedy (particularly his Caliphate: The History of an Idea*)
offers a fine introduction to this period.*

G.R. Hawting, *The First Dynasty of Islam, the Umayyad Caliphate,
  AD 661–750*, Routledge, 2000.
Hugh Kennedy, *Caliphate: The History of an Idea*,
  Basic Books, 2016; *The Prophet and the Age of the Caliphates*,
  Routledge, 2022; *The Court of the Caliphs:
  The Rise and Fall of Islam's Greatest Dynasty*, Weidenfeld &
  Nicolson, 2004.
Ira M. Lapidus, *A History of Islamic Societies*, Cambridge UP, 2004.
Wilfred Madelung, *The Succession to Muhammad: A Study of the
  Caliphate*, Cambridge UP, 1997.

PART THREE: The Emergence of the Three: Turkey, Persia and Saudi Arabia

If new to this subject, start with Jason Goodwin on the Ottomans, Michael Axworthy (Empire of the Mind) on Iran and Robert Lacey on Saudi Arabia.

Ottomans

Caroline Finkel, *Osman's Dream: The Story of the Ottoman Empire 1300–1923*, John Murray, 2005.

Jason Goodwin, *Lords of the Horizons: A History of the Ottoman Empire,* Holt, 1999.

Halil Inalcik, *The Ottoman Empire: 1300–1600*, Weidenfeld & Nicolson, 2000.

Iran

Abbas Amanat, *Iran: A Modern History*, Yale, 2017.

Michael Axworthy, *Iran: Empire of the Mind*, Penguin, 2008; *The Sword of Persia: Nader Shah, from Tribal Warrior to Conquering Tyrant*, I.B. Tauris, 2006.

Laurence Lockhart, *The Fall of the Safavi Dynasty and the Afghan Occupation of Persia*, Cambridge UP, 1958.

John Malcolm, *History of Persia*, London, 1829.

Moojan Momen, *An Introduction to Shi'i Islam*, Yale UP, 1985.

Saudi Arabia

Michael Crawford, *Ibn 'Abd al-Wahhab* (Makers of the Muslim World series), Oneworld, 2014.

Robert Lacey, *The Kingdom*, HarperCollins, 1982.

Madawi Al-Rasheed, *A History of Saudi Arabia*, Cambridge UP, 2010.

PART FOUR: Colonial Night, 1830–1979

*The three introductions recommended for Part Three cover much
of this period. For an outstanding overview of the Arab world, Tim
Mackintosh-Smith's* Arabs *is unrivalled.*

Iran

Ervand Abrahamiam, *A History of Modern Iran*, Cambridge UP,
 2009.

Ali Ansari, *Modern Iran Since 1921*, Longman, 2003.

Christopher de Bellaigue, *Patriot of Persia: Muhammad Mossadegh
 and a Tragic Anglo-American Coup*,
 Harper, 2002.

Saudi Arabia

David Holden and Richard Johns, *The House of Saud*, Macmillan,
 1981.

David Howarth, *The Desert King: The Life of Ibn Saud*,
 Quartet, 1980.

Madawi Al-Rasheed, *A History of Saudi* Arabia,
 Cambridge UP, 2010.

Alexei Vassiliev, *The History of Saudi Arabia,* Saqi, 2013.

Turkey

Patrick Kinross, *Ataturk: The Rebirth of a Nation,*
 Orion, 1964.

Bruce Masters, *The Arabs of the Ottoman Empire, 1516–1918,*
 Cambridge UP, 2013.

Hugh Pope, *Turkey Unveiled: A History of Modern Turkey,*
 Duckworth, 2012.

Eugene Rogan, *The Fall of the Ottomans (1914–1920),* Penguin,
 2015.

Broader horizons

Tim Mackintosh-Smith, *Arabs: A 3,000-Year History of Peoples, Tribes and Empires*, Yale UP, 2019.

Eugene Rogan, *The Arabs: A History*, Penguin, 2009.

PART FIVE: 1979 Revolutions: The Middle East Transformed

Key introductions here are Michael Axworthy on Iran, Robert Lacey on Saudi Arabia and Jeremy Seal on modern Turkey.

Iran

Said Amir Arjomand, *The Turban for the Crown*, Oxford UP, 1988.

Michael Axworthy, *Revolutionary Iran: A History of the Islamic Republic,* Penguin, 2003.

Kaveh Basmenji, *Tehran Blues: Youth Culture in Iran,* Saqi, 2005.

Christopher de Bellaigue, *In the Rose Garden of the Martyrs: A Memoir of Iran*, Harper, 2005.

Baqer Moin, *Khomeini: Life of the Ayatollah*, I.B. Tauris, 1999.

Roy P. Mottahedeh, *The Mantle of the Prophet*, Oneworld, 2008.

Azar Nafisi, *Reading Lolita in Tehran,* Penguin, 2008.

Iraj Pezeshkzad, *My Uncle Napoleon*, Random House, 2006.

Saudi Arabia

Natana J. Delong-Bas, *Wahhabi Islam: From Revival and Reform to Global Jihad*, Oxford UP, 2004.

Fouad Ibrahim, *The Shi'is of Saudi Arabia*, Saqi, 2006.

Robert Lacey, *Inside the Kingdom: Kings, Clerics, Modernists and Terrorists and the Struggle for Saudi Arabia*, Arrow, 2010.

Pascal Menoret, *Joyriding in Riyadh: Oil, Urbanism, and Road Revolt*, Cambridge UP, 2014.

Madawi al-Rasheed, *A Most Masculine State: Gender, Politics and Religion in Saudi Arabia*, Cambridge UP, 2013.

Alexei Vassiliev, *The History of Saudi Arabia*, Saqi, 2013.

Turkish Republic

Mehmet Ali Birand, *The Generals Coup in Turkey*, Brassey's, 1987.

Ahmad Feroz, *The Making of Modern Turkey*, Routledge, 1993.

William Hale, *Turkish Politics and the Military*, Routledge, 1993.

Gareth Jenkins, *Political Islam in Turkey: Running West, Heading East?*, Palgrave Macmillan, 2008.

David McDowall, *A Modern History of the Kurds*, I.B. Tauris, rev. edn., 2021.

Jeremy Seal, *A Fez of the Heart*, Picador, 1995; *A Coup in Turkey*, Chatto & Windus, 2021.

PART SIX: Twenty-First Century Battlefields: Syria, Iraq and Yemen

For modern Syria, Patrick Seale's biography of Assad is a first port of call, alongside the more recent work of John McHugo. Charles Tripp provides the best introduction to Iraq. For Yemen, look first to Paul Dresch and Tim Mackintosh-Smith.

Modern Syria

James Barr, *A Line in the Sand: Britain, France and the Struggle That Shaped the Middle East*, Simon & Schuster, 2011.

Nicholas Blanford, *Warriors of God: Inside Hezbollah's Thirty-Year Struggle against Israel*, Random House, 2011.

Joseph Daher, *Syria after the Uprisings: The Political Economy of State Resilience*, Pluto Press, 2016; *Hezbollah: The Political Economy of Lebanon's Party of God*, Pluto Press, 2015.

Robert Fisk., *Pity the Nation: Lebanon at War*, Oxford UP, 2001.

John McHugo, *Syria: A Recent History*, Saqi, 2015.

Patrick Seale, *Assad: the Struggle for the Middle East*, University of California Press, 1989.

Modern Iraq

Patrick Cockburn, *Muqtada Al-Sadr and the Shia Insurgency in Iraq*, Faber, 2008.

Con Coughlin, *Saddam: The Secret Life*, Macmillan, 2002.

John Devlin, *The Ba'th Party: A History from Its Origins to 1966*, Stanford UP, 1976.

Dilip Hiro, *The Longest War: The Iran–Iraq Military Conflict*, Routledge, 1990.

Justin Marozzi, *Baghdad: City of Peace, City of Blood*, Penguin, 2015.

Yitzhak Nakash, *The Shi'is of Iraq*, Princeton, 2003.

Rory Stewart, *Occupational Hazards: My Time Governing in Iraq*, Picador, 2006.

Charles Tripp, *A History of Iraq*, Cambridge UP, 2007.

Modern Yemen

Saeed Badeeb, *The Saudi–Egyptian Conflict over North Yemen, 1962–70*, Routledge, 1986.

Noel Brehony, *Yemen Divided: The Story of a Failed State in South Arabia*, I.B. Tauris, 2011.

Victoria Clark, *Yemen: Dancing on the Heads of Snakes*, Yale UP, 2010.

Paul Dresch, *A History of Modern Yemen*, Cambridge UP, 2000.

Doreen Ingrams, *A Time in Arabia*, John Murray, 1970.

Tim Mackintosh-Smith, *Yemen: Travels in Dictionary Land*, John Murray, 1997.

Robert Stookey, *South Yemen: A Marxist Republic in Arabia*, Routledge, 1982.

Jonathan Walker, *Aden Insurgency: The Savage War in South Arabia 1962–1967*, Spellmount, 2005.

PART SEVEN: The Enemy of My Enemy: Egypt, Israel, USA and Qatar

Two essential, highly readable authors here are Peter Hessler on contemporary Egypt and Ian Black on Israel/Palestine.

Modern Egypt

Anne Alexander, *Nasser: His Life and Times*, Haus, 2005.

John Calvert, *Sayyid Qutb and the Origins of Radical Islam*, Hurst, 2010.

Steven Cook, *The Struggle for Egypt from Nasser to Tahrir Square*, Oxford UP, 2011.

Peter Hessler, *The Buried: Life, Death and Revolution in Egypt*, Profile, 2019.

Afaf Lutfi Al-Sayyid, *A History of Egypt from the Arab Conquest to the Present*, Cambridge UP, 2007.

Eric Trager, *Arab Fall: How the Muslim Brotherhood Won and Lost Egypt in 891 Days*, Georgetown UP, 2016.

Israel and Palestine

Ian Black, *Enemies and Neighbours: Arabs and Jews in Palestine and Israel, 1917–2017*, Allen Lane, 2017.

Doreen Ingrams, *Palestine Papers, 1917–22: Seeds of Conflict*, John Murray, 1972.

Ghada Karmi, *In Search of Fatima: A Palestinian Story*, Verso, 2002.

Rashid Khalidi, *The Hundred Years War on Palestine: A History of Settler Colonial Conquest and Resistance*, Profile, 2020.

Benny Morris, *1948: The First Arab–Israeli War*, Yale UP, 2008.

Dervla Murphy, *A Month by the Sea: Encounters in Gaza*, Eland, 2013; *Between River and Sea: Encounters in Israel and Palestine*, Eland, 2015.

Raja Shehadeh, *Palestinian Walks*, Profile, 1997; *Where the Line is Drawn*, Profile, 2017.

Avi Shlaim, *Collusion Across the Jordan: King Abdullah, the Zionist Movement and the Partition of Palestine*, Oxford UP, 1988; *War and Peace in the Middle East*, Penguin, 1996; *The Iron Wall: Israel and the Arab Lands*, Penguin, 2000.

Qatar

Syed Ali, *Dubai, Gilded Cage*, Yale UP, 2010.

Mohammed Althani, *Jassim the Leader*, Profile, 2012.

Sean Foley, *The Arab Gulf States: Beyond Oil and Islam*, Lynne Rienner, 2010.

Donald Hawley, *The Trucial States*, Allen and Unwin, 1970.

Molly Izzard, *The Gulf: Arabia's Western Approaches*, John Murray, 1977.

Mehran Kamrava, *Qatar: Small State, Big Politics*, Cornell UP, 2013.

John Kelly, *Arabia, The Gulf and the West*, Weidenfeld & Nicolson, 1980.

Habibur Rahman, *The Emergence of Qatar: The Turbulent Years 1627–1916*, Routledge, 2005.

PART EIGHT: Far Frontiers and Distant Powers: Pakistan, Azerbaijan, Chechnya and China's New Silk Road

Jason Elliot provides a fine introduction to Afghanistan; Thomas de Wall, to Chechnya; and Morris Rossabi, to the Uighurs.

International horizons

Richard Bonney, *Jihad: From Qur'an to Bin Laden*, Macmillan, 2004.

Gilles Kepel, *Jihad: the Trail of Political Islam*, I.B. Tauris, 2002.

Malise Ruthven, *Islam in the World*, Oxford UP, 2006.

Pakistan and Afghanistan

David Edwards, *Before Taliban: Genealogies of the Afghan Jihad*, California UP, 2002.

Jason Elliot, *An Unexpected Light: Travels in Afghanistan*, Picador, 2007.

Larry Goodson, *Afghanistan's Endless War*, University of Washington Press, 2001.

Anthony Hyman, *Afghanistan Under Soviet Domination 1964–83*, Palgrave Macmillan, 1984.

Dennis Kux, *The United States and Pakistan: Disenchanted Allies, 1947–2000*, Oxford UP, 2001.

Ahmed Rashid, *Taliban, The Story of the Afghan Warlords*, I.B. Tauris, 2001.

Olivier Roy, *Islam and Resistance in Afghanistan*, Cambridge UP, 1986.

Ayesha Siddiqa, *Military Inc: Inside Pakistan's Military Economy*, Pluto Press Press, 2016.

Rory Stewart, *The Places In Between*, Picador, 2014.

Mullah Abdul Salem Zaeef, *My Life with the Taliban*, Hurst, 2011.

Azerbaijan and Chechnya

Oliver Bullough, *Let Our Fame Be Great*, Penguin, 2011.

Svetlana Chervonnaya, *Conflict in the Caucasus*, Gothic Image, 1994.

Thomas de Wall, *Black Garden: Armenia and Azerbaijan Through Peace and War*, New York UP, 2013; *The Caucasus: An Introduction*, Oxford UP, 2015.

Carlotta Gall and Thomas de Wall, *Chechnya: A Small Victorious War*, Picador, 1997.

Anna Politkovskaya, *A Small Corner of Hell: Dispatches from Chechnya*, University of Chicago, 2007.

Leo Tolstoy, *The Cossacks* and *Hadji Murat*, Penguin Classics.

Chinese Central Asia

Andrew Forbes, *Warlords and Muslims in Chinese Central Asia, 1911–1949*, Cambridge UP, 1986

Peter Frankopan, *The Silk Roads*, Bloomsbury, 2016.

Peter Hopkirk, *The Great Game*, John Murray, 2006.

Ahmed Rashid, *Jihad: The Rise of Militant Islam in Central Asia*, Yale UP, 2002.

Morris Rossabi, *China and the Uyghurs: A Concise History*, Rowman & Littlefield, 2022.

Acknowledgments

I am a heretic amongst historians, for I am as much interested in the believed stories that activate the living as the footnote battles that establish an exact chronicle of our past. I am also a follower of Apollinaire in his declaration 'I love men, not for what unites them, but for what divides them, and I want to know most of all what gnaws at their hearts.' I am as interested to hear what an articulate citizen makes of our world, as what an ambassador recollects saying to the Minister of Foreign Affairs as he descends the staircase. This desire to listen to random conversations of conviction has always empowered my travels. But they are rare, those moments when the public mask is dropped, eyes flash with animation and you hear stories from the heart.

Through accident, design and ambition, the last forty-five years of my life have included an enormous amount of travelling and chance conversations with people who live in the Middle East and North Africa. I have met more than my fare share of travel writers, academics, foreign correspondents, archaeologists, museum curators, editors, historians, researchers, diplomats and military attachés. I am not going to list any of these amazingly well-informed characters as sources, for I doubt many would wish to be associated with a book empty of footnotes and accents and full of personal opinions, and it has been my ambition to write about history as a tangible current of energy that affects life decisions. Almost all of my research has been done in a companionable huddle at an outdoor table of a restaurant or over a café table groaning with the many plates of a Levantine breakfast, scribbling down the best bits of transcribed conversation into a notebook with a fountain pen.

I was so engaged in passing on some of these stories that I have chanced upon that both the delivery date and intended size of the book got buried in my enthusiasm. My first draft was five years late and a quarter of a million words too long, but, assisted by the heroic labours of two young freelance editors, Hughie Rogers-Coltman and then Ella Carr, the task of editing was begun, and then completed by Rose Baring (a brilliant editor with whom I share my life). This now slim volume was finally quarried into its final shape through the tact and patience of Mark Ellingham, who is a cherished friend, accomplished editor and travelling companion. It has been a pleasure to work with him and everyone at Profile, which is an inspiration for small independent publishers (myself included).

Barnaby Rogerson, London, October 2023

Index

A

al-Abbadine, Ali ibn Husayn Zayn
90–91, 97, 312; *Al Sahifa
al-Sajjadiyya* 90–91
Abbas I, Shah of Persia 133–4, 149,
151, 276
Abbasid caliphate 20, 91, 95–6, 97,
98–104, 105, 107–8, 109, 111,
114, 174, 245, 276, 283, 376
Abd Shams clan 79
Abdal Malik, Caliph 97–8
Abdul Hamid II, Sultan 179, 248
Abdul Aziz bin Muhammad al-
Saud, Emir of Diriyah 140
Abdullah (son of Abu Bakr) 33
Abdullah (son of Muhammad) 46
Abdullah I, Emir of Jordan 252,
254, 256, 257
Abdullah II, King of Jordan 213
Abdullah bin Abdulaziz Al Saud,
King of Saudi Arabia 169, 209,
213–14, 215
Abdullah ibn Al Saud, Emir of
Diriyah 142
Abdurrahman, Sheikh 181
Abraham, Prophet 60, 88, 98n, 231
Abu Abbas (uncle of Muhammad)
36, 64, 98
Abu Abdallah (Shiite agent) 106
Abu Bakr, Caliph 109
  Aisha and 43, 47–8, 50, 68
  caliph, rule as 71, 72–3, 74, 77–8
  Haj and 59, 64
  house of 165
  ISIS and 305, 306
  Jafar al-Sadiq and 20, 103
  Kuswa and 26

Muhammad (son of) and 80
Muhammad, Prophet and 32–3,
38–9, 59, 64
Shia and 69, 74, 79
succession to Prophet Muhammad
and 65–9, 69n, 71, 72–3, 74,
77–8, 79, 80
Sunni and 19, 20, 65, 68, 69n, 103,
109
Zaydi tradition and 311
Abu Jahl (uncle of Muhammad) 75
Abu Yazid 28
Abyssinia, Empire of 72
Acre 246
Al-Adbaa (racing camel) 27
Aden 169–70, 244, 308, 309, 310,
314–15, 317–24, 351
  Aden Insurrection (1962–70)
  309–10, 314, 317–23, 324
Afghani, Jamal al-Din 152
Afghanistan 12, 13, 55n, 101,
112, 115, 134, 149, 152, 184,
220–26, 268, 324
  Abbasid Dynasty and 98–9
  Buyid emirates and 110
  civil war (1989–92) 205, 220,
  222–3
  Communist Party 220–21, 222
  ethnic groups 205, 225–6
  Iran and 149, 156, 205, 211, 221,
  224, 226
  KHAD secret police 222
  Mujahadin in 188, 211, 221, 222,
  223, 300, 306, 367, 368–9
  Pakistan and 188, 204, 205, 211,
  221, 223n, 224, 225, 226, 351,
  363, 367–9
  Saadabad pact and 156

Saudi Arabia and 188, 204, 221, 223n, 224
Soviet-Afghan War (1979–89) 187, 188, 204, 205, 211, 212, 220–22, 270, 297, 299, 300, 306, 351, 352, 368–9
Taliban in 55n, 188, 205, 217, 220, 223–5, 356, 365, 369, 370, 374
Trump government signs truce with Taliban 225
ungovernable nature of 226
US foreign aid to 329n
US war in (2001–21) 205, 220, 224–5, 301
Aflaq, Michel 255
Agha Khan 91, 103, 107, 247
Ahmadinejad, Mahmud 205–6
Ahmed ibn Yahya, Imam 314
AIOC (Anglo-Iranian Oil Company) 158
AIPAC (American Israel Public Affairs Committee) 350
Aisha (wife of Muhammad) 43–4, 45, 47–50, 48n, 64, 65, 68, 80, 143
Akar, Hulusi 238
Akbar, Mughal emperor of India, Shah 138
AKP (Justice and Development Party) 234–5, 237
Alawites 116, 247, 253, 254, 255, 259, 262, 265, 270
Al Azhar University, Cairo 106, 335
alcohol 107, 114, 163, 318, 369, 375
Al-Dawa Party 293–4
Aleppo, Syria 118, 246, 249, 256, 270
Alevi Islam 130, 183
Alexander the Great 28, 72, 134, 245
Algeria 12, 81n, 106, 247, 252, 319, 320, 321, 331, 334, 350, 377
Al Haqq party 315
Ali al-Hadi, Imam 105
Ali ibn Abi Talib, Caliph
  Abbasid dynasty and 98, 99
  Aisha and 43, 49, 50, 80
  Asad-Ullah ('Lion of God') 57–8
  bravery 32, 41, 53, 57, 58, 65, 82

Buyid emirates and 110
as caliph 80–81
children 58, 81, 82–4, 83n, 85, 86
death 8, 80–81, 82, 91–2
death of Muhammad and 64–6, 68
dynasty of Shia imams and 102, 103, 107
Fatima and 43, 45, 46, 57, 58
Fatimid dynasty and 107
First Imam of the Shia and Fourth Caliph of the Sunni 71
Four Companions of Ali 74–7
Ghadir Khum declaration and 61–2, 131
Hasan and 81, 82–4, 83n, 85, 86
Hyder Karrar ('warrior who attacks time and again') 56
Kaaba and 59
Khomeini and 203
Muawiya and 81, 82, 84
Muhammad, Prophet and 32, 39, 41, 51–2, 53, 54–6, 57, 64–5, 66, 68
Nahjul Balagha and 77
name 51
Omar and 65, 74, 77, 78–9
Ottoman Empire and 276
reigns of the first three caliphs and 77
rightful succession to the Prophet and 24, 28, 47, 51, 57–8, 68–71, 69n, 77, 81, 99
Sayyid or Shorfa and 45
Shia belief system and 91–2, 102
Sufi brotherhoods and 126
Sunni–Shia divide and 8, 19, 23, 24, 28, 51–8
tomb at Najaf 81, 276
Trench, Battle of and 58
Truce of Hudaybyah and 58, 59
'twin to the Koran' 52–3
Uhud battle and 57
Umm Salamah and 49
Uthman and 79, 80
Wahhabism and 143
Wells of Badr battle and 56
Yemeni tribes and 311–12
Zulfiqar ('master of the spine'), Muhammad presents to 57–8
Aliyev, Ilham 376

Al Jazeera 339, 355, 357, 357*n*, 358
alliance system, neo-colonial 148
Al Murrah tribe 162
Alp Arslan, sultan 112
al-Qaeda 212, 224, 270*n*, 300–301, 316, 317, 355
Amasya, Treaty of (1555) 132
Amina (Muhammad's mother) 35
amir (military commander) 61
Amman 374
Ammar ibn Yasir 74, 75
Amnesty 218
amsar (garrison cities) 78, 88, 101
Anatolia 112, 115, 119, 128, 142, 148, 175, 177–80, 182, 183–4, 231, 232, 235, 236, 243, 273, 274, 332
Al-Anfal campaign, Iraq (1988) 295–6
Anglo-Persian Petroleum Company 281–2, 359
Ansar ('helpers') 39, 40, 65
Antalya 128
Antioch 245, 254
Aqaba, oaths at 36, 37, 61–2, 65
Arab Empires. *See individual empire and ruler name*
Arab federation 258
Arabian peninsula 15, 26, 29, 30, 34–5, 37, 48, 58, 59, 63, 66–7, 69–70, 72–3, 73*n*, 81, 100, 105, 108, 109, 121, 147, 161, 162–5, 168, 208, 217, 243, 244, 289, 312*n*, 323, 342*n*, 356
  pagan 24, 53, 60
  united 16, 141–2
  Wahhabi 136–44
  See also individual nation name
Arabic language 4, 15, 16–17, 84, 97, 99, 100, 116, 117, 176, 177, 180, 230, 231, 249, 271, 273, 290, 319, 320, 331, 333–4, 345
Arab–Israeli War (1948–9) 11, 256–7, 286, 344–5, 350
Arab–Israeli War (1973). *See* Yom Kippur War
Arabistan 196, 290. *See also* Khuzestan
Arab League 264, 334

Arab nationalism 255–6, 319, 320
Arab Revolt (1916) 164, 175, 249, 278, 279, 280, 343
Arab Spring (2011) 13, 206, 214, 218, 236, 237, 267–8, 269, 304, 309, 316, 335, 356, 381
Ararat rebellion (1927–30) 181
architecture 26, 110, 118, 127, 138, 141, 155, 276, 308
Ardabil 126
Arif, Abdal-Salam 288
Armenia 112, 116, 132, 133, 150, 151, 228, 376–7
Armenians 116, 174, 175, 176, 178–9, 180, 183, 248, 253, 282
al-Arsuzi, Zaki 255
art 110, 113, 114, 150
al-As, Amr ibn 73
As-Sahabah ('the Companions') 19, 70–71, 70*n*, 72, 74, 85, 88, 95, 163, 208
Ashkenazi Jews 341, 342, 343
Ashura 12, 86–7, 109, 127–8, 190, 209
al-Askari, Jafar 280–81
al-Assad, Bashar 199, 236, 265, 268, 270, 272, 316, 339
al-Assad, Basil 264
al-Assad, Hafiz 259, 260, 261, 262, 263, 264–5
al-Assad, Maher 272
al-Assad, Rifat 264
Ataturk (Mustafa Kemal) 154–5, 156, 173, 175–8, 180, 181, 184, 227, 230, 231, 235, 339
Atlas Mountains 28
Awliat-i-Omar 78
Aws 36, 41
'Axis of Evil' speech, US (2002) 205
Ayyubid Empire 313
Azerbaijan 90, 151, 229, 363, 376–7
Azeri 130, 157, 376, 377
Aziz, Tariq 293

B

Ba'ath (Arab Renaissance) party 14
  Egypt and 339–40, 345, 359

Iraq and 196–7, 288–90, 288n, 291, 292, 293, 296, 299, 345
ISIS and 304, 306
Qatar and 359
Syria and 255–6, 258, 259, 261, 263, 265, 267, 268, 270, 271, 272, 345
Yemen and 319, 320
Babak 376, 376n
Babur 119
Al-Badr brigade 200, 296, 299, 302–3, 304
Baghdad 12, 13, 287, 288, 291, 314
  Abbasid caliphs of 91, 98–9, 102, 104, 111, 112, 114, 276
  Al-Mustan siriyyah in 113
  Arab Revolt and 278
  destruction of (1258) 114, 276, 279
  Iraq, node of power in 274
  Jews in 250, 277, 285
  Mahdi army in 303
  Ottoman Empire and 277
  publishing and newspaper printing in 248
  Tariq Aziz assassination attempt in (1980) 293–4
  Timur and 118
Baghdad pact/CENTO (1955) 158–9, 287
al-Baghdadi, Abu Bakr 55n, 305, 306–7
Bahrain 109, 131, 162, 214, 218, 267, 310n, 355, 358, 366
Bajkam, amir 103–4
Bakhtiar, Shapour 190–92, 196
Bakil tribe 311, 313, 315
al-Bakr, General Ahmed Hassan 196, 289, 292–3
Balkans 15, 229, 374
Balkan Wars (1912–13) 174–5, 229
Baluch 214, 225, 324, 366–7
Baluchistan 12, 107, 324, 366–7, 381
al-Banna, Hassan 337–8, 339
Banu Asad tribe 90
al-Baqir, Muhammad 91
Baradar, Mullah Abdul Ghari 225
Barger, Thomas 349

Barzani, Sheikh Ahmed 285, 290, 295
Barzani, Mustafa 285, 298
Barzanji, Mahmud 279
Barzanji, Sheikh Ahmed 281, 282
Basra 13, 80, 107, 135, 137–8, 274, 275, 277, 278, 358
Bayan, Jabr 302–3
bayat (public oath-taking) 61–2, 98
Bayat al-Nisa (personal oath of loyalty to Muhammad) 35–6
Bazargan, Mehdi 193, 194, 194n
Bedouin
  Abu Bakr and 33, 66, 73
  Aisha and 49
  Arab Revolt and 249
  Haj and 246
  hospitality 26
  Husayn and 86
  Islam and 30, 100
  non-aggression pacts with Muslims 40, 41
  Qarmatian Bedouin republic 108, 109
  Syria and 247, 249, 253
  Waddan patrol and 40
  Wahhabism/Saudi Arabia and 136, 138, 140, 143, 144, 152, 162–3, 164, 167, 212, 358
Beirut 199, 247, 248, 249, 249n, 250, 252, 262, 263, 266, 269, 314, 319, 323
Ben Ali, Zine El Abidine 214, 267
Beni Bekr tribe 73
Beni Hashim clan 35, 51, 53, 54, 56, 61
Beni Khalid tribe 136, 139
Beni Mustaliq tribe 49
Beni Nazzar clan 35
Beni Qurayzah clan 44
Berbers 106
Bhutto, Benazir 372
Bhutto, Murtaza 372
Bhutto political dynasty 366–8, 372
Bhutto, Shahnawaz 372
Bhutto, Zulfikar Ali 367, 368, 372
Bihan, Emir of 318
bin Laden, Osama 212, 300, 369
Bitar, Salah al-Din al 255
Black Death 117–18

Black Saturday, Cairo (1952) 158, 338
Black September (1970) 260, 263, 345, 368
Black Thursday (2011) 214
Bokhara 104
Bonyad Foundation for the Oppressed 193
Bosnia 126, 211
Bosphorus 120, 239
Bouzid, Sidi 267
BP (British Petroleum) 158, 282, 321–2, 377
Britain 17
  Aden Insurrection and 309–10, 314, 317–23, 324
  Arab Revolt and 175, 249, 278–9
  Azerbaijan, trade with 377
  China, historical relationship with 380
  Crimean War and 374
  Egypt and 248, 332, 332n, 338
  Falklands War and 297
  First World War and 278–9
  Iran and 149, 151–4, 156–8, 204
  Iraq and 148, 166, 182–3, 196, 277, 278–80, 281–7
  Israel and 250–52, 342–4, 342n, 346
  Pakistan and 368
  Qatar and 358–9
  Rushdie affair and 202, 203
  Saudi Arabia and 164–5, 167, 170
  Second Gulf War and 275, 306n
  Sèvres Treaty and 175, 183
  Suez crisis and 171, 258, 349, 350
  Sykes–Picot Agreement and 250–51
  Syria and 253–5
British East India Company 275, 277
British Royal Navy 152, 153, 157, 165
Brzezinski, Zbigniew 194
Bu'ath, Battle of (617) 36
Bush, George W. 205, 297–8, 301, 352
Buyid emirates 105, 108–10, 108n, 112

Byzantine Empire 27n, 29, 63, 72–3, 78, 84, 85, 97, 112, 120, 125, 125n, 178, 245, 341, 347

C

Cairo 89, 101, 105, 106, 107, 111, 114, 116, 118, 158, 165, 169, 174, 248, 313, 319, 332, 334, 335, 338
caliphates, medieval 93–120. See also individual caliphate name
Camel, Battle of the (656) 80
Camp David Accords (1978) 292
Carter, Jimmy 189, 369
Caucasus 147, 247, 248, 270, 363, 373–8
Cedar Revolution (2005) 266
ceramics 110, 113, 114–15, 118
Chaldiran, Battle of (1514) 125, 129–30
Chechnya 363, 374–6
Chiang Kai-Shek 383
China 14, 114, 119, 184, 200, 207, 277, 322, 364, 377, 379–83
Christianity 32, 72, 78, 87
  Caucasus and 374, 375, 376
  Coptic 27, 331–2
  Egypt and 251, 331–2
  Iraq and 276, 281, 283, 284, 288
  Maronite 247, 252, 254, 261, 262, 266
  Mongols and 116, 118
  Nestorian 74–5, 118
  Ottoman Empire and 126, 128, 137, 174
  Palestine and 343, 353
  Safavid Empire and 133
  Seljuk Empire and 112
  Syria and 245, 246, 247–8, 247n, 249, 250, 252, 254, 255, 261, 262, 265, 266
  Turkey and 176, 178, 229
  Wahhabism and 164
CIA 158, 195, 212, 297
Clinton, Bill 352
coinage 84, 97, 106, 108, 305, 318
Cold War (1946–91) 148, 157, 158, 227, 229, 230, 262, 264, 326, 349–50

Cole, USS 300–301
colonialism 145–84
  Persia and 149–60
  Saudi Arabia and 161–72
  Turkey and 173–84
Constantinople 29, 97, 120, 125
Constitution of Medina 32, 37–8
Constitutionalist Party 153
Council of Islamic Revolution 192
Crimean War (1853–56) 374
Crusades 113, 119–20, 245, 246, 253, 313
Cyprus 227, 227n, 229

D

Dabiq (ISIS online magazine) 305
Dagestan 151, 374
Dalyan 108–9
Damascus 253
  'Damascus Spring' 265
  French in 250, 251, 252, 253
  Great Mosque of 95
  Nasser visits 334
  Ottoman Empire and 246, 247–8, 247n, 249
  Syrian civil war (2011–) and 269
  Syrian coup (1963) and 259
  Syrian election (1947) and 256
  Timur and 118
  Umayyad dynasty rule from 84, 85, 87, 88, 89, 97, 116, 117
Darwin, Charles 148
Day of Judgement 34, 305
Delhi 118, 137
Deobandi 223, 223n
Dersim 181–3
Dervish tradition 75, 176
Dhala, Emir of 318
dhimmis (conquered peoples) 78
Dhofar war (1963–75) 323–5, 323n
Dhu al-Hijjah 61
al-Din, Badr 315
Diriyah, oasis of 139, 142
Diyarbakir 181
Dome of the Rock, Jerusalem 95, 97
Dostum, General 222
Drummond, David (Hamid Mirza) 157

Druze 247, 253, 254, 262
Duldul (mule) 27–8

E

Eagle Claw, Operation (1980) 195
East Africa embassy bombings (1998) 300
Egypt 14, 15, 27, 27n, 35, 52, 73, 78, 106, 137, 147, 148, 245, 246, 274, 329, 331–40
  9/11 and 301
  Al Azhar university 106, 335
  Arab League and 334
  Arab Revolt and 175, 278
  Arab Spring and 214, 236, 267, 335, 339
  Ayyubid dynasty and 313
  Black Saturday (1952) 158, 338
  British in 158, 248, 332, 332n, 337, 338
  China and 381
  Cold War and 350–51, 377
  Coptic Christians in 331–2
  coup (1952) 158, 168–9, 286–7
  cultural beacon 331, 335
  debt 334–5
  Farouk and *see* Farouk, King
  Fatimid dynasty and 109
  Haj caravan attacked by Ikhwan 165
  Mamelukes and 129, 136, 173–4
  Morsi as ruler of *see* Morsi, Mohamed
  Mubarak and *see* Mubarak, Hosni
  Muhammad Ali reforms and expands 142
  Muslim Brotherhood and 232, 236, 263, 335, 336–40, 356
  Nasser and *see* Nasser, General Abdel
  peace treaty signed with Israel (1979) 264, 292
  population numbers 207, 329, 331
  Qatar and 355
  River Nile and 331
  Sadat and *see* Sadat, Anwar
  Saudi Arabia and 169–70, 171, 256, 329
  Sisi regime 337

Six-Day War and 170, 260, 334
Suez Canal 251, 258, 321, 332, 337, 342
Suez crisis (1956) 171, 258, 287, 332, 349, 350
Sunni nation 14, 251, 331–2, 335, 336, 339–40
Syria and 256, 257, 258, 271
United Arab Republic (UAR) and 314–15, 334
US subsidies 334
Yom Kippur War and 41n, 170, 261, 334, 336, 344
Eid el-Fitr 190
Eisenhower, Dwight D. 171
Erdogan, Recep Tayyip 180, 183, 232, 234–40, 336, 356
Ethiopia 32, 167, 173, 314, 331, 350
Euphrates 81, 86, 90, 99, 250, 259, 273–4, 279, 306, 373
European Common Market 229
European Union (EU) 229

F

Fadhili Sultanate 318
Fahd, King of Saudi Arabia 169, 209, 213, 297
Faisal, King of Saudi Arabia 169, 171
Fajr offensives (1983) 200
Fakhita 52, 52n
Falklands War (1982) 297
Fallujah, battles of (2004) 304
Farazdac 86
Fardoust, Hossein 192
Farewell Sermon 60, 61
Farouk, King of Egypt 168, 286, 331, 339
al-Farisi, Salman 74–5
Fatima (daughter of Muhammad) 43, 44, 45, 46, 48–9, 50, 51, 55, 57, 58, 74, 89, 106, 312
Fatima bint Asad (mother of Ali ibn Abi Talib) 51
Fatimid Empire 8, 105, 106–7, 109, 111, 114, 245, 246
fatwa 202–4, 291

Faysal I, King of Greater Syria and Iraq 249–50, 252, 279–81, 284, 306
Faysal II, King of Iraq 287
Fighting Vanguard 263
First Gulf War (1990–91) 204, 211–12, 218, 274, 275, 296–300, 345, 351–2
First World War (1914–18)
Ikhwan and 164
Iraq and 278–9
Ottoman Empire and 148, 174–5, 179, 244, 248
Persia divided into two protectorates 153
Qatar and 358–9
Syria and 244, 245, 248–51
US and 349
Zionism and 342, 342n, 343
flight 655, shooting down of Iranian passenger plane 201
FLOSY (Front for the Liberation of Occupied South Yemen) 320–21
Four caliphs, First (Rashidun – the Rightly Guided) 19, 24, 72, 101. See also individual caliph name
Four Companions of Ali 74
France 4, 9, 17, 147, 157, 160, 175
Algeria and 247, 320
Crimean War and 374
Iraqi Petroleum Company and 281
ISIS and 306
Ottoman Empire and 175, 176, 179
Second Gulf War and 306n
Suez crisis and 258, 332, 350
Syria and 148, 175, 182–3, 199, 250, 251–7, 280, 285
Tunisia, annexation of 248
Free Syrian Army 268
Fustat, Egypt 78

G

Gabriel, archangel 29, 44
Gaddafi, Colonel 214, 236, 267, 271, 316, 334, 339, 372
Gallipoli campaign (1915–16) 120, 175, 278, 290

al-Gaylani, Rashid Ali 284–5
Gaza Strip 101, 175, 207, 257, 336, 346, 347, 356
Gazi, Osman 125
Gemayel, Bashir 262
Genghis Khan 111, 112, 114, 126, 130, 147, 173
Georgia 112, 116, 132, 133, 134, 151, 178, 179
Germany 153–4, 156, 175, 206, 302
Ghadir Khum, oath at 60–62, 65, 109, 131
al-Ghafari, Abu Dharr 74
Ghazi, King of Iraq 284
Gilgit massacres (1988) 371
Glaspie, April 297
global financial crisis (2008) 230
Golan Heights 260, 341
'golden chain' of scholarship 131
Golden Square 284–5
Gorbachev, Mikhail 222
'Great Game' 153
Great Mosque of Damascus 95
Greece 97, 99, 125n, 126, 174, 175, 176, 177, 178, 183, 227n, 228, 229, 332, 344
Grozny 375
Gujarat 139
Gulbenkian, Calouste 183, 282
Gulen, Fethullah 231, 232–40
Gulf States 14, 275, 322, 329–30, 331, 355, 378. See also individual state name

H

Habsburg Empire 173
Hadi, Abdrabbuh Mansur 310, 317
hadith (reported tradition or saying of the Prophet) 24, 44, 48, 100, 101, 102, 117, 137, 142, 143, 209, 305
Hadramaut 75, 310, 311, 324
Hafiz 118–19
Hafsa (third wife of Muhammad) 48, 50, 64, 68
Hafte Tir bombing (1981) 198
Hagar 60

Haj 45, 59, 60, 60n, 83, 98, 136, 141, 165–6, 167, 218, 246, 311, 335, 375
Halah 45, 46
Hamadan 152
Hamas 207, 213, 336, 347, 356
Hamidiye Alaylari 179
Hamad bin Khalifa al-Thani, emir of Qatar 357
Hamza (paternal uncle of Muhammad) 40, 56
Hanifa, Imam Abu 101, 134
Hanafi law code 101, 102
Hanbali Sunni 104, 117
Hanif (pre-Islamic searcher after God) 44
hans (caravanserais) 126
Hariri, Rifaq 266
Hariri, Saad 217
Harith, Muthana ibn 73
Harran 115, 116
al-Hasa 16, 109, 139, 162, 166
Hasan (son of Ali) 43, 58, 118, 312
Hasan, Imam 81, 82–4, 83n, 85, 86
Hasan al-Askari, Imam 103, 105, 131
Hashemites 164, 165, 170, 249, 253–4, 256, 257, 278, 279, 280, 342n, 344
Hashid tribe 311, 313, 315
Hassan, Abdel 293
Hatayi (pen-name of Ismail) 127
Hazara 205, 225–6
Hekmatyr, Gulbuddin 367–8
Herat 118, 119
Hezbollah 200, 213, 217, 266, 269, 270, 271, 272, 316, 336, 347, 355, 356
Hijrah 18n, 33
Hijra settlements 208
al-Hilli, Al Allama 131
Hira, Mount 141
Holland 133, 147, 281
Horns of Hattin, Battle of the (1187) 113
horse-power, era of 119
hospitality 26, 39, 103, 308
Hourani, Akram al- 255
Houthi, Abdul-Malik 316
Houthi Movement 16, 308–10, 315–17

Houthi, Sheikh Hussein Badreddin 315
al-Huda, Bint 293–4
hudud ordinances 369
hujar (Wahhabi villages) 163–4
Hulagu 112
Hunayn, Battle of (630) 28
al-Huq, Zia 365, 368
al-Hurriyah airbase, Iraq 197
Husayn, Imam (son of Ali) 43, 58, 81, 84, 85–90, 97, 127, 141, 190, 203, 276, 312
Hussaini, Arif Hussain 371
Hussein, Saddam 196, 200, 204–5, 264, 274, 288n, 289, 290, 291–8, 301–2, 303
Huyser, General Robert E. 191

I

Ibn Battuta 108
Ibn Baz 209
Ibn Hanbal 101–2, 276
Ibn Khaldoun 119
Ibn Saud (Abd al-Aziz ibn Abd al-Rahman ibn Faisal), King of Saudi Arabia 154–5, 156, 161–8, 161n, 171, 184, 210–11, 213, 215, 216
Ibn Taymiyyah 115–17, 137
Ibn Tumert 28
Idris, King of Libya 170
Ilkhanid dynasty 111, 114
imams 38, 45, 61, 63, 70, 91, 92, 105, 106–7, 109, 126, 127, 128, 131, 150, 162, 171, 232, 237. *See also individual imam name*
Imperial Bank of Persia 151–2
India 189, 202, 223n, 277
  Agha Khan dynasty and 107
  British Empire in 151, 154, 279, 317
  Ghaznavid army and 112
  Independence of 320, 343–4, 365
  Mughal Empire and 119, 129, 133, 135, 137, 138, 147, 148
  Ottoman Empire and 173
  Saudi Arabia and 139
Inonu, General Mustafa Ismet 178

Iran 41n, 90, 91, 107, 149–60, 189–207, 274, 279, 282, 284
  9/11 and 205
  Afghanistan and 205, 221, 224, 226
  Ahmadinejad as president 205–6
  Arab Spring and 267
  Azerbaijan and 376–7
  Azeri minority 130, 376
  Al-Badr Brigade and 296, 299, 302, 303, 304
  Baghdad pact/CENTO (1955) and 158–9
  British in 149, 151–8, 189, 196, 198n, 202, 203, 204, 285
  Buyid emirs and 105, 108–10
  Chaldiran Battle and 129–30
  China and 364, 379, 380, 381
  economy 201, 204
  Egypt and 336
  First Gulf War and 204
  First World War and 153–4
  gas reserves 207
  Greater Iran 105, 363
  Green Revolution 206, 267
  Hamas and 207, 213, 336, 347
  Hezbollah and 262
  Iran–Contra scandal and (1986) 199
  Iran–Iraq War (1980–88) 12, 17, 90n, 187, 196–202, 206, 211, 218, 219, 264, 274, 275, 293–6, 303, 330, 341, 345, 347
  Iranian Embassy, London siege (1980) 195–6
  Iraq and *see* Iraq
  Israel and 199, 200, 207, 330, 341, 347–8
  Kerbala and 140, 143
  Khomeini and *see* Khomeini, Ayatollah
  Khuzestan and 16–17, 153, 193, 196, 274, 275, 279, 283–4, 290, 294
  Kurds and 157, 183, 183n, 193, 298, 299
  Lebanon and 14, 16, 199, 200, 204, 207, 213, 217, 262, 272, 316, 347
  literacy 204
  modernisation 154–5

Mongol Ilkhanid dynasty and 111, 115
Mossadeq coup 157–8
nuclear programme 206–7, 330, 347
oil industry 17, 153–4, 156–9, 194, 196, 197, 201, 204, 207, 380
Pahlavi Shah as ruler of 156–9, 187, 189–91, 193
Pakistan and 202, 370, 381
Persian Spring 206
Persian-speaking 15
population numbers 15, 119, 207, 329
Qajar shahs and 150–53, 156–7, 258
Qatar and 355, 356
revolution (1906) 248
revolution, Islamic (1979) 16, 139, 159–60, 187, 189–207, 209, 293, 294, 295, 296, 351
Revolutionary Guard 187, 201, 262, 270, 356
Reza Shah as ruler of 154–5, 156, 184, 189
Rushdie affair and 202–4
Russia and 14, 149, 150–54, 156, 157, 205, 206, 207, 378, 379
Saadabad pact and 156
Saffarids and 104
Saudi Arabia and 213, 214, 217–19, 307, 308, 310, 316, 341, 354, 356
SAVAK (national intelligence and security organisation) 158
Second Gulf War and 205, 303, 304, 306, 352
Second World War and 156, 285
Shiite faction in Middle East led by 14, 15, 16, 17, 111, 123, 129, 130
Shiite rebellion against Saddam Hussein (1991) and 204–5
Soviet troops evacuated from (1946) 157
Syria and 199, 200, 206, 207, 264, 269, 270, 271–2, 378
trade sanctions imposed upon 206, 207
Tudeh party 157, 158, 192

Turkey and 154, 155, 156, 160, 180, 235, 238, 240
US hostage crisis 194–5, 347–8
USA and 156, 157, 158, 159, 189, 191, 192, 194–5, 198–9, 201, 202, 203, 204, 205, 206, 207, 347–8, 349
White Revolution (1963) 159
Yemen 207, 308–9, 310, 312n, 316, 324, 326
Zand dynasty and 149–50, 149n
See also Persia
Iraq 11, 14, 73, 77, 78, 81, 90, 91, 101, 105, 131, 244, 273–307, 309, 312, 325, 344
Abbasid caliphs in 107–9
Al-Anfal campaign in 295–6
Al-Badr Brigade and 200, 296, 299, 302–3, 304
Al-Dawa party and 293–4
Amasya Treaty and (1555) 132
Arab–Israeli War (1948–9) and 286
Arab Revolt and 175, 278
Ba'ath (Arab Renaissance) Party and 196, 197, 288–91, 292, 293, 296, 299, 302, 304, 306, 339, 345
Baghdad see Baghdad
British in 148, 165, 166, 250, 253, 278–87
Buyid emirates 109
as centre of the Islamic world 273
civil wars in (2013–17) 12, 13, 303–7
Cold War and 350, 377
coup (1936) 284
coup (1941) 284–5
coup (1958) 287–8
coup (1963) 288–9
coup (1968) 196, 292
coup (1973) 291
as cradle of humankind 243, 273
ethnic groups 273, 281
Euphrates and 273–4
Faysal placed on throne of 252 see also Faysal I, King of Greater Syria and Iraq and Faysal II, King of Iraq
First Gulf War (1990–91) and 204, 211–12, 274, 275, 278, 296–300, 345, 351

future of 307
Golden Square and 284–5
Ikhwan armies and 165, 166
independence (1932) 282
Iran–Iraq War (1980–88) 12,
    17, 90n, 187, 196–202, 206,
    211, 218, 219, 264, 274, 275,
    293–6, 303, 330, 341, 345, 347
Iranian Embassy, London siege
    (1980) and 195–6
ISIS in 13, 40n, 304–7, 352
Kerbala, Battle of (680) 86–9, 97
Kerbala, Wahhabi sack of (1801)
    140–41, 152
Ghazi as King of 284
Kurdan peace treaty (1746) and
    135
Kurds and 130, 182, 183, 183n,
    240, 270, 298–9
Nasser and 286–7
Nojeh camp plot and 196
oil industry 183, 251, 258, 273,
    275, 281–2, 283, 286, 288,
    290, 291, 292, 294, 295, 296,
    299, 301
Ottoman-Safavid wars and 276–7
population numbers 273
Qawmiyya and 283, 284
Republican Guard 289
revolts (1920) 279
Saadabad pact and 156
Saddam Hussein see Hussein,
    Saddam
Scud missiles launched at Israel
    (1991) 301–2
Second Gulf War and 12, 205,
    275–6, 300–307, 345, 351–2
Second World War and 284–5
Shah Abbas and 133, 134
Shatt al-Arab 200, 274–5, 290, 294
Shiite faction in Middle East and
    14, 16, 207
Shiite rebellion against Saddam
    Hussein (1991) 204–5
Shu'aiba, Battle of (1915) 278
Soviet Union and 291, 350, 377
Syria and 259, 264, 265, 268, 270,
    345
Tigris and 274
Wataniyya and 283, 284
Yom Kippur War and 292

Zanj rebellion (869) 107–8
Zuhab Treaty (1639) 276
Iraq Petroleum Company 183,
    281–2
Iraq War. See Second Gulf War
Iron Hand 254
Ironside, General 154
al-Iryani, Abdul Rahman 315
Isfahan 118, 130, 134
Ishmael (biblical character) 60
Isik Evler ('light houses') 233
ISIS 13, 16, 40n, 55n, 75n, 225,
    269–70, 270n, 272, 304–7,
    352, 355, 363, 374, 375
Islam
    caliphates, medieval 93–120 see
        also individual caliphate name
    colonialism and 145–84 see also
        individual colonial power name
    domestic space, respect for sanctity
        of 29
    dominant modern powers 121–44
        see also individual nation name
    imams see individual imam name
    Islamic fundamentalism see individual organisation name
    Islamism see Islamism
    jihad see jihad
    Koran and see Koran
    law codes 20, 77, 78, 101–3, 113,
        135, 136–7, 173, 176, 179
    marriage and 47
    modern battlefields of 241–326 see
        also individual conflict name
    Muhammad, life of Prophet see
        Muhammad, Prophet
    origins of 25–92
    pan-Islamic unity 20, 103
    revolutionary 185–240 see also
        individual revolution name
    rulers see individual ruler name
    scholarship see individual author
        name
    sects see individual sect name
Islamabad 366
Islamic jihad 199
Islamic Republican Party (IRP)
    192, 198
Islamic-Socialist party of reform
    (PPP) 366, 372

Islamism
 9/11 and 213, 224
 Afghanistan and 188, 193, 195,
  198, 212, 213, 224
 Caucasus and 363, 364, 373-8
 Egypt and 335, 336, 337, 339
 ISIS and 304–6
 Pakistan and 365, 367, 369, 370,
  371
 Palestine and 347, 348, 354
 Qatar and 356-7
 Saudi Arabia and 187, 210, 211,
  212, 213, 216, 223
 Syria and 263–5, 269–72
 Turkey and 183, 228, 231, 232,
  233–7, 239
 Yemen and 316–17
Islamist People's Mujahedin (MEK)
 193
Ismail, Abdal Fattah (Al Faqih)
 322, 325
Ismail I, Shah of Iran 126–7, 128,
 129, 130–31, 149, 276
Ismail II, Shah of Iran 113
Ismaili community 91, 103, 103n,
 107, 116, 247
Israel 14, 168, 207, 213, 243, 297,
 341–8
 Arab–Israeli War (1948–9) 11,
  256–7, 286, 344–5, 350
 Arab Revolt and 343
 British and 342–4, 346, 349, 350
 Cold War and 350–51
 Egypt, peace treaty with (1979)
  264, 292
 establishment of 250–51, 250n,
  341–4, 346
 First World War and 343
 Hamas and 347
 Hezbollah and 200, 347
 Iran and 330, 347–8
 Irgun 343, 346
 Israel Defense Forces 345
 Lebanon invasion (1982) 199–200,
  262–3, 266, 347
 Lehi and 343
 Likud Party and 346
 Morsi and 336–7
 nuclear deterrent 347
 Oslo Accords and 347
 Palestinians and 339, 343, 346–7,
  348, 354, 356, 380
 Saddam Hussein fires Scud missiles
  at 298, 301–2
 Six-Day War and 11, 170, 260,
  315, 321, 334, 344, 350
 size of 344
 Suez Crisis and 171, 258, 287, 332,
  349, 350
 Syria and 199, 200, 257, 272, 344,
  345
 US support for 329, 329n, 330,
  344, 347–8, 349, 350, 353,
  354, 379, 380, 382
 West Bank and 260, 297, 346, 353
 Yom Kippur War and 11, 41n,
  170–71, 261, 292, 334, 336,
  344
 Zionism and 249–50, 250n, 251,
  254, 257, 341–4, 345–6, 350
 See also Jews
Istanbul 11, 55n, 128, 141–2, 173,
 174, 175, 177, 216, 228, 229,
 234, 239, 247, 248, 251, 276,
 277–8

J

Al-Jadaa (racing camel) 27
Jadid, Salah 259, 260, 261
Jafar al-Sadiq, Imam 20, 91, 102–3
Janissary corps 128, 129, 174, 246
Japan 153, 302, 380, 383
Jasmine Revolution (2010–11) 267
Jassim, Abdullah bin 358
Jassim al-Thani, emir of Qatar,
 Sheikh 358
Jeddah 172
Jerusalem 27, 44, 95, 97, 98, 246,
 257, 342, 345
Jesus 27, 64, 76, 245
Jews
 Arab–Israeli War and 257
 Ashkenazi 341, 342, 343
 Baghdad and 250, 277, 285
 Beni Qurayzah clan 44
 Constitution of Medina and 37
 dhimmis 78
 Greater Syria and 250
 Iraq and 277, 281, 285

Jewish state and 250–51, 250n,
341–4, 346
Kurds and 180n
9/11 and 212
Ottoman Empire and 174
Ottoman–Safavid wars and 276
Russia and 341–2, 350
Salman al-Farisi and 75
Thessaloniki and 178
US and 350, 353
Zionism 249–50, 250n, 251, 254,
257, 341–4, 345–6, 350
jihad
Afghanistan and 222
Chechens and 223
Fatimid dynasty and 106
Golden Square and 284
Ibn Taymiyyah and 116
ISIS and 40n, 270n
Islamic jihad 199
Koran and 83
Ottoman dynasty and 126, 132,
154, 278
Sayyid Qutb and 339, 374
Umayyad dynasty and 97
Wahhabism and 138, 144
al-Jilani, Abdul-Qader 134, 143
Jordan 13–14
Arab–Israeli War and 256–7
Black September and 260–61, 368
Caucasus refugees in 374
Greater Syria and 243, 253–4
Hashemite monarchs 253–4, 256–7
Iran and 213
Iraq and 200, 273, 283, 286, 287
ISIS and 305–6
Israel and 342–6, 350
Pakistan and 366
Saudi Arabia and 170, 171, 258,
310n
Sunni Arab nation 14
Syria and 243, 253–4, 258,
260–61, 269
Yemen and 314, 322
Zayd ibn Ali and 91
Josh-e-Muhammad 370
Jumana 52
Al-Jumaila tribe 289
Jurf 63

K

Kaaba 59, 87–8, 108, 188, 208, 210
Kabir, Amir 151
Kabyle mountains, Algeria 106
kafir (unbeliever) 143–4
al-Karaki, Sheikh Ali al-Muaqqiq
131
Kazakhstan 229
KDP (Kurdish Democratic Party)
285n, 298–9
Kelly, John 297
Kerbala 12, 86–9, 97, 140–41, 152,
200, 218, 276, 312
Kerman 150
Khadija (first wife of Muhammad)
32, 44–7, 52, 54, 79, 165
al-Khattab, Zayd ibn 139
Khalid, King of Saudi Arabia 169
Al-Khalifa, Emir of Bahrain, Hamad
bin Isa 162, 214
Khalifat Allah ('deputy of God') 85
Khalifat Rasul Allah ('deputy of the
Messenger of God') 67, 85
Khamenei, Ayatollah 205–7
Khan, Daoud 367
Khan, Lotf Ali 150
Khan, Mohammed 150
Kharajites ('seceders') 81
Khashoggi, Jamal 216
al-Khateeb, Hamza 268
Khatemi, Muhammad 205
Al-Khayr (Musab ibn Umar) 36
Khayyam, Omar 113
Khaza'il, Sheikh of the Muhammara
279
Khazraj confederation 36, 41, 65
Khomeini, Ayatollah 159–60, 187,
189, 191, 192–7, 199, 201–5,
207, 234, 303
Koran 18
Ali and 52–4, 57, 69–70, 71, 77, 82
hadith and 100–101
Hafsa and 48
Hasan and 83
Ikhwan and 165
imam and 38
Miqdad ibn Aswad and 76
Muhammad and 24, 29, 32–4, 41,
44, 50, 57, 60–62, 67, 69–70

suras 33–4, 52–3, 70, 80, 83
Taliban and 224
Turkey and 176, 230, 231, 232, 233
Uthman and written 79–80
Wahhabism and 136–7, 142–4, 210
Khorasan 133
Khorramshahr, Battle of (1980) 197
Khusraw, Nasir 'Ruby of Bada-khshan' 108
Khuzaa confederation 49
Khuzestan 16–17, 153, 193, 196, 274, 275, 279, 283–4, 290, 294
Kinnana confederation 76
Kissinger, Henry 295
kizilbas 127–9, 131–2, 150
Knights of St John 118
Kocgiri tribal region 181
Konya 115
Korean War (1950–53) 158
Kufa 78, 81, 83, 84, 85–6, 87, 89, 91, 312
Kufic script 110
Kulthum, Umm 46, 58, 79, 333
Kurdan peace treaty (1746) 135
Kurdistan 15–16, 134, 175, 179, 182, 184, 279, 281, 282, 290, 298, 299
Kurds
  Iran and 157, 193
  Iraq and 273, 274, 278, 280, 281, 282, 283, 284, 285, 285n, 288, 290, 295, 296, 298–9
  ISIS and 306, 307
  Safavids and 126, 130
  Said Nursi and 231
  Saladin and 114
  Shah Abbas and 134
  Syria and 15–16, 247, 256, 270, 272, 306, 307
  Turkey and 175, 178, 180–83, 180n, 183n, 235–7, 239, 240
Kuswa ('split ears') (camel) 26–7, 48
Kut 175, 278
Kutahya 128
Kuwait 162, 279
  Black Thursday and 214
  Egypt and 335

First Gulf War and 204–5, 211–12, 218, 273, 274, 275, 296–300, 345, 351
Ikhwan and 165, 166
Iraq and 201, 204–5, 211–12, 218, 263, 273, 274, 275, 283–4, 296–300, 310n, 345, 351
Qatar and 355
Shatt al-Arab and 196n, 274–5
Six-Day War and 170
Yemen and 323
Kyrgyzstan 229

L

Lahej, Sultan of 317, 318
Lahoud, Emile 266
Lashkar-e-Jhangvi 370
Lashkare-Tayyaba 370
law codes 20, 77, 78, 101–3, 113, 135, 136–7, 173, 176, 179
Lawrence, T. E. 175
Layla al-Mabit 55
Laz 179–80, 182
League of Nations 182, 281
Lebanon 12
  9/11 and 301
  Armenians flee to 179
  British hostages released in (1990–91) 204
  Fatimid Empire and 107
  Hezbollah in 200, 213, 217, 266, 316, 336, 347, 356
  Iraq and 287, 290
  Israeli invasion of (1982) 199–200, 262, 347
  Saudi Arabia and 213, 217
  scholarship in 131
  Shiite faction in 14, 16, 90, 207
  Syria and 243, 246, 247–8, 249n, 252, 254, 255, 261–3, 264, 266–7, 268, 269, 272, 290
Lenin, Vladimir Ilyich 187
Levant 106, 113, 147, 178, 180, 255, 337, 341, 342, 343–4
Levantine Crisis (1945) 255
Libya 12, 170, 175, 214, 236, 265, 267, 271, 316, 325, 331, 334, 339, 350, 356, 372, 377

M

Ma Bufang 382–3
Mackintosh-Smith, Tim 107
Macmillan, Harold 314, 320
Madrasas (Islamic teaching colleges) 113, 113n, 117, 118, 173, 223, 369–70
Mahabad Kurdish Republic 285
Mahdi, Twelfth Imam (the awaited one) 91, 103, 106, 127, 131, 132, 303, 305
Mahdia 106
Mahdi army 303
Mahfouz, Naguib 338
Majlis (popular assembly) 153
Malaysia 147, 310, 380
Malik ibn Anas 101, 102
Maliki law code 101, 102
Malik Shah I, Sultan 112, 113
Mameluke sultanates 116, 129, 136, 173, 245
Al-Ma'mun, Caliph 99, 102
Manzikert, Battle of (1071) 112
Marir, Bara ibn 36–7
Marj Dabak, Battle of (1516) 129
Maronite Christians 247, 252, 254, 261, 262, 266
Mashhad 91, 133, 134
Massoud, Ahmed Shah 205, 224, 367–8
Mecca 18, 18n
  girl's school fire in (2002) 212
  Haj and see Haj
  Hijrah migration from Mecca to Medina/flight from Mecca (622) 18n, 32–42
  Ikhwan in 165
  Islamist uprising in (1979) 187, 188, 208–11, 368
  massacre in (1987) 218
  Muhammad, life of, and 24, 26, 28–9, 32–6, 38–41, 44, 45, 47n, 48, 51, 52, 52n, 53–7, 59, 60, 62, 66, 67, 68–9, 75, 77, 83, 87–8, 98, 100, 136
  Ottoman Empire and 141, 142, 173, 249, 375
  Qarmatians sack (930) 108
  Sulayhid dynasty and 311

Medes 180
Medina 18, 18n, 23, 101, 136–7, 223n, 312, 336
  Arab Revolt and 175
  Constitution of Medina 32, 37–8
  Hasan in 84
  Ikhwan in 165
  ISIS and 305
  Muhammad, life of, and 23, 24, 25–9, 32–41, 43, 45, 46, 47, 49, 55, 57, 58, 60, 63, 65–6, 66, 67n, 68–9, 75, 300
  Omar in 78, 79
  Ottoman Empire and 136–7, 141, 142, 173, 175
  Umayyad caliphate and 85–7
  Wahhabism and 136–7, 141, 142
Menderes, Adnan 230–32
Meriem 27
Mesopotamia 243, 273, 274, 275, 283, 284, 292, 296
Middle East
  caliphates, medieval 93–120 see also individual caliphate name
  climate change in 13
  colonialism and 145–84 see also individual colonial power name
  dominant powers 15, 121–44 see also individual nation name
  far frontiers of 361–83
  modern battlefields of 241–326 see also individual conflict name
  oil wealth 11, 15, 16–17 see also oil
  population size 12, 119
  revolutions in 185–240 see also individual revolution name
  Shiite crescent, emergence of 16, 213
  sources of tension within 17
  Sunni–Shia percentage of Muslim population 4
Miqdad ibn Aswad 74, 75–6
al-Missned, Moza bint Nasser 360
Mistra 125, 125n
Mizrahi communities 180n, 341
MKO 198
Mobile Oil 157
Mohammad Reza Pahlavi, Shah 156–9, 187, 189–91, 193
Moharram 86–7
Mohtashami, Ali Akbar 199–200

monafeqin ('hypocrites') 193
Mongolia 117, 119
Mongols 107, 111, 114–19, 129, 150, 226, 245, 276
Morgan Guarantee 171
Morocco 28, 108, 209, 252, 306, 310n, 312n, 331, 350
Morsi, Mohamed 335–7
Moses 27, 64, 245
Mossadeq, Mohammed 157–8
Mosul 114, 182, 197, 246, 274, 277, 280, 281, 282, 285, 304, 333
Moulid (celebration of the Prophet's birthday) 144
Mount Lebanon 246, 247, 252
Muattal, Safwan ibn 49
Muawiya, Caliph 80–81, 82, 84–5, 88, 97
Mubarak, Gamal 336
Mubarak, Hosni 214, 238, 267, 316, 335–6
Mubarrah al-Sabah, Emir of Kuwait 162, 279
Muezza 26n, 27
muezzins 106
Mughal Empire 119, 129, 133, 135, 137, 138, 147, 148
Muhajirun ('emigrants') 39, 40, 65–6, 67n
Muhammad, Prophet 18, 20, 23–71
  Abbasid dynasty and 98, 100
  Ali and *see* Ali (Ali ibn Abi Talib)
  Ammar ibn Yasir and 75
  Aqaba, midnight oaths at 61–2
  childhood 23–4
  Constitution of Medina and 32, 37–8
  converts, makes first 35–7
  death 25, 63–71, 72, 73, 85, 88, 141
  Farewell Sermon 59–60
  Fatimid Empire and 106
  first revelation 52
  Ghadir Khum, oath at 60–62, 65, 109, 131
  hadith see *hadith*
  Haj and 59–62
  Hasan and 83–4, 83n
  Hijrah migration from Mecca to Medina (622) 18n, 32–42

  house-mosque in Medina 25–7, 40, 113
  Koran and 24, 29, 32–4, 44, 50, 60–61, 62, 69, 70, 71
  Layla al-Mabit and 55
  Medina, life in 23–8
  as messenger for the divine 60–61
  Night Journey 44, 98n
  origins of Sunni–Shia schism and 23–92
  Ottoman Sultanate and 125, 126
  return to Mecca 59–62
  Salman al-Farisi and 75
  succession to 24, 28, 47, 51–92, 131
  Taliban and 223
  Uthman and 79
  Wells of Badr battle and 40–41
  women of his house 43–50
  'Year of Sorrow' 44
  Zaydi tradition and 103n
  Zulfiqar ('master of the spine') and 57–8
Muhammad (son of Caliph Abu Bakr) 80
Muhammad al-Badr, Iman 314–15
Muhammad Ali, viceroy of Egypt 142
Muhammad, Ali Nasir 325
Muhammad al-Saud, emir of Diriyah 139–40
Muhammad bin Nayef al-Saud, Prince of Saudi Arabia 168, 169, 215
Muhammad bin Salman al-Saud, Prince of Saudi Arabia (MBS) 208, 215–16, 215n, 217–18
Muhammad ibn al-Hasan al-Mahdi, Imam 91, 103, 106, 127, 131, 132, 305
Mujahadin 188, 198, 211, 221, 222, 223, 300, 306, 367, 368–9
Mulayda, Battle of (1891) 161–2
Muqawqis 27
Murtajaz (horse) 27
Al-Mustasim, Caliph 102
Musa al-Kadhim, Imam 91
Musaylimah 73n
Musharraf, Pervez 365, 372

Muslim Brotherhood 14, 217, 232, 234, 236, 263, 271, 335, 336, 337–9, 355, 356
Al-Mustan madrasa 113
Mu'tah, Battle of (629) 63
Mutair tribe 162–3
Mutawa 210–12, 215
Mutazalite theological position 101
Muttalib, Abdul (grandfather of Muhammad) 35

N

Nadir Shah 134–5, 137, 149, 151
Nahrawan, Battle of (658) 81
Najaf 81, 276, 291, 293, 303
Najd 136, 140, 142
Najibullah, Mohammad 223
Nasir ad-Din, Shah 151
Nasser, General Abdel
  assassination attempt (1954) 333
  Iraq and 286–9, 292
  military coup (1952) 286–7, 331
  Muslim Brotherhood and 338–9
  popularity 168
  Saudi Arabia and 168–9, 170
  Six-Day War and 260, 315, 334
  Suez Canal and 258, 332
  Syria and 258–60, 292, 333–4
  Umm Kulthum and 333
  United Arab Republic and 258, 287, 289, 314, 334
  US and 349–50
  'Voice of the Arabs' radio broadcasts 333
  Yemen and 314–15, 319, 320, 321, 322, 334
nationalism 156
  Azeri 376
  Egyptian 251, 258
  Iranian 195
  Iraqi 283
  Saudi 216
  Syrian 253, 255
  Turkish 178, 180, 236, 237, 240, 248, 278
  Yemeni 309, 319–22
NATO 229, 306
Al-Nazamiyyah madrasa 113
Nestorian Church 74–5, 118

al-Nimr, Nimr Baqir 218
Nine/Eleven (9/11) 205, 212, 220–21, 224, 265, 275, 301–2, 351, 352
Nizari imam 107
Nojeh camp plot (1980) 196
North Africa 106, 109, 113n, 119, 163, 173, 331
Northern Alliance 205
Northwest Frontier Province 366–7
nuclear power 206–7, 330, 347
Nuri, Ihsan 181

O

Obama, Barack 267
Oghuz Turks 112
oil
  Azerbaijan and 377
  British and 153, 156–8, 281, 359
  China and 364, 379–80, 382
  embargo (1973) and 170–71, 261, 292, 353–4
  Iran and 17, 153, 156–9, 194, 196, 197, 201, 207, 275, 281, 348
  Iraq and 17, 182, 201, 251, 258, 273–4, 281–2, 283, 286, 288, 290, 291, 292, 294, 295, 296, 299
  Khuzestan and 16–17
  Middle East wealth and 11, 15, 16–17
  Qatar and 359
  Russia and 377
  Saudi Arabia and 16, 156, 167–8, 170–71, 188, 210, 258, 261, 292, 349
  Six-Day War and 170
  Turkey and 182, 281
  US and 158, 167–8, 194, 258, 281–2, 349, 353–4
Oman 14, 81n, 147, 195, 323, 323n, 324, 325, 350, 366, 379, 381
Omar, Caliph 19, 48, 50, 64–5, 66, 67, 68–9, 69n, 71, 74, 77–9, 109, 311
Omar, Mullah 55n, 223, 225
Osama bin Zaid (son of Zaid) 50, 63, 73

al-Otaybi, Juhyaman 208–9, 210
Ottoman Empire 56, 375
  Arab Revolt and 164, 175
  Caucasus and 373, 374
  Chaldiran battle and 129–30
  Constantinople conquest (1453)
    120, 125
  Egypt and 332, 332n
  First World War and 148, 153–4,
    164, 175, 248–9
  Hanafi law code and 101
  Iraq and 276–81, 306
  origins of 125
  Qatar and 358, 359
  Safavid Empire and 123, 125–32,
    133, 135, 136, 137, 147, 276–7
  sultans, investiture of 58
  Sunni identity 51, 129
  Syria and 244, 245, 246, 247, 248,
    248–9, 253
  Turkish Republic and 15, 173–83,
    230, 231, 233, 278
  Wahhabism and 139, 141–2
  Yemen and 244, 313–14
Ottoman Petroleum Company of
  Mosul 281
Ozal, Turgut 228, 229

P

Paget, General 255
Pahlavi dynasty 149, 154, 156–7,
  193
Pahlavi Foundation 193
Pakistan 15, 41n, 107, 210, 324,
  365–72
  Afghanistan and 188, 204, 205,
    211, 221, 223n, 224, 225, 226,
    351, 363, 367–9
  Baghdad pact and 267
  Baluchistan and 366–7
  Bhutto political dynasty 366–8, 372
  bin Laden in 369
  China and 379, 381
  diaspora 366
  foreign aid and 366
  Gilgit massacres (1988) 371
  hudud ordinances and 369
  Hussaini assassinated (1988) 371
  ISIS and 13, 306

  Islamic-Socialist party of reform
    (PPP) and 366, 372
  Josh-e-Muhammad and 370
  Lashkar-e-Jhangvi and 370
  Lashkare-Tayyaba and 370
  madrasas in 369–70
  military in 365–6
  Musharraf and 365, 372
  Nazim Sharif and 371–2
  Northwest Frontier Province 366–7
  origins of 343, 365
  Pashtunistan campaign 367
  Rushdie affair and 202
  Saudi Arabia and 213, 214, 365,
    366, 368, 369
  Shia minority 366, 367
  Sipha-e-Sahaba (SAP) and 370
  Sunni Islamic power and 365, 371
  Taliban and 205, 369
  Zakat tax 370
  Zia-ul-Haq and 365, 368, 371, 372
Palestine 12, 101, 348, 380
  Al Jazeera and 357n
  Ba'ath Party and 290
  British occupation 148, 175,
    250–52, 254, 283, 284, 285,
    343–4
  Egypt and 336, 338, 339
  Gaza Strip 101, 175, 207, 257,
    336, 346, 347, 356
  Hamas in 207, 213, 336, 347, 356
  Iraq and 283, 284, 285, 286, 290,
    298
  Israel and 250–52, 254, 257, 260,
    264, 339, 341, 342, 343–4,
    346–7, 354, 356
  Muslim Brotherhood and 338
  Palestine Liberation Organization
    (PLO) and 200, 260–63, 347
  Qatar and 356
  Revolt (1936–39) 338
  Saudi Arabia and 171, 213
  Syria and 257
  West Bank 257, 260, 275, 297,
    346, 353
  Yemen and 316, 319, 322
Palestine Liberation Organization
  (PLO) 200, 260–63, 347
pan-Arabism
  Ba'ath Party and 14, 271, 292, 296,
    320–21

emergence of 248
Nasser and 287
peacekeeping forces 262
socialism 168
Panipat, Battle of (1525) 129
Pasha, Jamal 249
Pasha, Nureddin 181
Pashtun tribes 225–6
Pashtunistan campaign 367
Pathans 223, 225, 366, 367, 368
Persia 27n, 74, 84, 85, 99, 105,
    112, 114, 123, 149–60, 180,
    184, 213, 272, 280, 283
  British in 149, 151–4, 156, 157–8
  colonialism and 149–60
  First World War and 153–4
  Iran and *see* Iran
  Ottoman Empire and 127, 128,
    147, 148, 173
  Qajar shahs 150, 150n, 151, 153,
    156–7, 358
  Russian wars, nineteenth-century
    150–51
  Safavid Empire *see* Safavid Empire
  Sassanids and *see* Sassanid Empire
  Saudi Arabia and 139, 141
  shahs of *see individual names*
  See also Iran
Persian Gulf 109, 147, 152, 153,
    162, 163, 196, 196n, 201,
    214, 217, 219, 274–5, 278,
    298, 307, 318–19, 324, 351–2,
    353–4, 366, 373, 381
Persian language 15, 97, 119, 176,
    177, 195, 202
Peter the Great, Tsar 134
PKK party 237, 299
Popalzai Pashtun tribe 225
Popular Front 254
Portugal 119–20, 133, 147, 173,
    313
PSP (People's Socialist Party) 319
PUK (Patriotic Union of Kurdistan)
    298–9
Punjab 366, 370
Putin, Vladimir 375

Q

Qabus, Prince 324, 325
Qajar shahs 150, 150n, 151, 153,
    156–7, 358
al-Qaradawi, Sheikh Yusuf 339
Qarmatians 105, 108, 109
Qashqai tribe 153–4
Qasim (son of Muhammad) 46
Qasim, Abd al-Karim 287–8
Qataf 210
Qatar 14, 217, 235, 269, 270n,
    271, 310n, 329–30, 336, 339,
    355–60
Qawmiyya 283, 284
Qazvin 132
Qom 189
al-Otaibi tribe 162
al-Qadisiya, Battle of (636) 78
Quba 39
Qumm 109, 134
Quraysh tribe 23–4, 51, 53, 59, 66,
    73
Qutb, Sayyid 338–9
al-Quwwatl, Shukri 254, 256–7

R

Rabi al-Awwal 54–5
racism 148
al-Rachid, Haroun 98
Radio Cairo 169
Radio Mecca 169
RAF (Royal Air Force) 165, 282
Rafsanjani, Akbar Hashemi 201,
    204, 206
Rahimi, General Mehdi 192
Ramadan 40, 82, 162, 190, 200,
    211, 370, 371
Ramadan, Operation (1982) 200
Raqqa 55n, 75, 269, 304
Rashidi Emirate 142, 162, 164–5,
    171
Rashidun ('the Rightly Guided') 72
Rawzah ('the Garden') 90
Rayta 52
Rayy 109
Razi, Sharif 77
Reagan, Ronald 369

refugees 11
Afghanistan and 211, 220, 221,
223, 369
Caucasus and 374
Druze–Maronite massacre (1860)
and 247
early Islam and 33, 39, 40, 55–6
Iran–Iraq War and 200, 296
Kurdish 183
Middle East percentage of world-
wide 12
Ottoman Empire and 177–8
Palestinian 257, 261, 262, 290,
357n
Shiite rebellion against Saddam
Hussein (1991) and 205
Yemen and 310, 311, 323
Revolutionary Front for the
Liberation of Arabistan 196
Reza Shah of Iran 154–5, 156, 184,
189
Rida, Eighth Imam, Ali al 91, 99,
134
Riyadh 140, 162, 163
Riza, Seyid 182
Roosevelt, Franklin D. 167–8
Rouhani, Hassan 206
Royal Dutch Shell 281
Rughayabah 35
Rumi 113, 115, 143, 234, 305,
Mathnawi 115
Ruqayyah (daughter of Muham-
mad) 46
Rushdie, Salman 202–4
Shame 202
The Satanic Verses 202
Russia 17, 377–8
Ashkenazi Jews in 341–2, 350
Caucasus and 373–6
Chechnya and 363–4, 374–7
colonial empire 147, 149, 150–53
First World War and 153–4
Great Game and 153
Iran and 14, 149, 150–54, 156,
157, 205, 206, 207, 378, 379
ISIS and 305, 306, 363
Ottoman Empire and 137, 173,
174, 179
Persia, nineteenth-century wars
against 134, 150–52
revolution (1905) 248

revolutions (1917) 154
Second World War and 285
Syria and 247, 248, 270, 271, 272,
363, 375–6, 377–8, 379
Ukraine invasion (2022–) 12, 272,
377
Yemen and 322
Soviet see Soviet Union

S

Saadabad pact (1937) 156
Sabillah, Battle of (1929) 208
Sabra PLO refugee camp 262
Sadat, Anwar 331, 334, 336, 338
al-Sadr, Ayatollah Muhammad
Baqir 291, 293
al-Sadr, Muqtada 303–4
Safavid Empire 123, 126, 129, 130,
133–4, 135, 136, 137, 147,
149, 149n, 151, 183, 199, 244,
276
al-Saffar, Sheikh Hassan 209–10
Sahabi, Ezzatollah 194
Sahara 28, 106, 147, 274, 331
al-Said, Nuri 280–81, 286, 287
Said, Sheikh 181
Sakhb (stallion) 27
Saladin 113–14, 298
Salafi fundamentalist movement
19, 20, 51, 115, 270n, 300,
305
Saleh, Ali Abdullah 309, 315,
316–17
Salman, King of Saudi Arabia 215
Salma bint Amr 35
Samanid dynasty 104
Samarkand 118, 119
Sardar, Ziauddin 370
Sarraj 169
SAS 196, 314, 324
Sassanid Empire 27n, 29, 72, 73,
154, 245
Saud clan 136, 139–41, 142,
154–6, 161–72, 184, 208–19
Saudi Arabia 136–44, 161–72, 184,
208–19, 350, 383
9/11 attacks and 212
Afghanistan and 188, 204, 221,
223n, 224

Al-Qaeda and 212, 299–301
Arab oil embargo (1973–4) and
    170–71, 261, 292, 353
Arab-speaking 15
Arab Spring and 214, 218, 269
As-Sabalah, Battle of (1929) 166–7
China and 381
colonialism and 161–72
coup attempt (1969) 170
Egypt and 142, 165–71, 214, 329,
    331, 335, 336–7, 339
financial influence of 171
First Gulf War and 211–12, 297–8,
    299–300, 351–2
flight from Mecca and 32
future for 217–19
girl's school fire, Mecca (2002) 212
Haj pilgrimage and see Haj
Hejaz, Wahhabi invasion of (1805)
    165
hujar in 163–4
iconoclasm in 165
Ikhwan tradition 163–7, 188, 208,
    216, 224, 270, 280, 300
Iran and 16, 143, 205, 207, 209,
    211, 213, 214, 217, 218, 219,
    240, 275, 295, 307, 316, 345,
    354, 356, 357, 381
Iran–Iraq War and 211, 218, 275,
    295
Islamist uprising, Mecca (1979)
    187, 188, 208–10, 351, 366
Khashoggi murder 216
Kuwait, raids on (1928) 165
Lebanon and 213, 217, 266–7
Majlis al-Shura 172
Mecca massacre (1987) 218
modernising agenda 171–2
Mutawa 210–12, 215
National Guard/White Guard
    166–7
Nimr Baqir al-Nimr execution
    (2016) 218
oil industry 15, 16, 156, 167–8,
    170–71, 210, 292, 349
origins of 123, 136–44, 154–5,
    161–72
Osama bin Laden and 212
Pakistan and 365, 366, 368, 369
Public Investment Fund 216

Qatar and 217, 329–30, 355–7,
    359–60
rulers see *individual ruler name*
Russia and 378, 379
Saud dynasty and 136–44, 154–5,
    161–72
Shiite community in 15, 16, 108,
    109
Six-Day War and 170
Sunni–Shia divide in Middle East
    and 13, 14, 15, 16, 17
Syria and 254, 256, 258, 271, 272,
    356–7
Turabah, Battle of (1919) 164–5
USA and 156, 167–8, 171, 205,
    211–12, 213, 216, 349, 351,
    354
Wahhabism and see Wahhabi Islam
women and 164, 172, 210–11,
    213, 215
Yemen and 16, 165, 169, 217,
    308–9, 310, 310n, 314, 315,
    316, 322, 345
Yom Kippur War and 261, 292
Zakat and 167
Sawdah 47, 50
Sayyid or Shorfa 45
Second Gulf War (2003–11) 12,
    275–6, 301–7, 306n
Second World War (1939–45) 156,
    167–8, 254, 284–6, 343, 344,
    359, 379–80, 383
Selim, Sultan 128–9, 276
Seljuk Empire 111–15, 125, 173,
    178, 230, 245, 246
Sepah militia 192, 193, 197, 199,
    205
Sèvres, Treaty of (1920) 175, 183
Al Shahid al-Thani, emir of Qatar
    131
Shahbandar, Abd al-Rahman 253–4
Shamil, Imam 375
Shammar, Jabal 142
Shariatmadari, Ayatollah 194
Sharif, Nazim 371–2
Al-Shafi'i, Imam 101
Al-Shaikh 163, 169
Shatilla PLO refugee camp 262
Shatt al-Arab 200, 274–5, 290, 294

Shia Islam 11
Abbasid dynasty and 99, 102–3
Abu Bakr and 69, 71, 74, 79
Afghanistan and 205, 226
Aisha and 43–4
Ali and 24, 28, 47, 51, 57–8,
    68–71, 69n, 77, 81, 99
Ashura and 85–7
complexity of belief system 91–2
egalitarian nature of tradition 74
ethnicities of Middle East and 15
Fatima and 49, 74
Fatimid Empire and 106, 107, 114
Ghadir Khum and 61–2
hadith and 102
Haj and 60–62
Hasan and 83–4
Iraq and 13, 88–9, 134, 135, 140,
    244, 273, 274, 276, 278, 279,
    281, 282–3, 284, 286, 288,
    290–91, 293, 294, 296, 298,
    303, 304, 305, 306, 307, 309
ISIS and 269–70, 305, 306, 307
Jafar and 91, 102
Kerbala and 88–9, 140
Khadija and 46
Lebanon and 199, 200, 247,
    262–3, 266–7, 272, 309
Mahdi and 91, 131
Medina and 35
Muawiya and 88–9
Nadir Shah and 134–5
Nahjul Balagha and 77
Omar and 69, 71, 74, 78, 79
origins of Sunni–Shia schism
    21–92
Pakistan and 366–7, 370–72
as a percentage of Muslims
    worldwide 4
Persia/Iran and 123, 148, 150,
    152, 173, 200, 226, 240, 244
Prophet Muhammad and 18, 24,
    35, 46, 47, 60–62, 203
Saudi Arabia and 16, 136, 138,
    139, 140, 166, 209–10, 213,
    214, 217, 218
Shah Abbas and 133–4
succession to the Prophet and 24,
    28, 47, 51–92, 99
Sunni, common beliefs shared with
    18–19, 92

Syria and 200, 247, 250, 254, 259,
    262–3, 269–71, 272, 309
term 4
Turkey and 130, 183
Umayyad dynasty and 96, 99
Uthman and 79–80, 83, 125
Yemen and 308, 309, 311–12
Zaydi tradition and 91, 311–12
shirk (a sin) 138
Shu'aiba, Battle of (1915) 278
Shuba, Mughira ibn 73
Sicily 109
Sidqi, General Bakr 284
Siffin, Battle of (657) 75, 80–81
Sindh 366, 367, 372
al-Sindi, Muhammad Hayya 137
Sipha-e-Sahaba (SAP) 370
el-Sisi, General Abdel Fattah 337
Six-Day War (1967) 11, 170, 260,
    315, 321, 334, 344, 350
slavery 75, 77, 88, 103, 107, 113,
    116, 126, 133, 135, 143, 169,
    174, 269, 305
SOCAR (Azerbaijan state oil com-
    pany) 377
socialism, pan-Arab 168
Somalia 12, 325, 350, 351, 377
Soviet Union
    Aden and 323
    Afghan War (1979–89) 187, 188,
        204, 205, 211, 212, 220–22,
        270, 297, 299, 300, 306, 351,
        352, 368–9
    Baghdad pact and 287
    China and 383
    collapse of 228–9, 230, 264
    Egypt and 333, 336, 349–50
    Iran and 157, 198, 198n, 285,
        285n
    Iraq and 200, 201, 291
    ISIS and 305–6
    Israel and 350–51, 353
    Second World War and 156, 157,
        285
    Turkey and 156, 176, 228–9
    Yemen and 325
Spain 72, 95, 119, 133, 147, 173,
    178, 374
Standard Oil 167, 281
Stark, US frigate 201
Steineke, Max 349

Sudairi, Hussa 169
Sudairi Seven 169
Sudan 12, 147, 300, 310n, 331, 332
Suez Canal 251, 258, 321, 332, 337, 342
Suez crisis (1956) 171, 258, 287, 332, 349, 350
Sufi Islam 20, 23, 51, 75, 117, 126, 134, 137, 335, 338
Sukayna 89–90
Suleyman the Magnificent 276
Sullivan, William 195
Sultan bin Abdulaziz Al Saud, Prince of Saudi Arabia 168, 169
Sunni Islam
  Abu Bakr and 20, 33, 65, 68, 102
  Afghanistan and 223, 226
  Aisha and 43, 44, 49
  Ali and 24, 51, 57–8, 68–71, 69n
  'the Companions' and 19
  Deobandi and 223
  Egypt and 14, 251, 331–2, 335, 336, 339–40
  Fatimids and 106
  first four caliphs (Rashidun) and 19, 24, 72–4, 78, 81, 81n
  Ghadir Khum and 61
  Haj and 60–61
  Iraq and 13, 196, 273, 274, 276, 277, 278, 279, 280, 281, 283, 288, 290, 294, 295, 303, 304, 305, 306, 307, 352
  ISIS and 75n, 304, 305, 306, 307, 352
  Khadija and 46
  law codes 20, 100–102, 106, 113, 135
  Mecca, significance of 34–5
  Middle East ethnicities and 15
  Muhammad, Prophet and 18, 60–62, 64, 68–71, 69n
  Nadir Shah and 134–5
  Nahjul Balagha and 77
  origins of Sunni–Shia schism 21–92
  Ottoman Empire and 125, 126, 127, 128, 129, 173, 174, 244
  Pakistan and 363, 365–7, 370, 371, 372

  as a percentage of Muslims worldwide 4
  Qarmatian sack of Mecca and 108
  Qatar and 355
  Saudi Arabia and 14, 16, 123, 136, 138, 139, 141, 155, 213, 214, 217–18, 240, 270, 272, 308, 310, 336, 354, 381
  Sayyid or Shorfa and 45
  scholar-sheikhs 100–102
  Shah Abbas and 133–4
  Shia, common beliefs with 18–19, 92
  succession to the Prophet and 51–92
  'sultans' and 19
  Syria and 255, 259, 262, 263, 265, 270–72, 270n
  tenth day of Moharram and 87
  term 4
  Turkey and 111–12, 114, 123, 125, 126, 127, 128, 129, 173, 174, 180n, 183, 244, 246, 270, 272
  Uighurs and 382n
  Yemen and 308, 309, 310, 311, 312n, 313m, 317, 326
Sykes–Picot Agreement (1916) 250–52
Syria 23, 35, 40, 52, 63, 66, 67n, 73, 78, 87, 88, 107, 109, 245–72, 283
  Alawites and 116, 247, 253, 254, 255, 259, 262, 265, 270
  Arab–Israeli War (1948–9) and 257
  Arab Revolt and 249
  Arab Spring in 267–8
  Ba'ath Party and 255–7, 258, 259, 261, 263, 265, 267, 268, 270, 271, 272, 289, 292, 339, 345
  Bashar al-Assad becomes ruler 265
  Black September and 260
  Cedar Revolution and 266
  Christianity in 245
  cities, ancient 245–6
  civil war (2011–19) 12, 15–16, 75n, 199, 206, 214, 236, 239, 263, 264, 268–72, 304–6, 356–7, 363, 375, 377–8
  Cold War and 350, 351
  Corrective Movement 261

coup (1961) 258
coup (1963) 258–9
elections (1925) 253
elections (1947) 256
famine (1915–18) 249
First World War and 245, 248–51
French protectorate 148, 175, 248, 251–5, 280, 285–6
Greater Syria 243–4, 245, 249–54
Hafiz al-Assad assassination attempt (1980) 263
Hafiz al-Assad seizes power 261
Hama uprising (1982) 263–4
Iran and 199–200, 206, 207, 264, 267, 269, 270, 271, 272
Iraq and 250, 253, 256, 264, 268, 273, 274, 280, 283, 285–9, 290, 292–3, 299
Iron Hand 254
ISIS in 13, 16, 40n, 269–70, 304–6, 363
Israel and 199, 200, 257, 272, 344, 345
Lebanon and 199, 200, 260–62
Khan Maysalun caravanserai 252
King–Crane Commission 251
Kurds in 16, 130, 183, 183n, 239, 240, 299
Levantine Crisis and 255
Mongols and 115, 116
Muslim Brotherhood in 232, 236, 263, 271
Nasser and 258–60
National Party 256
Ottoman Empire and 129, 142, 173–4, 245, 246–9, 253, 332
parliamentary rule, return to (1954) 258
People's Party 253, 256
Qatar and 269, 356–7
rebellion (1925) 253
Russia and 247, 248, 270, 271, 272, 363, 375–6, 377–8, 379
Saudi Arabia and 169, 170, 171, 254, 256, 258, 261, 266–7, 269, 270–71, 272
Second World War and 254–5, 285–6
Shiite faction in the Middle East and 14
Siffin, Battle of and 80–81

Six-Day War and 259–60
Sykes–Picot Agreement and 250–52
Tammuz War and 266
UN founding member 255
United Arab Republic and 285–9, 292, 333–4
Yom Kippur War and 170, 261
Zaim and 257–8

T

Tabriz 127, 129, 132
Tahmasp I, Shah 131–2
Taif 32
Taj Mahal 135
Tajiks 205, 224, 225–6, 368
takfir 143
al-Takriti, Barzan 291
Talib, Al-Abbas ibn Ali ibn Abi 90
Talib, Abu Abd Manaf (uncle of Muhammad) 32, 51–4
Taliban 55n, 188, 205, 217, 220, 223–5, 356, 365, 369, 370, 374
Tamim bin Hamad al-Thani, emir of Qatar, Sheikh 357–8, 359
Tammuz War (2006) 266
Tehran 11, 151, 153, 154, 190–92, 194, 195, 198n, 205, 206, 209, 267, 293, 347–8
Thaqiq tribe 73
Thatcher, Margaret 228, 297
Timur (Tamburlaine or Tamerlane) 111, 112, 118–19, 126, 130, 134, 147, 173, 276
Timurid Empire 111, 118
Trans-Jordan, Emirate of 165, 252
Trebizond 125, 125n
Trench, Battle of (627) 58
Truce of Hudaybyah (628) 58
Trucial States 359
Trump, Donald 225
Tudeh party 157, 158, 192
Tughril Bey 112
Tunisia 28, 81n, 106, 209, 214, 248, 267, 305, 331, 335
Turabah, Battle of (1919) 164–5
Turaif 136
Turkestan 117, 381, 382, 383
Turkmenistan 229

Turkey 14, 15, 125*n*, 128, 155,
160, 173–84, 187, 214, 217,
227–40, 246, 250, 254, 269,
270, 282, 283, 284, 287, 329,
330, 336, 350, 356
  AKP (Justice and Development
Party) and 234–5, 237
  Alevi Shia in 130, 183
  Anatolia and *see* Anatolia
  Arab Spring and 236, 237
  Ararat rebellion (1927–30) 181
  Armenians and 176, 178–9,
180, 183
  Ataturk and *see* Ataturk (Mustafa
Kemal)
  Azeri and 377
  British in 175, 182–3
  Bylock app and 238
  China and 382
  Cold War and 227–9
  colonialism and 173–84
  coup (1960) 227, 230
  coup (1971) 227
  coup (1980) 187, 227–8
  coup (2016) 238–9
  Cyprus invasion (1974) 227, 227*n*
  Dersim massacre (1937) 181–2
  diplomatic isolation 235
  Eagle app and 238
  economy 229–30, 232, 239–40
  Erdogan and *see* Erdogan, Recep
Tayyip
  Ergenkon Plot 236
  EU membership process 229
  Gulen and *see* Gulen, Fethullah
  Kocgiri tribal region crushed
(1921) 181
  Kurds 15–16, 130, 178, 180–84,
236–8, 240, 270, 296, 298–9,
305, 306
  Laz 179–80
  Menderes and 230
  NATO 229
  origins of modern 15–16, 111, 112,
118, 123, 129–30, 154, 173–8
  Orthodox Christian minority
expelled 176
  Ottoman Empire and *see* Ottoman
Empire
  PKK party and *see* PKK party
  population numbers 15

  presidential election (2023) and
239–40
  Russia and 378, 379
  Saadabad pact and 156
  Said Nursi and 231–2, 235
  Soviet Union and 228–9, 230
  Syrian civil war and 15–16, 239,
270–71, 270*n*, 272, 378
  Turkic-speaking 15
  '24 January Decisions' 228
Turkic language 15, 178, 180, 226,
228–9, 244
Turkic people 103–4, 111–19, 125,
126, 129, 130, 134, 150, 227,
235, 239, 248, 276, 376, 382*n*
Tyre 245–6

U

United Arab Emirates (UAE) 214,
215*n*, 224, 271, 310*n*, 318,
355, 359, 381
Ubadayah, Saad ibn 65, 67*n*
Uhud, Battle of (625) 48, 57
Ukraine, Russian invasion of
(2022–) 12, 272, 377
Umar, Caliph 18*n*, 98, 139
Umar II, Caliph 98
Umayyad caliphate 79, 80, 89, 91,
95, 96, 97–9, 116, 245
Umm Habiba 50
Umm Kulthum 46, 58, 79, 333
Umm Salamah 48–9, 50
Ummah (worldwide community of
Islam) 95
United Arab Kingdom 251–2
United Arab Republic (UAR) 258,
287, 289, 314, 315, 334
United Nations (UN) 218, 223,
255, 297–8
Unwan al-Majd 140
USA 14, 349–54
  9/11 and 205, 212, 220–21, 224,
265, 275, 301–2, 351, 352
  Afghan War (2001–21) 205, 220,
224–5, 301, 351, 352
  Arab oil embargo (1974) and 353
  China and 379, 379*n*, 380, 382
  Cold War and 148, 349–51, 353

Egypt and 329–30, 329n, 334, 336, 337, 349–51
First Gulf War and 204, 205, 211–12, 275, 296–300, 351
First World War and 349
hostage crisis in Tehran 194–5, 347–8
Iran and 157, 158, 159–60, 189, 191, 192, 194–5, 198–9, 201, 202, 204, 205, 206, 207, 238, 347–8, 349, 351, 354
Iraq and 12, 183, 204, 205, 211–12, 275, 281–2, 292, 295, 296–307, 306n, 351, 352
ISIS and 306, 352
Israel and 168, 344, 346, 347–8, 350, 353, 354, 379
military bases in Middle East 225, 300, 351–2, 358, 359, 380
oil industry in Saudi Arabia and the Gulf, creation of and 349
Pakistan and 366, 369, 371
Qatar and 358, 359
Saudi Arabia and 156, 167–8, 169, 171, 188, 209, 211–12, 213, 216, 300, 336, 337, 349, 351–2, 354, 379
Second Gulf War and 12, 275, 301–7, 306n, 351, 352
Second World War and 156
shale extraction in 353
Suez crisis and 349, 350
Syria and 251, 260, 261, 264, 267, 269, 271, 272
Turkey and 227, 233–4, 238
Vietnam War and 321, 322, 329n, 348
Utba, Walid ibn 56
Uthman, Caliph 19, 46, 48, 57, 71, 77, 79–80, 82, 83, 125
Uzbekistan 229
Uzbeks 133, 205, 222, 225, 226
Al-Uyaynah 136, 138, 139

V

Valley of the Wolves (TV soap) 236
Vance, Cyrus 191
Vincennes, USS 201

Vietnam War (1955–75) 321, 322, 329n, 348

W

Waddan patrol 40
Wafd party 251
al-Wahad, Abd 314
Wahdi Haban, sultanate of 318
al-Wahhab, Muhammad ibn Abdul 135–40, 143–4; Kitab al-Tawhid 138, 143
Wahhabi Islam 23, 123
    Al-Qaeda and 300
    Deobandi and 223n
    Hejaz, Wahhabi invasion of (1805) 165
    hujar and 163–4
    Ibn Taymiyya and 115
    Iran and 203
    ISIS and 270n
    Kerbala, sack of (140–41, 152
    Khadija mausoleum and 45
    Muslim Brotherhood and 339
    origins of 16, 135, 136–44
    Qatar and 356, 358
    Saudi Arabia and 135, 136–44, 155, 163–4, 165, 166, 167, 169, 171, 188, 213, 216, 218
    ulema 166, 213
    women and 164, 172, 210–11, 213, 215
Wahidi Balhaf 318
al-Walid, Khalid ibn 73
al-Wathiq, Caliph 102
Wataniyya 283, 284
Wells of Badr, Battle of (624) 40–41, 41n, 48, 56
West Bank 257, 260, 275, 297, 346, 353
women
    Azerbaijan and rights of 376
    Iranian Revolution and rights of 193
    Iraq and rights of 291
    ISIS and 269–70, 305
    Muhammad and 37, 40, 43–50, 57
    Taliban and 224
    Turkey and rights of 176–7

Wahhabi Islam/Saudi Arabia and
rights of 164, 172, 210–11,
213, 215
Yemen and rights of 322
World Bank 228
Wudd, Amr ibn Abdu 58

X

Xinjiang province, China 364,
381–2

Y

Yafa 318
Yafur 27, 28
Yahya Muhammad Hamid ed-Din al
Mutawakil, Imam 313–14
Yalta conference (1945) 157
Yarmuk, Battle of (636) 73, 78
Yazid, Caliph 85, 87, 88, 89, 97,
210
Yazidis 180n, 269, 273, 281, 283,
305
Yeltsin, Boris 222
Yemen 12, 13, 15, 23, 52, 64, 66,
75, 91, 147, 148, 184, 207,
287, 301, 308–26, 333, 334,
350, 377, 381
Aden 169–70, 244, 308, 309, 310,
314–15, 317–24, 351
Aden Insurrection and 309–10,
314, 317–23, 324
Al Haqq party in 315
Arab Spring and 309, 316
al-Badr and 314
beauty of 308
border war between two Yemens
(1972) 309
British in 244, 309, 314, 317–23
civil war (1979) 309
civil war (2014–) 217, 308–9,
310–11, 317–18
coup (1962) 309–10, 314, 319
coup (1970) 324
Dhofar insurrection (1970–78)
323–5
election (2012) 309, 310

FLOSY (Front for the Liberation of
Occupied South Yemen) and
320–21
Houthi and see Houthi movement
Imam Ahmed ibn Yahya and 314
Imam Yahya Muhammad Hamid
ed-Din al Mutawakil and
313–14
Iran and 14, 16, 308, 310, 312n,
316, 324, 326
al-Iryani and 315
literacy in 322
Nasser and 315, 320–21
Operation Decisive Storm (2015–)
217, 308–9, 310–11, 317–18
Ottoman Empire take control of
Sanaa 313–14
People's Republic of Southern
Yemen, declaration of (1967)
321–2
rebellion (2004) 309, 315–16
Saleh as president of 309, 315,
316–17
Saudi Arabia and 165, 169–70,
217, 308–9, 310, 337, 345
Six-Day War and 321
Southern Arabian (Federation)
Army 321
Sulayhid rulers 311
union (1990) 309, 326
Zaydi in 16, 91, 244, 309, 311–15,
317
Yermolov, General 375
Yom Kippur War (1973) 11, 41n,
170–71, 261, 292, 334, 336,
344
Young Turks 248

Z

Zaim, Colonel Husni 257–8
Zayd ibn Ali, Iman 91, 312–14,
312n
Zakat (Islamic tithe) 167, 370
Zand dynasty 149–50, 149n
Zand, Karim Khan 149–50
Zangid Emirate of Mosul 114
Zanj rebellion (869) 107–8

Zaydi 16, 91, 103, 103*n*, 244, 309, 311, 312, 312*n*, 313–17
Zaynab (daughter of Muhammad) 46, 58, 89–90
Zayyad, Ubaydallah ibn 86
Zionism 249–50, 250*n*, 251, 254, 257, 341–4, 345–6, 350

Zoroastrians 74, 78
Zulfiqar ('master of the spine') 57–8
Zuljenah 89

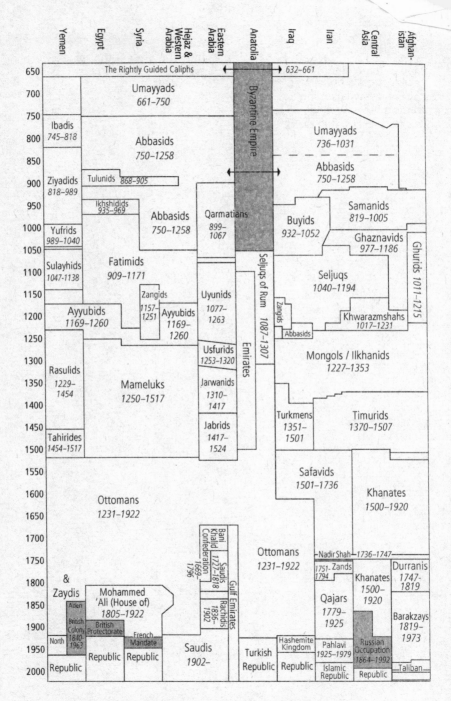

Timeline of Islamic Dynasties

Sunni and Shia populations in the Middle East

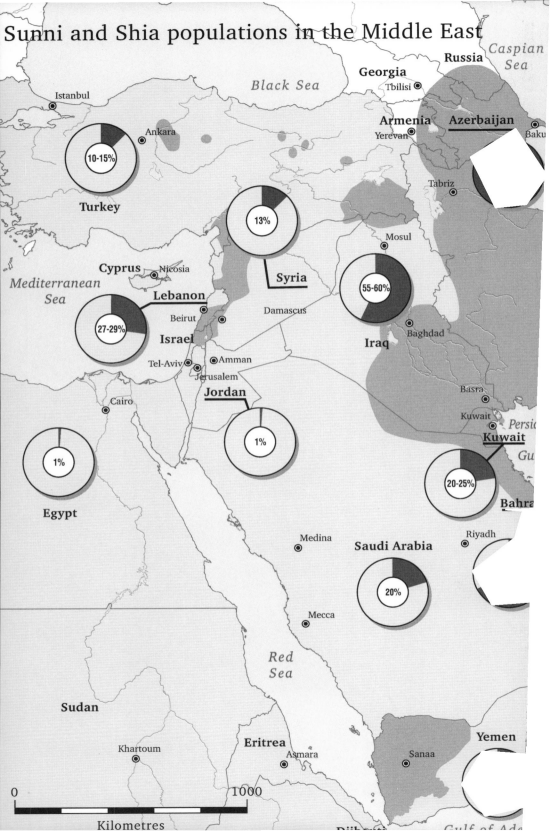

Caspian Sea

Russia

Black Sea

Georgia

Tbilisi

Istanbul

Armenia

Azerbaijan

Yerevan

Baku

Ankara

10-15%

Turkey

Tabriz

13%

Mosul

Cyprus Nicosia

Mediterranean Sea

Syria

Lebanon

Beirut

Damascus

55-60%

Baghdad

Israel

Iraq

Tel-Aviv

Amman

Basra

Jerusalem

Kuwait

Jordan

Persi

Cairo

1%

1%

Gu

Kuwait

20-25%

Egypt

Bahra

Medina

Riyadh

Saudi Arabia

20%

Mecca

Red Sea

Sudan

Eritrea

Yemen

Khartoum

Asmara

Sanaa

0

1000

Kilometres

Gulf of Ade